THE STRUCTURE OF OBJECTS

The Structure of Objects

KATHRIN KOSLICKI

OXFORD
UNIVERSITY PRESS

OXFORD

UNIVERSITY PRESS

Great Clarendon Street, Oxford OX2 6DP

Oxford University Press is a department of the University of Oxford.
It furthers the University's objective of excellence in research, scholarship,
and education by publishing worldwide in

Oxford New York

Auckland Cape Town Dar es Salaam Hong Kong Karachi
Kuala Lumpur Madrid Melbourne Mexico City Nairobi
New Delhi Shanghai Taipei Toronto

With offices in

Argentina Austria Brazil Chile Czech Republic France Greece
Guatemala Hungary Italy Japan Poland Portugal Singapore
South Korea Switzerland Thailand Turkey Ukraine Vietnam

Oxford is a registered trade mark of Oxford University Press
in the UK and in certain other countries

Published in the United States
by Oxford University Press Inc., New York

First published 2008
First published in paperback 2010

British Library Cataloguing in Publication Data
Data available

Library of Congress Cataloging in Publication Data
Data available

Typeset by Laserwords Private Limited, Chennai, India
Printed in the United Kingdom by
Lightning Source UK Ltd., Milton Keynes

ISBN 978-0-19-953989-5 (Hbk)
ISBN 978-0-19-959251-7 (Pbk)

To my parents,
Eleonore and Karli Pongratz

In gratitude for all the love and support I
have received from them over the years.

The Author

Kathrin Koslicki was born in Munich, Germany; she is currently Associate Professor of Philosophy at the University of Colorado, Boulder, and is the author of many articles in metaphysics, the philosophy of language and Ancient Greek philosophy, particularly Aristotle. Her work has appeared in *History of Philosophy Quarterly*, *Synthese*, *Nous*, *Mind and Language*, *Philosophical Studies*, the *Journal of Philosophy*, *Philosophy and Phenomenological Research* and *Dialectica*, among other publications.

ADDRESS

Kathrin Koslicki,
Department of Philosophy,
University of Colorado, Boulder,
Hellems 169
UCB 232
Boulder, CO 80309-0232
E-mail: Kathrin.Koslicki@colorado.edu

Preface

The main purpose of this book is to give an analysis of ordinary material objects, those material objects to which we take ourselves to be committed in ordinary, scientifically informed discourse. In pursuing this task, I want to focus in particular on the question of how the *parts* of such objects, assuming that they have parts, are related to the *wholes* which they compose. That most, or possibly all, ordinary material objects have parts I take to be an obvious intuitive datum: we would commonly say, for example, that among the parts of a tree are its branches, its trunk, its leaves and its roots; among the parts of a table are its legs and its top; among the parts of an H_2O molecule are its two hydrogen atoms and its single oxygen atom. As I understand it, then, to ask the question, "What *are* ordinary material objects?", is at least in part to ask, "How are these wholes related to the parts that compose them?", or "What is the nature of the relations of *parthood* and *composition* for material objects?".

Many philosophers today find themselves in the grip of an exceedingly deflationary conception of what it means to be an object, according to which any plurality of objects, no matter how disparate or gerrymandered, itself composes an object, even if the objects in question fail to exhibit interesting similarities, internal unity, cohesion or causal interaction amongst each other. To illustrate, according to this approach, George W. Bush's left hand together with the Eiffel Tower compose a further object, their sum, aggregate or fusion, which is partially located in the White House and partially located in Paris. The commitment to such initially counterintuitive objects follows from the belief that no principled set of criteria is available by means of which to distinguish the intuitively gerrymandered objects from the commonsensical ones; my project in this book is to persuade the reader that systematic principles by means of which composition can be restricted can be found and hence that we need not embrace this deflationary approach to the question of what it means to be an object.

To this end, I develop in what follows a more full-blooded neo-Aristotelian account of parthood and composition according to which objects are structured wholes: it is integral to the existence and identity of an object, on this conception, that its parts exhibit a certain manner of arrangement. For example, in order for there to be an H_2O molecule, the two hydrogen atoms and one oxygen atom that compose it must be arranged in the particular manner of chemical bonding, which requires the atoms in question to share electrons. This structure-based conception of parthood and composition, along with some of its historical precursors as well as some of its contemporary competitors, are explored in detail below.

The material put forth in this book, over the years, has been presented at numerous talks and conferences and has benefited from the help of many friends and colleagues. I express my gratitude to: Jody Azzouni, Lynne Rudder Baker, David Barnett, Nancy Bauer, Karen Bennett, Hagit Borer, Tyler Burge, Myles Burnyeat, Alex Byrne, Vince Cheng, Elijah Chudnoff, Dan Dennett, Harry Deutsch, Cian Dorr, Steve Downes, Betsy Duquette, Delia Graff Fara, Michael Fara, Michaele Ferguson, Malcolm Forster, Cody Gilmore, Michael Glanzberg, Ned Hall, John Hawthorne, Chris Heathwood, Mark Heller, Benj Hellie, Chistopher Hitchcock, Hud Hudson, Ray Jackendoff, Robin Jeshion, Ed Johnson, Jeff King, Christian Lee, Tucker Lentz, Janet Levin, Andrew Loxley, Kirk Ludwig, Ned Markosian, Jim Mazoué, Kris McDaniels, Brad Monton, Michael Nelson, Bob Pasnau, Laurie Paul, Jim Pryor, Greg Ray, Mark Richard, Nathan Salmon, Barry Schein, Ori Simchen, Peter Simons, Jim Stone, Leopold Stubenberg, Zoltan Szabo, Jan Szaif, Paul Teller, Mariam Thalos, Achille Varzi, Kadri Vihvelin, Ralph Wedgwood, Jessica Wilson and Dean Zimmerman. I have found my conversations with Kit Fine, Graeme Forbes, Verity Harte, Mark Johnston, Elijah Millgram and Ted Sider, as well as my engagement with their work, to be particularly influential in developing the philosophical approach presented here. Thanks also to an anonymous reader for Oxford University Press for helpful comments.

I would furthermore like to acknowledge the support of the following foundations and institutions which have had a hand in making this research possible. During the academic year of 1998/99, I held an Andrew Mellon Postdoctoral Fellowship in Linguistics and Philosophy at the University of Southern California. I received the support of Tufts University and the Andrew Mellon Foundation during the academic year of 2003/4 in the form of a Tufts Junior Faculty Research Leave as well as an Andrew Mellon Research Semester Fellowship. Finally, I am grateful to the Tanner Humanities Center for inviting me to spend the academic year of 2005/6 at the University of Utah on a Visiting Research Fellowship.

Portions of the material contained in this book are based on previously published work as follows. Chapter II contains some excerpts from Koslicki (2003a). Chapter III presents an expanded version of Koslicki (2005a). Chapter IV appeared in print as part of Koslicki (2007). Chapter V substantially elaborates on my condensed remarks in Koslicki (2004b) concerning Plato's mereology and its interpretation in Harte (2002). My take on Aristotle's mereology, as laid out in Chapter VI, was especially developed for this monograph; a small portion of it is incorporated into Koslicki (2006b) and (2007), the latter of which also makes use of some of the results I reach in Chapter V and Chapter VII. Chapters VIII and IX are completely new. I am grateful to *Philosophical Studies*, the *Journal of Philosophy* and *Dialectica* for allowing me to reproduce previously published material.

The intended audience for this book consists of anyone who is intrigued by the question of how best to analyze the notions of part, whole and object. It presupposes only a minute amount of basic logic, much less than would be imparted to a typical undergraduate philosophy major. With the heavy emphasis on Plato's and Aristotle's mereology, I hope that my project will also speak to those with a historical inclination. Finally, parts of this book, especially the discussion of natural kinds in Chapter VIII and that of structure in Chapter IX, touch on issues that are of relevance not only to metaphysicians, but also to philosophers of language and semanticists, epistemologists, philosophers of science, linguists, psychologists, and cognitive scientists in general.

K. K.

Summary Contents

Detailed Contents   xv

Part One   Standard Mereology   1
Introduction   3
I   The Standard Conception of Composition   9
II   Ordinary Objects as Mereological Sums   23
III   Composition as Non-Identity   45

Part Two   A Contemporary Structure-Based Mereology   69
IV   A Different Kind of Whole   71

Part Three Ancient Structure-Based Mereologies   91
V   The Role of Structure in Plato's Mereological Writings   93
VI   Aristotle's Refinements of Plato's Theory   122

Part Four   An Alternative Structure-Based Theory   165
VII   Objects as Structured Wholes   167
VIII   In Defense of Kinds   200
IX   Structure   235

Conclusion   261

Bibliography   265

General Index   281

Index of Names   286

Detailed Contents

I. STANDARD MEREOLOGY

Introduction   3

I.   **The Standard Conception of Composition**   9

§I.1   Introductory Remarks   9

§I.2   Standard Mereology   10

     §I.2.1   The Basic Concepts of Standard Mereology   11

     §I.2.2   The Basic Principles of Standard Mereology   15

     §I.2.3   A Gradual Statement of the Theory   17

§I.3   The Application of Standard Mereology to Ordinary Material Objects   20

II.   **Ordinary Objects as Mereological Sums**   23

§II.1   Introductory Remarks   23

§II.2   Thomson's Three-Dimensionalist Approach   23

§II.3   Lewis' Four-Dimensionalist Approach   29

     §II.3.1   Support for Unrestricted Composition   29

         §II.3.1.1   The Lewis/Sider Argument from Vagueness   30

         §II.3.1.2   The Controversial Premise (P3)   34

         §II.3.1.3   The Matter of Vague Existence   37

     §II.3.2   The Composition-as-Identity Thesis   40

§II.4   Concluding Remarks   43

III.   **Composition as Non-Identity**   45

§III.1   Introductory Remarks   45

§III.2   The Suspect Strategy   47

     §III.2.1   The Suspect Strategy and Leibniz's Law   47

         §III.2.1.1 Contingent Identity   47

         §III.2.1.2 Temporary Identity   48

         §III.2.1.3 Indeterminate Identity   51

     §III.2.2   The Suspect Strategy and Existence Principles: Non-Existent Objects   52

     §III.2.3   The Suspect Strategy and Restricted Indiscernibility Principles   54

         §III.2.3.1 Coincident Objects   54

         §III.2.3.2 Relative Identity   56

§III.3 What's Wrong with the Suspect Strategy?   58
        §III.3.1   The Purely Stipulative Response   58
        §III.3.2   Gibbard's Appeal to Failures of Substitutivity   61
        §III.3.3   Parsons' Appeal to the Paradoxes of Naive Set
                   Theory   65
        §III.3.4   Deutsch's Expansion Principle   66
§III.4 Concluding Remarks   67

II. A CONTEMPORARY STRUCTURE-BASED MEREOLOGY

IV. A Different Kind of Whole   71
     §IV.1   Introductory Remarks   71
     §IV.2   Parting Ways with the Standard Conception   72
             §IV.2.1   Fine's "Aggregative Objection"   72
             §IV.2.2   Fine's "Monster Objection"   73
     §IV.3   Fine's Theory of Embodiments   75
             §IV.3.1   Rigid Embodiments   76
             §IV.3.2   Variable Embodiments   78
     §IV.4   Discussion   82
             §IV.4.1   The Proliferation of *Sui Generis* Relations   82
             §IV.4.2   The Superabundance of Objects   83
             §IV.4.3   The Mysterious Nature of Variable Embodiments   85
             §IV.4.4   The Formal Properties of Parthood   88
     §IV.5   Concluding Remarks   89

III. ANCIENT STRUCTURE-BASED MEREOLOGIES

V.   The Role of Structure in Plato's Mereological Writings   93
     §V.1   Introductory Remarks   93
     §V.2   The Negative Mereological Undercurrent   94
     §V.3   The Positive Mereological Undercurrent   96
     §V.4   Platonic Wholes   100
            §V.4.1   Normativity, Teleology, Intelligibility and Unity   100
            §V.4.2   Structure and Content   105
                     §V.4.2.1 The Aristotelian Regress in *Met.* Z.17   108
                     §V.4.2.2 Parts as "Structure-Laden"   112
                     §V.4.2.3 A Final Word on Content   117
     §V.5   Concluding Remarks   119

VI.   Aristotle's Refinements of Plato's Theory   122

§VI.1   Introductory Remarks   122

§VI.2   The Centrality of "Part" and "Whole" in the
        Aristotelian Corpus   123

§VI.3   The Problem of the One and the Many   125

§VI.4   A Reading of the Text   126

    §VI.4.1   One, Divisibility, Part, Quantity and Measure   126
    §VI.4.2   Kinds of Measure and Principles of Unity   128
    §VI.4.3   The Ways of Being a Part: *Met.* Δ.25   134
    §VI.4.4   The Ways of Being a Whole: *Met.* Δ.26   139
        §VI.4.4.1 Wholes and Totals   140
        §VI.4.4.2 Degrees of Wholeness   142

§VI.5   Summary of Sections VI.3–4: The Highlights   150

§VI.6   Discussion   157

    §VI.6.1   The Formal Properties of Parthood   157
    §VI.6.2   In Search of the Ultimate Mereological Atom   159

§VI.7   Concluding Remarks   162

IV. AN ALTERNATIVE STRUCTURE-BASED THEORY

VII. Objects as Structured Wholes   167

§VII.1   Introductory Remarks   167

§VII.2   Outlines of the Theory   167

    §VII.2.1   Mereological Non-Proliferation: A Single Relation of
               Parthood   167
    §VII.2.2   The Restricted Nature of Composition   168
    §VII.2.3   An Ontology of Kinds   170
    §VII.2.4   Ontology and Mereology   171
    §VII.2.5   Form and Matter   172
    §VII.2.6   An Ontology of Structured Wholes   174
    §VII.2.7   The Dichotomous Nature of Wholes   176
        §VII.2.7.1 Material Components as Proper Parts   176
        §VII.2.7.2 Formal Components as Proper Parts   179
        §VII.2.7.3 Material and Formal Components as
        Proper Parts   183
    §VII.2.8   The Hierarchical Nature of Composition   186
    §VII.2.9   Change over Time   188
    §VII.2.10 Synchronic and Diachronic Identity   191
    §VII.2.11 Composition as Non-Identity   192

§VII.2.12 The Unified Nature of Wholes   192
§VII.3 Concluding Remarks   198

VIII. **In Defense of Kinds**   200

§VIII.1 Introductory Remarks   200
§VIII.2 What Are Natural Kinds?   201
§VIII.3 The Special Features of Natural Kinds   203
    §VIII.3.1 Induction and Projectibility   204
    §VIII.3.2 Laws of Nature   205
    §VIII.3.3 Causation and Explanation   207
§VIII.4 Biological Taxa   210
    §VIII.4.1 The Ontological Status of Species   210
    §VIII.4.2 Species as Kinds   214
§VIII.5 What Sorts of Entities Are Natural Kinds?   219
    §VIII.5.1 The Semantics of Natural Kind Terms   220
        §VIII.5.1.1 Rigid Designation   223
§VIII.6 Incommensurability and Indeterminacy: Physical and
    Chemical Kinds   227
    §VIII.6.1 Impurities and Isotopes: Scientific and Ordinary
        Classifications   227
    §VIII.6.2 Meaning-Change and Theory-Change   230
§VIII.7 Concluding Remarks   233

IX. **Structure**   235

§IX.1 Introductory Remarks   235
§IX.2 Some Preliminaries   236
    §IX.2.1 Related Notions   236
    §IX.2.2 Different Grammatical Roles   238
    §IX.2.3 The Gestalt Theorists: Rescher and Oppenheim   239
§IX.3 Some Case Studies   240
    §IX.3.1 Mathematical Structure   240
    §IX.3.2 Logical Structure   241
    §IX.3.3 Chemical Structure   244
    §IX.3.4 Musical Structure   246
    §IX.3.5 Linguistic Structure   248
§IX.4 Structures as Objects   252
§IX.5 The Grounding Problem Revisited   254
    §IX.5.1 A Potential Problem Case   256
        §IX.5.1.1 The Detachability of the Grounding
        Problem   256
        §IX.5.1.2 Giving Up the Transitivity of Parthood   257

§IX.5.1.3 Individual Forms and Haecceities   257
§IX.5.1.4 Denying the Existence of Heaps   258
§IX.6   Concluding Remarks   259

Conclusion   261

Bibliography   265

General Index   281

Index of Names   286

Part One

Standard Mereology

Introduction

The 2003 Honda VFR 800 Interceptor is an intricately designed motorcycle and, in the minds of the motorcycle community, a very successful piece of engineering. It consists of literally hundreds of parts, most of which have been given explicit names. Among these parts are the gauges, indicators and displays (e.g., the tachometer, right and left turn signal indicator, digital clock, etc.); the controls and features (e.g., the ignition switch, start button, engine stop switch, etc.); and the components (e.g., the coveted fuel-injected V-Tech engine, the seat, battery, fuses, generator, drive chain, side stand, center stand, gear shift pedal, fairing, fuel tank, air filter, throttle, clutch, suspension, transmission, brakes, wheels and tires, catalytic converter, etc.). These parts are described in some detail in the owner's manual and in much greater detail in the sort of documentation that would be handed to a Honda mechanic in training or to a worker at the Honda factory. Such documentation also specifies exactly which part must go where in the assembly of the motorcycle and how each part is connected to the parts surrounding it.

It is completely obvious to those not in the grip of a philosophical theory that there is a vast and important difference between a heap of disassembled motorcycle parts, piled up, as they might be, at the Honda factory or in someone's garage, and the motorcycle in running condition that results from assembling these parts in a particular, fairly constrained, way. Anyone who is at all mechanically inclined or who is interested in actually riding their motorcycle will attest to the importance of the distinction between a motorcycle in running condition and its disassembled parts. Surprisingly, this vast difference, which must strike the uninitiated as both trivial and nevertheless crucial, has been de-emphasized, almost to the point of completely disappearing, in much of the philosophical theorizing about parts, wholes and objects that has taken place in metaphysics during the last one hundred years or so.

How can this be? Part of the story, as outrageous as this might sound to the outsider, is simply historical accident. As one learns by working through Peter Simons' excellent book, *Parts: A Study in Ontology* (Simons 1987), the most popular and well-worked-out theory of parts and wholes, which came to dominate this corner of metaphysics in the 20th century, just happened to be designed by people who were not particularly interested in the distinction between, say, a motorcycle in running condition and its disassembled parts.

Rather, for various theoretical reasons, their theory of parts and wholes was intended primarily for the purposes of replacing set theory, and, as we all remember from learning elementary set theory, it makes no difference to the existence and identity of a set how its members are arranged; in this way, wholes came out looking as much like sets as they possibly could, without carrying with them set theory's commitment to an infinite hierarchy of abstract objects. Since the founders of this most popular theory of parts and wholes were not inclined to assign any importance to the distinction between, say, a motorcycle in running condition and its disassembled parts, they built their theory in such a way that it lacks the resources to recognize this distinction. (The theory in question, which I call "standard mereology", will be laid out and discussed in detail in Chapter I.)[1]

Standard mereology is an attractively simple, elegant and powerful theory; as we shall see below, it requires only a single primitive notion and in its standard formulations consists of a mere three axioms. However, from the point of view of those interested in characterizing the relation between, say, a motorcycle and its parts, this system also has some counterintuitive consequences. For example, it follows from one of the axioms of standard mereology, commonly known as the Uniqueness of Composition, that there is no difference between a heap of unassembled motorcycle parts piled up in someone's garage and the motorcycle in running condition that results from assembling these parts in a particular way: for the heap and the motorcycle, by hypothesis, have the very same parts and, according to the Uniqueness of Composition, objects with the same parts are numerically identical. Thus, standard mereology cannot tell the difference between the motorcycle in running condition and the heap of disassembled parts; from the point of view of theory, they are the very same thing.

Moreover, it also follows from another one of the axioms of standard mereology, commonly known as Unrestricted Composition, that *any* plurality of objects, no matter how disparate, dissimilar or gerrymandered, itself counts as an object, even if these objects fail to exhibit interesting similarities, internal unity, cohesion or causal interaction amongst each other. Thus, according to this axiom, the American President's left hand together with the Eiffel Tower compose a further object, their mereological sum, fusion or aggregate, which is partially located in the White House and partially located in Paris. This object is just as real and respectable from the point of view of standard mereology as the President's left hand or the Eiffel Tower taken individually; from the point of view of the theory, there is no difference in ontological status between them.

How could a theory which has these counterintuitive consequences have become the most widely used theory of parts and wholes among metaphysicians

---

[1] The word "mereology" literally means the study or theory of parts and wholes, deriving from "*meros*", the Greek word for part, and "*logos*", which in this context may be taken to mean study, theory, science or rigorous inquiry.

today? The other part of the story, at least for the last few decades, is due to the philosophical genius and charisma of David Lewis. David Lewis believed that insofar as we have any understanding of the notions of part and whole at all, this understanding derives from the theory I have been calling "standard mereology": for Lewis, there is no other mereology besides standard mereology." This conception of parts and wholes, despite its austerity, or rather precisely because of it, proved to be a perfect fit with Lewis' more general ontological outlook. Together, standard mereology, combined with Lewis' four-dimensionalism and his way of thinking of necessity and possibility, gave rise to something akin to a "movement" among contemporary metaphysicians, an approach to many of the classical problems in metaphysics that has proven to be simply irresistible to several generations of philosophers.'''

My project in this book is to help reverse this trend in contemporary metaphysics and to put the notion of *structure* or *form* squarely back at the center of any adequate account of the notions of part, whole and object.'' To this end, I propose in what follows a conception of ordinary material objects as *structured wholes*: it is integral to the existence and identity of an object, according to this approach, that its parts exhibit a certain configuration or manner of arrangement.' For example, in order for there to be an H_2O molecule, the two hydrogen atoms and one oxygen atom that compose it must be arranged in the particular manner of chemical bonding, which requires the atoms in question to share electrons. Moreover, in what is perhaps the most radical feature of my view, I argue below that the structure which dictates how the remaining parts of a whole are to be arranged is itself, literally and strictly speaking, *part* of the whole it organizes.

" See, for example, Lewis (1986a) for an expression of this sentiment; the passage in question is cited in Chapter I below.

''' *Three-dimensionalism* (also known as "*endurantism*") and *four-dimensionalism* (also known as "*perdurantism*" or "the *doctrine of temporal parts*") are competing theories concerning the *persistence* of ordinary material objects over time, i.e., they aim to provide an answer to the question of how an object that exists at one time can be numerically identical to an object that exists at another time, as we say, for example, of the young Socrates and the old Socrates. According to the four-dimensionalist, objects persist over time by *perduring*, i.e., by having temporal parts, in addition to their ordinary spatial parts, at all those times at which they exist. The three-dimensionalist, on the other hand, holds that ordinary material objects persist by *enduring*, i.e., by being (as they say) "wholly present" at each time at which the object exists. For detailed discussion and references, see Sider (2001). The dispute between three-dimensionalists and four-dimensionalists will come up again below; it is, however, not one of the main themes of this book. The present inquiry is conducted within a three-dimensionalist framework; for discussion, see Koslicki (2003a) and (2003b).

'' The contemporary philosophers most sympathetic to this project are Verity Harte, Kit Fine and Mark Johnston (see the Bibliography for references); however, in each case, there are significant differences between my approach and theirs. Harte and Fine are discussed in detail below.

' In what follows, whenever I speak of "ordinary material objects", I take myself to be including those objects to which our best scientific theories take themselves to be committed. For reasons of simplicity, I will not always explicitly specify that I intend the phrase "ordinary material object" to be understood in this wide sense.

The main historical inspiration for this view is, of course, Aristotle and, as it turns out, Plato as well, though, for reasons that will be spelled out in detail below, to a somewhat lesser extent. In Aristotle's view, an object, such as a bronze sphere, consists of two components, its *matter* (the bronze) and its *form* (sphericity); as I read him, both the matter and the form of an object are taken by Aristotle to be strictly and literally *part* of the object, just as my hand is part of my arm. Something counts as an object, on this view, only if its material components display a certain kind of *unity* which is imposed on the matter by the form. Thus, not every collection of objects itself qualifies as a single object; the Eiffel Tower and the President's left hand, for example, fail to exhibit the necessary unity required by these stricter criteria, since they lack a single form. Similarly, the heap consisting of disassembled motorcycle parts would be strongly distinguished by this theory from the motorcycle in running condition.

Although the richness of Aristotle's views is of course beyond dispute, contemporary metaphysicians have found it difficult to make sense of his notions of form and matter. Thus, one of the main challenges for any neo-Aristotelian approach is to develop a conception of what it means to be an object which divorces itself from those elements of Aristotle's system which would now strike us as puzzling, foreign or unmotivated, in particular his strong normative and teleological commitments. To this end, I attempt to show below that the notion of structure or form, far from being the mysterious and causally inert philosophical invention ridiculed by Descartes and numerous thinkers since then, in fact lies at the very center of many scientific and other rigorous endeavors, such as mathematics, logic, linguistics, chemistry and music.

Once we realize that an object is more than simply the sum of its material parts, arranged any which way, much that has so far puzzled us about the nature of objects themselves as well as their interaction with one another can be seen to fall into place. One of the advantages of the neo-Aristotelian conception of objecthood is that it answers certain long-standing questions in metaphysics; in particular, it provides a solution to a classical problem in metaphysics known as the *Problem of Constitution*. The Problem of Constitution concerns the nature of the relation which obtains between an object and what it is made of, e.g., a statue and the clay which constitutes it. Metaphysicians are puzzled by this relation, because, on the one hand, the statue and the clay are sufficiently similar to one another to make it tempting simply to identify them; on the other hand, there are sufficient differences between them to make us think that we cannot simply be dealing with a single object. The neo-Aristotelian thesis that objects are compounds of matter and form yields a solution to the Problem of Constitution: the clay now turns out to be merely a proper part of the statue (viz., its matter); the "remainder" of the statue is made up of those of its formal or structural components which distinguish it from the clay. But the fact that the clay and the statue are two distinct objects which occupy the very same region of space-time, according to this view, is no more worrisome than the fact that, say, my hand occupies a region of space-time also occupied by my arm: in both cases, one of the objects in question is a proper part of the other.

Moreover, my account also helps to generate a solution to what I call the *Problem of the One and the Many*, the problem of how an object that has many parts can nevertheless be one.[vi] The search for a response to this problem was one of the driving forces in ancient accounts of parts and wholes, and it has recently been revived by Peter van Inwagen under the heading "The Special Composition Question" (van Inwagen 1990a). I argue that the Problem of the One and the Many actually dissolves once we recognize that the notion of unity is conceptually separate from that of indivisibility into parts: far from posing a threat to its unity, the presence of parts in an object is in fact a requirement to building a unified specimen of a kind. To illustrate, there could be no H_2O molecule, unless two hydrogen atoms and one oxygen atom entered into the particular configuration of chemical bonding. Objects of this kind are unified in the sense that they are one specimen of the kind in question, precisely because they are composed of the right sorts of material components arranged in the manner required by the structural components associated with the kind in question.

The following is a play-by-play description of what happens in each chapter. Chapter I gives an exposition of the basic concepts and principles of standard mereology; my main source for this chapter is Simons (1987). I also borrow from Simons his instructive gradual development of standard mereology, which shows how stronger and stronger principles may be added gradually to a minimal core, until we arrive at the full-strength theory of standard mereology.

In Chapter II, I consider the application of standard mereology to the case of ordinary material objects: my representative for the three-dimensionalist camp is Thomson (1983); my representative for the four-dimensionalist camp is Lewis (1986b) and (1991). I argue in Chapter II that neither the argument in favor of Unrestricted Composition in Lewis (1986b), which has recently been creatively adopted and elaborated in Sider (2001), nor the considerations in favor of the Composition-as-Identity Thesis in Lewis (1991), should persuade us to adopt standard mereology. My case against the Composition-as-Identity Thesis is further supported in Chapter III with a defense of the position that, by Leibniz's Law, wholes are in no way numerically identical to their parts.

Chapter IV continues my case against the thesis that ordinary material objects are mereological sums in the standard sense and begins my exploration of alternative systems. I turn in particular to the work of Kit Fine, who, in a series of papers, has provided powerful reasons for parting ways with standard

---

[vi] This name, "The Problem of the One and the Many", or something close to it, is usually reserved for the question of how a *universal* like redness is related to the many *particulars* that instantiate it, e.g., the red roses, fire trucks and tomatoes, etc.; however, this latter problem is unrelated to the question about parts and wholes that is at issue here.

conception. In the later sections of the chapter, I discuss in detail Fine's own positive proposal, in particular his theory of embodiments as developed in Fine (1999), and indicate where I take myself to be departing from it.

The methodological and ontological concerns arising from Fine's theory of embodiments provide motivation to search for an alternative approach which preserves the neo-Aristotelian spirit of Fine's theory of embodiments while avoiding its troubling features. Since the kind of theory we are seeking has its historical roots in Aristotle, and as it turns out in Plato as well, I examine the rich and rewarding writings of these two ancient authors on parts and wholes in detail in Chapters V and VI, respectively.

Chapter VII states the main tenets of the view I have in effect been gradually assembling over the course of the previous six chapters: it provides a defense of my main thesis that ordinary material objects are structured wholes and describes in detail the conception of parthood and composition to which I am committed. Since this conception is ultimately grounded in an ontology of kinds, I continue in Chapter VIII with a defense of this commitment for the special case of natural kinds.

Given the centrality of the concept of structure in what has come before, Chapter IX provides a general characterization of this notion and considers some of its most visible and instructive applications, in particular in the fields of mathematics, logic, linguistics, chemistry and music.

I

The Standard Conception of Composition

§1.1 INTRODUCTORY REMARKS

The objects we encounter in ordinary life and scientific practice — cars, trees, people, houses, molecules, galaxies, and the like — have long been a fruitful source of perplexity for metaphysicians. The purpose of this book is to give an analysis of those material objects to which we take ourselves to be committed in our ordinary, scientifically informed discourse. My focus will be on *material* objects in particular or, as metaphysicians like to call them, "*concrete particulars*",[1] i.e., objects which occupy a single region of space-time at each time at which they exist and which have a certain range of properties that go along with space-occupancy, such as weight, shape, color, texture and temperature.

In giving an analysis of ordinary material objects, I want to focus in particular on the question of how the *parts* of such objects, assuming that they have parts, are related to the *wholes* which they compose. That most, or possibly all, ordinary material objects have parts I take to be an obvious intuitive datum.[2] We would commonly say, for example, that among the parts of a tree are its branches, its trunk, its leaves and its roots; among the parts of a table are its legs and its top; among the parts of an H_2O molecule are its two hydrogen atoms and its single oxygen atom. Let's call objects which have parts *mereologically complex*,

---

[1] *Concrete* is typically taken to contrast with *abstract*; *particular* with *universal*. Although it is difficult to make precise exactly what is meant by these distinctions, it is sufficient for present purposes to proceed with the rough and ready characterization given above. Thus, I understand "concrete" as entailing space-occupancy and the possession of a certain range of physical properties that we take to go along with space-occupancy. Since the defining feature of universals is typically taken to be that they are multiply located, i.e., that they are simultaneously present in their entirety in each of their instances, we can take particulars, in contrast, to be capable of being wholly present in only a single region of space-time at each time at which they exist. Due to my appeal to such notions as "space-occupancy", "being an instance of" and "being wholly present", I don't take anything I have just said to be particularly illuminating or *definitive* of the "concrete/abstract", "particular/universal" distinctions; I hope nevertheless that what I have said will give the reader at least a rough idea of the starting point of my analysis. As will become clear shortly, the current inquiry is not meant to answer the question, "What concrete particulars are there?", but assumes as given an ontology of material objects to which we take ourselves to be committed in ordinary life and scientific discourse.

[2] Though one which would be denied by the Nihilist, who holds that nothing composes anything, i.e., that the world consists of mereological simples. I take on a particular version of the Nihilist position, as defended recently by Cian Dorr (e.g., in Dorr 2005), in Koslicki (2005b).

compound or *composite* objects, or *wholes*. Then, as I understand it, to ask the question, "What *are* ordinary material objects?", is at least in part to ask, "How are these wholes related to their parts?", or "What is the nature of the relation of *composition* for material objects?".

§I.2 STANDARD MEREOLOGY

One prominent answer to these questions which has been embraced by three-dimensionalists and four-dimensionalists alike is that ordinary material objects are *mereological sums*, *fusions* or *aggregates*, according to a particular, standard conception of mereology.[3] The standard conception of mereology I have in mind is the family of systems which Simons (1987) calls "Classical Extensional Mereology" (CEM), and I shall follow him in this usage. The first formulation of CEM appears to have been given by Stanislaw Leśniewski, informally in Leśniewski (1916) and formally in Leśniewski (1927–30), though Simons speculates, based on some remarks by Russell in 1914, that Whitehead's mereology may actually have been developed not only independently of Leśniewski's but may also have preceded it (cf. Russell 1914, Simons 1987, p. 82). Leśniewski's system is not widely known to contemporary writers, due to the fact that it is based on his formal system, "Ontology", which is generally found to be relatively inaccessible (but see Simons 1987, ch. 2, for a very clear and detailed exposition of Leśniewski's systems "Ontology" and "Mereology"). The classical statement of CEM in English, using the language of first-order predicate-logic, is Henry Leonard and Nelson Goodman's "Calculus of Individuals" (Leonard and Goodman 1940), of which the first version appeared in 1930 in Leonard's doctoral dissertation. Leonard and Goodman's (1940) Calculus of Individuals is formulated with appeal to set theory, as is Tarski's version of CEM in Tarski (1937) and (1956); but a nominalistic formulation of the same theory, in which reference to sets is replaced by reference to predicates, is given in Goodman (1977).[4, 5]

---

[3] To avoid confusion, I shall use the term "mereology" neutrally to mean what it literally means, viz., the study of parts and wholes; according to this usage, *any* theory concerning the logic of the part/whole relation is *a* mereology. The terms "whole", "part" and "composition" are to be understood in an equally non-theory-specific way: a (non-trivial) whole is simply any object which has parts; a part is that which (if it is a *proper* part) composes a whole and is non-identical with it. What it means to be a whole or a part may be spelled out differently by different mereologies; i.e., wholes and parts will have whatever properties the particular mereology specifies for its relations of parthood and composition. Finally, I shall use the terms "sum", "fusion" and "aggregate", interchangeably; unless otherwise indicated, I shall reserve these terms for the composite objects described by the particular theory I call "standard mereology"; what I mean by "standard mereology" will be explained shortly.

[4] Mereology can also be formulated by means of plural quantification, as illustrated for example in Lewis (1991) or van Inwagen (1990a) and (1994).

[5] Other work that deals more or less directly with mereology includes (in alphabetical order): Bostock (1979); Bunt (1985); Cartwright, H. M. (1996); Casati and Varzi (1999); Chisholm (1973,

§I.2.1 The Basic Concepts of Standard Mereology

The basic concepts of standard mereology are as follows:[6]

Proper Part:	$x < y$	"x is a *proper part* of y"
Proper or Improper Part:	$x \leq y$	"x is a *proper or improper part* of y"
Overlap:	$x \circ y$	"x *overlaps* y"
Disjointness:	$x \mid y$	"x is *disjoint* from y"
Binary Product:	$x \cdot y$	"the *product* of x and y"
Binary Sum:	$x + y$	"the *sum* of x and y"
Difference:	$x - y$	"the *difference* of x and y"
General Product (Nucleus):	$\pi x \, [F(x)]$	"the *product* of all the x's which are F"
General Sum:	$\sigma x \, [F(x)]$	"the *sum* of all the x's which are F"
The Universe:	U	"the *Universe*"
Complement:	$U - x$	"the *complement* of x"
Atom:	$At(x)$	"x is an *atom*"

The relation of *proper part*, $<$, does not require much illustration, since it is firmly embedded in our ordinary way of conceptualizing the world; it holds, for example, between a man and his forearm. The most obvious formal properties of $<$ are *transitivity*, *asymmetry* and hence *irreflexivity*:

Transitivity of Proper Parthood:	$(x < y \;\&\; y < z) \rightarrow (x < z)$
Asymmetry of Proper Parthood:	$(x < y) \rightarrow \sim(y < x)$
Irreflexivity of Proper Parthood:	$\sim(x < x)$

In other words, if one object is a proper part of another and the second is a proper part of a third, then the first is a proper part of the third as well; if one

---

1975, 1976); Clarke (1981); De Laguna (1922); Eberle (1970); Fine (1982, 1983, 1992, 1994a, 1994c, 1999, 2003); Harte (2002); Hudson (2000, 2001); Husserl (1900–1); Lejewski (1982); Lewis (1991); Markosian (1998a, 1998b); Menger (1940); Merricks (1993, 2003); Moltmann (1997, 1998); Needham (1981); Oliver (1994); Plantinga (1975); Rea (1998, 2002); Scaltsas (1990); Sharvy (1980, 1983); Sider (1993, 2001); Smith (1982, 1997); Smith and Varzi (2000); Thomson (1977, 1983, 1998); Tiles (1981); Tranöy (1959); van Benthem (1983); van Inwagen (1981, 1987, 1990a, 1993, 1994, 2002); Varzi (2000); Whitehead (1919, 1920, 1929); Wiggins (1979); and Zimmerman (1995). (Again, the reader is referred to Simons 1987, ch. 2, for a detailed discussion and explicit comparison of several alternative mereological systems, some classical, some non-classical, and some of which extend mereology into the realm of topology.)

[6] This section follows very closely Simons (1987, ch. 1), which should be consulted for a more detailed exposition of the basic mereological vocabulary.

object is a proper part of another, then the second is not also a proper part of the first; and, finally, nothing is a proper part of itself. Thus, the relation of proper parthood is a *strict partial ordering*. However, as Simons points out, not every strict partial ordering can be described as a relation of parthood; thus, the question arises of what further formal properties distinguish proper parthood from other strict partial orderings. We shall turn to this question shortly. Though there are some writers who entertain the possibility of a relation of parthood which does not even satisfy these minimal properties,[7] I side with Simons in taking transitivity, asymmetry and irreflexivity to be partially constitutive of the relation of proper parthood; thus, any relation which fails to satisfy these rather weak formal requirements by its very nature ought not to be counted as a genuine notion of proper parthood. To illustrate, if a particular cell is a proper part of a particular body and a particular nucleus is a proper part of the cell, then I take it to be obvious that the nucleus is also a proper part of the body, even if there are plenty of *other*, more loaded, relations in the vicinity which cannot be so easily extended to hold both between the nucleus and the cell and between the cell and the body.

If identity is taken as given, then the relation, $\leq$, of *proper or improper parthood* can be understood in terms of identity and proper parthood: "$x \leq y$" holds just in case x is either a proper part of y or x is identical to y. Like the relation "is less than or equal to", to which it is formally analogous, $\leq$ is *transitive*, *non-symmetrical* and *reflexive*:

Transitivity of Proper or Improper Parthood:	$(x \leq y \ \& \ y \leq z) \rightarrow x \leq z$
Non-Symmetry of Proper or Improper Parthood:	$(\exists x)(\exists y) (x \leq y \ \& \ y \leq x) \ \&$ $(\exists x)(\exists y) (x \leq y \ \& \ \sim y \leq x)$
Reflexivity of Proper or Improper Parthood:	$x \leq x$

In other words, if an object is a (proper or improper) part of another, and the second is a (proper or improper) part of a third, then the first is also a (proper or improper) part of the third; if an object is a (proper or improper) part of another, then in some cases the second is also a (proper or improper) part of the first and in other cases the second is not also a (proper or improper) part of the first; and, finally, any object is a (proper or improper) part of itself.

Two objects *overlap* just in case they have a (proper or improper) part in common; thus, "x∘y" holds in any of the following scenarios: (i) x and y share a proper part; (ii) x and y are identical; (iii) x is a proper part of y; or (iv) y

---

[7] See, for example, Rescher (1955), Lowe (1989, p. 94, n. 9), Moltmann (1997, 1998) and Johnston (2002), for approaches that question whether parthood is in general transitive.

is a proper part of x. The notion of overlap is *reflexive* and *symmetric*, but not *transitive* (since, for example, in scenario (i), objects x and y may share a proper part, as do y and z, without z sharing a proper part with x):

Reflexivity of Overlap:	$x \circ x$
Symmetry of Overlap:	$(x \circ y) \rightarrow (y \circ x)$
Intransivity of Overlap:	$\sim[(x \circ y\ \&\ y \circ z) \rightarrow (x \circ z)]$

In other words, every object overlaps itself; if an object overlaps another, then the second overlaps the first; and, finally, it does not in general follow that if one object overlaps a second, and the second overlaps a third, that the first object also overlaps the third. Although the notion of overlap (along with that of disjointness and possibly even that of parthood itself) is easily taken to have *spatial* overtones, it is important to keep in mind that this is merely an artifact of the natural language expression that is used to render this formal relation in ordinary English; according to the original theory of CEM, all of the basic mereological vocabulary is intended to be understood in an entirely *neutral* fashion, to allow for application across a wide range of cases.

Two objects are *disjoint* just in case they do not overlap, or share no (proper or improper) part in common. Disjointness is *symmetric*, but neither reflexive nor transitive:

Symmetry of Disjointness:	$(x \rfloor y) \rightarrow (y \rfloor x)$
Irreflexivity of Disjointness:	$\sim(x \rfloor x)$
Intransitivity of Disjointness:	$\sim[(x \rfloor y\ \&\ y \rfloor z) \rightarrow (x \rfloor z)]$

In other words, if an object is disjoint from another, then the second is also disjoint from the first; nothing is disjoint from itself; and if an object is disjoint from another, and the second disjoint from a third, it does not in general follow that the first is also disjoint from the third.

As can be seen from the occurrence of the definite article in the paraphrases above, the remaining items in the list—*product, sum, difference, universe* and *complement*—are all used to form *singular terms* (with the exception of "At", which plays the role of a *predicate*). The singular term "x·y", which denotes the (binary) *product* of x and y, denotes that object which is part of both x and y, and which is such that any common part of both x and y is a part of it. Such an object will only exist, of course, if x and y have a common part; if they lack a common part, then "x·y" is a non-referring singular term and can be dealt with in whatever manner is chosen to apply to other non-referring singular terms. The notion of product is the mereological analogue of set-theoretic intersection, with the exception that two disjoint sets always have an intersection, viz., the null-set, whereas most mereologies want no truck with such a thing as the "null-object" (which would be defined as that object which is part of everything). The notion of binary product can be generalized to apply to the infinite case by means of the variable-binding operator, π, so that "$\pi x\ [F(x)]$" denotes the product or nucleus (if there is one) of all the objects satisfying the predicate in question. The singular term "$x + y$", which denotes the (binary) *sum* of x and y, denotes that object which is such that something overlaps it just in case it overlaps at least one of x and y. The notion of sum is the mereological analogue of set-theoretic union. Here, no proviso for non-referring singular terms or null-objects is needed, since it is a central thesis of CEM, and possibly its most notorious claim, that any two objects, no matter how disparate and dissimilar, have a sum. Again, the relation of binary sum can be generalized to the infinite case by means of the variable-binding operator, σ, so that "$\sigma x\ [F(x)]$" denotes the object which is the sum of all the objects satisfying the predicate in question.

The singular term "$x - y$", which denotes the *difference* of x and y, denotes the largest object contained within x which has no part in common with y. This difference exists only if x is not a part of y; if x and y overlap and x is not a part of y, then $x - y$ is a proper part of x.

If arbitrary sums exist (that is, if any collection of objects has a sum), then there exists an object which is the sum of all objects whatsoever; this object, of which all other objects are part, is the *Universe*. Since CEM endorses not only the *existence* of arbitrary sums, but also their *uniqueness*, it also follows that there is only *one* such object, *the* Universe. The Universe functions algebraically as the Boolean unit element. In a non-classical system, in which the existence of arbitrary sums is not guaranteed, the existence of the Universe would have to be postulated separately. Assuming that differences and the Universe exist, then the singular term "$U - x$" denotes the *complement* of x, i.e., that object (if there is one) which comprises the remainder of the Universe outside of x.

Our final piece of basic mereological vocabulary consists of the notion of an *atom*: the predicate "$At(x)$" applies to an object just in case the object has no proper parts, i.e., the object is indivisible from the point of view of the theory. Anything may be taken as an atom for the purposes of the theory, whether or not it in fact has parts. (Compare, for example, the case of sentential logic versus predicate-logic: in sentential logic, sentences are taken as atomic for the purposes of the theory, even though we in fact take them to have parts. Predicate-logic, in turn, represents sentences as non-atomic, but construes the objects over which the variables range as atomic, even though, again, many, most or all of them in fact have parts.) Thus, to be a mereological atom simply means to be treated as indivisible by the theory. Whether there *in fact* are any atoms is an open question; certainly, the objects physicists call "atoms" have turned out not to be atoms in the mereological sense, since they have, for example, electrons and protons as parts. Mereology as such is neutral on the question of atomism; but a mereology can be explicitly turned into an *atomic, atomless* or *non-atomic* system, by means of further assumptions:

Atomicity:	$(\forall x)(\exists y)\ (At(y)\ \&\ y \leq x)$
Atomlessness:	$(\forall x)(\exists y)\ (y < x)$
Non-Atomicity:	$(\exists x)(At(x))\ \&\ (\exists x)\ (\forall y)\ (y \leq x \rightarrow (\exists z)(z < y))$

An *atomic* mereology requires that every object either is itself an atom or is composed of atoms. An *atomless* mereology requires that every object is infinitely divisible into further proper parts. A *non-atomic* mereology requires that, among the objects over which it ranges, some are atomic and some are atomless. In an atomic mereology, the cardinality of the domain can be determined on the basis of the cardinality of atoms: for n atoms, there are $2^n - 1$ objects. Atomless and non-atomic mereologies of course have infinite domains.

§I.2.2 The Basic Principles of Standard Mereology

CEM is a very simple, elegant and surprisingly powerful theory. It requires only a single primitive notion in terms of which the remainder of the mereological concepts just introduced (along with others, if so desired) can be defined. In its standard formulations, CEM consists of a mere three axioms; all other statements of the theory follow as theorems from the definitions and axioms of the system. The single primitive can be chosen to be parthood (either $<$ or $\leq$), overlap, disjointness or sum; the other notions are definable in terms of whichever one is taken as primitive. Identity is either assumed as given or (more controversially) as definable in terms of the primitive mereological notion. Although some formulations of CEM make use of set theory, reference to sets can be avoided, as can be seen, for example, from the definitions given above as well as from the formulation of CEM proposed in Goodman (1977). Algebraically speaking, while parthood is a mere partial ordering, CEM has the strength of a complete Boolean algebra, with the zero element deleted.

Historically, the development of CEM was motivated, first, by a desire to avoid the paradoxes of naive set theory and, secondly, by a desire to formulate a thoroughly nominalistic system. It is important to keep in mind, however, that especially the second goal is associated with mereology merely by historical accident and is in no way intrinsically connected with mereology as such; this is an important theme in Simons (1987) and is also visible in the work of others, most prominently perhaps that of Husserl, whose mereology is steeped in modal and other notions which would cause traditional nominalists great discomfort (cf. Husserl's third *Logical Investigation*, 1900–1). Both of these major goals of CEM are achieved by having the variables of the system range over entities of only a single, viz., the lowest, logical type; these entities are referred to by Leonard and Goodman (1940) as *individuals*. (Thus, somewhat misleadingly, the reference of Leonard and Goodman's term "individual" includes mereological sums, i.e., objects which have proper parts.) CEM itself, however, remains completely neutral as to what is taken to be an individual for the purposes of the theory, as the closing passage from Leonard and Goodman (1940) reminds us:

> . . . [The Calculus of Individuals] performs the important service of divorcing the *logical* concept of an individual from metaphysical and practical prejudices, thus revealing that the distinction and interrelation of classes and wholes is capable of a purely formal definition, and that both concepts, and indeed all the concepts of logic, are available as neutral tools for the constructional analysis of the world. Then, for example, it becomes clear that the practice of supposing that *things* are what the x's and y's of *Principia mathematica* denominate and that qualities are necessarily to be interpreted as logical predicates thereof, rather than vice versa, is purely a matter of habit. The dispute between nominalist and realist as to what actual entities are individuals and what are classes is recognized as devolving upon matters of interpretative convenience rather than upon metaphysical necessity.
>
> (Leonard and Goodman 1940, p. 55)

Whatever may have become of Leonard and Goodman's further ambitions for their theory, the basic point of this passage is surely correct: like any formal system, CEM itself of course makes no pronouncements as to what its own variables range over, and hence what gets to count as an individual with respect to the theory. Thus, the theory may in principle be applied to anything which we are willing to regard as an individual and which can be appropriately characterized by means of mereological concepts.

Leonard and Goodman's version of CEM, which is called the "Calculus of Individuals", uses as its single primitive the relation, $|$, of disjointness; identity is assumed (as defined independently, in accordance with the method given in *Principia Mathematica*). Then, "parthood", "overlap", "sum" and "product" can be defined in terms of disjointness as follows:

<u>Definition of Parthood:</u>	$x \leq y \equiv_{def} (\forall z)(z \mid y \rightarrow z \mid x)$
<u>Definition of Proper Part:</u>	$x < y \equiv_{def} x \leq y \ \& \ x \neq y$
<u>Definition of Overlap:</u>	$x \circ y \equiv_{def} (\exists z)(z \leq x \ \& \ z \leq y)$
<u>Definition of Sum:</u>	$xFu\alpha \equiv_{def} (\forall z)((z \mid x) \leftrightarrow (\forall y)(y \in \alpha \rightarrow z \mid y))$
<u>Definition of Product:</u>	$xNu\alpha \equiv_{def} (\forall z)((z \leq x) \leftrightarrow (\forall y)(y \in \alpha \rightarrow z \leq y))$

In other words, an object is a *(proper or improper) part* of another object just in case anything that is disjoint from the second is also disjoint from the first. An object is a *proper part* of another just in case the first is a (proper or improper) part of the second and they are not identical. Two objects *overlap* just in case they have a (proper or improper) part in common. An object *fuses* a set, a, just in case everything that is discrete from the fusion is also discrete from every member of the set and vice versa. An object is the *product* or *nucleus* of a set, a, just in case everything that is a (proper or improper) part of the product is also a (proper or improper) part of every member of the set, and vice versa. The notions of "difference", "universe" and "complement" can also be defined straightforwardly in terms of those already cited; for the sake of brevity, I omit these definitions since they will not be of immediate concern to us in what follows.

We can now state the three axioms of the Calculus of Individuals, assuming any axiom system sufficient for first-order predicate-logic with identity and set theory:

Axiom 1 (Fusions): $(\exists x)(x \in a) \to (\exists y)(yFua)$
Axiom 2 (Parthood): $(x \leq y \ \& \ y \leq x) \to x = y$
Axiom 3 (Overlap): $x \circ y \leftrightarrow \sim(x \mid y)$

The first axiom, which insures the *existence* of fusions (for all non-empty sets), is perhaps the most notorious among the three axioms; though the second axiom, which guarantees their *uniqueness*, has also generated some interesting discussion. The controversy surrounding both of these axioms will concern us further below. The third axiom merely lays down the formal properties of overlap in relation to the primitive notion of disjointness.

A very accessible formulation of CEM, which is slightly different from, but formally equivalent to, that of Leonard and Goodman (1940), is also given in Lewis (1991), where the three basic axioms of standard mereology are stated informally as follows:

Axiom 1 (Unrestricted Composition): Whenever there are some things, then there exists a fusion of those things.
Axiom 2 (Uniqueness of Composition): It never happens that the same things have two different fusions.
Axiom 3 (Transitivity): If x is part of some part of y, then x is part of y.

In what follows, I will, whenever convenient, refer to the first two axioms of CEM using Lewis' terminology, as "Unrestricted Composition" and "Uniqueness of Composition".[8]

§I.2.3 A Gradual Statement of the Theory

Even though, as we have seen, the full-strength theory of CEM can be stated in a very economical way in terms of the definitions and axioms given above, it is actually quite instructive to lay out the theory in a more round-about fashion, by gradually adding stronger and stronger principles to a minimal core, until we arrive at the full-strength version of CEM. Such a gradual exposition of CEM is given in Simons (1987, Sect. I.4). Its purpose is to bring out, for the benefit

---

[8] In the Leonard/Goodman Calculus of Individuals, the transitivity of parthood follows as a theorem from the axioms and definitions of the system.

of those who do *not* view CEM as the ontologically harmless theory it is often advertised to be, how much mereology they can embrace before they arrive at the full-strength principles of CEM which they may find controversial. In what follows, I will present only some of the most important landmarks in Simons' gradual statement of the theory; for a full development, the reader is referred to my source.

We begin by assuming any set of axioms sufficient for first-order predicate-logic with identity; in order to preserve neutrality on the question of whether identity can and should be defined in terms of parthood, we take identity as given. We assume as our single primitive notion proper parthood, $<$. Since proper parthood (or so at any rate we presuppose) is at least a strict partial ordering, we assume that any mereology must accept the *asymmetry* and *transitivity* of $<$,

<u>Axiom 1</u> (Asymmetry): $x < y \rightarrow \sim(y < x)$
<u>Axiom 2</u> (Transitivity): $(x < y \,\&\, y < z) \rightarrow x < z$

from which the *irreflexivity* of proper parthood follows. To capture the characteristics of proper parthood, however, more is needed than what is already encapsulated in Axioms 1 and 2. For one thing, Axioms 1 and 2 are satisfied by models in which an object has only a *single* proper part. And while not all writers agree on this point, Simons at least takes it to be *constitutive* of the notion of proper parthood that an object cannot have merely a single proper part:

How could an individual have a *single* proper part? That goes against what we mean by "part". An individual which has a proper part needs other parts in addition to *supplement* this one to obtain the whole.

(Simons 1987, p. 26; his italics)

Since there are different ways of expressing this point formally, Simons proposes a series of what he calls "Supplementation Principles", of increasing strength. Two such principles, which in Simons' view are clearly too weak, are as follows:

<u>Overly Weak Supplementation Principle I:</u> $(x < y) \rightarrow (\exists z)(z < y \,\&\, z \neq x)$
<u>Overly Weak Supplementation Principle II:</u> $(x < y) \rightarrow (\exists z)(z < y \,\&\, \sim(z \leq x))$

The first principle is too weak, because it does not rule out models in which there is an infinitely descending linear chain of objects; and while each of these objects has more than a single proper part, these are themselves proper parts of its other proper parts. The second principle is too weak because it does not rule out models in which all proper parts overlap each other. To rule out all three sorts of models, we require a principle of at least the strength of the "Weak Supplementation Principle" (WSP),

<u>Axiom 3</u> (Weak Supplementation Principle): $\quad (x < y) \rightarrow (\exists z)(z < y \ \& \ z \lfloor x)$

which requires that an object which has a proper part has at least another proper part disjoint from the first. While this axiom rules out the three models just considered, it still permits models in which distinct objects are made of exactly the same parts, which contradicts the second axiom of standard mereology. In order to exclude this possibility, one must assume either the "Proper Parts Principle" (PPP) or the "Strong Supplementation Principle" (SSP), from which both PPP and WSP follow:

<u>Axiom 4</u> (Proper Parts Principle): $\quad ((\exists z)(z < x) \ \& \ (\forall z)((z < x) \rightarrow (z < y))) \rightarrow x \le y$

<u>Axiom 5</u> (Strong Supplementation Principle): $\quad \sim(x \le y) \rightarrow (\exists z)(z \le x \ \& \ z \lfloor y)$

The axiom system which results from assuming Axioms 1, 2 and 5 still falls well short of CEM, in part because it does not guarantee the existence of unique products. Since the assumption that any two overlapping objects have a unique product appears plausible in an *extensional* mereology, i.e., one which has already accepted, in accordance with PPP or SSP, that no two distinct objects can be made of exactly the same proper parts, it would be natural to supplement Axioms 1, 2 and 5 with a further principle to this effect:

<u>Axiom 6</u> (Products): $\quad (x \circ y) \rightarrow (\exists z)(\forall w)((w \le z) \leftrightarrow (w \le x \ \& \ w \le y))$

In this stronger context, SSP can now be derived from Axioms 1, 2 and 6. Simons refers to the axiom system consisting of Axioms 1, 2 and 6 as "Minimal Extensional Mereology" (MEM). That MEM still has not reached the strength of CEM can be seen from the fact that MEM does not guarantee the conditional or unconditional existence of arbitrary sums, not only in infinite models (since MEM lacks provisions for infinitary operators) but also in small finite models. According to CEM, for example, there is only a single seven-element model (which is built up from three atoms), whereas according to MEM there are many such models (twenty-eight, to be precise). Thus, the remainder of Simons' gradual exposition consists in adding stronger and stronger principles to MEM which concern the conditional or unconditional existence of sums, binary or generalized (as well as the weaker notion of "upper bound", which we can ignore here), such as the following:

<u>Axiom 9</u> (Conditional Binary Sums): $\quad (x \circ y) \rightarrow (\exists!)(x + y)$

<u>Axiom 14</u> (Unconditional Binary Sums): $\quad (\exists!) \ (x + y)$

<u>Axiom 16</u> (Universe): $\quad (\exists x)(\forall y) \ (y \le x)$

<u>Axiom 18</u> (Conditional General Sums): $\quad (\forall x)(\forall y)(((F(x) \ \& \ F(y)) \rightarrow (x \circ y)) \rightarrow (\exists!)(\sigma x[F(x)]))$

Eventually, with Axiom 24 or the "General Sum Principle" (GSP), we reach the full strength of CEM:

<u>Axiom 24</u> (General Sum Principle): $(\exists x)(F(x)) \rightarrow (\exists x)(\forall y)((y \circ x) \leftrightarrow$
$(\exists z)(F(z) \ \& \ (y \circ z)))$

GSP states that for any of the objects that satisfy the predicate in question, there exists a sum of these objects (provided that the predicate has a non-empty extension). Once Axiom 24 is added to Axioms 1, 2 and 3, the resulting system is formally equivalent to CEM and the intermediary stages have thereby become redundant.[9]

§1.3 THE APPLICATION OF STANDARD MEREOLOGY TO ORDINARY MATERIAL OBJECTS

Given its simplicity and strength, CEM no doubt has its attractions as a theory characterizing such formal notions as $<$, $\leq$, $\circ$, $\mathfrak{l}$, $+$, $\cdot$, $-$, π and σ. But whether CEM in fact correctly characterizes our *ordinary* mereological concepts is by no means obvious. For, whatever its merits as a formal theory, it is of course a further question whether the variables of CEM ought to be interpreted as ranging over anything to which we take ourselves to be committed in our ordinary, scientifically informed discourse or which is of any interest to metaphysicians. To anticipate, my own answer to these questions will be negative, and our next goal will be to motivate and defend the thesis that standard mereology does *not* provide the correct tool for the analysis of ordinary material objects. However, while a small minority of philosophers would agree with this assessment (e.g., Armstrong 1978, 1986, 1989, 1991, 1997; Fine 1982, 1994a, 1999; Harte 2002; Husserl 1900–1; Johnston 2002; Simons 1987; van Inwagen 1981, 1987, 1990a, 1993, 1994, 2002), it is fair to say that the vast majority would protest that insofar as we have any understanding of the notions of parthood and composition at all, this understanding derives from standard mereology. The following passage from Lewis (1986a) will do as a representative expression of this sentiment; it is

---

[9] In the context of disputing Lewis' mereological interpretation of set theory in Lewis (1991), Oliver (1994) quite rightly points out that it is doubtful whether even the full-strength system of CEM has really succeeded in *formal* terms in capturing what is characteristic of mereology. For just as not all mere partial orderings are plausibly interpreted as genuine relations of parthood, so similarly not all axiom systems that have the strength of a complete Boolean algebra minus the zero element are plausibly interpreted as being genuinely mereological in character. Oliver gives as an example to illustrate this point any finite set of prime numbers, together with their products: it is not obvious in a case of this sort that a number is *part* of another *merely* because the former *divides* the latter. Thus, it should be kept in mind that it is no objection against weaker systems of mereology that they fail to capture what is genuinely mereological about the relation of parthood in purely formal terms, since the same objection can arguably be launched against the stronger systems as well.

taken from a context in which Lewis is concerned primarily with the Uniqueness of Composition and Armstrong's work on *structural universals* (by "mereology", Lewis means what we have called CEM; and by "mereological composition", he means "composition" in the sense specified by CEM):

My objection [to the idea that there are several different, non-standard senses of composition] is that I do not see by what right the operations are called *combining* operations. An operation applies to several universals; it yields a new universal. But if what goes on is unmereological, in what sense is the new one *composed* of the old ones? In what unmereological sense are they present in it? After all, not just any operation that makes new things from old is a form of composition! There is no sense in which my parents are parts of me, and no sense in which two numbers are parts of their greatest common factor; and I doubt that there is any sense in which Bruce is part of his unit set. [. . .] . . .[If the friend of *"sui generis* composition"] does insist that his unmereological composition is nevertheless composition, in a perfectly literal sense, then I need to be told why. Saying so doesn't make it so. **What is the *general* notion of composition, of which the mereological form is supposed to be only a special case? I would have thought that mereology already describes composition in full generality.** If sets were composed in some unmereological way out of their members, that would do as a precedent to show that there can be unmereological forms of composition; but I have challenged that precedent already.[10]

Thus, in Lewis' view, there is only one genuinely mereological notion of composition and it is that specified by CEM. And while I have tried to be as neutral as possible in my exposition of standard mereology, the reader has perhaps already noticed that there are some reasons for thinking that a skeptical attitude towards Lewis' stance might be justified. For one thing, we have seen that basically *any* assumption concerning the question of which axiom system correctly characterizes the logic of parthood is surrounded by controversy, down to even the seemingly most innocuous requirement that proper parthood be characterized formally as a strict partial ordering: for every assumption concerning parthood that has appeared obvious to some, there are others in the literature who have been willing to challenge it. Moreover, as Simons' gradual exposition of CEM brings out, provided sufficient independent motivation is given, there are various places in the evolving axiom system, short of the full-strength theory of CEM, at which one could stop and still end up with something which arguably deserves to be called a mereology; a weaker mereology of this sort will also come with an associated weaker sense of "composition", which may nevertheless deserve to be viewed as genuinely mereological. We will in what follows encounter reasons for thinking that an adequate analysis of ordinary material objects dictates precisely such a strategy. Without going into Lewis' arguments in any detail at this juncture, it thus seems reasonable to believe that there is at the very least room for other genuinely mereological notions of composition besides that of CEM.

[10] Lewis (1986a, p. 97); his italics, my bold-face; page numbers come from the reprinted version in Lewis (1999).

But suppose, for the moment, that Lewis is right in thinking that standard composition is the only genuinely mereological form of composition there is. We began by taking it as an intuitive datum that ordinary material objects are *wholes* composed of parts; and everyone except the Nihilist (who believes that nothing has proper parts) will concur. If we combine this intuitive datum with Lewis' thesis that standard composition is the only genuinely mereological notion of composition, then we of course get the result that ordinary material objects must be wholes in the standard sense of composition, i.e., that ordinary material objects must be *mereological sums*.

The thesis that ordinary material objects are mereological sums has been remarkably popular among three-dimensionalists and four-dimensionalists alike. From a three-dimensionalist perspective, perhaps the most well-known defense of this approach can be found in Judith Jarvis Thomson's influential article "Parthood and Identity Across Time" (Thomson 1983). Among the four-dimensionalist tradition, the arguments provided by David Lewis, especially in Lewis (1986b) and (1991), have had a wide following; some of Lewis' main arguments in defense of standard mereology have also been adopted and elaborated in creative ways in Theodore Sider's recent book, *Four-Dimensionalism: An Ontology of Persistence and Time* (2001). Thus, we shall turn next to Thomson, Lewis and Sider's arguments in favor of the thesis that ordinary material objects are best viewed as mereological sums, in the standard sense.

II

Ordinary Objects as Mereological Sums

§II.1 INTRODUCTORY REMARKS

The last chapter has been devoted mainly to an exposition of the main concepts and principles of standard mereology. By "standard mereology", I mean the system referred to in Simons (1987) as "Classical Extensional Mereology" or CEM, originally developed by Leśniewski and introduced to the English-speaking world primarily in the guise of Leonard and Goodman's "Calculus of Individuals" (Leonard and Goodman 1940). Despite CEM's considerable merits as a formal theory, it remains to be seen whether it is of any use to the metaphysician in characterizing our ordinary mereological concepts, as they apply to our scientifically informed, common-sense ontology. One of my main theses in what follows is that CEM is the wrong theory for this purpose. However, since this view goes against a powerful trend within contemporary metaphysics, we would do well to examine first what motivates the position that ordinary material objects are mereological sums in the standard sense. To this task, we will turn next.

§II.2 THOMSON'S THREE-DIMENSIONALIST APPROACH

From a three-dimensionalist perspective, a prominent defense of the view just outlined can be found in Judith Jarvis Thomson's classic paper, "Parthood and Identity Across Time" (Thomson 1983). In this essay, Thomson proposes that ordinary material objects, such as Tinkertoy houses, ought to be regarded as mereological sums according to the standard conception, though she finds that in order for the application of standard mereology to the case of ordinary material objects to have any plausibility at all, the standard conception must be extended and weakened in certain respects. Let's examine Thomson's support for this position.

Her argument begins with the following two observations, which she takes to be intuitively compelling:

A Tinkertoy house is made of Tinkertoys. And surely a Tinkertoy house is made only of Tinkertoys: surely it has no additional ingredients, over and above the Tinkertoys it is made of. (Perhaps there is such an entity as 'house-shape'. Even if there is, it certainly is not literally part of any Tinkertoy house.)

It is an attractive idea that the logic of parthood is the Leonard–Goodman Calculus of Individuals, . . .

(Thomson 1983, p. 201)

The two ideas Thomson finds to be intuitively compelling are, first, that a Tinkertoy house is made of Tinkertoys and *only* of Tinkertoys; and, secondly, that the logic of parthood is correctly captured by CEM. The second assumption is not taken by Thomson as set in stone and is modified in crucial respects in the remainder of her essay, though I suspect she would not want to give up the first one under any but the most dire circumstances. (To anticipate, my own view in what follows will be that both assumptions must be rejected.) Thomson doesn't at this point say why we should think of CEM as the correct theory of parthood; but, in addition to the considerations she provides to this effect in the remainder of the essay, she also may have in mind that CEM, in the guise of the Leonard–Goodman Calculus of Individuals, arguably was at the time at which her essay was written, and possibly still is, the most widely known and well-worked-out theory of parthood available.

Once we accept the two assumptions just stated, (i) that the parts of the Tinkertoy house are all and only the Tinkertoys, and (ii) that CEM correctly characterizes the logic of parthood, then we get the following result. If the Tinkertoy house exists and is composed only of Tinkertoys, then (by the Principle of Unrestricted Composition) it follows that there is such a thing as the unique fusion of the Tinkertoys which compose the house. And once we are committed to the fusion of Tinkertoys, it would of course be natural to suggest that the Tinkertoy house be identified with the fusion, since we are otherwise committed to the result that the single region of space-time in question is occupied by both the Tinkertoy house and the numerically distinct Tinkertoy fusion.

However, this simple view, which preserves both the spirit and the letter of (i) and (ii), faces an immediate obstacle, viz. the problem of *change over time*: intuitively, Tinkertoy houses can change their parts over time, but CEM-style mereological sums cannot, since numerical identity according to CEM requires sameness of parts and no allowances are made within CEM for sensitivity to time. Thus, it seems that the simple view must be abandoned and Tinkertoy houses cannot be fusions in exactly the sense of CEM.

One way out of this quandary is to endorse the doctrine of temporal parts, a four-dimensionalist metaphysic. The four-dimensionalist may continue to view ordinary material objects as mereological sums in the standard sense *and* account for the problem of change over time in the following way. The spatio-temporally extended Tinkertoy house persists over time, according to this approach, by having, in addition to its ordinary spatial parts, numerically distinct temporal parts at each of the different times at which the Tinkertoy house exists. (We are to understand the temporal parts of the Tinkertoy house roughly on analogy with its spatial parts: just like the Tinkertoy house has a left half and a right half, so we are to think of it as also having an "earlier half" and a "later half"; see Thomson 1983 and Sider 2001 for a more detailed exposition of the four-dimensionalist outlook.) Now, for the Tinkertoy house to change its parts over time, on this view, just means for its earlier temporal parts to have different (spatial) parts from those of its later temporal parts; but since the earlier temporal parts and the later temporal parts are numerically distinct objects, no violation of Leibniz's Law is thereby incurred.

This would be a fine way of preserving assumptions (i) and (ii), if only the doctrine of temporal parts were an acceptable metaphysical theory concerning the nature of ordinary material objects (as opposed to, say, that of events like football games). But Thomson famously objects that the doctrine of temporal parts is "a crazy metaphysic—obviously false" (Thomson 1983, p. 210), since it entails that material objects are constantly being generated *ex nihilo* (or, at least, the stuff of which they are composed is). I won't comment here on Thomson's classic *ex nihilo* objection (but see Koslicki 2003a and 2003b for further discussion), since our main concern presently is Thomson's own positive proposal as to how the three-dimensionalist can best preserve assumptions (i) and (ii) in the face of the problem of change over time.

In response, Thomson offers a *temporalized* version of the Calculus of Individuals, which she calls the "Cross-Temporal Calculus of Individuals". Since, as she observes, it really is intuitively obvious that ordinary material objects can change their parts over time, parthood (for the three-dimensionalist) must be a *three-place* relation between pairs of objects and times, not the timeless *two-place* relation at work in the original Calculus of Individuals. In this way, the logic of parthood cannot be *quite* that of the original Calculus of Individuals, but it can nevertheless be something reasonably close to it, something which preserves the spirit of the original Calculus of Individuals while allowing for the phenomenon of change over time.

The new Cross-Temporal Calculus of Individuals now defines "fusion" as relativized to times in terms of its primitive notion, temporalized disjointness, in the following way:

Fusion at a Time: $xFuS@t \equiv_{def} xE@t \ \& \ (\forall y) \ [(y \vert x@t) \leftrightarrow (\forall z)((z \in S \ \& \ zE@t) \rightarrow (y \vert z@t))]$

In other words, a mereological sum, x, fuses a set, S, at a time, t, just in case x exists at t and anything that is at t disjoint from x is also disjoint at t from every member of S, and vice versa. In place of the old fusion-axiom, Thomson suggests indefinitely many axioms of the following form:

Cross-Temporal Fusions: $[t_1 \neq t_2 \ \& \ (\exists x)(x \in S_1 \ \& \ xE@t_1) \ \& \ (\exists y)(y \in S_2 \ \& \ yE@t_2)] \rightarrow (\exists z)(zFuS_1@t_1 \ \& \ zFuS_2@t_2)$

Each new fusion-axiom of this form states that for any two non-empty sets whose members exist at two distinct times, there is a mereological sum which fuses the members of the one set at the one time and the members of the other set at the other time. In place of the old Uniqueness Axiom, Thomson proposes the following temporalized version:

Temporalized Uniqueness: $(x = y) \leftrightarrow (\forall t) [((xE@t) \lor (yE@t)) \rightarrow ((x \leq y@t) \lor (y \leq x@t)]$

In other words, objects x and y are numerically identical just in case they are parts of each other at every time at which they exist. (See also Simons 1987, for another version of a temporalized three-dimensionalist mereology.) With the temporalized version of CEM in hand, the three-dimensionalist now has the option of viewing the Tinkertoy house as a *cross-temporal* fusion of Tinkertoys, which may, without contradiction, fuse different sets of Tinkertoys at different times.[1]

This is not quite the end of the story, though. For, in analogy with the temporal problem, the three-dimensionalist who takes Thomson's position also faces the problem that the *modal* properties of the Tinkertoy house are intuitively different from those of a cross-temporal fusion of Tinkertoys. For suppose that an object and the parts that compose it happen to have exactly the same spatio-temporal extent; that is, they go out of existence and come into existence at exactly the same times. (It helps to think of ice-sculptures in this context; see also Gibbard 1975 for a well-known illustration of a scenario of this kind.) It now follows from Thomson's Cross-Temporal Calculus of Individuals that the objects in question are numerically identical, since they have the same parts *at all times* at which they exist. But this looks to be intuitively the wrong result, since we might ordinarily agree, for example, that the very same ice *might have* never composed an ice-sculpture at all, that it *might have* composed a different ice-sculpture, that the very same ice-sculpture *might have* been made of slightly different ice, and so on (though Thomson doesn't seem to think our intuitions are crystal-clear in this respect). (A modal objection of this sort is raised against the four-dimensionalist in van Inwagen 1990b.)

Those who accept the intuition that ice-sculptures and the ice that composes them have divergent modal properties, it seems, must now extend the Cross-Temporal Calculus of Individuals in some fashion to make room for modal notions, i.e., they must adopt a "Modal Cross-Temporal Calculus of Individuals".

---

[1] Thomson's Cross-Temporal Calculus of Individuals still carries a commitment to coinciding objects, i.e., numerically distinct objects which occupy exactly the same region of space-time. For if it is the case that the parts that currently compose the Tinkertoy house needn't always compose the Tinkertoy house, then the current parts are fused into lots of distinct cross-temporal fusions whose careers at other times diverge from that of the Tinkertoy house itself. These cross-temporal fusions are numerically distinct from one another, but coincide spatio-temporally during certain periods of time. One might think that their coincidence is made somewhat more bearable by the fact that they are mutual parts of each other during the times at which they coincide; alternatively, one might also find it even more puzzling how objects can be parts of each other during certain periods of time and yet not be numerically identical.

Thomson ends her paper by suggesting that such a modalized version of CEM should endorse a new, further weakening of the Uniqueness Axiom, according to which objects are numerically identical just in case they *necessarily* have the same parts at all times at which they exist:

Modalized Uniqueness: $\quad (x = y) \leftrightarrow \Box(\forall t)[((xE@t) \lor (yE@t)) \rightarrow ((x \leq y@t) \lor (y \leq x@t)]$

This further modification would get us around the modal problem just raised, since it would allow, for example, that the ice and the ice-sculpture are numerically distinct even though their actual spatio-temporal extent happens to be exactly the same.[2]

Given our exposition of Thomson's views, we can now state her support for the thesis that ordinary material objects are best analyzed as mereological sums, in a suitably weakened and extended sense, as follows. The idea that the parts of a Tinkertoy house are all and only the Tinkertoys that compose it is intuitively attractive. Arguably the most widely known and well-worked-out theory of parthood is CEM, in the guise of the Leonard–Goodman Calculus of Individuals. CEM appears to run into trouble with the problem of change over time. A popular fix for this difficulty, the doctrine of temporal parts, has unacceptable consequences of its own. But a temporalized version of CEM, which is still reasonably close to the spirit of the original theory, can get around the problem of change over time. The temporalized version of CEM now runs into a modal analogue of the problem of change over time; but this difficulty can be addressed in parallel fashion by modalizing CEM. The thesis that ordinary material objects are mereological sums in the (extended) standard sense thus seems to have survived the major temporal and modal hurdles intact.[3] The only remaining matter is to lay to rest the worries of those who believe that CEM isn't the ontologically innocent theory it is often made out to be. To this end, Thomson tries at various places in her essay to address the concerns of those who are troubled by CEM's commitment to arbitrary sums by pointing out that her argument could run equally well with a more restricted commitment to

---

[2] It does so of course only at the price of further commitment to coincident objects. For, just as in the temporal case, a single this-worldly fusion of parts may be associated with many different other-worldly fusions of parts; the resulting objects are all strictly speaking numerically distinct even though they share exactly the same this-worldly spatio-temporal extent. Depending on one's outlook, their coincidence is again either mitigated or made even more puzzling by the fact that they are this-worldly parts of each other. The nature of some of these numerically distinct coinciding objects is investigated further in Thomson (1998).

[3] Of course, Thomson's proposal is not the only option available to the three-dimensionalist. For example, another possibility would be to argue that modal and temporal arguments for distinctness using Leibniz's Law, such as those considered by Thomson, can be defeated in another way. Views of this kind will be taken up for discussion and rejected below (see also Koslicki 2005a for arguments to this effect). Assuming that arguments from Leibniz's Law really do establish numerical distinctness, though, Thomson is right to think that parthood for the three-dimensionalist must be temporalized and modalized.

sums. Thomson herself, however, does not mind CEM's full-blown Unrestricted Composition Principle one bit and remarks that "one only has to live with fusions for a while to come to love them" (Thomson 1983, p. 217).

We thus find in Thomson (1983) a three-dimensionalist defense of the thesis that ordinary material objects are temporalized and modalized mereological sums. And although Thomson's version of standard mereology modifies the original formulation of CEM developed in Leonard and Goodman (1940) in certain important respects, it is not too far-fetched to continue to regard such a Modal Cross-Temporal Calculus of Individuals as a working out of what I have been calling the standard conception of mereology. A modalized version of CEM of course does more violence to the intentions of its original founders than does a temporalized version; but we have already noted that extreme nominalism was associated with mereology purely by historical accident and thus comes as an independent theoretical commitment of this particular group of philosophers. Thomson's Calculus still makes provisions for the existence and uniqueness of mereological sums, two of the most characteristic features of CEM, even if her Uniqueness Principle is weakened to allow for temporary or contingent coincidence and full-blown commitment to arbitrary sums is not required by anything she says in her essay (though Thomson herself is happy to accept Unrestricted Composition). Most importantly, though, the original analogy between the identity- and existence-conditions of mereological sums and those of sets is preserved in crucial respects by Thomson's modified version of CEM: just as the existence and identity of a set depends on nothing more than the existence and identity of its members, so the existence and identity of a mereological sum depends on nothing more than that of its parts. Correspondingly, since ordinary material objects on Thomson's view just are temporalized and modalized sums, their existence and identity too depends on nothing more than the existence and identity of their parts at a time and in a world. I take the preservation of this characteristic analogy between sets and sums to be sufficient grounds for regarding Thomson's Calculus as a manifestation of standard mereology.[4]

Despite the merits of Thomson's Calculus, we shall find in what follows that a three-dimensionalist analysis of ordinary material objects in terms of CEM, even in this suitably extended and weakened form, cannot be sustained. First, however, I turn to Lewis' four-dimensionalist approach, which will also give us occasion to consider in more detail how standard mereologists might try to convince those who are skeptical that their theory is in fact as ontologically innocent as it is advertised to be, even when it embraces the full-blown commitment to arbitrary sums.

---

[4] If anything, mereological sums according to the standard conception are even *less* structured than sets, since standard mereology makes no room for a distinction analogous to that between subset and membership; in order to avoid the set-theoretic paradoxes and to satisfy the nominalist commitments of the standard mereology's original founders, all the entities quantified over within standard mereology were taken to be of the same ontological type, viz., individuals.

§II.3 LEWIS' FOUR-DIMENSIONALIST APPROACH

David Lewis has been among the most visible four-dimensionalist defenders of the thesis that ordinary material objects are mereological sums in the standard sense. Lewis' defense of this approach has several detachable components: (i) his defense of *four-dimensionalism* over three-dimensionalism as the most promising theory of persistence (see especially Lewis 1983a and 1986b); (ii) his defense of the principle of *unrestricted mereological composition* (see especially Lewis 1986b); (iii) his defense of the *Uniqueness of Composition* primarily against Armstrong's alternative conception in the realm of properties (see especially Lewis 1991 and 1986a); and, finally, (iv) his *Composition-as-Identity* thesis which is intended to establish that standard mereology is ontologically innocent (see especially Lewis 1991).[5]

In the present chapter, our main concern is with components (ii) and (iv) of Lewis' view. Since I am not currently engaged directly in the dispute between three-dimensionalists and four-dimensionalists, I will not take up component (i), i.e., the so-called "problem of temporary intrinsics" of Lewis (1986b) or the condensed argument in favor of temporal parts in the Postscript to Lewis (1983a). We can also leave aside, for present purposes, component (iii) of Lewis' defense of four-dimensionalism: since four-dimensionalism is precisely designed to avoid commitment to numerically distinct spatio-temporal coinciding objects, violations of Uniqueness of Composition do not arise for Lewis in the realm of material objects; he only has to worry about them in the context of his preference for a nominalist conception of properties as classes of possible and actual concrete particulars, over Armstrong's alternative conception of properties as Aristotelian universals. Assuming then that (i) has been dealt with sufficiently in another setting and by other writers, and that a discussion of (iii) has been deferred to another occasion, let's turn to components (ii) and (iv) of Lewis' approach.

§II.3.1 Support for Unrestricted Composition

Along with everyone other than the Nihilist, Lewis accepts the intuitive datum that ordinary material objects are *wholes* composed of parts. Component (i) of Lewis' analysis leads to a certain conception of what sorts of things ordinary material objects are and what sorts of things they number among their parts: in

---

[5] Components (i) and (ii) are the main focus in Sider (2001); see also Koslicki (2003a) and (2003b) for discussion. A less condensed version of the argument in Lewis (1983a) can be found in Hawthorne, Scala and Wasserman (2004). Unrestricted Composition is opposed in van Inwagen (1990). For interesting discussion of component (iv), see, for example, Baxter (1988a) and (1988b); Harte (2002); Oliver (1994); and van Inwagen (1994). Contribution to the lively debate over universals include Armstrong (1978, 1980a, 1986, 1988, 1989, 1991, 1997); Bigelow (1986); Devitt (1980); Forrest (1986a) and (1986b); Quine (1980); and Williams (1953).

addition to their more familiar spatial parts, they also have less familiar temporal parts at each time at which they exist. But their four-dimensional nature in itself doesn't settle the question of *how* ordinary material objects are composed of these temporal and spatial parts, i.e., what the notion of mereological composition is that is operative in this context. We have already quoted Lewis earlier, at the end of Chapter I, as being of the firm opinion that there is only a single genuine kind of mereological composition, namely that captured by the axiom system of CEM. In Lewis' formulation, the three axioms of CEM are (i) Unrestricted Composition, (ii) the Uniqueness of Composition and (iii) the transitivity of parthood. Among these axioms, we follow Lewis in taking the third to be unassailable, despite the fact that even this axiom has not gone completely unchallenged in the literature. Thus, if Lewis wants us to follow him in taking composition, as it applies to ordinary material objects, to be the notion described by CEM, he must convince us that there is no way around accepting the first two axioms of standard mereology along with the third. Given Lewis' four-dimensionalism, the Uniqueness of Composition is inert in the context of ordinary material objects. For all the usual non-Gibbard-style cases of putative coincidence (e.g., cases of constitutionally related objects with different spatio-temporal extents) present us with mere temporary overlap, while Gibbard-style cases are dealt with by invoking counterpart theory. (See Sider 2001, ch. 5 for a more detailed exposition of the four-dimensionalist response to the puzzles of coincidence.) Either way, ordinary material objects, according to the four-dimensionalist picture, don't threaten to violate the Uniqueness of Composition. Thus, if Lewis wants to convince us that ordinary material objects are four-dimensional mereological sums in the standard sense, the most important item on his agenda is a defense of the first axiom, the principle of unrestricted mereological composition, according to which any plurality of objects whatsoever, no matter how disparate and gerrymandered, composes a further object, their sum.[6]

§II.3.1.1 *The Lewis/Sider Argument from Vagueness*

Lewis' argument to this effect can be found in a very condensed passage in Lewis (1986b, ch. 4, pp. 211 ff), which is helpfully summarized by Sider as follows:

> If not every class has a fusion then there must be a restriction on composition. Moreover, the only plausible restrictions on composition would be vague ones. But there can be no vague restrictions on composition, because that would mean that whether composition occurs is sometimes vague. Therefore, every class has a fusion.

(Sider 2001, p. 121)

Very briefly, Lewis' reason for thinking that any plausible restriction on mereological composition would have to be vague is as follows. We are intuitively

---

[6] My remarks in the following section against the Lewis/Sider argument in favor of unrestricted mereological composition are drawn from Koslicki (2003a).

more comfortable with certain fusions than with others: the fusion of all the molecules that are currently part of my body, for example, seems acceptable using such intuitively plausible principles as physical contact, adjacency, unified action, contrast with the environment, and the like; Lewis' legendary "trout-turkey" (an object which fuses the upper half of a trout with the lower half of a turkey), on the other hand, makes us queasy. But there is no principled line to be drawn between fusions that make us queasy and those that do not; any plausible candidate for a restriction on mereological composition would therefore need to reflect this fuzziness in our intuitions.

Lewis' reason for thinking that it can never be indeterminate whether composition takes place is this. The only acceptable account of vagueness is one which locates the source of vagueness in language and thought: vagueness is a matter of semantic indecision. But the question of whether a given plurality of objects composes something can be formulated in a part of language which does not contain any vague vocabulary. Therefore, the question of whether a given plurality of objects composes something can never receive a vague answer.

Many of us find that Lewis' argument goes by a bit fast. In only a little over two pages, he reaches the (to some of us) startling conclusion that composition *always* occurs, whenever there is a plurality of objects. It is thus helpful to examine a less condensed statement and justification of Lewis' argument, as proposed in Sider (2001, ch. 4). Sider refers to this argument as the "argument from vagueness". The role of this argument in Sider's defense of four-dimensionalism cannot be overestimated, since, as I have argued in Koslicki (2003a), a creatively adopted, temporalized version of it in effect becomes Sider's main strategy of breaking the dialectical stand-off between endurantists and perdurantists. Sider's (non-temporalized) version of Lewis' argument goes as follows:

(P1) If not every class has a fusion, then there must be a pair of cases connected by a continuous series such that in one, composition occurs, but in the other, composition does not occur.

(P2) In no continuous series is there a sharp cut-off in whether composition occurs.

(P3) In any case of composition, either composition definitely occurs, or composition definitely does not occur.

This argument uses several technical notions: that of a "case of composition", that of a "continuous series" of cases of composition, and that of a "sharp cut-off" point between cases of composition. A "case of composition" is simply a possible situation involving a class of objects which have certain properties and stand in certain relations; one can ask with respect to various such possible situations whether or not the objects in question compose anything. (Somewhat confusingly, something can be a case of composition, even though composition does not take place in it.) A "continuous series" is taken to be a finite series of cases of composition connecting a case, C_1, with a case, C_2, such that each case in the series is extremely similar to the case immediately adjacent to it in all relevant respects (e.g., qualitative homogeneity, spatial proximity, unity of action, comprehensiveness of causal relations).[7] A "sharp cut-off" in a series of cases of composition is a pair of adjacent cases, such that in one composition definitely occurs and in the other composition definitely fails to occur.

The first premise of Sider's argument states that, if composition were to be restricted, there would be at least one continuous series of cases, which connects a case of composition with a case of non-composition. Premise (P2) says that the shift from composition to non-composition in such a series does not happen suddenly. Premise (P3) rules out that any such shift could happen gradually. But if the shift can neither happen suddenly nor gradually, then it cannot happen at all. Thus, the requirements which would need to be met in order for composition to be restricted cannot be met; hence, composition is unrestricted.

(In what follows, let's call the subscriber to the Lewis/Sider line, according to which mereological composition is unrestricted and takes place under all circumstances, a "Universalist" about mereological composition. I will refer to the position of their main opponent as "the intermediary position", according to which composition takes place under certain circumstances but not under others; the boundary between circumstances in which composition takes place and those in which composition fails to take place may, but needn't, be vague. As mentioned earlier, "Nihilism" about mereological composition is the position that composition never takes place; there are only mereological simples.)

One of Sider's biggest challenges is to show why his argument should not in fact be likened to the following strikingly bad argument:[8]

(P1′) If baldness is restricted, then there must be a pair of cases connected by a continuous series such that in one baldness occurs and in the other baldness does not occur.

(P2′) In no continuous series is there a sharp cut-off in whether baldness occurs.

(P3′) In any case of baldness, either baldness definitely occurs or baldness definitely does not occur.

---

[7] As a possible example for such a continuous series, take C_1 to be a case involving the molecules that are now part of my body and C_2 to be a case involving those same molecules long after I have died, when they are scattered into different regions of the Milky Way; it is likely that supporters of restricted composition would agree that the first is a case of composition, while the second is a case of non-composition, and that the two cases can be connected by some continuous series. If this example is not to the liking of those supporting restricted composition, they are invited to pick their own example: all Sider requires is that there is *at least one* such case which can be connected by a continuous series.

[8] In analogy with the definition of "a case of composition", I understand the phrase "case of baldness" in such a way that it leaves open whether baldness occurs in it or not; thus, a "case of baldness" is simply a possible situation involving the "ingredients" for baldness or non-baldness, i.e., people and their hair, or lack thereof.

Here, of course, the most intuitively plausible view is precisely that "baldness is restricted", so to speak; both "Universalism" and "Nihilism" about baldness are extremely counterintuitive, to say the least. Thus, the most reasonable position concerning baldness seems to be precisely the kind of intermediate position which is supposed to be untenable in the case of composition. The existence of a continuous series of cases involving baldness should also not be in doubt, since in typical cases of baldness one and the same man goes bald slowly over time, which at the same time gives plausibility to (P2')'s assumption that this process takes place gradually. What we would of course balk at is (P3'), the assumption that there can be no indeterminacy in whether or not baldness occurs; "is bald" is, after all, everyone's favorite example of a vague predicate.[9]

Sider's main work, in my view, therefore lies in defending the plausibility of (P3) in the case of composition. In what follows, I will simply grant to him the truth of (P1) and (P2).[10] I will also grant to him two "local" presuppositions he uses in his argument: (i) that the only plausible account of vagueness is the linguistic one (according to which vagueness is always a matter of semantic indecision); and (ii) that logic can never be a source of vagueness (though we will have to be careful about what exactly granting this assumption comes to in this context). We will furthermore not dispute two more "global" presuppositions Sider makes throughout his book: (i) Lewis' "best-candidate" theory of meaning, according to which meaning supervenes on use and intrinsic eligibility (see, for example, Lewis 1983b); and (ii) the anti-Carnapian assumption defended in the introduction of Sider (2001), according to which genuine ontological disagreement is possible between two feuding factions.[11]

Why, then, should we not think that there is a region somewhere between the definite case of composition, C_1, and the definite case of non-composition, C_2, in which it is indeterminate whether composition occurs? Perhaps, some years after I have been buried, the molecules that were part of my body just before I died are still fairly close together but not so close that they clearly compose the remains of a human body, for example; some may have been carried off by winds or rains. If the Lewis/Sider line concerning mereological composition is correct, it seems that one would in fact *expect* there to be such an indeterminate region in a series connecting a case of composition with a case of non-composition, since any restricted account of composition must match the indeterminacy present in our intuitions concerning composition.

---

[9] Sider himself turns out to be a "Nihilist" about baldness (see Sider and Braun 2007); however, his position on this issue does not affect the present discussion, since we are not currently debating the plausibility of any particular theory of vagueness.

[10] This is not to say, however, that the question of whether the truth of (P2) should be granted to Sider does not also raise questions which are worth pursuing; see, for example, Markosian (1998a) and Hudson (2000) and (2001), especially Chapter Three, for interesting discussion of the status of (P2).

[11] The nature of ontological disagreement is pursued further in Koslicki (2005b).

§II.3.1.2 *The Controversial Premise (P3)*

Let's see, then, what Sider has to say in defense of (P3). We have of course already heard Lewis' justification: the question of whether composition occurs can never have a vague answer, since it can be stated in a part of language which contains no vague vocabulary. But Lewis' justification contains a step which looks to be blatantly circular:

> Vagueness is semantic indecision. But not all of language is vague. The truth-functional connectives aren't, for instance. Nor are the words for identity and difference, *and for the partial identity of overlap.* Nor are the idioms of quantification, so long as they are unrestricted. How could any of these be vague? What would be the alternatives between which we haven't chosen?
>
> (Lewis 1986b, p. 212; my emphasis)

As we saw in Chapter I, composition can be defined either in terms of overlap or in terms of one of the other basic mereological vocabulary items (which in turn can be used to define the notion of overlap). Thus, it would seem that in a context in which the question at issue is whether the mereological notion of composition can ever be vague, it cannot legitimately be taken for granted that the mereological notion in terms of which it is defined (overlap or parthood or disjointness) is not vague.[12]

Sider attempts to bypass Lewis' illicit assumption in his defense of (P3). The crucial move in Sider's justification of (P3) is to attempt to show that Lewis' assumption (that composition can never be vague) can be restated in a part of language which only contains *logical* vocabulary (and no longer any objectionable *mereological* vocabulary). Given Sider's presupposition that logic can never be a source of vagueness, the truth of (P3) would then follow.

Let's now consider Sider's proposed circumvention of Lewis' illicit assumption. If it ever were a vague matter whether composition takes place (so Sider argues), then it would also be a vague matter how many concrete objects exist. For consider a collection, C, of objects; if the world contains the fusion of C, in addition to the objects in C, then the world would contain one more object. But if it is indeterminate whether C has a fusion, then it is also indeterminate whether the world contains this additional object, the fusion of C, over and above the objects in C. That is, there would be some numerical sentence of the form "There are *n* concrete objects" (for some finite value of "*n*"), whose truth-value is indeterminate. But a numerical sentence of the form "There are *n* concrete objects", according to Sider, contains no mereological vocabulary, only logical

---

[12] Perhaps, Lewis is less troubled by this move than I am because he also sometimes sounds as though he takes mereological notions themselves to be logical. This goes along with his Composition-as-Identity Thesis, which will be examined in the next section. Unfortunately, Sider seems to embrace Lewis' arguments in favor of the Composition-as-Identity Thesis (Sider 2001, pp. 160–1), though he does not invoke them in the context of his justification of (P3).

terms and the predicate "is concrete". Thus, Lewis' assumption that composition can never be vague can thus be reformulated in non-mereological terms, since (C) can be justified by way of (N):

(C) Composition is never vague.

(N) No numerical sentence of the form "There are *n* concrete objects" (for some finite value of "*n*") is ever indeterminate in truth-value.

Conversely, instead of focusing our attention on (~C), the claim endorsed by this version of the intermediary position, we can instead debate the truth of (~N):

(~C) Composition is sometimes vague.

(~N) Numerical sentences of the form "There are *n* concrete objects" (for some finite value of "*n*") are sometimes indeterminate in truth-value.

Now, if Sider's claim is correct and (N) contains no mereological vocabulary, then the assumption that logic is non-vague, in conjunction with the claim that no vagueness can result from the concreteness-predicate, should buy him his conclusion, that (N) is true.[13]

Suppose now that there is a particular numerical sentence (X) of the form "There are *n* concrete objects" (for some finite value of "*n*"), whose truth-value is in dispute between the Universalist and the holder of the intermediary position. The Universalist (let's suppose) says that (X) is definitely true (because he thinks that the questionable fusion at issue definitely exists), while the holder of the intermediary position believes (X) is indeterminate in truth-value. What could the two of them possibly be disagreeing over? (X), so Sider would argue, contains nothing but logical vocabulary (ignoring the concreteness predicate): the existential quantifier, logical connectives and the identity relation; but none of these (in Sider's view) is a plausible candidate for a term which has different possible precisifications. Thus, anyone who grants that logic is non-vague must also agree that (X) has a determinate truth-value.

---

[13] In my view, Sider's use of the concreteness-predicate in this context is in fact illegitimate; however, since my objection to his use of the concreteness-predicate is really just another version of the objection to (P3) I am about to raise, I will not elaborate in detail my reasons for taking his use of this predicate to be illegitimate. Most importantly, it seems to me that the concreteness-predicate is implicitly mereological and that a stipulative definition of "is concrete" in terms of "is abstract" of the kind Sider attempts to give is hopeless. However, Sider's main purpose in adding the concreteness-predicate to the numerical sentences in question is merely to assure the existence of *finite* instances of such sentences (i.e., to keep out all the sets and other abstract objects, which would make all finite instances of "bare" numerical sentences false). The question of whether there is a way of making finite instances of the numerical sentences at issue true is independent of the dispute between the Universalist and the proponent of the intermediary position. To see this, assume, for instance, that both participants in the dispute are radical nominalists: they might agree that there are no infinite hierarchies of abstract objects and still disagree over whether composition is non-vague.

While I am willing to grant Sider that logic is non-vague, we must consider carefully what granting this assumption really comes to, in this context. Let's put aside, again, the notions that are not central to this dispute: the identity relation and the logical connectives; what is central to this dispute is surely the existential quantifier. So how do the participants in this dispute stand with respect to the existential quantifier?

The Universalist and the holder of the intermediary position can, I think, agree on the *meaning* of the existential quantifier, in the sense that they can agree on which logical operation is denoted by the symbol "∃". They can also agree that the existential quantifier is non-vague, in the sense that it can be precisely specified which logical operation it denotes. But settling on the meaning of the existential quantifier by itself does not settle what its *range* is: two philosophers can perfectly well agree on what the symbol "∃" means, while still carrying on a thoroughly sensible dispute over the *size and the nature of the domain of quantification* (while both of them are talking about *unrestricted* quantification). This is exactly the kind of situation in which the Universalist and the holder of the intermediary position find themselves. They are not merely equivocating on the meaning of "∃"; rather, they are engaged in a genuine ontological dispute over *what* exists and *how many* things exist: in other words, they disagree over what it means to be an *object*.

The same situation obtains with respect to the notion of a fusion. The Universalist and the holder of the intermediary position can, again, agree on what the term "fusion" means, e.g., that it denotes the operation defined in the first chapter. But this does not mean that they agree on *which* fusions exist: here, the holder of the intermediary position will insist that the relation "x fuses a class, α" only applies in conditions in which a certain *further* constraint is met (i.e., the restriction on composition must be satisfied). The Universalist, on the other hand, believes that the relation "x fuses a class, α" applies in every situation in which we are dealing with a plurality of objects; no further constraints need be satisfied. They therefore agree on the *meaning* of the term "fusion", but they disagree on its *range*.

Nothing has been gained by reformulating the dispute between the Universalist and the holder of the intermediary position in terms of (N), instead of (C). For the truth-value of a numerical sentence like (X) cannot be settled in the absence of taking a position on the question of whether composition is restricted or unrestricted. Whichever way we put it, the two philosophers disagree on which objects exist and on what it means to be an object. Given Sider's anti-Carnapian outlook, the dispute between the Universalist and the defender of the intermediary position therefore looks to be as genuine as any ontological dispute. But the numerical sentence in question only serves to *mark* the dispute between the Universalist and the defender of the intermediary position; it is just another way of formulating the point on which they disagree. To settle the truth-value of the numerical sentence at the center of the debate, the ontological dispute itself must be settled, *by other means*.

In the end, it therefore seems as though Sider ends up with a more elaborate version of what has already bothered us about Lewis' illicit move. In the context of a discussion over whether composition could ever be vague, one cannot take for granted that mereological vocabulary is never vague. But, in the same context, one also cannot take for granted that no numerical sentence of the form "There are n concrete objects" (for some finite value of "n") is ever indeterminate in truth-value, since that is merely a restatement of what is at issue.[14]

§II.3.1.3 *The Matter of Vague Existence*

When presented with these arguments in Koslicki (2003a), Sider responds in his paper "Against Vague Existence" as follows (see Sider 2003). According to Sider, the proponent of the intermediary position faces, first, a break-down of the existing paradigm under which the linguistic theory of vagueness is conceptualized as *requiring precisifications*; secondly, he faces a conflict with an independently plausible picture of existence as a *natural kind*. I think that the first of these considerations poses a fair challenge to the holder of the intermediary position and to supporters of the linguistic theory of vagueness, to spell out exactly how a sentence like "There are n concrete objects" (for some finite

---

[14] One might think that my rendition of the Lewis/Sider argument above does not present the argument in its most charitable light. The argument might appear less question-begging than it does in my rendition of it, if we take its goal to be to establish that Universalism about composition must be embraced because the intermediary position can be found to lead to *ontological* vagueness, i.e., the thesis that there is vagueness in the world. This would be an unwelcome consequence for the holder of the intermediary position, since all participants in the dispute have agreed to sign on to the linguistic theory of vagueness, for the time being. I am equally unpersuaded by this version of the Lewis/Sider argument, however. For notice that the thesis endorsed by the holder of the intermediary position—that a sentence like (X) can sometimes be indeterminate in truth-value—does not by itself commit its proponent to ontological vagueness any more than does the parallel claim about bald men: to agree that a sentence of the form "There are n bald men" can sometimes be indeterminate in truth-value, by itself, is not yet to endorse a particular theory of vagueness, such as the theory that there is vagueness in the world. Similarly, there is no reason to think that the apparent indeterminacy in numerical sentences of the form "There are n concrete objects" (for some value of "n") could only be resolved by means of a single strategy, viz., the ontological theory of vagueness. For example, take the dispute between the Universalist and the holder of the intermediary position to be of the kind imagined in Putnam (1987, pp. 18–19): in this scenario, we are to consider a world, w, which contains three atoms, a, b and c; the question under dispute is, "How many *objects* does w contain?". The Universalist unhesitatingly answers "seven"; the holder of the intermediary position, on the other hand, may view it as a determinate matter that w contains at least six objects, but wavers over whether w also contains a seventh object, viz., the sum of a, b and c. It's important to be clear that this dispute need not be construed as committing the holder of the intermediary position to ontological vagueness for the following reason: what this philosopher may view as indeterminate is whether w's domain is correctly described as one containing six objects or as one containing seven objects; i.e., what he regards as indeterminate is the question of which of two domains, both of which contain a determinate number of objects (either six or seven), is correctly described as the domain of objects existing in w. This sort of situation is very different, however, from being committed to w's containing a vague seventh object.

value of "*n*") can be indeterminate in truth-value. I am less moved by Sider's second consideration, however, which to my mind utilizes a bizarre conception of natural kinds.

As Sider points out, there is an interesting asymmetry between the purported indeterminacy of the "bare" numerical sentence (X) and the more familiar indeterminacy of, say, a sentence like (Y):

(Y) There are exactly three bald men in the room.

In the case of (Y), those who believe that vagueness is a matter of semantic indecision can express what the various available candidate-meanings of the predicate "is bald" are in a "relatively precise *background-language*" (Sider 2003, p. 138), without using the predicate itself. For various numerical values, *n*, there is the set containing men with *n* hairs on their head; and although it is a precise matter for each of these sets whether the men in the room are members of it, none of these sets has an overwhelming claim to being considered *the* one and only legitimate precisification of the meaning of "is bald". Thus, the indeterminacy of a sentence like (Y) can be traced to the role played in the sentence by one or more of its constituents; and it can be described in a way which doesn't itself make use of the constituent in question.

In the case of a "bare" numerical sentence like (X), on the other hand, this attractive model which traces the source of indeterminacy to multiple precisifications of one or more of its constituents seems to break down. For once a sentence like "There are *n* concrete objects" (for some finite value of "*n*") is translated into logical notation, it contains nothing but logical vocabulary (ignoring the concreteness-predicate): the existential quantifier, variables, identity and logical connectives. For example, if the value of "*n*" in question is three, then (X) would become something along the lines of (X′):

(X′) $(\exists x)(\exists y)(\exists z)((x \neq y \;\&\; x \neq z \;\&\; y \neq z) \;\&\; (\forall w)(w = x \lor w = y \lor w = z))$

If a "bare" numerical sentence of this kind turned out to be indeterminate in truth-value, it is difficult to see how the source of its indeterminacy could be traced to a single one of its constituents and, moreover, how this indeterminacy could be expressed by means of multiple precisifications which don't themselves use the constituent in question; for it seems that any adequate paraphrase of a sentence like (X) or (X′) would itself have to contain the same logical vocabulary, viz., the existential quantifier, variables, identity and logical connectives. What, then, is the "relatively precise background language" in which the multiple candidate-meanings for the constituent responsible for the indeterminacy in question could be expressed? I take this to be, in essence, Sider's first challenge for the intermediary position.

Sider's point against the intermediary position is certainly justified. However, it is also not surprising to find that there are interesting asymmetries between the sort of indeterminacy which manifests itself in more familiar cases of vagueness and the purported indeterminacy present in the kind of "bare" ontological disagreement we are considering. If I was forced to point to a single constituent to which the indeterminacy of the English sentence (X) could be traced, my response would be that the culprit is the term "object". But, of course, when (X) is translated into logical notation, as illustrated in (X'), there is no explicit occurrence of a predicate like "is an object"; rather, this notion is already built into our conception of the domain over which the existential quantifier, the variables and the identity relation are defined. As became clear in the last section, the situation we face here is indeed significantly different from that posed by the more familiar cases of indeterminacy, in that the Universalist and the holder of the intermediary position *agree* on the (precise) meaning of the logical vocabulary in question; their disagreement is over its range. If we compare this to an analogous dispute over (Y), on the other hand, between, say, someone who takes (Y) to be determinately true and someone who takes the same sentence to be indeterminate in truth-value, the disputants would in effect be quarreling over the *meaning* of the predicate "is bald", e.g., over whether a man with 100 hairs is sufficiently hairless to be counted as bald.

What Sider's first objection shows, then, is that the linguistic theory of vagueness must in some fashion be made to accommodate certain special cases of "bare" ontological disagreements in which the source of the indeterminacy cannot be straightforwardly located in a single constituent that is explicitly represented in the logical form of the disputed statements and whose indeterminacy may be exorcized by means of multiple precisifications stated in a "relatively precise background language" in which the term in question need not occur. Rather, in such cases, the indeterminacy resides not in the meaning but in the application of notions that are implicitly at work in specifying the domain over which the explicit constituents range. I acknowledge that this objection presents an interesting challenge for the linguistic theory of vagueness, but I leave the details for a context which is more directly concerned with the phenomenon of vagueness than our present discussion (but see note 14 for a brief suggestion on how the indeterminacy at issue might be handled).

Sider's second argument can, I think, be dealt with more briefly. Using the Lewisian picture of meaning as "intrinsic eligibility plus use" (see Lewis 1983b and 1984), Sider argues that it is implausible to think of the term "existence" (as well as the term "object", I assume) as having multiple precisifications, as required by the linguistic theory of vagueness, due to the fact that existence, in his view, is a *natural kind*. This, he remarks, fits nicely into his anti-Carnapian picture of the world as consisting of a ready-made domain of objects, along with their natural properties and relations (Sider 2003, p. 144).

However, at least according to extant notions of natural kind, *existence* would not be classified as such; rather, paradigmatic examples of natural kinds are typically taken by those that play some prominent role for the purposes of explanation and prediction, e.g., biological, chemical or physical kinds, such as *tiger* or *water*. According to the classical treatment of the semantics of natural kind terms in Putnam (1975b) and Kripke (1980), for example, these expressions are said to be similar in their semantic properties to proper names, in that both are considered to be *directly referential rigid designators*. Natural kind terms like "water" or "tiger", on this view, denote entities whose members are empirically discovered to share certain theoretically interesting properties or "hidden essences", with the consequence that theoretical identity statements like "Water is H_2O" or "Tigers are animals with genetic code C" acquire the status of *necessary a posteriori* truths.

Regardless of the details of the Kripke/Putnam account, it is difficult to see how any substantive conception of natural kinds could be extended to include the notion of existence. Like self-identity, existence applies to everything there is (ignoring, for the moment, unrelated complications concerning allegedly non-existent objects). How, then, could such a property mark a natural kind, at least if the conception of natural kinds operative in this context is to have any *bite*? What could be the scientifically discoverable, theoretically interesting properties that the members of this alleged natural kind have in common? Perhaps Sider has a different conception of natural kinds in mind, in which case we would need to be told what it is; in the absence of a viable alternative notion, however, it is difficult to make sense of his suggestion that existence be regarded as a natural kind.[15]

§II.3.2 The Composition-as-Identity Thesis

To complete our discussion of Lewis' four-dimensionalist approach to ordinary material objects, it remains for us to examine component (iv) of his program, the so-called "Composition-as-Identity Thesis", whose primary defense is mounted in Lewis (1991, Sect. 3.6). The dialectical role of this component is to make the commitment to Unrestricted Composition, which was supposed to follow from component (ii) of Lewis' analysis, more palatable to those who are skeptical of CEM's supposed ontological innocence. For if, contrary to my remarks in the last two sections, Lewis' defense of Unrestricted Composition were successful, then it would follow that the material world is far more densely populated than we ordinarily assume it to be, with all manner of gerrymandered and intuitively bizarre mereological sums (such as the notorious "trout-turkey", whose parts are the, still undetached, upper half of a trout along with the, still undetached, lower half of a turkey). Most of these counterintuitive sums of course never turn out to be of any interest to us, outside of philosophical disputes over ontology, and thus, as Lewis allows, they never make it into the ordinarily restricted (and frequently fuzzy) range of our everyday quantifiers. But, whether talked

---

[15] I am equally mystified by the recent suggestion in Dorr (2005) to the effect that *parthood* be considered a natural kind.

about or not, they exist nonetheless. The aim of the Composition-as-Identity Thesis now is to convince those who are not yet on board that the commitment to arbitrary sums is thoroughly harmless from an ontological point of view.

Lewis' defense of the Composition-as-Identity Thesis in Lewis (1991) has already been subjected to detailed discussion and criticism, for example in Oliver (1994) and van Inwagen (1994) (see also Harte 2002 for a more condensed discussion which reaches the same conclusion). Since I agree with much of what these philosophers have said, my treatment of Lewis' thesis will be brief. Lewis' Composition-as-Identity Thesis is that commitment to arbitrary sums ought to be viewed as ontologically harmless because composition is either, as he sometimes puts it, a *kind* of numerical identity, or it is at any rate *analogous*, in a sufficiently interesting sense, to numerical identity. Somewhat confusingly, he slides back and forth between these two designations. Either way, however, as Lewis repeatedly points out, commitment to sums is "not a *further* commitment", since sums are "nothing over and above" the objects that compose them.

In support of his Composition-as-Identity Thesis, Lewis invokes work by Donald Baxter and David Armstrong (Baxter 1988a and 1988b; Armstrong 1978), both of whom, for different reasons, allow that there is a sense or kind of identity, according to which *many* objects can be identical to *one* object. In Baxter's case, the reason for this extended notion of identity is that, like Bishop Butler and Roderick Chisholm, he recognizes, in addition to the familiar "identity in the strict and philosophical sense", also a kind of "identity in the loose and popular sense"; it is in this latter sense that many objects can turn out to be identical to one object. Armstrong, on the other hand, emphasizes that strict identity and strict distinctness are merely the endpoints of a spectrum of cases, whose middle-portions are occupied by objects which overlap more or less extensively; in this sense, a sum and its parts are not completely distinct, since they are not disjoint.

Neither of these considerations, however, is going to move those who are skeptical of CEM's purported ontological innocence. For when they claim that one object can never be identical to many objects, they have in mind Baxter's first "sense" of identity, viz., "identity in the strict and philosophical sense"; and this, they will maintain, is the *only* genuine kind of numerical identity there is, our ordinary talk involving "sameness" notwithstanding. Moreover, when they deny that many things can be identical to one, according to their understanding of "identity" and "distinctness", they have in mind, not the mereological concepts of "overlap" or "disjointness", which everyone agrees to be notions of degree, but rather "numerical identity" and "numerical distinctness", which the philosophers in question will take to be absolute notions. Thus, rhetoric aside, no one—not even Lewis, Baxter or Armstrong themselves—would disavow the claim that mereological sums are *not identical* to their parts, when this claim is properly disambiguated to involve "identity" in the strict and numerical sense; in this sense, then, a commitment to sums clearly *is* a further commitment "over and above" the commitment to the objects that are said to compose the sums in question.

To illustrate, consider a world which, by hypothesis, contains two (and only two) mereological atoms, a and b. Those who accept the principle of unrestricted mereological composition, would hold that the world in question also contains a *third* object, c, which is the sum of a and b. All parties agree that the sum, c, is "in the strict and philosophical sense" numerically distinct from a and b, despite the fact that c is of course not disjoint from a and b. Thus, when "$\neq$" is interpreted in the usual way to denote strict numerical distinctness, then it is true to say that a $\neq$ c and b $\neq$ c. Moreover, if identity is understood in the same strict numerical fashion, then the claim that a and b "taken together" just are c can only be interpreted to be the uncontroversial claim that *the sum* of a and b is identical to c, i.e., that c is self-identical. To the extent, then, to which the world in question is said by the supporters of Unrestricted Composition to contain an additional, *third* object numerically distinct from the two atoms, whose existence the detractors of Unrestricted Composition may well wish to deny, commitment to sums does indeed carry a *further* ontological commitment "over and above" the commitment to the two atoms. We may of course still believe that such a commitment is harmless from an ontological point of view, or worth its price, but this shouldn't detract from the fact that commitment to sums *is* a further commitment "over and above" commitment to the objects that are said to be its parts.

In addition to his reference to the work of Baxter and Armstrong, Lewis cites as further support for his thesis that composition is a *kind of*, or *analogous to*, strict numerical identity the following five considerations (Lewis 1991, pp. 85 ff; my italics). (i) First, the purported *ontological innocence* of CEM: ". . . just as it is *redundant* to say that Possum exists and something identical to him exists as well, so likewise it is *redundant* to say that Possum and Magpie both exist and their fusion exists as well". (ii) Secondly, the "automatic" existence of sums which follows from an acceptance of *Unrestricted Composition*: "If Possum exists, then *automatically* something identical to Possum exists; likewise if Possum and Magpie exist then *automatically* their fusion exists". (iii) Thirdly, the *extensional* nature of CEM, which follows from the *Uniqueness* of Composition: "Just as there cannot be *two different* things both identical to Possum, likewise there cannot be *two different* fusions of Magpie and Possum". (iv) Fourthly, the *ease of describing* fusions: "*Describe* Possum *fully*, and thereby you *fully describe* whatever is identical to Possum. *Describe* Magpie and Possum *fully*—the character of each, and also their interrelation—and thereby you *fully describe* their fusion". (v) And, finally, the *multiple location* of fusions in exactly the places in which its parts are located: ". . . if it turns out that Mary and her lamb are identical, then there is no mystery at all about their *inseparability*. Likewise if it turns out that the lamb is part of Mary, and if Mary is <u>wholly</u> present wherever she goes, then again the *inseparability* is automatic, and in no way mysterious."

Clearly, only the last two of these considerations are dialectically appropriate, as addressed to a philosopher who doubts the ontological innocence of CEM. For the Composition-as-Identity Thesis is precisely meant to convince such a philosopher that he can put aside his qualms and accept Unrestricted Composition (consideration (ii)) as well as the Uniqueness of Composition (consideration (iii)) because commitment to fusions is ontologically harmless (consideration (i)). Thus, considerations (i), (ii) and (iii) simply beg the question against the kind of philosopher to whom this discussion is addressed.

This leaves considerations (iv) and (v). Consideration (iv) seems to make use of a kind of supervenience thesis, according to which the characteristics of sums supervene on the characteristics of their parts; consideration (v), on the other hand, can be understood to pose a kind of challenge to those who deny the Composition-as-Identity Thesis: if sums, according to their view, are not in some sense identical to their parts, then the inseparability of sums and their parts seems to become mysterious. But neither of these considerations would change the mind of someone who does not believe that many objects can ever, in any interesting sense, be identical to one object. For it could nevertheless be the case that the characteristics of the one object supervene on those of the many, or that the one object is located wherever the many objects are located, even though the relation between the one and the many is nothing like that of numerical identity (to illustrate, witness the example of sets and their members or that between mental states and physical states). Thus, while considerations (iv) and (v) do not share the obviously question-begging character of (i), (ii) and (iii), they do not by themselves turn the tide in any way in favor of Lewis' view.

§II.4 CONCLUDING REMARKS

This concludes our discussion of Lewis' four-dimensional approach to the metaphysics of material objects. We have, in this chapter, encountered two prominent defenders of the thesis that ordinary material objects are best viewed as mereological sums in the standard sense. Thomson's three-dimensionalist version of this thesis was found to modify the standard conception of mereology in the sense of CEM in certain crucial respects, to account for the temporal and modal properties of ordinary material objects. In Chapter IV, we will see why this suitably extended and modified version of CEM nevertheless does not yield an adequate analysis of ordinary material objects. The considerations provided in this chapter, however, should, if successful, have established that Lewis' four-dimensionalist case for a CEM-style analysis of ordinary material objects can be resisted on the grounds that both his argument in favor of Unrestricted

Composition as well as his arguments in favor of the Composition-as-Identity Thesis are ultimately question-begging. We did not, in the present context, address the two remaining aspects of Lewis' four-dimensionalist picture, viz., the argument in favor of perdurance over endurance or the argument in favor of the Uniqueness of Composition, both of which lie outside the scope of the present study.

III

Composition as Non-Identity

§III.1 INTRODUCTORY REMARKS

In the foregoing remarks, I have aligned myself with a conception of parthood and composition which carries genuine ontological commitment: contrary to the Lewisian Composition-as-Identity model, wholes according to this conception are in no way to be identified with their parts; rather, a commitment to wholes is a commitment to entities that are numerically distinct from their parts. A crucial piece in the apparatus which supports this ontologically loaded conception of parthood and composition is a certain style of argument which I term Leibniz's Law-style argument for the numerical distinctness of wholes and their parts: on my reading of this style of argument, wholes and their parts are numerically distinct by Leibniz's Law, because they do not share all of their properties (e.g., for one thing, while the parts typically do exist, the whole does not exist prior to the creation of the whole). The purpose of the present chapter is to defend this style of argument for the numerical distinctness of wholes and their parts.[1]

My game plan for this chapter is as follows. I will argue against philosophical positions which oppose the argument from Leibniz's Law to the conclusion that wholes and their parts are numerically distinct on general grounds: such positions are forced to make use of a particular, surprisingly widespread, strategy in metaphysics which I will refer to in what follows as "The Suspect Strategy" (TSS); this strategy is suspect for various reasons, which I will detail below, and hence ought to be abandoned.

In very broad strokes, situations which give rise to TSS contain as one of their ingredients a general metaphysical principle of some form whose truth the proponent of TSS wishes to uphold; the nature of the principle differs from context to context, but examples include the following:

(LL) Leibniz's Law:

    If $x = y$, then every property of x is a property of y.[2]

(RI) Restricted Indiscernibility:

---

[1] This chapter presents an expanded version of the argument defended in Koslicki (2005a).
[2] For the sake of simplicity, I am omitting relations.

If a certain relation, R, holds between x and y, then every Φ-property of x is a property of y.

(EP) Existence Principle:

For any set of Φ-properties, there exists an object which has all the properties in the set and no other Φ-properties.[3]

The second ingredient which is needed to give rise to TSS is a certain troublesome class of contexts, Σ (e.g., contexts like "____ is essentially a statue"). These contexts appear to satisfy the purely formal syntactic and semantic well-formedness conditions expressions must satisfy in order to play the semantic role of predicates. (For example, they are "unsaturated", in Frege's sense, i.e., when combined with singular terms, they yield statements that can bear a truth-value; they apparently do not lead to paradox, and so forth.) However, to allow that these contexts straightforwardly determine *properties* and that these properties straightforwardly *fall under the scope of* the general metaphysical principle in question would conflict with certain *other* metaphysical priorities of the proponent of TSS.

To resolve this tension, the philosopher in question invokes TSS, with the intended result that the troublesome contexts in Σ be *excluded* from the reaches of the general principle in question, either because these contexts fail to determine properties at all or because the properties they do determine fail to fall under the scope of the general principle at issue. What makes the strategy in question *suspect* is that, as we shall see, the different kinds of methods by which the troublesome contexts are excluded from the reaches of the general principles raise serious methodological concerns or are objectionable for other reasons.

We should draw two conclusions from the failure of TSS. First, the need to invoke TSS by itself counts as a strike against a philosophical theory; hence, competing philosophical theories which require no such appeal are preferable in this respect. Secondly, unless other independently motivated considerations are provided, the rejection of TSS presents a good reason to accept that the contexts in Σ determine properties and that these properties fall under the scope of the general principle (provided of course that this principle is taken to be true):

---

[3] RI and EP are *schemata* of which particular restricted indiscernibility principles or existence principles are instances. As it stands, RI contains at least two open places. (i) The place marked by "R" is to be filled in by a relation which is similar to but weaker than numerical identity (e.g., the relation of constitution); if R is taken to be numerical identity, then "Φ" can be taken to mark no restriction at all, and RI simply collapses into LL. (ii) The family of properties with respect to which the R-related objects are indiscernible must be explicitly specified, i.e., "Φ" must be filled in in some way (e.g., in the case of constitution, one will want to exclude the property of being essentially a statue from the family of Φ-properties; such "ordinary" intrinsic and relational properties as weight and spatiotemporal location, on the other hand, should be included in the family in question). Similarly, with respect to EP, there are different ways of specifying the relevant class of properties in Φ.

this second consequence of the failure of TSS further commits us to a universe populated with numerically distinct yet almost indiscernible objects.[4]

§III.2 THE SUSPECT STRATEGY

I now turn to some representative illustrations of contexts in which TSS is applied with respect to the three general principles mentioned above, LL, RI and EP. For example, we find TSS implemented with respect to LL in the following contexts: (i) Alan Gibbard's defense of *contingent identity* (Gibbard 1975); (ii) George Myro's and André Gallois' defense of *temporary identity* (Myro 1986; Gallois 1990, 1998); as well as (iii) Terence Parsons' defense of *indeterminate identity* (Parsons 2000). Our example of TSS as implemented with respect to EP is (iv) Terence Parsons' defense of *non-existent objects* (Parsons 1979, 1980). Finally, an example of TSS, as implemented with respect to an instance of RI, can be found in (v) the *coincidence-theorist's* analysis of the problem of constitution, as developed, for example, in Baker (1999, 2000), Fine (1982, 1999), and Yablo (1987); as well as in (vi) a recent development of Geach's *relative-identity* view (Geach 1962, 1967) in Deutsch (1998) (see also Deutsch 2002).

§III.2.1 The Suspect Strategy and Leibniz's Law

§III.2.1.1 Contingent Identity

In his classic paper "Contingent Identity" (1975), Alan Gibbard argues that certain identities are best interpreted as contingent, despite Kripke's powerful arguments to the contrary (cf. Kripke 1971). As an example of such a contingent identity, Gibbard offers the case of a statue, Goliath, and the piece of clay, Lumpl, of which it is made, which are stipulated to have exactly the same temporal extent; their relation, in Gibbard's view, is best described as in (1):

(1) Goliath = Lumpl & $\Diamond$(Goliath $\neq$ Lumpl)

Of course, as Gibbard points out in Section V of his paper, one's immediate reaction is that (1) cannot possibly be the correct interpretation of the relation between Lumpl and Goliath, on the grounds of the following style of argument:[5]

(2) $\Box$(Lumpl = Lumpl)
Lumpl = Goliath

$\Box$(Goliath = Lumpl)

---

[4] See also Fine (2003), for a recent critique of various attempts to block inferences using LL to conclude that coincident objects are numerically distinct.

[5] For simplicity, I omit relativization to existence in this and all following arguments.

The argument in (2) states that because Lumpl is necessarily self-identical, so anything that is identical with Lumpl, viz., Goliath, also must be necessarily identical to Lumpl. This argument depends on taking the context in (3),

(3) $\Box$(_____ = Lumpl)

in conjunction with LL, to generate the conclusion in (2), which contradicts Gibbard's central thesis in (1). (Gibbard 1975 is specifically addressed to an argument of this sort that is given in Kripke 1971; Kripke uses this argument to conclude that such pairs of objects as Lumpl and Goliath must be numerically distinct.) In other words, if the argument in (2) is correct, then the context in (3) points us to a property with respect to which the objects in question are not indiscernible (viz., necessary identity with Lumpl); LL would then seem to lead us to conclude that Lumpl and Goliath are numerically distinct and hence not contingently identical, contra (1).

Gibbard calls this the "most prominent objection" to the contingent-identity view; his response is an instance of TSS:

The usual answer will serve my purpose here. Leibniz' Law settles very little by itself: put as a general law of substitutivity of identicals, it is just false; in its correct version, it is a law about properties and relations: *If x = y, then for any property, if x has it, then y has it, and for any relation and any given things, if x stands in that relation to those things, then y stands in that relation to those things.* The law so stated yields substitutivity of identicals only for those contexts that attribute properties and relations. [The conclusion in (2)] follows from [the two premises] by Leibniz' Law, then, only if [the context in (3)] attributes a property. We can block the inference to [the conclusion in (2)] by denying that [the context in (3)] attributes a property.[6]

In case someone should worry about the possible "arbitrariness" of this response, Gibbard remarks that whether the context in (3) denotes a property is precisely what is at issue in the dispute between the essentialist and the anti-essentialist. A context denotes a property, so Gibbard argues (plausibly, of course), only if it applies to an object *independently of the way in which it is designated*; and whether *de re* modal contexts apply to objects in this fashion is precisely the point over which anti-essentialists like Gibbard and Quine disagree with essentialists like Kripke. The battle between them must therefore be fought on other grounds.

§III.2.1.2 Temporary Identity

According to the temporary-identity view developed, in different ways, in Myro (1986) and Gallois (1990, 1998), statements of identity in general must be viewed as being relativized to times. As a result, one can sometimes run into situations in which statements of the following sort are true (for some objects, A and B, and some times, t and t′):

---

[6] Gibbard (1975, p. 201) (his italics; the numbering of examples has been adjusted to my text).

(4) [at t: A = B] & [at t′: A ≠ B]

The benefits of this view are that it can be used to solve many of the traditional puzzles concerning identity, e.g., change over time, constitution, fission, fusion, and the like.

Again, perhaps the most prominent objection to a view of this sort comes from an analogue of the argument from LL in (2) above:

(5) For all times t′: [at t′: A = A]
At t: A = B

For all times t′: [at t′: A = B]

The argument in (5) states that, since object A is always self-identical, any object (viz., B) which is at any time identical to A must be so at all times. Again, this argument depends on taking a context like (6),

(6) At all times t′: [at t′: A = _____]

and conjoining it with LL, which itself must be relativized to time on this view,

(LL$_{Temp}$) For all times t′: If x = y at t′, then every property of x at t′ is a property of y at t′.

to yield the conclusion in (5), which contradicts the main tenet of the temporary-identity view as expressed in (4).[7]

Myro and Gallois respond to the challenge posed by the argument from (LL$_{Temp}$) by endorsing slightly different versions of TSS. Myro's response is in fact quite close to Gibbard's:

So the general way of dealing with the complication is to divide properties into those which are "*time-free*"—like being on the mantelpiece—which are represented by open sentences

----

[7] Since the temporal case is slightly more tricky than the modal one, let me lay out the analogy very explicitly. The first premise of (5) states that A always has the property of being identical to A; the second premise of (5) states that A is identical to B at a particular time, t. Now take the following instance of (LL$_{Temp}$):

[at t: A = B] → [[at t: ∀t′ (at t′: A = A)] ↔ [at t: ∀t′ (at t′: A = B)]].

We use this instance to infer:

[at t: ∀t′ (at t′: A = A)] ↔ [at t: ∀t′ (at t′: A = B)]

Since A is always identical with itself, I assume that it is also true *at t* that A is always identical with itself; in that case, (LL$_{Temp}$), in conjunction with the assumption that the context in (6) denotes a property, permits the inference to the conclusion that if A is ever identical to B, then it is so always. The temporalized identity theorist may of course attempt to block this inference in one of the ways laid out in the main text, either by rejecting the following, seemingly innocuous principle,

∀t (at t: A = A) → ∀t′ [at t′: ∀t [at t: A = A]]

or by questioning the substitution of contexts like (6) into (LL$_{Temp}$).

not containing temporal qualifications, and those which are "*time-bound*"—like being on the mantelpiece on Tuesday—which are represented by open sentences which do contain temporal qualifications. And what must be done is that "Leibniz's Law subject (like other statements) to temporal qualification" is to be, in addition, *restricted* to properties which are "*time-free*"—properly represented by open sentences (or "predicates") which do not (relevantly) contain temporal qualifications.

(Myro 1986, pp. 392–3; his italics)

Unlike Gibbard, Myro allows that the "time-bound" contexts in question denote properties, but proposes to restrict (LL$_{Temp}$) to exclude such properties. The result, however, is the same: contexts which, when conjoined with (LL$_{Temp}$), seem to yield the conclusion that the objects under consideration are numerically distinct are removed somehow from the field of contexts governed by (LL$_{Temp}$).

Gallois blocks the inference in (5), not by overtly restricting (LL$_{Temp}$) or by openly declaring that contexts of a certain kind fail to denote properties, but rather by opposing a certain pre-theoretically plausible principle concerning the transmission of properties through times:

(TP) $(\forall F)(\forall x)(\forall t)(\forall t')$ [at t': Ex $\rightarrow$ [at t : F(x) $\leftrightarrow$ [at t': F(x) at t]]]]

The "Transmission Principle" (TP) states that an object has a property, F, at some time, t, just in case, at any other time, t', at which the object exists, it has at those times, t', the property of having the property of being F at t; in other words, having the property of being F at t "transmits" to other times. For example, if I have the property of wearing yellow socks on Monday, then, by TP, it is still true of me on Tuesday (even if I am now wearing pink socks) that it was true of me on Monday that I wore yellow socks then.[8]

Although Gallois' careful treatment of the issues in question deserves separate discussion, his position nevertheless strikes me in the end as a slightly more elaborate version of the view that there is no automatic passage from contexts of a certain purportedly questionable kind to properties of the corresponding kind, where the contexts in question are now those involving *nested* temporal qualifications. Given our present purposes, I will thus classify Gallois' opposition to the "Transmission Principle" as a version of the same general strategy as that found in Gibbard (1975) and Myro (1986).[9]

---

[8] Given Gallois' rejection of TP, the following instance of this principle, appealed to in the previous note,

$\forall t$ (at t : A = A) $\rightarrow$ $\forall t'$[at t' : $\forall t$ [at t : A = A]]

is now no longer available.

[9] For insightful and detailed discussion of Gallois' views, see Sider (2001, ch. 5).

§III.2.1.3 Indeterminate Identity

Parsons (2000) defends the view that, under certain circumstances, identities can be indeterminate, i.e., that statements of the following kind can be true (where the operator "∇" is taken to mean "it is indeterminate that"):

(7) $\nabla(B = A)$

Once again, the defender of indeterminate identities faces an objection from LL, structurally analogous to those reviewed above, except for the fact that the argument in question this time makes use of LL in its *contrapositive* form (cf., Evans 1978, for the original statement of this argument):

(LL_{Contra}) Contrapositive Leibniz's Law:

If some property, F, is a property of x but not of y, then x $\neq$ y.

The identity sign, "$=$", is read by the defender of indeterminate identity as applying to objects which are *determinately* identical; correspondingly, "$\neq$" applies to objects which are *determinately* distinct. Normally, the equivalence between LL and LL_{Contra} is of course taken for granted. In the context of disputes over the determinacy of identity, however, this equivalence is no longer uncontroversial; Parsons, for example, accepts LL but denies that inferences using LL_{Contra} are always valid.

Now assume, for reductio, that objects A and B are indeterminately identical, i.e., that (7) is true. Then, the argument from LL_{Contra} can be stated as follows:

(8) $\nabla[B = A]$
      $\neg\nabla[A = A]$

      $B \neq A$

The argument in (8), again, proceeds by way of taking contexts like (9),

(9) $\nabla[\underline{\quad\quad} = A]$

in conjunction with LL_{Contra}, to lead to the conclusion in (8), according to which A and B are determinately distinct, which contradicts the assumption in (7). This argument is used by the opponent of indeterminate identity to show that objects can never be merely indeterminately identical; i.e., that identity is always determinate.

In response to this Evans-style argument, Parsons proposes the familiar strategy of denying that contexts like that in (9) denote properties. He does, however, introduce a novel consideration in support of his version of TSS. What makes contexts like (9) suspicious, according to Parsons, is that they bear some structural similarity to contexts which are used to generate the paradoxes of naive set theory. Since Parsons also accepts that (determinate) identity can be *defined* as the sharing of properties as in (10),

(10) $A = B \equiv_{def} \forall P[P(A) \leftrightarrow P(B)]$

contexts like (9), in his view, involve implicit quantification over all properties. Parsons explains the analogy between the Evans-style argument and set-theoretic paradoxes as follows:

> The force behind the reasoning thus comes from the fact that identity is defined in terms of what properties there are, and a problematic property is defined using an abstract that quantifies over *those* properties. The condition in the abstract is cleverly designed to conflict with its yielding one of the properties quantified over (if any objects are indeterminately identical with A). The reasoning thus resembles that of the Russell paradox in set theory. (Identity between sets is defined in terms of what sets they have as members, and a problematic set is defined using a set abstract that quantifies over *those* sets. The condition in the set abstract is cleverly designed to conflict with its yielding one of the sets quantified over.)

> (Parsons 2000, p. 51)

Given the analogy with the paradoxes of naive set theory, Parsons takes himself to be justified in adopting his version of TSS, viz., that contexts which have this apparently impredicative character cannot always be expected to determine a property.

§III.2.2 The Suspect Strategy and Existence Principles: Non-Existent Objects

In an unrelated earlier work by Terence Parsons, "Referring to Non-Existent Objects" (1979), we see an application of TSS with respect to EP (cf. also Parsons 1980 for a more detailed elaboration of the view). Parsons' aim in this context is to preserve the plausibility of our pretheoretic intuition to the effect that terms like "Sherlock Holmes" and "Zeus" function in many ways exactly like terms which we view as unproblematically referential; he proposes to solve this quandary by expanding our ontology to include both *existent* and *non-existent* objects. Parsons' defense of non-existent objects relies crucially on a distinction he introduces between *nuclear* and *extra-nuclear* properties. The nuclear properties determine, via the following two principles, which (existent and non-existent) objects there are and how to tell the difference between them (P1 is Parsons' *strengthened* version of the controversial Identity of Indiscernibles (II), the converse of LL; P2 is Parsons' version of EP):[10]

(P1) Strengthened Identity of Indiscernibles:

---

[10] P1 is a *strengthened* version of II because it states that indiscernibility of *nuclear* properties alone is sufficient for numerical identity; II, in its original version, requires indiscernibility of *all* properties *whatsoever* for numerical identity. This brings out one of the two ways in which the nuclear properties are very "powerful stuff", since they by themselves can induce numerical identity; P2 brings out their forceful nature with respect to the existence of objects.

For every (existent or non-existent) object, x and y, if every *nuclear* property of x is a *nuclear* property of y, then x = y.

(P2) Parsons' Existence Principle:

For any set of *nuclear* properties, there is an object that has all of the properties in the set and no other *nuclear* properties.

For example, principles P1 and P2 predict that, if the property of being golden and the property of being a mountain are nuclear properties, then there is exactly one (non-existent) object which satisfies the set {goldenness; mountainhood}, i.e., exactly one (non-existent) golden mountain. This non-existent golden mountain is indeterminate with respect to all nuclear properties that are not in the set, but it determinately has the properties of being golden and of being a mountain.

But which are the nuclear properties? P1 and P2 bring out the central role played by the notion of a nuclear property in determining the existence and identity of objects; but not all predicates stand for nuclear properties. How, then, do we tell the difference between predicates which denote nuclear properties and those which denote extra-nuclear properties? In response to this question, Parsons first gives us a list of examples of nuclear predicates (NPs) and extra-nuclear predicates (ENPs):[11]

(NPs) Nuclear Predicates:

"is blue", "is tall", "kicked Socrates", "was kicked by Socrates", "kicked somebody", "is golden", "is a mountain", . . .

(ENPs) Extra-Nuclear Predicates:

Ontological: "exists", "is mythical", "is fictional", . . .

Modal: "is possible", "is impossible", . . .

Intentional: "is thought about by Meinong", "is worshiped by someone", . . .

Technical: "is complete", . . .[12]

When confronted with the question of how this list is to be continued, however, Parsons offers us only rough guidance: the category of ENPs includes mainly predicates which have been traditionally given special status (e.g., some have been thought by Russell and Frege to be higher-order predicates which do not denote properties of individuals) or which are surrounded by a history of philosophical controversy:

Our historical situation yields a very rough kind of decision procedure for telling whether a predicate is nuclear or extranuclear. It's this: if everyone agrees that the predicate stands

---

[11] A *predicate* is nuclear or extra-nuclear depending on whether it denotes a nuclear or extra-nuclear *property*.

[12] "Is complete" is Parsons' technical term for either having a nuclear property or its negation, for any nuclear property.

for an ordinary property of individuals, then it's a nuclear predicate, and it stands for a nuclear property. On the other hand, if everyone agrees that it doesn't stand for an ordinary property of individuals (for whatever reason), or if there's a history of controversy about whether it stands for a property of individuals, then it's an extranuclear predicate, and it does not stand for a nuclear property.

(Parsons 1979, p. 102)

Again, the basic procedure here is the same as that observed earlier: certain troublesome contexts are excluded from the reaches of the general metaphysical principle under discussion, by assigning to them a "second-class-citizen" status with respect to the principle at issue; in this case, the general principle under discussion is Parsons' version of EP in P2 and the contexts in question are those which are said to denote *extra-nuclear* properties.

§III.2.3 The Suspect Strategy and Restricted Indiscernibility Principles

§III.2.3.1 Coincident Objects

Whenever an object (e.g., a lump of clay) constitutes, composes or makes up another object (e.g., a statue), the objects in question are both strikingly similar in many respects and also apparently different from one another in other respects. The problem of constitution, according to my own conception of it, consists in the demand for an account of both the striking similarities and the apparent differences between constitutionally related objects. The coincidence theory, as developed, for example, in Baker (1999, 2000), Fine (1982, 1999) and Yablo (1987), is one possible response to the problem of constitution: it holds that the statue and the lump of clay are numerically distinct objects which occupy the same region of space-time. Their numerical distinctness serves to account for the apparent differences between constitutionally related objects; but this still leaves their striking similarities unexplained. To this end, Baker, Fine and Yablo each propose slightly different versions of a restricted indiscernibility principle of the following form:

(RI$_{Const}$) <u>Restricted Indiscernibility of Constitutionally Related Objects:</u>

If x constitutes y, then every Φ-property of x is a property of y.

The differences between the three accounts lie in precisely how "Φ" is to be filled in. According to Fine (1982), the family of properties in question is defined to include all and only those that are *normal*, where a "normal" property is one that is not *formal* and whose application concerns only the *time* and *world* in question. The notion of a "formal" property is not further elucidated by Fine, but I take it to include such purely "logical" properties as the property of being self-identical and the property of being either red or not red. (A similar principle is also to be found as "Postulate (V7)" in Fine 1999.) Baker (1999) and (2000) define the family of properties in question in a similar fashion, as those that include all properties *except* those that are ("alethic") *modal* properties, those that concern *identity* and *constitution*, and those that are *rooted outside* the times at which they are had. For Yablo (1987), the family of properties in question includes all and only those that are *categorical*, i.e., roughly those that concern what goes on in the *actual* world; the properties that are *excluded* from the family in question are the *hypothetical* ones, i.e., those that concern what goes on in *other* worlds.

I have developed my criticisms of the coincidence theorist's attempt to account for the similarities between constitutionally related objects in this fashion in detail elsewhere (see especially Koslicki 2004a).[13] For present purposes, the important point is just that the strategy employed by Baker, Fine and Yablo presents us with another instance of TSS. For in order to account for the striking similarities between constitutionally related objects, the coincidence theorist must explain the validity of inferences that are analogous to those considered earlier in the context of our discussion of LL:

(11) Lumpl has the Φ-property F.

 Lumpl constitutes Goliath.

 Goliath has F.

Just as numerical identity, via LL, is thought to transmit (apparent) properties like necessary identity with Lumpl (cf. context (3) above), so constitution is thought to transmit properties that number among the Φ-properties, in accordance with the restricted indiscernibility principle in RI_{Const}. What is crucial to the endeavor of accounting for the validity of inferences like (11) is that contexts like the following,

(12) Troublesome Contexts (Constitution):

 Modal: "_____ is essentially a piece of clay"

 Temporal: "_____ existed before the statue came into existence"

 Identity: "_____ is identical to the lump of clay"

 Constitution: "_____ constitutes a statue"

be *excluded* from the reaches of the restricted indiscernibility principle in RI_{Const}, since they will *invalidate* inferences like those in (11). The strategy used by Baker, Fine and Yablo to exclude the troublesome contexts in question

---

[13] I should note, however, as discussed in Koslicki (2004a), that Fine, Baker and Yablo are actually quite unusual among coincidence theorists, in that they pay any attention at all to the problem of how to capture the striking similarities among constitutionally related objects.

from the general metaphysical principle in RI_{Const}, whose truth they wish to uphold, is structurally analogous to earlier implementations of TSS, especially those encountered in Gibbard (1975) and Myro (1986).

§III.2.3.2 Relative Identity

The final context I want to consider occurs in a subtle and interesting recent development of Geach's relative identity view (Geach 1962, 1967) in Deutsch (1998). According to Deutsch, the relative identity theory can solve many classical metaphysical problems that concern numerical identity in an attractive way; examples he considers include the following:

(13) Metaphysical Puzzle Cases:

Change over Time: "The young Fido is *the same dog as* the old Fido."

Constitution: "Lumpl is *the same statue as* Goliath."

Types and Tokens: "My copy of *On the Road* is *the same literary work as* that originally written by Kerouac."

In each case, Deutsch proposes that the relation in question, e.g., *being the same dog as*, *being the same statue as*, and *being the same literary work as*, is best analyzed as a relation of *relative identity*. Thus, the relation in question does not dissolve, as the absolute identity theorist would have it, into a predicative component and a component that denotes absolute identity, as in "x is a dog and y is a dog and x = y"; rather, the relation in question is not further analyzable and simply denotes a feature of the world, viz., one of the ways in which objects that are numerically distinct in the absolute sense can be similar to one another. (Unlike Geach, Deutsch does not believe that absolute identity is incoherent or unintelligible and accepts that objects that are merely relatively identical are numerically distinct in the absolute sense.)

As Deutsch acknowledges, any plausible version of the relative identity theory must respond in some manner to David Wiggins' original challenge to Geach: to offer a suitable *restricted* indiscernibility principle which can be said to govern relative identity in place of the unrestricted LL (cf. Wiggins 1980, pp. 18 ff; 2001, pp. 24 ff). For if Lumpl and Goliath are not the same statue in the *absolute* sense, we of course have no right to expect them to be indiscernible in absolutely *every* respect, as LL would have it. But we do have a right to ask how the relative identity theorist will explain the fact that being similar in *this* respect (viz., the respect denoted by "is the same statue as") entails being similar in so many *other* respects, in an entirely predictable and systematic fashion: statues and the objects that constitute them can *always* be expected to have the same weight, shape, color, texture, chemical composition, and so forth. Thus, as in the case of the coincidence theorist considered above, the relative identity theorist bears the responsibility of offering a restricted indiscernibility principle of some kind, as in RI_{Rel},

(RI$_{Rel}$) Restricted Indiscernibility of Relatively Identical Objects:

If x is relatively identical to y, then every Φ-property of x is a property of y.

which will, among other things, validate inferences like those in (11),

Lumpl has the Φ-property F.

Lumpl is the same statue as Goliath.

Goliath has F.

Again, as in the case of the coincidence theory, the crucial question is how to fill in "Φ" in such a way as to *exclude* troublesome contexts like those mentioned above in (12) from the reaches of the restricted indiscernibility principle in RI$_{Rel}$, since they will in general *invalidate* inferences like the one just cited. Only in this case the task faced by the relative identity theorist is especially challenging, since "Φ" must be filled in such a way that it will simultaneously validate inferences in *all* the metaphysical contexts for which relative identity is intended to yield an analysis, e.g., contexts involving the phenomenon of *change over time* as well as those involving *constitution* and *identity among allographic objects*; whereas the coincidence theorist was faced only with the task of offering a version of RI which will validate inferences using the relation of constitution.

As his version of RI$_{Rel}$, Deutsch proposes the principle he calls "(T4)" which is here reworded in a more informal fashion (for reasons that shall become apparent momentarily, I label this principle Deutsch's "Expansion Principle"):

(RI$_{Rel-Deutsch}$) Deutsch's Expansion Principle:

If x is the same F as y, then y has all of those properties of x which satisfy the condition: if *some* F has the property in question, then *all* the Fs do.

The intuitive idea behind RI$_{Rel-Deutsch}$ is to isolate those properties which "spread through" the entire equivalence class singled out by a particular relative identity relation. For example, consider the equivalence class consisting of all the different objects (numerically distinct, in the absolute sense) which are *the same statue as* Goliath (at a particular time or over time). The Φ-properties with respect to this equivalence class are those which satisfy the condition: if one such "Goliath-object" has the property in question, then they all do. As we shall see below, Deutsch's version of RI$_{Rel}$ compares favorably, from a methodological point of view, to other strategies of excluding the troublesome contexts; but it is nevertheless suspect for other reasons.

§III.3 WHAT'S WRONG WITH THE SUSPECT STRATEGY?

In our illustrations of TSS above, we have encountered basically four different strategies of how to exclude the troublesome contexts from the reaches of the general principle at issue, viz., LL, RI or EP. (i) First, there is what I shall term the "Purely Stipulative Strategy"; this strategy is the most widespread in the literature and is here exemplified by Gibbard, Myro, Gallois, the Parsons of non-existent objects, Baker, Fine and Yablo. (ii) Secondly, we see in Gibbard an extremely condensed suggestion which, if it were elaborated more fully, might seem to point the way towards a non-stipulative response; I shall term this Gibbard's "Appeal to Failures of Substitutivity". (iii) Thirdly, we came across a novel and intriguing suggestion in the Parsons of indeterminate identity, viz., that the troublesome contexts in question are somehow analogous to those that give rise to the paradoxes of naive set theory and should be excluded from the reaches of the general principle on those grounds; I shall term this response Parsons' "Appeal to the Paradoxes of Naive Set Theory". (iv) Finally, we considered a creative proposal by Deutsch on behalf of the relative identity theorist, which I shall term Deutsch's "Expansion Principle". In what follows, it will be my aim to show that none of these strategies of excluding troublesome contexts from the reaches of the general principle is successful.

§III.3.1 The Purely Stipulative Response

I turn, first, to the Purely Stipulative Response, which is to be found in Gibbard, Myro, Gallois, the Parsons of non-existent objects, Baker, Fine and Yablo. In each case, the Purely Stipulative Strategy proceeds by way of excluding, on *purely stipulative grounds*, a set of troublesome contexts from the reaches of a general metaphysical principle, whose truth the philosopher in question wishes to uphold: it is simply legislated either that these contexts *fail to denote properties* altogether or that the properties they do denote *fail to fall under the scope* of the general metaphysical principle in question. The first strategy is taken by Gibbard; the second by everyone else.

Of course, the mere fact that this strategy is purely stipulative makes it seem ad hoc and hence methodologically suspect. I will, however, try to say more explicitly what it is about this strategy that should worry us, since its proponents might suggest that *some* purely stipulative maneuvers are worth their philosophical price. What makes the Purely Stipulative Strategy especially troubling is that it has the following feature: in each case, there is only a handful of contexts which, when combined with the general metaphysical principle at issue, will generate trouble for the philosopher in question. For example, in the case of the contingent identity theorist, the general principle is LL in its unrestricted, non-temporalized form, and the contexts in question are only those that would conflict with the thesis that coincident objects with the same spatio-temporal extent are contingently identical, e.g. contexts of the following sort (or whatever else the essentialist wishes to substitute):

(14) <u>Troublesome *De Re* Modal Contexts:</u>
 Necessary Identity: □ (_____ = A)
 Essential Kind-Membership: □ (_____ is a statue)
 Essentiality of Origin: □ (_____ was fashioned by artist so-and-so)

In response to the potential threat posed by contexts like those in (14), Gibbard adopts the view that *de re* modal contexts *in general* fail to denote properties. This strategy has momentous consequences, as it leads to a complete reinterpretation of much of our discourse: it requires, among other things, a new theory of proper names, a new notion of rigidity, a new conception of crossworld identity and a new conception of what goes on in contexts in which we seem to attribute *de re* modal properties to concrete objects directly. It does, however, achieve the intended result of effectively removing the troublesome contexts from the reaches of LL, since, as Gibbard remarks, LL is to be understood as a *metaphysical* principle ranging over objects, properties and relations, and not as a *linguistic* principle of substitutivity ranging over contexts and expressions.

 The difficulty for the contingent identity theorist now is that there are plenty of contexts which satisfy the purely formal criteria of being *de re* modal (viz., they involve an occurrence of a name or unbound variable within the scope of a modal operator), and which are completely harmless from the point of view of the contingent identity theorist, in the following sense: if they *were* to be included in the scope of LL, they would *not* conflict with the thesis of contingent identity; I have in mind contexts of the following sort (assuming, with Gibbard, that dispositional, counterfactual and causal contexts involve *de re* modality):

(15) <u>Harmless *De Re* Modal Contexts:</u>
 Dispositional: (_____ is fragile)
      (_____ conducts electricity thus-and-so)
 Counterfactual: (if _____ were dropped on my foot, my foot would swell)
 Causal: (_____ prevents my hand from passing through it)
      (_____ casts a shadow of length so-and-so when hit by the sun at angle thus-and-so)

If the contingent identity theorist were to exclude from the reaches of LL *only* the contexts in (14), and *not* those in (15), then the arbitrariness of his strategy would presumably be just too blatant: contexts would then be sorted into those which fall under the scope of LL and those which fail to do so simply by whether the result would conflict with the contingent identity theory.

To avoid this undisputably blatant arbitrariness, Gibbard adopts a more coarse-grained individuation criterion for troublesome contexts, which includes *all* contexts that satisfy the purely formal criteria for being *de re* modal, i.e., the harmless contexts in (15) along with the troublesome contexts in (14). In his very condensed remarks in Section V of his paper (some of which were quoted above), Gibbard seems to suggest that this more coarse-grained individuation criterion can actually be justified on independent grounds, viz., on the grounds that *de re* modal contexts in the eyes of the anti-essentialist fail to satisfy a generally plausible principle governing the relation between linguistic contexts and properties:

(16) Independently Plausible Principle Concerning Property-Formation:

> A context denotes a property only if it applies to an object *independently of how the object is designated.*

I will comment in more detail below on why I do not believe that (16) succeeds in accomplishing its intended goal. For now, I want only to note that the exclusion procedure Gibbard adopts in the interest of avoiding the undisputably blatant arbitrariness yields the wrong results by virtue of being *too* coarse-grained. For by excluding the harmless contexts in (15) from the reaches of LL, along with the troublesome contexts in (14), the contingent identity theorist has now done away with contexts with respect to which contingently identical objects can in general be *expected* to be indiscernible. If LL can no longer be used to provide an explanation of this datum, then some *other* explanation must take its place. This, of course, puts the contingent identity theorist in exactly the same boat as the coincidence theorist and the relative identity theorist: for he is now in need of a *restricted* indiscernibility principle like RI (only one that is formulated in terms of contexts rather than properties), which provides a systematic account of the ways in which contingently identical objects are indiscernible. This principle, again, must be formulated in such a way as to *exclude* the troublesome contexts in (14) and *include* the harmless contexts in (15).

But how do we formulate such a principle in a way that is not methodologically or otherwise suspect? The first group of philosophers we considered who attempt to propose a restricted indiscernibility principle of this kind, viz., Baker, Fine and Yablo, do so in terms which suffer from exactly the same weaknesses as Gibbard's own account: their proposal is (i) *purely stipulative* and (ii) *overly coarse-grained*. It is purely stipulative, because it is simply *legislated* that contexts of the troublesome kind are to be excluded from the reaches of RI, without any attempt at giving an independent justification for why *these* properties, and not others, deserve this special status with respect to the principle at issue. Moreover, the strategy is overly coarse-grained because it legislates again in the wrong way: by using purely formal criteria (e.g., the occurrence of particular operators in certain syntactically defined ways), it fails to distinguish between the harmless contexts in (15) and the troublesome contexts in (14), since both involve *de re* modal attributions. Thus, unless some other method of delineating contexts can be found which is neither (i) purely stipulative nor (ii) overly coarse-grained, we should be skeptical that the strategy adopted by Gibbard, Baker, Fine and Yablo can be made to work.

These conclusions transfer straightforwardly to our other examples of the Purely Stipulative Strategy in Myro, Gallois and the Parsons of non-existent objects, since all three accounts (i) simply *legislate* that certain kinds of contexts are to be excluded from the reaches of the general principle under discussion, without providing any independent motivation for this measure; and (ii) the contexts in question are once again individuated by means of purely formal criteria (viz., the occurrence of certain kinds of operators in certain syntactically defined ways), which, as we have observed, are too coarse-grained to achieve their purpose: they exclude, along with the troublesome contexts, also contexts which are harmless from the point of view of the position to be defended (e.g., temporal contexts like " _____ has the property today of having occupied a mantelpiece at some time or other" in the case of Myro and Gallois; and modal contexts like those listed above in (15) in the case of Parsons). While the arbitrariness of the Purely Stipulative Strategy may be slightly less blatant as a result of its more coarse-grained exclusion procedure, it also, as a result, draws the boundaries in the wrong place.

§III.3.2 Gibbard's Appeal to Failures of Substitutivity

With his very condensed remarks in Section V of his paper, Gibbard suggests that the anti-essentialist in fact has independent motivation for removing the troublesome contexts from the reaches of LL, by virtue of the general principle in (16) cited above which is to govern the relation between linguistic contexts and properties. It is not entirely clear how Gibbard imagines that (16) will help the contingent identity theorist with respect to the "most prominent objection" coming from LL; in what follows, I lay out what I take to be his implicit reasoning.

In addition to the *metaphysical* principle, LL, governing objects, properties and relations, there is also a *linguistic* principle concerning the substitutivity of co-referential expressions, which is sometimes called by the same name and occasionally even taken to be the same principle as LL; I shall call this principle "The Substitutivity of Co-Referring Expressions" (SCE):

(SCE) The Substitutivity of Co-Referring Expressions:

For all expressions, α and β, *$\alpha = \beta$* expresses a true proposition only if substitution of α for β is truth-preserving.[14]

The phrase, "substitution of α for β is truth-preserving", in SCE is to be understood as expressing the following condition:

(TPS) Truth-Preserving Substitution:

> For all expressions, α and β, substitution of α for β is truth-preserving if and only if, for all sentences, S and S', if S' is like S save for containing an occurrence of β where S contains an occurrence of α, then S expresses a true proposition only if S' does also.[15]

Gibbard remarks that the linguistic principle in SCE, as it stands, is simply false, and we can concur with him in his assessment, as the evidence to this effect is quite massive and convincing. Counterexamples to SCE are drawn primarily from contexts which are considered to be *opaque* in some fashion, e.g., "so-called" constructions such as the following:

(17) Giorgione is so-called because of his size.

(18) Barbarelli is so-called because of his size.

However, none of the counterexamples to SCE, as Gibbard correctly notes, are thought to affect the truth of LL: when properly understood, the sorts of considerations that are appealed to in order to reveal the falsity of SCE do not present us with cases in which one and the same object is said both to possess and not to possess a single property. For example, the truth of (17) and the falsity of (18) can hardly be used to conclude that the context "_____ is so-called because of his size" determines a single property, which one and the same object (i.e., the object variously referred to as either "Giorgione" or "Barbarelli") both has and lacks. In fact, LL is taken by many to be a principle, much like the Principle of Non-Contradiction, whose truth is so obvious and fundamental that nothing of an informative and non-question-begging nature could be said to justify it. Anything that, on the face of it, looks like a counterexample to LL must thus simply involve some sort of misunderstanding.[16]

If my interpretation of Gibbard's reasoning in Section V of his paper is correct, then his thought is that, for the anti-essentialist, troublesome contexts like (3),

(3) □ (_____ = Lumpl)

are, in the relevant respects, just like "so-called" contexts, in that both involve hidden reference to linguistic expressions. For to be so-called because of one's

---

[14] I take "*" to stand for corner-quotes.

[15] These formulations are taken from Cartwright (1971, p. 136); the page numbers refer to the reprinted version in Cartwright (1987), as in all subsequent quotations from Cartwright.

[16] See, for example, Cartwright (1971) and Richard (1987) for arguments to this effect.

size is to be called by some *name* or other because of one's size. Similarly, for the anti-essentialist of Gibbard's stripe, an occurrence of a name within the scope of a modal operator as in (3) induces a *non-standard* interpretation of the name, according to which it is taken to refer to a concrete object not directly, but only *via a sortal concept* of some sort, in this case something along the lines of "lump of clay". For objects in and of themselves, according to the anti-essentialist, do not have particular features necessarily or contingently; they do so only *as designated in a certain way*.

On this conception, then, a context like (3) may both apply and fail to apply to one and the same object, depending on whether the single object in question is designated under the name "Lumpl" or under the name "Goliath". And this feature is of course precisely the mark of a context which, according to the independently plausible principle (16), *fails* to determine a property. In this way, so the anti-essentialist reasons, contexts like (3) can at most be used to provide yet another counterexample to the already disproven linguistic principle in SCE, but they have no relevance to metaphysical principle in LL.

With Gibbard's reasoning reconstructed in this way, we can now see why the Appeal to Failures of Substitutivity does not provide independent motivation for TSS. My argument comes from three essays by Richard Cartwright—, "Some Remarks on Essentialism" (1968), "Identity and Substitutivity" (1971) and "Indiscernibility Principles" (1979)—in which he demonstrates that the falsity of the linguistic principle in SCE has in fact no bearing on the debate between the essentialist and the anti-essentialist. Cartwright's argument, very briefly, is as follows.

There is actually an important *disanalogy* between contexts like those in (3) and contexts like those in (17) and (18), which we can all agree provide a counterexample to the linguistic principle in SSE. For suppose we succeed in identifying a "so-called" context which is in fact both true and false of a single object, depending on whether the object is designated as "Giorgione" or as "Barbarelli"; suppose further the context in question is " _____ is so-called because of _____'s size". Then, on pain of *incoherence*, the context in question cannot be said to determine a property, since, in addition to the places marked by " _____ ", it contains another empty place marked by "so" which has yet to be filled in. Thus, there is *no one* property determined by the context " _____ is so-called because of _____'s size"; rather, there are *lots* of properties, depending on how the place marked by "so" is filled in, which have been misleadingly collected under the same heading: there is the property an object has if it is called "Giorgione" because of its size; the property an object has if it is called "Barbarelli" because of its size; and so on. However, once the hidden place marked by "so" has been explicitly filled in, so that we have in fact succeeded in determining a property, we are no longer dealing with a context which both applies and fails to apply to a single object, depending on how the object is designated. For " _____ is called 'Giorgione' because of _____'s size" truly applies to the object in question, no matter how it is designated; and "_____ is called 'Barbarelli' because of _____'s size" fails to apply to the object in question, no matter how it is designated. This is the reason why "so-called" constructions only provide a counterexample to SCE but not to LL.

In a similar vein, the anti-essentialist (according to the version of this view currently under consideration) conceives of *de re* modal contexts like (3) as containing a hidden ellipsis which must be filled in, in this case, by a particular sortal concept before the context in question succeeds in determining a property. For example, the context "_____ is necessarily identical to Lumpl", on this view, again denotes a multiplicity of properties, as in "_____, *when designated as a lump of clay*, is necessarily identical to Lumpl", "_____, *when designated as a statue*, is necessarily identical to Lumpl", etc. Once a context has been filled in in this way, we will again no longer be faced with a property which both applies and fails to apply to a single object; for it is true of the single statue-shaped object in the actual world, independently of whether it is designated as "Lumpl" or as "Goliath", that, *when designated as a lump of clay*, it is necessarily identical to Lumpl; and it is false of the single statue-shaped object in the actual world that, *when designated as a statue*, it is necessarily identical to Lumpl. In this way, the anti-essentialist avoids any conflict with the metaphysical principle LL.

The essentialist, on the other hand, takes a different view of modal contexts like those in (3). For him, such contexts contain no hidden ellipsis: thus, a context like "_____ is necessarily identical to Lumpl", all by itself, i.e., without the help of any sortal concept, already succeeds in specifying a property which either applies or fails to apply to an object. And, since Lumpl and Goliath are numerically distinct objects, according to the kind of philosopher we are imagining, there is again no conflict with LL, since the property determined by "_____ is necessarily identical to Lumpl" does not truly apply and fail to apply to a single object.

What makes the situation with respect to such modal contexts as (3) different from that of the agreed-upon counterexamples to SCE, however, is that, on pain of begging the question against their opponent, neither the anti-essentialist nor the essentialist can appeal to any sort of *incoherence* in the other's position. For the core of the disagreement between them lies precisely in whether *de re* modal contexts like (3) apply to objects in and of themselves, independently of how they are designated. To show that one of the two sides in this dispute is to be preferred over the other, one must appeal, as Gibbard in fact does, to independent, substantive considerations, e.g., the thesis that the essentialist is committed to an unattractive "ghostly" conception of physical objects or that he relies too heavily on questionable modal intuitions. The falsity of the linguistic principle in SCE and the plausibility of the principle concerning property formation in (16), however, can do nothing to resolve the dispute between the essentialist and the anti-essentialist; for the two parties can perfectly well agree on all of the following points: (i) that the linguistic principle in SCE is false; (ii) that SCE is shown to be false, among other things, by contexts like the "so-called" constructions; (iii) that none of this affects the truth of LL; and (iv) that the principle in (16) states a correct constraint on property formation. What they disagree on is whether (16) is applicable to *de re* modal contexts like (3); but this disagreement is independent of (i) to (iv). In short, whatever the plausibility of Gibbard's *other* considerations in favor of the contingent identity theory, the falsity of the Substitutivity of Co-Referring Expressions is simply irrelevant to the dispute between the essentialist and the anti-essentialist.[17, 18]

§III.3.3 Parsons' Appeal to the Paradoxes of Naive Set Theory

Parsons' Appeal to the Paradoxes of Naive Set Theory has the advantage of being methodologically more satisfying than the Purely Stipulative Strategy, since it introduces a systematic, independently motivated consideration by which contexts are to be classified: their apparently vicious impredicative character. It is, however, questionable whether the contexts at issue really are analogous to those that generate the paradoxes of naive set theory. For note, first, that Parsons' suggestion depends crucially on the assumption that identity can be *defined* as indiscernibility in all respects; unless we accept that the questionable contexts in fact do involve quantification over all properties, they would not be of the allegedly problematic form in which an entity is introduced by means of a definition that quantifies over a domain of elements which is already supposed to include the entity to be defined. By most philosophers' lights, a second-order principle in the manner of (10) is unproblematic only if numerical identity is itself included among the properties to be quantified over; if numerical identity is not so included, then the truth of the principle depends on the very controversial assumption that there can be no numerically distinct, qualitatively indiscernible objects. It is therefore open to the opponent of indeterminate

---

[17] Cartwright (1979) contains a further, powerful objection against Gibbard's particular style of anti-essentialism. Cartwright argues in this essay that the question of whether a context denotes a property is entirely *irrelevant* to the question of whether the corresponding indiscernibility principle is true; for, according to Cartwright, *all* (coherently formulated) indiscernibility principles are true, independently of whether the contexts that occur in them denote properties, and the principle we are accustomed to single out under the name "Leibniz's Law" has no special status among these indiscernibility principles. Gibbard may of course respond to this objection by adopting the more common position of conceding that the contexts in question denote properties, while nevertheless insisting on their exclusion from LL. However, this concession would not only force a drastic reorientation in many of his other commitments; Gibbard would then still be faced with the task of having to explain why this exclusion of properties from LL ought not to be viewed as suspect.

[18] One may worry that my reconstruction of Gibbard's condensed reference to SCE results in a position that is not the most favorable to the anti-essentialist; perhaps the anti-essentialist is better off adopting a position that relativizes *de re* modal contexts in a less overtly *linguistic* manner. In that case, however, one wonders why it is pertinent at all, in this otherwise thoroughly metaphysical context, to point to the falsity of the linguistic substitution principle as well as the independently plausible constraint concerning property formation.

identity to block Parsons' reasoning at this point by resisting the *definition* of identity as indiscernibility in all respects.

Moreover, Parsons' analogy is also questionable in the following further respect. Suppose we were to accept that inferences using LL_{Contra} are valid, that contexts like (9) denote properties, and that identity can be defined in terms of quantification over all properties. Then, the only thing that follows from these assumptions is the conclusion of the Evans-style argument against the possibility of indeterminately identical objects; since the object, A, determinately shares all properties with itself, any object which does not determinately share all properties with A must be *determinately distinct* from A. But no *paradox* ensues from jointly accepting these assumptions. Thus, it seems that Parsons' strategy suffers from the same weakness as Gibbard's Appeal to Failures of Substitutivity, in that it introduces a consideration that is simply irrelevant to the purpose at hand.

Finally, Parsons' strategy, like the Purely Stipulative Strategy above, unsurprisingly also suffers from the weakness of being *overly coarse-grained*, since it too uses purely formal criteria of individuation (viz., the occurrence of a universal quantifier ranging over properties among which the property to be defined is itself included). Even if we were to grant that *some* contexts involving attributions of indeterminate identity lead to paradox, it seems that there are again plenty of *other*, completely harmless, contexts which are defined in the characteristically self-referential manner. For example, suppose an object, A, and an object, B, have exactly the same number of properties; then, presumably, the context "_____ has the same number of properties as A" specifies a property which is itself included among B's properties, and correspondingly for A. But there is nothing paradoxical about this sort of property.[19]

§III.3.4 Deutsch's Expansion Principle

The final proposal I want to consider is Deutsch's *restricted* indiscernibility principle governing objects that are identical merely in the relative sense. Such objects, as we know from $RI_{Rel-Deutsch}$, must share all those properties which, if instantiated by *any* members of a particular equivalence class, must be instantiated by *all* the members of this class.

Like the Parsons of indeterminate identity, Deutsch's proposal is methodologically less suspect than the Purely Stipulative Strategy, in that it introduces a completely general, systematic constraint on LL; it does, however, suffer from the other weakness we have identified, viz., that of being *overly coarse-grained*. To see why, consider the equivalence class containing all those objects (numerically

---

[19] A similar lesson may be learned from those solutions to the semantic paradoxes which trace their source to the phenomenon of self-reference and proceed by legislating that all such contexts are disallowed. Since not all self-reference is problematic (e.g., "This sentence is true"), an approach which proceeds by way of such purely formal criteria of individuation contexts tends to rule out too much.

distinct, in the absolute sense) that are the same literary work as Jack Kerouac's *On the Road* (at a particular time or over time). This equivalence class will consist of a highly non-uniform collection of objects: yellowed paperback copies with missing pages that smell of cigarette smoke and have torn covers, coffee stains and scribbles in the margins; pristine and beautifully illustrated hardcover, first-edition collectors' items, signed by the author; and so on. The regions of space-time occupied by the books themselves are also of course inhabited by the various quantities of matter that constitute them: quantities of paper, cardboard, printer's ink, glue, fabric, etc. Since Deutsch invokes the relative identity theory to solve the problem of the identity of allographic objects as well as the problem of change over time and the problem of constitution, the different copies of the book themselves as well as the quantities of matter coincident with them are all assigned to the same equivalence class, viz., the class unified by the *being-the-same-literary-work-as* relation. If we now apply Deutsch's restricted indiscernibility principle RI$_{\text{Rel-Deutsch}}$ to this heterogeneous bunch, we find that the only properties that satisfy it are properties of a rather *general* sort, viz., those that are commonly taken to be *essential* properties of the literary work in question: e.g., kind properties, such as "_____ is a book", "_____ is an artwork", "_____ is an artifact"; origin properties, such as "_____ was authored by Jack Kerouac"; and the like. And while Deutsch's principle perhaps says as much as any principle *of logic can* say about the ways in which relatively identical objects can generally be expected to be indiscernible, it would not, for example, satisfy the philosopher who was looking for a response to Wiggins' challenge. For such a philosopher wants to know, for example, when, in general, inferences like those in (11) can be expected to be valid; but Deutsch's principle doesn't tell us why constitutionally related objects *always* share the same weight, shape, texture, color, and so on, since relatively identical objects are not always indiscernible in these respects. I thus conclude that Deutsch's principle is too coarse-grained for the purposes at hand, in that it fails to yield a satisfying explanation for the striking similarities that are conferred upon objects by the various identity-like relations collected under the heading "relative identity".

§III.4 CONCLUDING REMARKS

This chapter examined a variety of contexts in metaphysics which employ a strategy I consider to be suspect. In each of these contexts, "The Suspect Strategy" (TSS) aims at excluding a series of troublesome contexts from a general principle whose truth the philosopher in question wishes to preserve. We saw TSS implemented with respect to Leibniz's Law (LL) in the context of Gibbard's defense of contingent identity, Myro and Gallois' defense of temporary identity, as well as Parsons' defense of indeterminate identity. Our example of TSS as implemented with respect to the Existence Principle (EP) was Terence Parsons' defense of non-existent objects. Finally, the coincidence theorist's analysis of the problem of constitution as given by Baker, Fine and Yablo, as well as Deutsch's recent defense of the relative identity theory, provided examples of TSS as implemented with respect to restricted indiscernibility principles of the form in RI.

On the basis of these examples, we discerned four different forms TSS can take: (i) the most widespread Purely Stipulative Strategy; (ii) Gibbard's Appeal to Failures of Substitutivity; (iii) Parsons' Appeal to the Paradoxes of Naive Set Theory; and (iv) Deutsch's Expansion Principle. I discussed in detail why I believe that TSS remains suspect in all four types of approaches considered above.

And while of course we cannot conclude from our exposure to extant versions of TSS that *no* exclusion procedure could ever overcome the troubling features we encountered, my remarks here should, I think, at least give us reasons to be skeptical that any strategy which proceeds by means of *purely formal* (e.g., syntactic) individuation criteria could achieve its intended purpose; for we have seen that such strategies are in general *too coarse-grained* to individuate contexts correctly into those that should and those that should not be excluded from the reaches of the general principle under discussion. I suspect, moreover, though I did not argue for this stronger claim, that any strategy which does *not* proceed by means of purely formal criteria would in some way succumb to the charge of *circularity*.

Supposing then that no non-suspect strategy can be found to exclude the troublesome contexts from the reaches of the general principle, where does this leave us? As I see it, we have basically two options: (i) we can either accept that the general principle in question is true, that the relevant contexts denote properties and that these properties fall under the scope of the general principle; or (ii) we can deny the truth of the general principle in question. The second option, I take it, is not one that many philosophers would take seriously in the context of LL or certain instances of RI, but it may be one that is attractive in the case of EP.

If, as in the case of LL, the truth of the general principle is non-negotiable, then option (i), in the absence of further independently motivated considerations, naturally leads to a universe populated with a surprising multitude of numerically distinct yet almost indiscernible objects, such as statues and the lumps of clay that constitute them, as well as wholes and their parts more generally. For, assuming the preceding remarks are correct, TSS can no longer be invoked in order to bracket those contexts, such as "_____ is essentially a statue", by means of which these objects are apparently discernible; and, by Leibniz's Law, objects which are *almost*, but not quite, indiscernible are numerically distinct.

Part Two

A Contemporary Structure-Based Mereology

IV

A Different Kind of Whole

§IV.1 INTRODUCTORY REMARKS

So far, we have been concerned primarily with the main concepts and principles of standard mereology or CEM as well as the cogency of a certain style of argument which reasons from Leibniz's Law to the numerical distinctness of wholes and their parts. Chapter II examined both three-dimensionalist and four-dimensionalist applications of standard mereology to the case of ordinary material objects. Our main representatives there were Thomson, for the three-dimensionalist camp, and Lewis, for the four-dimensionalist camp. Two components of Lewis' approach were found to be directly relevant to the present discussion: his argument in favor of Unrestricted Composition, which has recently been creatively adopted and elaborated in Sider (2001), in what Sider calls the "argument from vagueness"; and Lewis' so-called "Composition-as-Identity Thesis" in Lewis (1991). Both components are independent of Lewis' endorsement of four-dimensionalism and could therefore, if successful, also persuade the three-dimensionalist to embrace a CEM-style analysis of ordinary material objects. However, as I hope my arguments in Chapter II have established, the three-dimensionalist need not feel moved by either of these components of Lewis' view, since both are ultimately founded on question-begging reasoning. It remains to be seen, however, why, from a three-dimensionalist perspective, the properties of ordinary material objects are not already adequately accounted for by Thomson's modified and weakened version of standard mereology. To this end, I turn next to the work of Kit Fine, who, in a series of papers, has provided powerful reasons for abandoning the standard conception of composition; in its stead, Fine proposes an alternative, neo-Aristotelian, model, which is in some respects close to my own (see also Johnston 2002 for a related framework). I begin this chapter by examining Fine's reasons for parting ways with the standard conception; I consider these reasons to be utterly persuasive and fatal to the standard conception. In the later sections of this chapter, I turn to a detailed discussion of Fine's own positive proposal and indicate where I take myself to be departing from it.

§IV.2 PARTING WAYS WITH THE STANDARD CONCEPTION

In a series of papers, starting in the early 1980s, Kit Fine has developed a novel, neo-Aristotelian conception of ontology and mereology, which differs in certain crucial respects from the more mainstream, CEM-inspired analyses of ordinary material objects (see especially Fine 1982, 1983, 1992, 1994a, 1994c, 1999, 2003). Fine believes that an adequate analysis of ordinary material objects calls for new, *sui generis*, relations of composition; it cannot be couched in terms of the old, CEM-style conception, in his view, because the conditions of existence, spatio-temporal location, and part–whole structure of ordinary material objects simply do not match those of standard mereological sums. In fact, once Fine brings to our attention just how blatantly ordinary material objects diverge from standard mereological sums with respect to their conditions of existence, location and part–whole structure, one wonders how the standard conception could ever have had such a powerful hold on the minds of so many philosophers. Whatever the psychological, historical and sociological reasons for this curious preference for austerity, it is high time that we follow Fine's lead and look towards alternative conceptions of composition which are not blind to certain obvious features exhibited by ordinary material objects; such alternative conceptions will turn out to have much closer affinity to those developed more than two thousand years ago by Plato and Aristotle than they do to those which enjoyed popularity in the 20th century.

Fine's main motivation for the introduction of new primitives is that he believes extant conceptions of parthood to suffer from the following two shortcomings: (i) they are committed, first, to an *aggregative* or *disjunctive* conception of parthood, which assigns the wrong conditions of existence and spatio-temporal location to ordinary material objects; and (ii) even when patched up in certain obvious ways, they misrepresent the part–whole structure of ordinary material objects, as brought out by what Fine calls the *monster objection*. (The second, but not the first, objection applies to Fine's earlier conception of parthood, as developed in Fine 1994a, as well.)

§IV.2.1 Fine's "Aggregative Objection"

Fine's first objection is stated in the following passage:

... [O]n [the standard, "aggregative"] understanding, a sum of material things is regarded as being spread through time in much the same way as a material thing is ordinarily regarded as spread out in space. Thus the sum $a + b + c + \ldots$ will exist *whenever* any of its components, a, b, c, . . . , exists (just as it is located, at any time, *wherever* any of its components are located). It follows that under the proposed analysis of the ham sandwich, it will exist as soon as the piece of ham or either slice of bread exists. Yet surely this is not so. Surely the ham sandwich will not exist until the ham is actually placed between the two slices of bread. After all, one *makes* a ham sandwich; and to make something is to bring into existence something that formerly did not exist.

(Fine 1999, p. 62)

Fine has in mind the following problem. Suppose, for example, the ham sandwich is analyzed as a standard mereological sum, $s = s_1 + s_2 + h$, consisting of two slices of bread, s_1 and s_2, and a slice of ham, h. Given the standard conception of parthood and mereological composition, it seems that we will thereby have assigned to the ham sandwich simply the wrong conditions of existence and spatio-temporal location, at least if we take our ordinary beliefs and utterances about such objects as ham sandwiches as a guide. For a mereological sum, according to the standard conception, exists wherever and whenever *at least one* of its parts does. Thus, if the slice of ham, h, comes into existence at time, t, before the two slices of bread, s_1 and s_2, have come into existence, and h is located at t in the spatio-temporal region, p, then the mereological sum, $s = s_1 + s_2 + h$, also exists at t, in the region, p, occupied by h, and has as parts all and only the parts of h: for the mereological sum, $s_1 + s_2 + h$, according to the standard conception, is that object, s, which has as parts all and only the parts of s_1, s_2 and h; since only h exists at t, the parts of s at t simply are the parts of h at t. But we would not ordinarily say that the ham sandwich has already come into existence at t, when the two slices of bread have not yet come into existence. Of course, we would ordinarily also not say that the ham sandwich has come into existence, even when all of s_1, s_2 and h already exist, unless s_1, s_2 and h were *arranged* in a characteristically sandwich-like manner, with h being between s_1 and s_2. Thus, as far as ordinary material objects are concerned, it is not enough simply to tack onto the standard conception of parthood the requirement that the parts of a sum must all exist at the same time in spatial proximity to one another; the parts must also be arranged in certain specific ways, depending on the kind of object at hand.

§IV.2.2 Fine's "Monster Objection"

Fine's second objection, the "monster objection", is precisely a way of bringing out why simply tacking on an additional requirement of spatio-temporal cohabitation is not sufficient to turn the standard conception of parthood into one that becomes useful for an analysis of ordinary material objects. The problem Fine points to in this objection is the following. Consider an *extended* sense of parthood, according to which, for any two objects, o_1 and o_2, o_1 is (in the extended sense) part of o_2 if the *restriction*, $o_{1\text{-restr}}$, of o_1 to the times at which o_2 exists is (in the unextended sense) a part of o_2, i.e., $o_1 <_{ext} o_2$, if $o_{1\text{-restr}} < o_2$. The extended notion of parthood provides a way, so to speak, of cutting out, by brute force, the spatio-temporally non-cohabiting parts of an object from the mereological sum it helps to compose. We may thus wonder what the merits of such a notion are for the analysis of ordinary material objects, since a proponent of what I have been calling "the standard conception" may well take this extended notion of parthood to be sufficiently close to the original one to feel that his approach can triumph after all. Fine's "monster objection" shows why this won't work:

> In any case, the proposed sense of part will not deliver the correct results. Consider the sum of the ham and Cleopatra or, more dramatically, the sum of the ham and all objects that existed only before or after the ham sandwich existed. Then the restriction of this sum to the time the sandwich exists is the same as the restriction of just the ham and hence must also be a part of the sandwich. But it is ludicrous to suppose that this monstrous object—of which Cleopatra and all merely past and future galaxies are parts—is itself a part of the ham sandwich.
>
> (Fine 1999, p. 63)

Consider the restriction of the mereological sum, $s = s_1 + s_2 + h$, to those times at which the ham sandwich exists; the result of this restriction is another mereological sum, s_{restr}, which exists at all and only those times and places at which the ham sandwich exists and which has at those times all and only the parts of s. Now consider the restriction, h_{restr}, of the ham to those times at which the ham sandwich exists. According to the new notion of parthood, the ham, h, is a part in the extended sense of the restricted sum, s_{restr}, (even though it exceeds s_{restr}'s spatio-temporal boundaries) because the restriction, h_{restr}, of h to the times at which s_{restr} exists is a part in the unextended sense of s_{restr}: i.e., $h <_{ext} s_{restr}$, since $h_{restr} < s_{restr}$. This, of course, is a welcome consequence, since we would like to be able to say that the ham is part of the ham sandwich, even though the ham already existed before the ham sandwich did; we just don't want it to follow from this claim that the ham sandwich therefore *also* already exists as soon as the ham comes into existence.

So far so good. But now, as brought out by the "monster objection", it turns out that, according to the same modified notion of parthood, various "monster objects" also count as parts in the extended sense of the restricted sum, s_{restr}, e.g., the object that has as parts the ham along with *all* objects *whatsoever* that ever have existed or will exist at times at which the ham sandwich doesn't exist (since these will be "cut out" in the restriction). And why, so Fine rightly asks, should we consider a relation which has these consequences to be a relation of parthood at all? It is certainly not one that holds much promise for an analysis of ordinary material objects.

The "aggregative" objection and the "monster objection" evidently provide strong motivation for abandoning the standard conception of parthood and composition. The lesson we learn from these two objections is that an analysis of ordinary material objects requires a notion of parthood which is sensitive not only to the *spatio-temporal proximity* of objects but also to their *manner of arrangement*.

Even after the standard conception has been suitably weakened and modified by Thomson to meet the temporal and modal arguments for distinctness from Leibniz's Law, the conditions of existence, identity, spatio-temporal location and part–whole structure that are assigned to ordinary material objects by the Modalized Cross-Temporal Calculus of Individuals still retain too much of the original analogy between sums and sets to make room for both of these crucial elements. Fine's first objection brings out that ordinary material objects simply do not exhibit the "aggregative" conditions of existence and spatio-temporal location of mereological sums according to the standard conception, since ordinary material objects exist and are located at those times and places at which *all* of their parts *together* are located. Thus, as Fine (1994a) already urged us, an adequate analysis of ordinary material objects evidently requires *conjunctive* conditions of existence and spatio-temporal location. But the "monster objection" shows that the standard conception of mereology cannot be saved merely by means of tacking onto the standard notion of parthood and composition a "conjunctive" requirement of spatio-temporal cohabitation, because the result is still missing a crucial feature: it fails to represent the *manner of arrangement* which the parts of ordinary material objects must exhibit in order for the object in question to exist.

I take these two considerations to be fatal for the standard conception of mereology as it applies to ordinary material objects. And while I of course have no interest in quibbling over terminology, I assume that any conception of parthood and composition that is rich enough to represent explicitly the *manner of arrangement* of an object's parts is too far removed from the original incarnations of CEM to be regarded as an extension of the standard conception. Such an alternative model may of course take over certain minimal requirements on parthood and composition from the standard conception; but it will impose further, richer conditions which must be satisfied in order for one object to compose or be part of another. These richer conditions no longer make it possible to hold on to the original analogy between wholes and sets: for the existence and identity of a set of course in no way depends on the *spatio-temporal proximity* of its members; nor does it impose any special requirements on the *manner of arrangement* which its members must exhibit.

§IV.3 FINE'S THEORY OF EMBODIMENTS

I now want to discuss Fine's own alternative conception of composition in some detail and indicate what I take to be its strengths and weaknesses. I focus in particular on his discussion in "Things and Their Parts" (1999), since this is Fine's most recent and comprehensive exposition of his views concerning the topics that are relevant to the present discussion.

Fine's aim in this and earlier papers (especially Fine 1982) is to "sketch a theory of the general nature of material things"; the more specific entry into this theory taken in Fine (1999) is through consideration of the question, "How are objects capable of having the parts that they do?", or, "What in an object's nature accounts for its division into parts?". The theory is broadly divided into the following two components: (i) the first part, the theory of *rigid embodiments*, is intended to apply to objects which have their parts *timelessly*; (ii) the second part, the theory of *variable embodiments*, is intended to apply to objects whose parts can vary over time. As examples of the former, we are given such objects as ham sandwiches, bouquets of flowers, molecules, suits, nuts and qua-objects (e.g., "personages" such as airline passengers, mayors, and the like; for the theory of "qua-objects", see Fine 1982). As examples of the latter, Fine cites such objects as the water in a particular river (where this phrase is to be understood not as denoting a particular quantity of water, but as denoting a variable quantity of water, one about which it could be meaningfully said, for example, that it is rising) as well as artifacts such as cars.

§IV.3.1 Rigid Embodiments

The theory of rigid embodiments analyzes such composite objects as the ham sandwich as having the constituent structure, "$< a, b, c, \ldots /R >$", where a, b, c, ... are objects, R is a property or relation, and "$/$" denotes a *sui generis* relation of rigid embodiment, a particular way in which wholes may be formed out of parts.[1] Even though the relation, "$/$", of rigid embodiment is taken as primitive, we may nevertheless derive an implicit understanding of it from the following six postulates, which specify conditions for the existence, location, identity and part–whole structure of rigid embodiments:[2]

(R1) Existence-Postulate:

The rigid embodiment, $< a, b, c, \ldots /R >$, exists at a time t iff R holds of a, b, c, ... at t.

(R2) Location-Postulate:

If the rigid embodiment, $e = < a, b, c, \ldots /R >$, exists at a time t, then e is located at the point p at t iff at least one of a, b, c, ... is located at p at t.[3]

---

[1] I add the brackets merely as a device of notational convenience, not to be confused with the notation used for ordered pairs.

[2] About the character of rigid embodiments, i.e., the properties they have and how these properties are related to those of their constituents, nothing of a general nature can be said, according to Fine. In contrast, the earlier theory of "qua-objects" proposed in Fine (1982) contained a principle to this effect called the "Inheritance Principle", according to which a qua-object inherits a certain class of properties (the so-called "normal" properties) from its objectual component (see Koslicki 2004a and 2005a for criticisms of Fine's "Inheritance Principle").

[3] By (R2), the location *in space* of a rigid embodiment still retains the "aggregative" character of standard mereological sums, since the objectual components of a rigid embodiment may of course occupy non-overlapping regions of space. However, its location *in time* is required to be *conjunctive* by force of (R1): I take it that the property or relation component, R, can only hold of the objectual components, a, b, c, ..., at t, if all of a, b, c, ..., *exist* at t.

(R3) Identity-Postulate:

The rigid embodiments, $< a, b, c, \ldots /R >$ and $< a', b', c', \ldots /R' >$, are the same iff $a = a', b = b', c = c', \ldots$, and $R = R'$.

(R4) 1st (Timeless) Part–Whole Postulate:

The objects, a, b, c, ..., are (timeless) parts of $< a, b, c, \ldots /R >$.

(R5) 2nd (Timeless) Part–Whole Postulate:

The relation R is a (timeless) part of $< a, b, c, \ldots /R >$.

(R6) 3rd (Timeless) Part–Whole Postulate:

Any timeless part of $< a, b, c, \ldots /R >$ is a timeless part of one of a, b, c, ... or of R.

Postulate (R1) requires that in order for a rigid embodiment, e, to exist at a certain time, all of e's object components must exist at that time and be arranged in the manner specified by e's intensional component, R. (Following Fine's usage, I refer to the property or relation component of a rigid embodiment as its "intensional component"; I shall have more to say about the nature of this component below.) Postulate (R2) ties the location of the rigid embodiment to the location of its object components, since presumably the intensional component doesn't have spatio-temporal location, at least not in the same straightforward sense as the object components. The identity-postulate (R3) places very strict conditions on the identity of rigid embodiments and results in what Fine himself admits is an "embarrassing diversity" of rigid embodiments. To illustrate, the region of space-time which we would ordinarily say is occupied by a ham sandwich will be inhabited by multiple rigid embodiments composed of the same object components, depending on how the intensional component is specified: the rigid embodiment composed of the two slices of bread, the slice of ham, and the relation of being between, for example, is distinct from the rigid embodiment composed of the two slices of bread, the slice of ham, and the relation of being surrounded, since the relation of being between is distinct from the relation of being surrounded.

Given this "embarrassing diversity" of rigid embodiments, Fine offers an alternative formulation of (R3) (and, correspondingly, (R4)) which delineates the identity conditions and mereology of rigid embodiments on the basis of the identity conditions of the *states* into which their components enter:

(R3′) Alternative Existence-Postulate:

The rigid embodiments, $< a, b, c, \ldots /R >$ and $< a', b', c', \ldots /R' >$, are the same iff the state of a, b, c, ..., standing in the relation R is the same as the state of a', b', c', ... standing in the relation R'.

(R4′) Alternative 1st (Timeless) Part–Whole Postulate:

The rigid embodiment, $< a, b, c, \ldots /R >$, is a (timeless) part of the rigid embodiment, $< a', b', c', \ldots /R' >$, if the state of a, b, c, ... standing in the relation R is a part of the state $a', b', c', \ldots$ standing in the relation R'.

Of course, these alternative formulations are only helpful if we can somehow get a handle on the identity conditions of states independently of those of the objects, properties and relations that participate in them.

Postulate (R5) brings out what is perhaps the most Aristotelian aspect of Fine's theory, namely that the intensional component of a rigid embodiment is a genuine part of it, in the same sense of "parthood" in which its objectual components are parts of the rigid embodiment. Postulate (R6) states that all of the parts of a rigid embodiment derive from their objectual and intensional components. And while the theory of rigid embodiments itself doesn't contain an explicit postulate to the effect that *every* timeless part of a timeless part of a given whole is itself a timeless part of the whole, the transitivity of timeless parthood (and parthood in general) is simply presupposed by Fine as an independently given formal requirement on the part-relation as a strict partial ordering. In fact, Fine's alternative system in general simply presupposes standard mereology and imposes on it further conditions.[4]

§IV.3.2 Variable Embodiments

The theory of variable embodiments analyzes such objects as the water in a particular river or a particular car as having the following more complex constituent structure. A variable embodiment, $f = /F/$, is an object consisting of a principle, F, of variable embodiment as well as a series of "manifestations", f_t, determined by F at the times, t, at which /F/ exists. The principle, F, of a variable embodiment, /F/, is described by Fine as a "function" from times to objects (ibid., p. 69); however, we are to understand the term "function" in this context in a neutral, non-committal way, and not (necessarily) according to its strict, mathematical usage. The manifestation, f_t, of /F/ determined by F at t may itself be a rigid embodiment or a variable embodiment.

Metaphorically speaking, variable embodiments may be thought of along the lines of containers and their contents: the principle, F, of variable embodiment plays the role of the container (which is to be understood not as yet another physical object alongside the content; and not as merely a passive holding-device, but rather as an active participant in determining its content); the manifestations, f_t, are likened to the content (which may vary over time); and the variable embodiment, /F/, itself may be compared to the container together with its content.[5]

---

[4] Professor Fine has assured me (personal communication, October 9, 2003) that this was his intention. All of my comments in what follows that go beyond what Fine explicitly says in his written work are based on his verbal remarks on this occasion; I hope that I have represented his views with accuracy.

[5] Unlike the theory of rigid embodiments, the theory of variable embodiments does not explicitly state that the intensional component of an object, its principle of variable embodiment, is a genuine

Although the operation, $/\ldots/$, of variable embodiment is again taken as a primitive, *sui generis* way of forming wholes out of parts, we gain an implicit understanding of this notion by means of the following postulates governing the existence, location, identity, part–whole structure, and character of variable embodiments:

(V1) Existence-Postulate:

The variable embodiment, $f = /F/$, exists at a time t iff it has a manifestation at t.

(V2) Location-Postulate:

If the variable embodiment, $f = /F/$, exists at t, then its location is that of its manifestation, f_t (assuming that f_t has a location).

(V3) Identity-Postulate:

The variable embodiments, $/F/$ and $/G/$, are the same iff their principles, F and G, are the same.

(V4) 1st (Temporary) Part–Whole Postulate:

Any manifestation of a variable embodiment at a given time is a temporary part of the variable embodiment at that time (in symbols: $f_t \leqslant_t f$).

(V5a) 2nd (Temporary) Part–Whole Postulate:

If a is a timeless part of b that exists at t and if b is a part of c at t, then a is a part of c at t.

(V5b) 3rd (Temporary) Part–Whole Postulate:

If a is a part of b at t and if b is a timeless part of an object c that exists at t, then a is a part of c at t.

(V6) 4th (Temporary) Part–Whole Postulate:

If a is a temporary part of b at t, then there is a mereological chain at t connecting a to b.

(V7) Character Postulate:

The pro tem properties of a variable embodiment, f, at a given time t are the same as those of its manifestation f_t.

The last two postulates involve the technical terms, "mereological chain" and "pro tem property", which are defined as follows:

part of the object; Fine accepts, however, that this is the case (p.c.). The intensional component of a variable embodiment cannot be a part of the variable embodiment in the same sense of "parthood" as that which applies to its manifestations, since these are *temporary* parts of the variable embodiment. It is therefore a *timeless* part of the variable embodiment; to state this explicitly, the theory would need to be supplemented with a postulate corresponding to postulate (R5) from the theory of rigid embodiments. Unless a postulate to this effect is added to the theory, the nature of the relation which holds between a variable embodiment and its principle remains mysterious, since it would otherwise make no pronouncements as to how each such object has its very own principle "attached" to it.

(D6a) Definition of "Fundamental Link":

A link between two objects is a fundamental link at t if it holds between the manifestation, f_t, of a variable embodiment and the variable embodiment itself.

(D6b) Definition of "Auxiliary Link":

A link between two objects is an auxiliary link at t if it holds between two objects, a and b, where a and b both exist at t and a is a timeless part of b.

(D6c) Definition of "Mereological Chain":

A sequence, $(a_1, a_2), (a_2, a_3), \ldots, (a_{n-1}, a_n)$, of connected links is a mereological chain at t if (i) each link in the sequence is either a fundamental link or auxiliary link at t, and (ii) at least one link in the sequence is fundamental.

(D7) Definition of "Pro Tem Property":

A property of an object is a pro tem property if its holding at a time depends only upon how the object is at that time.

Postulates (V1) and (V2) tie the existence and location of a variable embodiment, /F/, at a time t to the existence and location of its manifestation, f_t, at t. Postulate (V3) ties the identity of a variable embodiment, /F/, to the identity of its principle, F, of variable embodiment: two variable embodiments, /F/ and /G/, are the same just in case their principles, F and G, are the same, i.e., just in case they determine for each time for which they are defined the same manifestation.

Postulates (V4), (V5a), (V5b) and (V6) tell us about the part–whole structure of variable embodiments: they serve to relate the two notions of parthood, timeless part and temporary part, which correspond to the (at least) two sorts of wholes, rigid embodiments and variable embodiments; moreover, they also serve to reconstruct a restricted form of transitivity across the two notions of parthood. (V4) states that variable embodiments have their manifestations as temporary parts;[6] this link, between variable embodiments and their manifestations, as

---

[6] Is the manifestation, f_t, selected by F at t a *proper* temporary part of the variable embodiment, /F/? If so, we may wonder, what (if any) are its *other*, non-overlapping, proper temporary parts? (I am appealing here to Simons' Weak Supplementation Principle, which in Simons' view is constitutive of the notion of parthood; this principle states that nothing can have just a single proper part (excluding the overlapping ones); for any proper part of a whole, there must be at least one other, non-overlapping proper part that makes up the remainder of the whole.) The variable embodiment, /F/, cannot be *identical* to its manifestation, f_t, at t, since this would turn numerical identity into a temporalized relation. What exactly, then, is the object to which the variable embodiment, /F/, is identical at each time at which it exists? In the case of rigid embodiments, the theory explicitly answers this question: a rigid embodiment is an object which is composed, by means of the primitive *sui generis* relation, "/", out of other objects, along with an intensional component; the objectual components are arranged in the manner required by the intensional component; the intensional component is itself a genuine part of the resulting composite object; the object in question has its parts timelessly. But the nature of variable embodiments is not settled to the same extent by Fine's

brought out by Postulate (V6), is also the fundamental mereological link which grounds all other relations of temporary part. Postulates (V5a) and (V5b) state that timeless parts of temporary parts are themselves temporary parts, and that temporary parts of timeless parts are themselves temporary parts; thus, chaining temporary with timeless parts itself results in temporary parts.

Finally, Postulate (V7) connects the character of a variable embodiment to that of its manifestations: a variable embodiment inherits those properties from its manifestations which depend only on "how the object is at that time" (whatever exactly that means).[7] Thus, Postulate (V7) is the successor of the principle that was called "Inheritance" in Fine (1982) (see Koslicki 2004a and 2005a for critical discussion of Fine's "Inheritance" principle). In general, the theory of Fine (1999) extends the theory of Fine (1982) by allowing for variation of parts over time; the qua-objects of Fine (1982) are all, in the language of Fine (1999), rigid embodiments.

Since the theory of variable embodiments, with its hierarchical part-structure, is difficult to comprehend, let's consider how it applies, first, to the (variable) water in the river and, then, to the particular car. The (variable) water in the river, according to Fine, is to be analyzed as a variable embodiment, $/F/$, whose principle, F, selects at each time, t, at which the river exists a particular quantity of water, the manifestation, f_t, of $/F/$ at t. We are not explicitly told whether the particular quantities of water selected by F at the different times at which the river exists are themselves rigid embodiments or whether they are objects that lack an intensional component altogether (if there are such objects). I assume that Fine takes the particular quantities of water not to be capable of changing their parts over time, and thus not to be variable embodiments; but whether they are themselves rigid embodiments or objects of another kind is left open.

The car, on the other hand, is analyzed as a variable embodiment, $/F'/$, whose manifestations, f'_t, are rigid embodiments of the form, $< a, b, c, \ldots /R >$. We are to think of the objectual components, $a, b, c, \ldots$, of these rigid embodiments as the "major" parts that are characteristically associated with cars, e.g., the engine, the chassis, the wheels, etc.; the relation, R, reflects the fact that these "major" parts must be arranged in a characteristically "automotive" fashion. The

---

theory as that of rigid embodiments. (See also note 5 for a similar complaint; we will return to these issues below.)

[7] Presumably, a principle of this sort does not apply to rigid embodiments, because what a rigid embodiment is like at each time at which it exists depends not only on what each of its objectual components is like individually at that time, but also on how the objectual and the intensional components interact when combined; and about this (so Fine seems to think) nothing general can be said beyond the fact that the objectual components must instantiate R (Postulate (R1)). For example, even though having a temperature of $100°F$ presumably counts as a "pro tem property" of an object, one cannot infer from the fact that an objectual component, a, has this property that the rigid embodiment, $< a, b, c, \ldots /R >$ it helps to compose also has this property; for its other objectual components, $b, c, \ldots$, may have different temperatures, so that it would be wrong to say the rigid embodiment as a whole has the temperature $100°F$.

objects which are part of each of these rigid embodiments, on the other hand, i.e., the engine, chassis, wheels, etc., are themselves variable embodiments, i.e., objects whose parts may vary over time. The resulting car is thus a hierarchical arrangement of variable and rigid embodiments.

§IV.4 DISCUSSION

As we saw earlier in this chapter, Fine's two main objections against standard mereology, the "aggregative" objection and the "monster objection", certainly provide strong motivation for abandoning a traditional, CEM-style analysis of ordinary material objects. However, once this realization is granted as a starting point, there are of course various directions in which one can go to seek such an alternative conception of parthood and composition. The question now at hand is therefore whether the particular alternative conception developed by Fine yields the most attractive analysis of ordinary material objects.

§IV.4.1 The Proliferation of *Sui Generis* Relations

From a methodological point of view, Fine's analysis raises the worry that it leads to a proliferation of primitive, *sui generis* relations of parthood and composition. Fine's general strategy is to presuppose standard mereology and to impose on it further, more stringent conditions, in the form of postulates specifically tailored to the demands of a particular domain of objects.[8] As we saw in the preceding sections, the domain of ordinary material objects alone, in Fine's view, already calls for two distinct, primitive, *sui generis* relations of parthood and composition: the relations of composition by which rigid embodiments and

---

[8] Fine doesn't actually say in writing which principles of standard mereology he presupposes. Since, as will become clear shortly, he rejects the Weak Supplementation Principle, the version of standard mereology accepted by Fine must be exceedingly weak: for, as we saw in Chapter I, WSP is entailed by the full-strength version of CEM; but both WSP and the Proper Parts Principle (PPP) are also already entailed by the Strong Supplementation Principle (SSP), which results in a system much weaker than full-strength CEM, since it doesn't make provisions for the conditional or unconditional existence of arbitrary products and sums. Presumably, Fine accepts Unrestricted Composition for *his own* relations of composition; i.e., those governing the formation of rigid and variable embodiments. But since these relations of composition have placed upon them a system of postulates, composition in the sense of embodiment of course only takes places when these postulates are satisfied. Uniqueness of Composition would seem to be inert in the case of Fine's *sui generis* relations; for while we have a superabundance of coinciding objects which occupy the same region of space-time, quite possibly in *every* possible world, I presume that even these necessary coincidents would not share the same part-structure. Arbitrary sums, according to the standard conception, on the other hand, can be taken to be *postulated* entities (according to the "method of postulation" mentioned in note 9); and while Fine would presumably not be opposed to the existence of arbitrary sums in the standard sense, as such, when conceived of in this way as postulated entities, I assume that he would insist that none of these mereological sums in the standard sense serve to represent ordinary material objects.

variable embodiments are formed out of their respective components; as well as the relations of timeless part and temporary part that go along with these. Rigid embodiments have only timeless parts; variable embodiments have both timeless and temporary parts. Since the two sorts of embodiments can enter into hierarchical arrangements with one another, various postulates are required in order to connect the two notions of parthood, to reconstruct a restricted form of transitivity. Whatever connections there are between the two notions of composition and parthood thus do not follow from the general formal properties of the basic mereological vocabulary, independently of the domain of objects to which this vocabulary is currently applied; rather, they are explicitly imposed on these relations via postulates specifically tailored to the realm of ordinary material objects. Thus, even within this single domain of objects, Fine's strategy already leads on a (comparatively) small scale to a proliferation of distinct, primitive relations, which are not obviously needed in order to capture the conditions of existence, identity, location, character and part–whole structure of ordinary material objects. Since mereological vocabulary also applies outside of the realm of ordinary material objects, however, Fine's strategy would appear to lead to further distinct, primitive, *sui generis* relations of composition and parthood for each such domain of objects, accompanied by a system of postulates specifically tailored to the particular kinds of objects at issue. Such an approach takes on an overly stipulative and fractured air.

§IV.4.2 The Superabundance of Objects

Fine's strategy of solving long-standing metaphysical problems by introducing new primitive notions thus raises *methodological* concerns; but there are also serious *ontological* reasons for wanting to resist Fine's theory. (For an insightful discussion, among other things, of the problematic ontology of the earlier theory of qua-objects in Fine 1982, see Ray 2000b.) As Fine himself admits, the ontology to which his theory of embodiments is committed far outstrips that of traditional mereology, which many of us, with its endorsement of arbitrary sums, already find troubling. We saw earlier that each occupied region of space-time is inhabited by numerous rigid embodiments which share their objectual components and only differ in how their intensional component is specified. (Exactly *how* numerous the rigid embodiments occupying a given region of space-time are depends on how finely properties, relations or states are individuated.) But now, with the addition of variable embodiments, each such region of space-time is even more densely populated, with both rigid and variable embodiments, whose current manifestations again share many of their parts with each other and with their rigid cohabitants. And although the theory does not spell out the *modal* character of these coincident objects, it seems that many of them will turn out to be *necessarily* coincident, and yet numerically distinct (Fine 1999, p. 73).

To illustrate, consider again the region of space-time occupied by a car. (To recall, a car is analyzed as a variable embodiment, $/F'/$, whose manifestation, f_t', at a time t is itself a rigid embodiment, of the form, $< a, b, c, \dots /R >$; the objectual components, a, b, c, $\dots$, of f_t', are variable embodiments, viz., the "major" parts of a car, its chassis, engine, etc., arranged in a characteristically "automotive" fashion indicated by R.) The same region of space-time that is occupied by the car, $/F'/$, is also occupied, for example, by the variable embodiment, $/G/$, the (variable) quantity of metal, plastic, rubber, etc. of which the car consists throughout its lifetime. The manifestations of $/F'/$ and $/G/$ share some, but not all, of their objectual components; $/F'/$, for example, has a chassis as a temporary part, while $/G/$ merely has as a temporary part the quantity of matter that constitutes the chassis.

But the car, $/F'/$, and the variable quantity of matter, $/G/$, that constitutes the car throughout its career, are only the tip of the iceberg, so to speak. To get a sense of just how densely the single region of space-time in question is populated, consider the existence principle endorsed by Fine: "In general, we will suppose, *given any suitable function or principle F* (taking times into things), that *there is a corresponding object* standing in the same relationship to F as the variable water of the river stands to its principle" (Fine 1999, p. 69; my italics). What makes a principle *suitable*? No boundaries are set, other than a type-restriction on the entities to which the principles apply: the principles must take times as arguments and determine objects as values. Perhaps Fine is pessimistic that any principled line can be drawn between those principles (which relate times to objects) that select ordinary material objects and those that don't, and so decides to accept the whole lot. Without any further restriction on which principles are "suitable", however, the single region of space-time will be occupied by a dizzying array of objects, many of which determine objects with persistence-conditions that strike us, from an ordinary point of view, as quite bizarre. For example, there is also in the particular region of space-time under discussion an object, $/H/$, whose principle, H, divides up cars like sandwiches: it selects at time t a manifestation, h_t, which is a rigid embodiment, $< d, e, f/S >$, whose objectual components, d, e and f are (the quantity of matter constituting) the left half of the car, a thin middle "slice" and (the quantity of matter constituting) the right half of the car, respectively, and whose intensional component, S, requires that the thin middle "slice", e, be between the left half, d, and the right half, f. Since this principle, H, takes times to objects, it constitutes, for all we know, a "suitable" way of selecting an object which occupies the region of space-time inhabited by the car, $/F'/$, and the variable quantity of matter, $/G/$; and who knows how H behaves at other times: it might, for all we know, select at the next time a flower bouquet on a different continent. It thus seems that Fine's theory of embodiments, with its exceedingly tolerant existence principle, generates plenty of "monsters" of its own.

We can also appreciate now how Fine answers the original questions he sets himself, "How are objects capable of having the parts that they do?" or "What in an object's nature accounts for its division into parts?". Fine's answer is that an object has the parts that it does because its intensional component yields this particular way of partitioning the occupied region of space-time in question. However, talk of "nature", in this context, is misleading at best, since the theory predicts that, given our apparently never-ending supply of principles, for any imaginable way of partitioning an occupied region of space-time, there is an object whose intensional component yields this particular division into parts.

To make his "vast superstructure" of objects somewhat more palatable, Fine suggests that we might take the intensional component of an object (i.e., the properties, relations and functions) to be of a *conceptual* nature, and that the commitment to these objects need not be regarded as *ultimate*. However, from the point of view of those who believe that ordinary material objects deserve a privileged ontological status, this suggestion will be no less disconcerting; for, in that case, trees, houses and people will of course suffer the same fate as "car-sandwich-flower-bouquets".[9]

§IV.4.3 The Mysterious Nature of Variable Embodiments

The goal of Fine's theory is to provide an analysis of the "general nature of material things", which answers the question of why material things are divided into parts in the particular ways that they are. But the theory of variable embodiments leaves unanswered several central questions concerning the nature of variable embodiments, their principles and their manifestations (see also notes 5 and 6 for comments to this effect).

---

[9] Current work by Fine on postulation may help address the worries raised in the last two sections concerning the proliferation of primitive *sui generis* relations as well as the superabundance of objects. According to Fine's "method of postulation", what there is (in the unrestricted sense) is relative to postulation. Postulation is a means of extending one's ontology, but it is not a method by which objects are merely "created"; it is an interpretative act, by which existing quantifiers are interpreted as ranging over new objects. Only some relations can be used for the postulation of objects; relations which are legitimate for this purpose satisfy certain constraints. Some of these constraints are general, others are specific to particular domains. For example, within the confines of set theory, set formation is an acceptable method of postulating objects; but this operation must satisfy the following formal constraints: (i) extensionality: one cannot postulate a set that is distinct from and has the same members as an already existing set; (ii) new set-theoretic objects may only be postulated on the basis of already existing objects, but not vice versa; and (iii) any object which has a member must be taken to be a set. While Fine's "method of postulation" may indeed make the proliferation of objects and relations less burdensome, it also appears to lead to a certain form of ontological relativism. (Fine's remarks concerning the "conceptual" nature of intensional components and the non-ultimate commitment to the resulting compounds already foreshadow a certain skeptical attitude to ontology; moreover, further evidence for this development can be gleaned from Fine 2001.) For those of us who are not attracted to relativism in ontology, Fine's "method of postulation" therefore provides little comfort. Instead of letting a zillion entities bloom and then dealing with this fantastic multiplicity by invoking a relativistic stance, the absolutist is best served by opting for a different strategy from the outset, which prevents the proliferation of objects and relations from even getting off the ground.

Let's think first about the principles of variable embodiment themselves. We know that they are principles or functions (in a neutral sense) from times to objects. But what are these principles and how is it that each object has such a principle associated with it? Some of Fine's remarks towards the end of the paper suggest that the answer to this question might ultimately refer back to us, if the intensional components of embodiments are to be thought of as being of a conceptual nature and commitment to them is not "ultimate" (but see the remarks on Fine's "method of postulation" in note 9). I take it, however, that these remarks are not intended to touch on the ontological status of the principles themselves, only perhaps on the mechanism by which specific principles are selected in particular contexts.

The principles which play the role of associating each variable embodiment with its current manifestation cannot be thought of along the lines of Aristotelian forms, at least as long as these are conceived of as *universals*. For variable embodiments are identical just in case their principles of variable embodiment are identical. Thus, no two distinct variable embodiments can have the same principle; but this is precisely not what Aristotelian forms, as universals, are like: all members of the same species, according to this conception, have the same form. (See Fine 1994c for discussion of some puzzles which arise in connection with the Aristotelian conception of matter and form.)

Thus, the principles of variable embodiment may be likened more plausibly to Aristotelian forms, thought of as *individuals*, perhaps something along the lines of *individual essences*. The essences in question must be so specific that they select exactly one current manifestation (barring issues of vagueness) for each time at which the variable embodiment exists. If we think of individual essences as collections of properties, one wonders what collection of properties, short of haecceities, could be sufficiently specific to do this job; certainly, such non-trivial essential properties as those concerning origin will not be nearly fine-grained enough.

Moreover, think again in this context of the "monster objects" to which Fine's theory gives rise. To illustrate, consider a function, f, which selects an object with roughly the persistence conditions of what we ordinarily refer to as a car. Suppose further the car in question comes into existence in the year 1957 and goes out of existence in the year 2000; then, f is not defined before 1957 and after 2000. However, given the never-ending supply of principles from times to objects, there are of course other principles, $g_1, \ldots, g_n$, which agree with f in their 1957-to-2000 portion but which are defined before the year 1957 or after the year 2000; these principles, $g_1, \ldots, g_n$, combine their 1957-to-2000 car-portion with all sorts of other objects (umbrellas, sunflowers, rain drops, what have you) in every way imaginable. If the principles of variable embodiment are thought of as individual essences, then each of these principles, $g_1, \ldots, g_n$, counts as the individual essence of some object; in fact, in general, since no restrictions have been placed on which principles (from times to objects) are "suitable" for selecting objects, *every* such principle which takes times to objects, as far as we know, is the individual essence of some object. I take it that this outcome would make most essentialists uncomfortable.

My second comment concerns the nature of the connection between a variable embodiment, its principle and its manifestations. We know that the relation between a variable embodiment and its manifestations is that of temporary parthood; we know furthermore that the relation between a principle of variable embodiment and a manifestation at a time is something resembling function application. But what is the relation between a variable embodiment and its principle? The variable embodiment presumably is not *identical* to its principle, since this principle is something like a function, i.e., an abstract object, and variable embodiments are (often) material objects. A natural candidate for the relation that holds between a variable embodiment and its principle is of course that of *timeless parthood*. But, in that case, we face the analogue of the worry raised already in note 6 for manifestations and temporary parthood: if a variable embodiment has its principle as a *proper* timeless part, then what are its other, non-overlapping proper timeless parts? According to Simons' Weak Supplementation Principle, an object cannot have just a single proper part; every object that has a proper part must have at least another proper part disjoint from the first. If, on the other hand, the principle is a timeless part of the variable embodiment, but not a proper part, then (assuming WSP holds) it is identical to the variable embodiment and we are back to the worry that material objects have been identified with abstract principles. Finally, if the relation between a variable embodiment and its principle is neither that of identity nor that of timeless parthood, then the nature of this relation has been left mysterious by the theory. In that case, however, Fine's goal of providing a "theory of the general nature of material things" has not been met in a crucial way, as long as we are left in the dark on this question. The worry is, of course, that the theory might at this point be forced to appeal to yet another primitive, *sui generis* relation of composition.

As a matter of fact, although this is not explicitly stated in Fine (1999), Fine's position is that each variable embodiment has both its principle as a *proper timeless part* and its current manifestation as a *proper temporary part*. Fine opts to resolve the dilemma just raised by rejecting the Weak Supplementation Principle; this rejection, in his view, is in any case independently motivated. Consider, for example, a domain of time intervals which are not to be thought of as composed of instants. Now, a particular closed interval, T, may be a proper part of an open interval of time, T′, without there being at least one further interval that is both a proper part of T′ and disjoint from T. In Fine's view, even when WSP is satisfied, the question of what the whole is over and above the parts remains: this mystery is not resolved by pointing to additional parts; rather, it is addressed only by means of elucidating the particular relation of composition at work in the context at hand. The work of elucidating a particular composition relation is accomplished by providing a system of postulates, of the kind Fine develops for rigid and variable embodiments. This latter point can be illustrated by means of the following set-theoretic example. Assume for the moment that the members of a set are, at least in some sense, part of the set (even though this assumption is of course not beyond challenge and contradicts, for example, assumptions made in Lewis 1991). Now consider the relation between Socrates and his singleton set. In this case, WSP is not satisfied: the singleton set containing nothing but Socrates is distinct from its only proper part, Socrates; but it has no other proper parts, disjoint from Socrates. If we now consider instead a set containing as members two sets, Socrates' singleton set and any other set, the presence of the additional proper part, in Fine's view, in no way makes it easier to understand the original mystery, namely how a whole—in this case, a set—is related to its proper parts, even though WSP is satisfied in the latter case. Examples of this kind illustrate why Fine believes that his rejection of WSP as a necessary constituent of any genuine parthood relation is independently justified.

§IV.4.4 The Formal Properties of Parthood

Among the attractive features of Fine's theory of embodiment are (i) its wide applicability across the domain of both material and abstract objects; as well as (ii) its "sparse" and hierarchical conception of parthood. To illustrate, Fine's notion of rigid embodiment is tailored to apply not only to material objects such as ham sandwiches, but also to acts such as Oswald's killing of Kennedy, and to abstract objects such as the "law of the land". For example, Oswald's killing of Kennedy is analyzed as Oswald's act of shooting the gun (its objectual component) under the description of causing Kennedy's death (its intensional component); the "law of the land", on the other hand, is analyzed as a variable embodiment whose manifestations are different bodies of law.

The "sparseness" and hierarchical nature of parthood, on Fine's model, can be brought out by considering the resemblance parthood bears to the relation of *set membership*, rather than to the *subset* relation, to which it is traditionally likened (Fine 1999, p. 72). Thus, embodiments are viewed by Fine as "sparsely" and hierarchically structured objects which may be composed of further "sparsely" and hierarchically structured objects. At each level in the hierarchy, an object's division into parts is prescribed by the particular intensional component that is operative at that level, with the result that not every arbitrary way of dividing up an embodiment results in a division into *parts*.

Given this hierarchical and "sparse" conception of parthood, Fine's model allows for an attractive distinction between parts in a *vertical* sense and parts in a *horizontal* sense. Consider, for example, a tree and the wood (and other biological substances) of which it is composed. The tree has as its immediate, horizontal (temporary) parts its trunk, branches, leaves, etc.; the (variable quantity of) wood, on the other hand, has as its immediate, horizontal (temporary) parts the cellulose molecules of which it is composed at each time at which it exists, but not the more highly structured parts of which the tree consists. In the non-immediate, vertical sense, however, the parts of the wood are also parts of the tree. This situation is to be compared, for example, to the set-theoretic analogue of {a, b, c, d} and {{a, b}, {c, d}}: even though the two sets, in some sense, are built up out of the same basic constituents, the latter is more highly structured than the former and the two do not coincide in their part structure (assuming, again, that the members of a set are, in some sense, parts of it).[10]

While I take the "sparse" and hierarchical nature of Fine's notion of parthood as well as its wide applicability across diverse ontological domains to be attractive features of his theory, there is I think a legitimate worry as to whether this theory preserves to a sufficient extent the formal properties that have at least a strong claim to being considered constitutive of any genuine relation of parthood. We have seen already that, despite the fact that Fine accepts unrestricted transitivity for each parthood relation individually, due to the proliferation of distinct parthood relation, transitivity *across* the different notions of parthood cannot in general be presupposed but must be reconstructed, where it holds at all, by means of separate postulates. Moreover, we have also observed that Fine's theory leads to the rejection of the Weak Supplementation Principle, which has at least a plausible claim at being a mark of any genuine relation of parthood and which forms the distinctive formal core of Simons' most minimal mereology. Thus, in addition to the methodological and ontological worries I have raised in the preceding sections, Fine's theory might legitimately make us wonder why its so-called relations of parthood and composition should in fact be considered to be genuinely mereological at all, given their formal profile.

§IV.5 CONCLUDING REMARKS

Given the methodological and ontological consequences of Fine's theory of embodiments, the question thus arises as to whether such commitments are in fact needed to accomplish the tasks Fine sets himself: to give an analysis of the "general nature of material things", which answers the question of why material things are divided into parts in the particular ways that they are. Unless one is already accustomed to the outlook of standard mereology, it is not obvious that the theory of rigid embodiments is really required for an analysis of *material* objects (as opposed to, say, abstract objects which have their parts essentially), since the objects of our scientifically informed common-sense ontology (even,

---

[10] The analogy with set theory is, in Fine's view, only that, an analogy. Sets are not rigid embodiments; rather, they are governed by their own *sui generis* relation of composition, associated with its own relation of parthood. Fine does not believe that the membership relation can be defined in terms of parthood; rather, if anything, the direction of analysis is reversed: parthood for set-theoretic objects can be defined as the ancestral of the membership relation.

arguably, such things as ham sandwiches, flower bouquets, suits, and nuts) generally seem to be capable of surviving the gain and loss of parts. Whether there are material objects (such as, possibly, very small subatomic particles) which are counterexamples to this claim is, I take it, an empirical question; and even if there turn out to be such objects, it is not clear that their analysis requires the introduction of an additional timeless notion of parthood into the domain of material objects, since such objects otherwise exist in time and may be capable of persisting through changes with respect to some of their remaining characteristics; thus, using the same, time-relative notion of parthood that applies to such objects as trees, which can change their parts over time, we may simply say of these mereologically inflexible objects that they must have the same parts at all times at which they exist.

Thus, from the point of view of those not yet in the grip of the mereological rigidity of traditional sums, it would seem that the material world in general is composed, in the terminology of Fine's theory, of variable embodiments, which are in turn hierarchically composed of further variable embodiments. But in order to reflect an object's ability to survive change of parts over time, all that is required is that the part relation be relativized to time, just as property instantiation in general (according to the three-dimensionalist picture) is relativized to time. Thus, the only consideration so far which seems to favor Fine's theory of variable embodiments over standard alternatives is its widely applicable "sparse" and hierarchical conception of parthood, which allows for a response to the "monster objection" by taking into account not only the spatio-temporal proximity of an object's parts but also their *arrangement*. But we have encountered reasons to be doubtful of the success of this alternative conception of parthood. For we have seen that Fine's theory gives rise, first, to a proliferation of primitive *sui generis* relations of parthood and composition, whose characteristics must be imposed on them stipulatively by means of distinct systems of postulates, tailored to different domains of objects. Secondly, we noted that, given its "superabundance" of objects, Fine's theory is committed to its very own population of "monsters". Thirdly, once rigid embodiments are abandoned, the neo-Aristotelian flavor of Fine's theory is preserved only at the cost of abandoning the Weak Supplementation Principle. This, along with the other formal properties of Fine's system, makes us wonder why one should consider the primitive, *sui generis* operations introduced by Fine's theory to be genuinely mereological at all. In sum, there are thus good reasons to look for an alternative analysis of material objects which preserves the neo-Aristotelian flavor of Fine's embodiments, but avoids their methodological and ontological excesses.[11]

---

[11] The contents of this chapter have appeared in print as part of Koslicki (2007) and are followed by brief responses to some of my criticisms by Professor Fine.

Part Three

Ancient Structure-Based Mereologies

V

The Role of Structure in Plato's Mereological Writings

§V.1 INTRODUCTORY REMARKS

The object of Chapter IV was two-fold: first, to present what I take to be convincing reasons for abandoning a CEM-style analysis of ordinary material objects as three-dimensional or four-dimensional mereological sums; and, secondly, to evaluate the most explicit and detailed modern-day alternative to a CEM-style theory, which takes these considerations into account, viz., that developed by Kit Fine in a series of papers over the past twenty years or so. The two main considerations which motivate Fine's own departure from the standard CEM-style approach are, first, the "aggregative" objection, according to which the standard approach assigns simply the wrong, set-like conditions of existence and spatio-temporal location to ordinary material objects; and, secondly, the "monster objection", which brings out a crucial element in the analysis of ordinary wholes that is completely absent from the standard account, viz., that of *structure* or *manner of arrangement*.

In response to the "aggregative" objection and the "monster" objection, Fine proposes an alternative account, which takes both the idea of structure, or manner of arrangement, as well as the requirement of spatio-temporal proximity very seriously. The resulting theory of *rigid* and *variable embodiments*, whose most detailed statement is found in Fine (1999), was evaluated in detail in the previous chapter. While the neo-Aristotelian spirit of this theory, with its widely applicable, "sparse" and hierarchical conception of parthood is quite attractive and ought to be preserved, it also gives rise to a number of serious methodological and ontological concerns. First, it leads to a methodologically suspect proliferation of primitive, *sui generis* relations of parthood and composition, distinct ones for different domains of objects, whose characteristics and connections must be explicitly imposed on these relations by means of separate bodies of postulates, specifically tailored to each domain; the resulting approach takes on an overly fractured and stipulative air. Secondly, Fine's theory, in part because of its acceptance of an exceedingly liberal existence principle, is committed to a superabundance of objects, an ontology which far outstrips the (to many of us) already over-abundant ontology of standard mereology: each region of space-time turns out to be occupied by a dizzying array of numerically distinct (and yet, in some cases, *necessarily coextensive*) objects, whose persistence conditions from an ordinary point of view look quite bizarre; as a result, Fine's theory gives rise to plenty of "monsters" of its own. Thirdly, given their formal profile, we are left to wonder, especially in light of the considerations noted in the first objection, what makes these primitive, *sui generis* relations posited by Fine's system genuinely *mereological* in character: certainly, to recall a remark by Lewis quoted in Chapter I, a philosopher who already harbors doubts that any system other than CEM could capture a genuinely mereological operation might react to Fine's theory of embodiments in this fashion; but even those of us who are open to the possibility of genuinely mereological non-CEM-style systems, in this case, I think would be sympathetic to the Lewisian challenge.

These methodological and ontological considerations provide motivation to search for an alternative approach which preserves the neo-Aristotelian spirit of Fine's theory while avoiding its troubling features. Since the kind of theory of composition for which we are aiming has its historical origins in Aristotle, and, as it turns out in Plato as well, I want to examine, in the next two chapters, some of the rich and rewarding writings of these two ancient authors on parts and wholes. Even though the texts in question of course raise numerous interesting and difficult interpretive questions and have generated a voluminous literature in ancient philosophy, I will in what follows be less concerned to participate in these scholarly debates than to approach Plato's and Aristotle's remarks from the point of view of a contemporary metaphysician who is interested simply in finding the *right* theory of parthood and composition for ordinary material objects. I turn first to Plato's mereological writings and Verity Harte's recent insightful readings of them (especially Harte 1994, 1996 and 2002); Aristotle's treatment of parts and wholes will be the subject of the following chapter.[1]

§V.2 THE NEGATIVE MEREOLOGICAL UNDERCURRENT

Although neither Plato's nor Aristotle's corpus includes a separate treatise that is devoted specifically to the discussion of parts and wholes, questions of mereology were clearly very much on their minds and suggestive remarks concerning mereology can be found scattered throughout many of their works. In some cases, these remarks are extremely condensed and mystifying; in other cases, the discussion is quite extensive and, despite the absence of explicit axioms and theorems, might fairly be viewed as adding up to something close to a theory, or at least a conception, of parthood and composition.

---

[1] The material in the current chapter constitutes a more detailed development of the points made in a very condensed fashion in my review of Harte (2002) (see Koslicki 2004b).

In Plato's case, Harte (2002) identifies both what she calls a *negative mereological undercurrent* and a *positive mereological undercurrent*: in the former, Plato is concerned to explore conceptions of composition he finds to be lacking in some respect; in the latter, he aims to develop his own positive proposal. Harte locates texts that belong to the first group primarily in passages from the *Theaetetus, Parmenides*, and *Sophist*;[2] those that belong to the second group, she argues, can be found in the *Parmenides, Sophist, Philebus* and *Timaeus*.[3] Harte impressively weaves together these diverse and difficult contexts to construct a reading of Plato which portrays him as being concerned precisely to take a stand on what we would now describe as Peter van Inwagen's "Special Composition Questions", the question "Under what conditions do *many* things compose *one* thing?" (van Inwagen 1990), and to come out against David Lewis' Axiom of Unrestricted Composition, according to which *any* plurality of objects whatsoever, no matter how disparate and dissimilar, composes a further object, their mereological sum (Lewis 1991). Moreover, if Harte is right, Plato should be regarded not only as a serious contender in the contemporary debate over the nature of mereological composition, alongside such current theorists as David Lewis, David Armstrong and Peter van Inwagen; Plato's theory in fact, she argues, has an edge over contemporary alternatives precisely because of the prominent role it assigns to the notion of *structure*.

In the negative phase of his mereological writings, Plato is, in Harte's view, primarily concerned to problematize a particular view of composition that is in fact surprisingly close to that of David Lewis, a kind of Composition-as-Identity view, whose ancient proponents turn out to be the commitment-shy Eleatic philosophers, the followers of Parmenides and Zeno. The central premise on which this view turns is the principle Harte calls the "Pluralizing Parts Principle" (PPP), according to which a whole is *many*, as many as its parts. A sample appeal to PPP can be found, for example, in the First Deduction of the *Parmenides*:

Then, on both grounds, the One would be composed of parts, both being a whole and having parts? – Necessarily. – Then on both grounds the One would thus be *many and*

---

[2] The specific texts Harte groups into the negative mereological undercurrent are as follows. (i) *Theaetetus* 203–206: a passage that occurs in the third part of the *Theaetetus*, while considering the definition of "knowledge" as true judgment with an account ("λόγος"), during Socrates' "Dream-Argument"; it concerns the relative unknowability or knowability of "elements" over "complexes". (ii) *Parmenides*: Harte identifies four different mereological puzzles that mark out the negative undercurrent in the *Parmenides*; they occur in the initial conversation between Socrates and Zeno (*Prm.* 129b ff), in the "Dilemma of Participation" (*Prm.* 131a–c), as well as in the First and Second Deduction (*Prm.* 137c–142a, 142b–155e). (iii) *Sophist*: the relevant passages occur in the discussion of the "Monists" (viz., those philosophers who hold, like Parmenides and Zeno, that what is is one) at *Sph.* 244b6–245e2.

[3] The specific texts belonging to Harte's positive mereological undercurrent are as follows. (i) *Parmenides*: passages from the Second, Third, Fourth and Seventh Deductions (especially *Prm.* 146b2–5, 157b7–c8 and 158b5–c7). (ii) *Sophist*: the discussion of the "Late Learners" (*Sph.* 251a5 ff). (iii) *Philebus*: the discussions of "limit", "unlimited" and "mixture", which dominate large sections of the dialogue. (iv) *Timaeus*: the first creation story, which concerns the creation of the body of the cosmos (beginning at *Tim.* 29d7), and the second creation story, which concerns the creation of the four elements (beginning at *Tim.* 53a7).

not one. —True. —But it must be not many, but one. —It must. —Then *if the One will be one, it will neither be a whole nor have parts.* —It won't.

(*Prm.* 137c9–d3)[4]

Due to the implicit acceptance of PPP, the mere presence of *many* parts in an object (in this case, the Parmenidean "One") is here seen as a threat to that object's unity, to its being genuinely *one*: in other words, parts in and of themselves are viewed as pluralizing an object, according to PPP. The result is a paradoxical-seeming "many-one" entity, reminiscent of what we found in Lewis' wavering discussion of the Composition-as-Identity Thesis discussed earlier in Chapter II, in which he is tempted both straightforwardly to *identify* an object with its many parts (leaving us with an object that would appear to be *many*, as many as its parts) and to draw a mere *analogy* between composition and identity (leaving at least a precarious opening for complex wholes that are *one* despite their many parts). Plato eventually finds this model of composition to be untenable precisely because it fails to make room for wholes that are genuinely *one* despite the fact that they have *many* parts.

While the Composition-as-Identity model seems to be the one which most occupies Plato in these passages, Harte also notices other conceptions that crop up here and there: a *container*-model, briefly entertained in the Second Deduction of the *Parmenides* (*Prm.* 144e3–145a3), according to which wholes are viewed as completely disjoint from their parts;[5] a sort of *Nihilist* conception, sometimes at work for example in the *Theaetetus'* Dream-Argument and in the *Parmenides'* First Deduction, according to which (trivially) the only wholes are *mereological atoms*; and, finally, a picture of wholes, which makes an appearance, for example, in the *Parmenides'* Seventh Deduction, according to which wholes are *bare pluralities*, i.e., not really one at all. All of these models are ultimately rejected by Plato, sometimes without explicit discussion; but, in other cases (particularly that of the Composition-as-Identity model), we see Plato going to great lengths to bring out the paradoxical results to which these unacceptable models lead.

§V.3 THE POSITIVE MEREOLOGICAL UNDERCURRENT

The positive mereological undercurrent in Plato's writings takes up a suggestion briefly made, but not further developed, in the *Theaetetus*, according to which wholes are to be viewed as something that is genuinely *one*, viz., as *some single form* (μίαν τινά ἰδέαν):

---

[4] Unless otherwise noted, the translations in what follows are Harte's; the italics mine.
[5] Recall in this context that Fine also likens his principles of variable embodiments to "containers", which actively pick out their manifestations at each time at which the variable embodiment in question exists.

Look here, what do we mean by "the syllable"? The two letters (or if there are more, all the letters)? Or do we mean *some single form* [μίαν τινά ἰδέαν] produced by their combination?

(*Tht.* 203c4–6; Levett/Burnyeat translation)

We come across this conception of wholes as genuinely unified again in sections of the *Parmenides* and *Sophist*; but these discussions pale in comparison with the wealth of detail that is provided in the *Philebus*' treatment of "limit", "unlimited" and "mixture", as well as in the *Timaeus*' creation stories. From these texts, Harte assembles for us the following positive characterization of Platonic wholes.

(i) *Unity.* As against the pluralized wholes of the Composition-as-Identity model, wholes according to the new conception are genuinely *unified*. To bring out the intimate relation into which the parts of such a genuinely unified whole must enter, Plato invokes, especially in the *Sophist* and *Philebus*, a rich and suggestive vocabulary consisting of terms like "weaving together" (συμπλέκειν), "blending" and "mixing" (συγκεράννυσθαι, συμμείγνυσθαι), "communing" and "combining" (ἐπικοινωνεῖν, κοινωνεῖν), as well as "fitting together" or "harmonizing" (συναρμόττειν, συμφωνεῖν). Some of these terms have connotations which also relate to feature (vi) below.

(ii) *Ontological Commitment.* When parts of the right kind enter into the intimate relationships described by Plato's body of metaphors cited in (i), the result is the *creation* of a new object, to which we were in no sense already committed previously; thus, contra Lewis, the Platonic conception of composition is *ontologically loaded*. Plato's new conception of wholes as clearly numerically distinct from their parts is brought out well in the following passage from the *Parmenides*:

Everything, I take it, is related to everything else as follows: it is either *the same* [ταὐτόν] or *other* [ἔτερον], or, if it is neither the same nor other, it would either be a *part* [μέρος] of that to which it is thus related or be related as *whole* [ὅλον] to part.

(*Prm.* 146b2–5)

As highlighted by Harte, Plato in this passage explicitly disassociates himself from the Composition-as-Identity conception which endorses PPP, since he specifically differentiates the relations of parthood and composition from those of numerical identity and distinctness.

(iii) *Restricted Composition.* Again contra Lewis, composition, for Plato, is also *restricted*, in that not all pluralities of objects are capable of entering into the requisite relationship; only certain combinations of objects result in a genuinely unified whole. The restricted nature of composition is of special concern to Plato, for example in the *Sophist*, in the context of the discussion of the "mixing" of the "kinds" (here, "Being", "Change" and "Rest") in connection with the so-called "Late Learners":

Then shall we not fasten being to change or rest, nor anything to anything else, but rather take them to be unmixed (ἄμεικτα) and thus incapable of having a share of each other in our assertions (λόγοι)? Or shall we gather them all together in the same, as being capable of combining (ἐπικοινωνεῖν) with each other? Or shall we suppose that *some can* and *some cannot*? Which of these shall we say that these people choose, Theaetetus?

(Spht. 251d5–e1)

The options Plato is here outlining are that composition be conceived of either (i) as *never* occurring (as on the Nihilist model) or (ii) as *universal* (as on the Composition-as-Identity model) or (iii) as *restricted* (as, for example, on the model of van Inwagen 1990, according to which only parts whose activity constitutes a single *life* compose an object). The option Plato explicitly chooses is the third, that of restricted composition: only *some* things can combine to form a genuine whole. One of Plato's examples in the *Sophist* to illustrate the restricted nature of composition is that of letters and syllables; another one that of musical sounds:

Since some things are willing to do this [to combine] and some things are not, they will be affected in just the same way as the *letters of the alphabet*; for some of these do not fit together with each other and some do fit together (συναρμόττειν).

(Spht.252e9–253a2)

Again, isn't it the same as regards *sounds* of high and low pitch? Isn't the one who has the skill (τέχνη) to know which blend (συγκεραννυμένους) and which do not musical (μουσικός), whereas the one who does not know is unmusical?

(Spht. 253b1–3)

(iv) *Structure/Content Dichotomy.* Perhaps most centrally, a Platonic whole consists of two components, which Harte identifies as *structure* and *content*. "Structure" tends to be characterized by Plato as something that is *mathematically* expressible (number, measure, ratio, proportion and the like); "content", that on which structure is imposed, remains a bit murky, since not much of a positive nature is said about it. In the *Philebus*, the structure/content dichotomy is aligned by Harte with the distinction between *limit* (πέρας) and *unlimited* (τὸ ἄπειρον), that which admits of the "more and less", a domain delineated by pairs of opposing qualities such as hot and cold; a whole resulting from the combination of the two is called a *mixture* (μίξις or τὸ μεικτόν). The following passage illustrates the three elements of "limit", "unlimited" and "mixture" in the *Philebus*' analysis of complex wholes:

Whatever seems to us to become "more and less", or susceptible to "strong and mild" or to "too much" and all of that kind, all that we ought to subsume under the genus of the *unlimited* as its unity. This is in compliance with the principle we agreed on before, that for whatever is dispersed and split up into a multitude, we must try to work out its unifying nature as far as we can, if you remember. –I do remember. –But look now at what does not admit of these qualifications but rather their opposites, first of all "the equal" and "equality" and, after the equal, things like "double", and all that is related as number to number or measure or measure: If we subsume all these together under the heading of "*limit*", we would seem to do a fair job. Or what do you say? –A very fair job, Socrates. –Very well, then. But what nature shall we ascribe to the third kind, the one that contains the *mixture* (τὸ μεικτόν) of the two?

(*Phlb.* 24e7–25b6; Frede translation)

In the *Timaeus*, Harte sees structure manifesting itself as the demiurge's *geometrical proportion* ("ἀναλογία") or *order* ("τάξις"), which she reads as "configurations of space". Content is that which is being configured, i.e., either the *four elements* (in the story surrounding the creation of the body of the cosmos) or (in the story surrounding the creation of the four elements) the *receptacle* (ὑποδοχή), which Harte reads simply as *space*.[6]

(v) *Priority of Wholes over Parts.* Platonic wholes, on Harte's reading, are in some way *prior* to and more *basic* in Plato's ontology than their parts; parts, as she puts it, are *structure-laden*; their existence and identity is in some sense (whose precise nature remains unspecified) *dependent* on the wholes of which they are part. One of Harte's main direct pieces of textual evidence for the attribution of this feature to Plato is the following intriguing passage from the *Philebus*:

Any blend (σύγκρασις) which does not have measure (μέτρος) or the nature of proportion (σύμμετρος) in any way whatsoever, of necessity *destroys both its ingredients and, primarily, itself.* A thing of this sort is truly *no blend at all*, but a kind of *unblended disaster*, a real disaster for the things which acquire it.

(*Phlb.* 64d9–e3)

In this passage, Plato appears to be saying that the very same object cannot at one point be a part (or "ingredient") of a genuine whole or "mixture", i.e., one which has "measure" and "proportion", and at another point cease to be a part of such a mixture, but nevertheless survive intact; for without the mixture, so Plato seems to be saying, the "ingredients" themselves are "destroyed" as well.

(vi) *Normativity and Teleology.* As is widely documented by Harte, especially across the *Philebus* and *Timaeus*, Platonic wholes have a *normative* and *teleological* character: they are described by Plato as "complete" or "perfect" (τέλειος), "harmonious" (σύμφωνα), "commensurate" (σύμμετρα), "ordered" (διακεκοσμισμένα) and "good" (καλά); on a literal reading of these texts, their creation is governed by a divine agent who arranges everything for the best.

---

[6] Plato, in the *Timaeus*, views the cosmos as an ensouled, living being that is created by a teleologically driven divine demiurge out of geometrical proportions and the "receptacle"; the body of the cosmos consists of the four elements, as arranged in certain geometrical proportions. The four elements themselves are viewed as non-basic: they consist of triangles and cubes, as arranged in certain geometrical proportions (fire consists of pyramids; air consists of octahedrons; water consists of icosahedrons; and earth consists of cubes); the possibility is left open that the triangles and cubes themselves may be non-basic as well.

(vii) *Proper Objects of Science.*   Due to the mathematical nature of structure and the teleological cause underlying the creation of Platonic wholes, these wholes are *intelligible*, and they are in fact the *proper objects of science*; all of Plato's examples of wholes are chosen from such domains as grammar, music, medicine, meteorology, philosophy and cosmology to bring home this point. To illustrate, recall the passage from the *Sophist*'s discussion of the "Late Learners" quoted above (*Spht.* 253b1–3) in which Socrates emphasizes the "skill" (τέχνη) of someone who has the requisite knowledge concerning the proper combination of high and low pitches; such a person is called a "μουσικός", someone who is versed in the science of music. References of this kind are abundant especially in the *Sophist*, *Philebus* and *Timaeus*.

In sum, Platonic wholes, as they have been described in this section, have the following features: they are (i) genuinely *unified*; (ii) *ontologically loaded*; (iii) governed by a *restricted* notion of composition; (iv) comprised of the two components of *structure* and *content*; (v) ontologically *prior* to their parts; (vi) *normative* and *teleological* in nature; as well as (vii) inherently *intelligible* and the *proper objects of science*. I turn now to a discussion of some of the substantive features of this theory, as viewed from a contemporary perspective, as well as to some questions I want to raise about Harte's account of it.

§V.4 PLATONIC WHOLES

While some of the features of Platonic wholes could be incorporated quite easily into a contemporary neo-Platonic theory of parthood and composition, others may strike us as peculiar or controversial, perhaps most of all those in (vi) and (vii).

§V.4.1 Normativity, Teleology, Intelligibility and Unity

(vi) *Normativity and Teleology.*   Plato's thesis in the *Philebus* that *all* genuine mixtures have normative and teleological features and, even more controversially, that these normative and teleological features are exclusively *positive* (viz., all genuine mixtures are "complete" or "perfect", "commensurate", "ordered" and "good"), is surely impossibly strong and not particularly plausible, from a contemporary point of view; its justification relies on the invocation of a centralized, and apparently theological, teleology, whose existence could not be taken for granted by a modern-day mereologist. We may well wish to attribute normative and teleological features to *some* wholes, but such an attribution would need to be argued for, with much ingenuity, on a case-by-case basis, and could not with any credibility be restricted only to positive characteristics.

What, for example, might be the positive normative or teleological features present in a cancer cell or in a quantity of radioactive waste? There are different

ways in which Plato could approach such entities, depending, first, on whether
he does or does not view them as having the relevant positive normative and
teleological features and depending, secondly, on whether he does or does not
assign to them genuine whole status of some kind. (a) First, Plato could insist on
viewing such entities as cancer cells or quantities of radioactive waste as genuine
wholes or "mixtures" which are "complete" or "perfect", "commensurate",
"ordered" and "good", just like musical melodies and health, even though they
may not appear that way to us (presumably in virtue of our limited epistemic
perspective). (b) Secondly, he could treat them as *unities* of some kind, though
not as genuine "mixtures", precisely because they lack the requisite positive
normative and teleological features; in that case, we end up with what seems to
be suggested in the passage from *Phlb.* 64d9–e3 quoted above in connection
with feature (v), in which Plato distinguishes between genuine wholes or
"mixtures" and "unblended disasters":[7] a kind of "two-tiered" system of wholes,
the "full-fledged" ones which have positive normative and teleological features
(the "mixtures") and the more "marginal" ones which lack such features (the
"unblended disasters").[8] (c) Thirdly, he could deny such entities "whole" status
altogether and view them instead as "mere" "bare pluralities". (The remaining
possibility, to view them as mereological atoms, does not plausibly apply here,
since it would surely strike us as quite ad hoc to claim that such entities as
cancer cells and radioactive waste lack parts altogether.) In the case of (c), we
are left again with a "one-tiered" system of wholes, all of which can be viewed
as exhibiting the requisite normative and teleological features. Thus, in sum, the
different options again are: to view such entities as cancer cells and quantities of
radioactive waste either as (a) genuine "mixtures" which, despite appearances,
are "complete" or "perfect", "commensurate", "ordered" and "good"; or as
(b) "second-class" wholes of some kind, precisely because they lack the positive
normative and teleological features required for genuine "whole" status; or,
finally, as (c) "bare pluralities", i.e., as entities which are not unities of any kind
and which lack the normative and teleological features in question.

All of these strategies raise difficult questions for Plato. (a) If he takes the first
route, we begin to wonder whether calling something "complete" or "perfect",
"commensurate", "ordered" and "good" really has much bite at all, or whether
it is in fact exceedingly easy for an entity to get a hold of these features. In a way,
Plato's construal of the structural component of a whole as what is mathematically
expressible (number, measure, ratio, proportion) lends itself to this "deflationary"
reading of what it means to be "complete" or "perfect", "commensurate",
"ordered" and "good", since *any* plurality of objects whatsoever can be viewed

---

[7] At least on one reading of the passage; but one might also read the "unblended disasters" in
the manner of (c).

[8] Plato's "unblended disasters" are of course reminiscent of Aristotle's mere heaps (on which
more below); the latter might also be read either as "marginal" wholes of some kind, as in (b), or in
the manner of "bare pluralities", as in (c).

as standing in *some* mathematically expressible relation to one another. Hence, unless further constraints are imposed on *which* numbers, measures, ratios and proportions are the ones that lead to perfection, commensurability, order and goodness, it would seem that *any* plurality of objects whatsoever will come out as composing a genuine "mixture" with positive normative and teleological features. (This, of course, conflicts, among other things, with Plato's desire that composition be *restricted*.) If, on the other hand, certain numbers, measures, ratios and proportions are in fact singled out as the ones which give rise to the relevant normative and teleological features, then Plato faces the unattractive challenge of having to justify why *these* and not others; and there may be nothing further to be said in response to this challenge than that these mathematical objects are simply the ones which please the divine demiurge more than others, because, as a matter of fact, they are the ones that give rise, more so than any others, to the greatest possible cosmic harmony.[9]

(b) Secondly, suppose Plato goes the route of endorsing a "two-tiered" system of wholes, according to which some unities (the "mixtures") have positive normative and teleological features and others (the "unblended disasters") do not. The resulting theory of parthood and composition would require a radical departure from what we find in Plato's texts; for the status of something as a whole of some kind and the presence of positive normative and teleological features in that object are now completely divorced from one another. This new situation would call for a completely new explanation, first, of what accounts for the presence of positive normative and teleological features in an object, when we do find them, since the mere fact that that object is a whole of some kind can no longer be held responsible for the presence of these features; rather, their presence must now be traced to the particular *kind* of object with which we are dealing (e.g., that it is an object with a conscious mind, a work of art, etc.) and to its other characteristics. Secondly, a completely new account is now called for to explain the mereological features of the "second-class" wholes, i.e., one which makes no reference whatsoever to a centralized teleology in which everything is arranged for the best, since the "marginal" wholes of course require, just as much as their "full-fledged" cousins, their own theory of parthood and composition,

---

[9] Plato's situation here is interestingly similar to that of Kit Fine, as described in Chapter IV. For Fine also endorses an exceedingly liberal conception of what it means to be the structural component of some whole. Fine's "principles of variable embodiment" are the analogue in his system to Plato's number, measure, ratio and proportion; they are likened to *functions* from times to objects and no restrictions whatsoever are placed on *which* function-like operations make suitable "principles of variable embodiment". This feature of Fine's system, combined with his extremely tolerant existence principle, according to which *any* such principle determines an object, yields the superabundant ontology to which we objected earlier. The lesson we learn from both of these writers is that a theory of composition which assigns a central role to structure cannot construe the structural component in purely mathematical terms (or in analogy with a mathematical object of some kind); as we shall see below, Aristotle seems to have incorporated this lesson into his treatment of parts and wholes.

their own account of what binds the many parts of a whole together into one unified thing, and so on. Given the prominence of normativity and teleology in Plato's existing analysis of wholes, we have no indication of what sort of shape this new theory of wholes would take or whether Plato would have been sympathetic to this second option.

(c) Further, suppose the "unblended disasters" are excluded from "whole" status altogether and are viewed instead as "mere" "bare pluralities" of some kind, leaving us once again with a "one-tiered" system of wholes, all of which can be viewed as exhibiting the relevant positive normative and teleological features. This strategy, among other things, raises concerns similar to those cited under consideration (a) above; for, given Plato's construal of the structural component of a whole in purely mathematical terms, one wonders of course whether the assignment of cancer cells and quantities of radioactive waste to the category of "bare pluralities" proceeded on principled grounds, or whether they were simply given this status to avoid problems for Plato's thesis that all genuine wholes (i.e., the "mixtures") are "complete" or "perfect", "commensurate", "ordered" and "good".

In sum, whichever way Plato goes, there seem to be serious problems lurking around the corner for his thesis that all genuine wholes are "complete" or "perfect", "commensurate", "ordered" and "good". Needless to say, from a modern-day perspective, a mereologist who wants to follow Plato in viewing wholes as intrinsically normative and teleological (though not, presumably, in exclusively positive ways) would need to make contact with what, in our times, have been widely debated issues in areas like ethics and the philosophy of mind, viz., whether objects have irreducibly normative and teleological features at all and how to accommodate the presence of such features within a naturalistic world-view in a way that is compatible with current scientific theory, especially evolutionary biology.

(vii) *Proper Objects of Science.* Feature (vii) of Plato's account, the inherent intelligibility of wholes and their relevance to scientific study (in the broad, Greek sense of "science" which includes such domains as music and philosophy) is also tied too closely for modern tastes to Plato's particular kind of centralized teleology. For once we disassociate ourselves from this feature of Plato's account, we lack the a priori guarantee that all wholes will be in principle accessible to or, for that matter, of any interest to a rigorous discipline. For all we know, the mathematical structure of some wholes may simply exceed our cognitive abilities; others may not in themselves make suitable subject matters for scientific study (e.g., works of art or artifacts), though their microscopic constituents of course would fall into the domain of some such discipline (e.g., physics, chemistry, biology, and the like).

(i) *Unity.* The feature of unity, in contrast, is one that must be represented in some fashion by any theory (other than Nihilism) which is concerned to address van Inwagen's Special Composition Question, "Under what conditions do *many* objects compose *one* object?". The trouble with respect to this feature is that it is not clear how satisfying Plato's remarks are as a response to van Inwagen's question. To be sure, we do find in Plato's texts a rich and suggestive body of metaphors to *describe* the intimate relation into which the parts of a genuinely unified whole must enter ("weaving", "blending", "mixing", "communing", "combining", "fitting together" and "harmonizing"). Moreover, we are also presented by Plato with a wide and interesting range of *examples* of cases in which composition takes place: (i) syllables and letters as well as "things composed of number" (such as twice three and six) and "things measured by number" (such as acres, miles and armies) in the *Theaetetus*; (ii) "Being", the "One" and the "Many" in the *Parmenides*; (iii) the five "great kinds"—"Being", "Same", "Other", "Change" and "Rest"—as well as examples from language and music (syllables and letters; statements and terms; musical sounds and the chords or melodies they compose) in the *Sophist*; (iv) examples from music, medicine and meteorology (again, musical sounds and the chords and melodies they compose; health; and the weather) in the *Philebus*; (v) as well as the body of the cosmos and the four elements in the *Timaeus*.

Plato's body of metaphors, along with his elaborate discussion of examples, certainly goes *some* of the way towards delineating a response to van Inwagen's Special Composition Question. But, unlike Aristotle, Plato is not as obviously concerned to confront the question of how a plurality of objects can yield a unity of some kind in the most *general* of terms. For consider the kind of information we *are* given by Plato (where the open slots in what follows are often fleshed out with remarkable detail): under particular conditions, certain kinds of letters (consonants and vowels), when combined in the right way, compose a word; certain types of expressions (names and verbs), when combined in the right way, compose a statement; sounds that exhibit certain contrary qualities (e.g., high and low, slow and fast, loud and soft), when combined in the right way, compose a chord or a melody; other contrary qualities (e.g., hot, cold, moist, dry), when combined in the right way, compose a state of the body we call health or meteorological phenomena like heat waves and thunderstorms; the receptacle, when configured in the manner prescribed by certain geometrical proportions, composes the four elements; and the four elements, when configured in the manner prescribed by certain geometrical proportions, compose the body of the cosmos.

But if we ask now, "How is this list to be *continued*?" or "Why in *these* cases under *these* conditions and not in others?", no completely *general* answer is clearly forthcoming from Plato's account, except one which appeals again to the centralized teleology ("Because it is for the best this way"). In fact, as mentioned earlier, given the nature of Plato's structural component, unless some such stricture is put into place, nothing might stand in the way of composition taking place under *all* conditions and in *all* cases: for if structure is understood simply as something that is mathematically expressible (number, measure, ratio, proportion), then what is to prevent *any* plurality of objects whatsoever from composing a further object, their "mixture", unless some of these mathematically expressible relations are assigned a privileged status? In sum, while the feature of unity in itself is a desirable component of Plato's theory, we do not seem to find in Plato an explicit attempt to confront van Inwagen's question in its full *generality*, as we do in Aristotle.

(ii) *Ontological Commitment/*(iii) *Restricted Composition.* Features (ii) and (iii) require less comment than the other components of Plato's theory. For one thing, they are more easily intelligible from a contemporary point of view than some of the other features of Plato's theory. Moreover, we have already encountered indirect evidence for thinking that Plato is exactly on the right track by proposing a theory that satisfies (ii) and (iii): for we saw in Chapter II that both the Lewis/Sider argument in favor of Unrestricted Composition as well as Lewis' defense of the Composition-as-Identity Thesis are flawed in that they rely on implicitly circular reasoning; there are thus good reasons to follow Plato in accepting a restricted and ontologically committing conception of composition.

§V.4.2 Structure and Content

(iv) *Structure/Content Dichotomy.* We come then to what is perhaps the most central feature of Plato's account, the dichotomy of structure and content. And it is in connection with this feature that we encounter an aspect of Harte's account of Platonic wholes which, to my mind, is quite puzzling. Recall that the structural component of a Platonic whole (that which is mathematically expressible: number, measure, ratio, proportion) is aligned by Harte with "limit" in the *Philebus* as well as with geometrical proportions in the *Timaeus*; content (that which is being configured in these mathematically expressible ways) with the "unlimited" in the *Philebus* as well as with the "receptacle" and the four elements in the *Timaeus*.[10, 11]

But we also find in Harte *two* very different ways of speaking of Platonic wholes. On the one hand, she often characterizes Platonic wholes as having the

---

[10] For reasons that will become apparent below, Harte stresses the role of the "receptacle" as content more than that of the four elements; since the four elements are themselves already structured, they don't fit as easily as the "receptacle" into her conception of content as something that is in itself completely unstructured.

[11] As mentioned above, Harte reads the *Timaeus'* "receptacle" simply as *space*; the geometrical proportions by means of which the demiurge arranges the "receptacle" as *configurations of space*. This reading of the *Timaeus* seems to commit Plato to generation of something out of nothing: for how could space by itself be configured geometrically in such a way as to give rise to *material* bodies, if there is nothing which *fills* the space? Harte considers this worry (p. 258) and declares it to be confused; I disagree. Harte's reading of the *Timaeus* may be connected to her adoption of the "wholes as *identical* to structures" model, which, as I argue in what follows, does not make room for a genuine distinction between content and structure. An alternative reading, which does not follow the "wholes as *identical* to structures" model, would, in the case of the *Timaeus*, allow for a genuine distinction between the content that is being configured in the manner of these geometrical proportions, i.e., what *fills* the space, and the ways in which that which fills the space is being configured (structure).

"two-fold" nature just noted, according to which they consist of both structure and content. Under this conception, Harte refers to Platonic wholes as *contentful structures*, i.e., as the result of *combining* content with structure. On the other hand, she also takes the central thesis of her book to be that Platonic wholes *are* (to be *identified* with) structures. On the first of these readings, the relation between a Platonic whole and its structural component is that of *composition*, not identity: if a whole is conceived of as the result of combining content with structure, then clearly structure is merely one of the *components* of a whole, not all there is to the whole. According to the second thesis, on the other hand, structure is literally all there is to a whole: a whole is *identical* to structure (*a structure*?).[12] In the following passage, for example, we see Harte endorsing both of these conceptions:

What emerges from this general theorizing and from the illustrative examples of combining and of mixing, I have argued, is a conception of wholes as *contentful structures*. Structure, according to this conception, is essential to the constitution of a whole. Indeed, wholes, I have argued, are here best thought of as *being* (instances) of [sic] structures and not as things that "have" structure in a way that makes structure seem more or less detachable from the whole and its parts.

(Harte 2002, p. 268; my italics)[13]

Harte's explicit endorsement of the second conception ("wholes as *identical* to structure") is certainly not difficult to document; for example, in the "Introduction" to her book, she describes Plato's alternative model of composition as being one according to which "wholes *are* structures" (Harte 2002, p. 3; my italics).

Quite clearly, Harte's alignment of structure with the Phileban "limit" as well as the geometrical proportions of the *Timaeus* favors the *first* of these interpretations, the "wholes as *composed* of structure" model. For if structure is

[12] Note that English actually recommends two different uses of the term "structure", in connection with the two formulations of Harte's thesis: in connection with the first conception ("wholes as *composed* of structure"), the term is most naturally used as a *mass* noun, i.e., as a noun which has a "bare" or unquantified singular occurrence, without the indefinite article; in connection with the second conception ("wholes as *identical* to structures"), on the other hand, it is most naturally used as a *count* noun, in a quantified singular or plural occurrence accompanied in the singular by the indefinite article, as in "*A* whole = *a* structure", the plural version of which is "Wholes = structures".

[13] Whether or not structure is *detachable* from the whole is of course a different issue and the "wholes as *composed* of structure" model need not be read in a way which makes the structural component merely a *contingent* ingredient of a whole, i.e., one which one and same whole could gain or lose without thereby ceasing to exist. Rather, the "wholes as *composed* of structure" model may very well take structure to be an *essential* ingredient of the whole, as for example both Fine and Aristotle do (see below, for a defense of this reading of Aristotle). If, on the other hand, "detachable" does not mean "contingent", then I am not sure quite what to make of its meaning. Perhaps, Harte is instead, in the passage just quoted, launching an implicit *criticism* against the "wholes as *composed* of structures" model, viz., that the opposing conception of wholes has an easier time *explaining* the modal status of structure with respect to the whole; this is of course correct (given the necessity of identity), but the disadvantages of the "wholes as *identical* to structures" model nevertheless outweigh this particular advantage.

understood as what is mathematically expressible (number, measure, ratio and proportion), it simply cannot be all there is to a whole; otherwise, all wholes will literally turn out to *be* mathematical objects and we will end up with a universe populated with mathematical objects that is perhaps more Pythagorean than even Plato would want it to be: for example, the bathwater Harte considers as an example of a perfect Phileban mixture of hot and cold water will then be *identified* with, say, the mathematical ratio 2:1; but, as Harte herself acknowledges, it is of course difficult and ultimately not very satisfying to bathe in a mathematical ratio.

In addition to yielding an overly Pythagorean universe populated with mathematical objects, the "wholes as *identical* to structures" reading also does violence to several of the main tenets of Plato's analysis of wholes. For one thing, it leaves no room for any genuine content/structure *distinction*, since the identification of wholes with structures puts content out of its job of acting as the *second* member of the structure/content dichotomy. Moreover, this way of thinking of wholes would of course also remove the need for an application of the composition relation, i.e., the relation Plato describes by means of the body of metaphors ("weaving together", "mixing", "blending", etc.) discussed earlier in connection with feature (i), the unified nature of wholes: for if wholes are literally *identical* to structures, then structures do not need to be *combined* with anything else to yield wholes. Of course, there may still be occasion for the composition relation to apply *within* the structural component, if, as we will observe explicitly in the case of Aristotle's treatment of parts and wholes, structures themselves are viewed as mereologically complex. However, Plato's purpose in invoking his body of metaphors does not seem to be to describe how, say, one number is "woven together" with another number; rather, like Aristotle, he seems to want the relata of the "weaving together", and other, relations to be of *distinct ontological kinds*, e.g., numbers, on the one hand, and musical sound, on the other. Given the overwhelming evidence in favor of the "wholes as *composed* of structure" model, let's investigate why Harte is nevertheless tempted to endorse the "wholes as *identical* to structures" model as well, leaving us with two distinct and incompatible characterizations of Platonic wholes.[14]

---

[14] Of course, one possibility, which would resolve the tension between her two readings of Plato is that Harte is simply using the term "structure" in two distinct ways. And there is in fact some indication that this is precisely what is going on in Harte's text, when she speaks, for example, of the "structure *of* a structure". She explicitly discusses the potential danger of equivocation that lies in this apparent double use of the term "structure" (e.g., Harte 2002, p. 166) and decides that this practice is not harmful to her thesis that wholes *are* structures. For the reasons indicated above, however, I disagree. Of course, Harte is free to introduce another use of the term "structure" according to which wholes *are* structures, but then *these* structures are merely the result of combining the *other* structures (i.e., in the sense of what is mathematically expressible) with content. "Structure" in this new use is then merely another term for "whole", and I don't see what is to be gained from giving wholes another name: certainly we don't thereby understand the relation between a whole and its parts any better, since structure, in the new sense, would feature as the *analysandum* in Plato's analysis of wholes, while structure, in the first sense of what is mathematically expressible, would be that (in conjunction with content) in terms of which wholes are *to be explained*.

§V.4.2.1   The Aristotelian Regress in Met. Z.17[15]

Harte of course has good reason to be tempted by the "wholes as *identical* to structures" model. She puts forth several arguments in favor of this conception in the beginning of Chapter 4 of her book, to which I turn in the next section. However, it seems that the main motivation which drives Harte to the identification of wholes with structures is the Aristotelian regress argument from *Metaphysics* Z.17. Since this argument occurs in the context of a passage that contains many of Aristotle's most central distinctions for the purposes of his treatment of parts and wholes, I will cite a longer segment of the text within which the regress argument occurs; the regress itself is marked in boldface:

As regards that which is compounded [σύνθετον] out of something so that the whole [τὸ πᾶν][16] is one—not like a heap [σωρός], however, but like a syllable,— the syllable is not its elements [στοιχεῖα], "ba" is not the same as "b" and "a", nor is flesh fire and earth; for when they are dissolved the wholes, i.e., the flesh and the syllable, no longer exist, but the elements of the syllable exist, and so do fire and earth.[17] The syllable, then, is something—not only its elements (the vowel and the consonant) but also something else [ἕτερόν τι], and the flesh is not only fire and earth or the hot and the cold, but also something else. Since, then, that something must be either an element or composed of elements [ἐκ στοιχείων εἶναι], **(1) if it is an element the same argument will again apply;** for flesh will consist of this and fire and earth and something still further, **so that the process will go on to infinity;** while **(2) if it is a compound, clearly it will be a** compound not of one but of many (or else it will itself be that one),[18] so that again in this case we can use the **same argument** as in the case of flesh or of the syllable. But it would seem that this is something, and not an element, and that is the *cause* [αἴτιον] which makes *this* thing flesh and *that* a syllable. And similarly in all other cases. And this

---

[15] For an expanded version of my reading of the regress argument in *Met.* Z.17, see Koslicki (2006b).

[16] "Τὸ πᾶν", literally "the all", is also the term used by Plato and Aristotle to distinguish "mere" mereological sums or aggregates from genuine wholes (ὅλον); τὸ πᾶν is for example used in Aristotle's entry on "whole" in *Met.* Δ.26 for what Ross there translates as "totals", i.e., entities such as water which in Aristotle's view lack the requisite degree of unity to be considered genuine wholes. But in the current context, Aristotle is clearly using the term "τὸ πᾶν" in a broader sense, to include genuinely unified wholes as well, and is primarily interested in differentiating such wholes from mere heaps (σωρός). We will return to these distinctions below, in connection with Aristotle's entries under "part" and "whole" in his "Philosophical Lexicon" in *Met.* Δ.

[17] Notice that Aristotle is here appealing to a Leibniz's Law-style argument for the numerical distinctness of wholes and their elements. Aristotle's reasoning is that because a whole and its elements do not share all of the same characteristics (in this case, persistence conditions), they cannot be numerically identical (reading "the same", in this context, as denoting the relation we would now call "numerical identity"); for the elements can survive "dissolution", while the whole cannot.

[18] I read Aristotle here as appealing to the Weak Supplementation Principle, according to which an object which has a proper part must have at least another proper part disjoint from (i.e., not overlapping or sharing parts with) the first. Similarly, a compound, Aristotle says, cannot be composed of just one element, since the object in question would then be identical to its sole element (reading "being that one" again as denoting in this context the relation contemporary metaphysicians call "numerical identity").

is the *substance* [οὐσία] of each thing; for this is the primary cause of its being; and since, while some things are not substances, as many as are substances are formed naturally and by nature, their substance would seem to be this nature [φύσις], which is not an element but a principle [ἀρχή]. An *element* is that into which a thing is divided and which is present in it as matter [ὕλη]; e.g. "a" and "b" are the elements of the syllable.

(*Met.* Z.17, 1041b11–33; Ross translation; his italics, my boldface)

Without attempting to do justice to all the intricacies of this rich and difficult passage, I want for now simply to comment on the role the Aristotelian regress plays for Harte's conception of Platonic wholes; she reads it as in essence preventing us from taking structure to be yet another *part* of the whole, i.e., as a decisive argument against the "wholes as *composed* of structure" model:

To say that a whole is more than the sum of its parts, on any ordinary understanding of the phrase "more than", is to say that a whole has something extra in addition to its parts (or indeed to the sum of its parts). Is this something extra a *part*? It had better not be, for the familiar reason that, if it is, then all that we have is another sum of parts (the original ones plus the something extra). So, either we should concede that a whole is, after all, the sum of its parts—and if it is this one, why not the original one? or regress threatens: the whole is more than this new sum also. (To my knowledge, the first person to formulate this argument explicitly was Aristotle . . .)

(Harte 2002, p. 11; my italics)[19]

But notice that Aristotle does not actually argue in the cited passage that a regress results in itself from taking the "something extra" (which, in Harte's terminology, turns out to be *structure*) to be a *part*: rather, a regress threatens, in his view, if the "something extra" in question is *of the same ontological kind* as the other components which make up a genuinely unified whole, be they mereologically basic (i.e., elements) or mereologically complex (i.e., compounds of . . . compounds that are themselves composed of elements).[20] Thus, the point of Aristotle's regress argument is to argue that genuinely unified wholes must not only be mereologically complex but also *ontologically complex*, in that they consist of entities which belong to distinct ontological categories. The two distinct types of entities that go into a genuinely unified whole are here identified by Aristotle as (i) *elements* (στοιχεῖα), which are later in the same passage aligned with *matter* (ὕλη); and (ii) *cause* (αἴτιον), *principle* (ἀρχή), *nature* (φύσις) and *substance* (οὐσία), which are concepts normally associated jointly with *form* (εἶδος), though Aristotle does not explicitly mention form in the passage under discussion.[21]

---

[19] Harte goes on to refer to the passage from *Met.* Z.17 just cited.

[20] The second case, as Aristotle points out, of course reduces to the first: for suppose we are dealing with a compound that is composed of further compounds; we can then ask about each of these smaller compounds what *they* are in turn composed of, etc., until we get to a compound which is composed, not of further compounds, but of elements, in which case we now have something that has the shape of the first case.

[21] Aristotle, in this passage, seems to take heaps, as contrasted with genuinely unified wholes, to be entities which are mereologically complex but ontologically simple, in that they consist merely

Harte's reading of Aristotle's regress argument thus turns on reading "element" as synonymous with "part".[22] And while Z.17 itself does not explicitly legislate on the question of whether form and matter are themselves *part* of the compound, a reading which takes "part" to be intersubstitutable with "element" in fact creates unnecessary tensions with what Aristotle says elsewhere, as the following passage from *Met.* Δ.25 (his fourth notion of "part") illustrates:[23]

> Those into which the whole is divided, or of which it consists—"the whole" meaning either the form or that which has the form; e.g. of the bronze sphere or of the bronze cube both the bronze—i.e. the matter in which the form is—and the characteristic angle are *parts* [μέρος].
>
> (*Met.* Δ.25, 1023b19–22; Ross translation; my italics)[24]

of elements, but lack a principle that "ties together" the elements into a genuinely unified whole. Wholes, on the other hand, in Z.17 are taken to be exclusively objects that are unified under a single form. In light of what Aristotle says in the texts to be examined in Chapter VI, however, we will have occasion to construe both the term "whole" and the term "heap" differently below: the term "whole" will be seen to apply more broadly to objects that are mereologically complex and unified under *some* principle of unity (though not necessarily form); the term "heap" will be taken to apply to objects that are mereologically complex and not unified under a single form (though possibly under a different, weaker principle of unity). The details of Aristotle's conception of wholes will be the subject of the next chapter; what matters for present purposes is only whether the regress argument in Z.17 must be read as having any impact on the "wholes as *composed* of structure" model.

   [22] This feature of her reading comes out quite clearly, for example, in the following passage from Chapter 3 of Harte's book; after quoting a section from Aristotle's text, she says:

> This "something else" is not a further *part* of the whole (cf. 1041b25–7), but it is rather its nature (φύσις) and principle (ἀρχή) (1041b30–1); and this, although Aristotle does not here explicitly use the term, is form (εἶδος).
>
> (Harte 2002, p. 133; my italics)

Although she doesn't say this explicitly in her book, her dissertation suggests that Harte may have had in mind a reading of Aristotle which holds that form is a part of the compound according to a sense of parthood ("formal part") distinct from that which applies to matter ("material part"). This reading leaves open the possibility that "element" in Z.17 may be taken as synonymous with "part", as long as we are careful to understand "part" in this context as meaning material part; moreover, on this reading, form would still come out as a proper part of the compound according to its own separate sense of "part" ("formal part"). Although I acknowledge that Aristotle often talks as if he means by "part" material part, I take him in these contexts merely to be using a convenient short-hand; in what follows, I offer both textual and conceptual reasons against distinguishing a "formal" from a "material" sense of parthood.

   [23] In fact, given Aristotle's endorsement of the Weak Supplementation Principle, as documented above, he does not have much of a choice in this matter, if he wants to avoid inconsistency: if he were to view only the matter as part of the compound and not the form as well, not only would the relation between the compound and form have been left mysterious (see my earlier comment in Chapter IV along the same lines concerning Fine's principles of variable embodiment); we would also have a violation of the Weak Supplementation Principle, viz., a compound which is composed of only one thing as part, viz., matter.

   [24] I have here emended Ross' translation by rendering his "the *elements* into which the whole is divided", in the first sentence of the cited passage, simply as "*those* into which the whole is divided", which, though less elegant in English than Ross' rendition, is closer to the text. The text does not contain an occurrence of the word "στοιχεῖα", with which we have just been concerned in the

This passage, somewhat obscurely, makes the point that both matter (the bronze) and form (the characteristic angle) are *part* of the compound (the bronze sphere or cube). And while Aristotle speaks less often explicitly of the form as being itself part of the compound than he speaks of the matter as being part of the compound, both of these commitments can fairly be regarded as official Aristotelian doctrine. (We will return to these issues in more detail in the next chapter.)

I conclude, then, that the Aristotelian regress does not present convincing evidence against the "wholes as *composed* of structure" model. It does, of course, raise the difficult question of how the unity of a whole *is* to be explained on a model which takes the "something extra", the *source* of the unity of the whole, as itself a component of the whole, alongside the remaining, non-structural components: certainly, the mere recognition of a particular kind of ontological complexity within a genuinely unified whole by itself does not yet solve the mystery of *why* it is that these entities of distinct ontological types (in Aristotle's case, form and matter) can come together to produce a single genuinely unified thing. But the existence of this *further* question does not in itself show that the "wholes as *composed* of structure" model must be abandoned in the face of the Aristotelian regress. Certainly, Aristotle himself did not interpret his own regress argument in that fashion, since he does take both form and matter to be part of the compound. Rather, he seems to have thought that his distinction between "elements" and "principles" solves the regress and that other aspects of his metaphysics would speak to the question surrounding the unity of wholes. Given the disadvantages of the "wholes as *identical* to structures" model noted above, we should therefore stick with composition over identity, despite the regress, and deal with the problem of unity as best as we can. After all, not even the proponent of the "wholes as *identical* to structures" model can completely escape the problem of unity, if he is willing to allow, as seems plausible, that the structural component may itself exhibit mereological complexity: for the problem of unity arises for anyone who recognizes genuinely unified wholes that are composed of many parts, even when both the whole and the parts in question are structural.[25]

---

context of *Met.* Z.17; rather, it contains merely a neuter plural relative pronoun, i.e., something closer to the more literal "*those* into which the whole is divided"; "elements" is inserted by Ross simply to fill out the meaning of the pronoun and is thus best construed in a neutral non-technical fashion. Since Ross' insertion of "the elements" might be confusing in the context of the present discussion, as we have also been concerned with the technical use of the term, I have found it best simply to omit it from the passage at issue.

[25] My characterization of Aristotle's loyalties as lying unambiguously with the "wholes as *composed* of structure" model is of course over-simplified; the actual situation is in fact more messy. (Note, for example, that Aristotle offers *two* characterizations of "whole" in the passage from Δ.25 cited above: (i) whole as form; and (ii) whole as the compound of matter and form.) For one thing, he does, as we shall see below, take some wholes to *be* structures, e.g., when he speaks of form in the sense of "definition" or "formula of the essence", which he usually takes to be a composite

§V.4.2.2 Parts as Structure-Laden

(v) *Priority of Wholes over Parts.* I turn now to the final remaining feature of Harte's account of Platonic wholes that has yet to be discussed, the *priority* of wholes over parts. As pointed out above, Harte takes wholes to be, in some sense (whose precise nature is left unspecified), *prior* to and more *basic* in Plato's ontology than their parts; parts are, as she puts it, "structure-laden", in that their existence and identity is in some way dependent on the wholes of which they are part. Harte takes this feature of Platonic wholes to be closely tied to the thesis that wholes *are* structures, which has been the subject of the preceding section. The priority of wholes over parts is of course highly reminiscent of Aristotle's *Homonymy Principle*, according to which a severed hand (say) is a hand "in name alone";[26] a modern-day version of the priority of wholes over parts can be found, for example, in Fine (1994).

Harte's thesis that parts, for Plato, are structure-laden is somewhat difficult to evaluate in detail. First, on the whole, the direct textual evidence in favor of Plato's endorsement of the structure-laden nature of parts (as, for example, in the

---

entity, composed of genus and differentiae: definitions thus seem to present us with an example of a complex whole which is itself structural in nature; however, even in this case, Aristotle appears to be driven by his general views on composition to identify a component within the definition that is aligned with *matter* (the genus) and a component that is aligned with *form* (the differentiae), or at least we see him going through great contortions in his attempt to come up with a satisfying account of the apparently composite, yet unified, nature of form, when understood in the manner of definition. (More on this below.) Moreover, in many contexts in the *Metaphysics* (especially Book Z), Aristotle seems to come close to an outright *identification* of substance with form (at least substance in the *relative* sense of the term, according to which we speak of the substance *of* a thing). However, this conception of substance as form does not entail that wholes in general are now to be identified with form; for, in those contexts in which Aristotle is tempted to privilege form in this manner, he tends to be more concerned with deciding what sort of entity deserves *primary substance* status, and not so much with the task of providing an analysis of composition (in fact, even in these contexts, he seems to take for granted his analysis of composition in terms of matter and form); thus, even when he gravitates, with some hedging, towards *identifying*, say, Socrates with Socrates' form (the soul) (as he does, e.g., at *Met.* Z.11, 1037a5 ff), Aristotle would not for that reason do away with *compounds* of matter and form (e.g., as another way of looking at Socrates); these compounds of matter and form still have their rightful place within his ontology, and along with them so does his analysis of composition in terms of matter and form, only such compounds would now rank lower than form alone in the hierarchy of substances.

²⁶ See, for example, *De Anima* II.1, 412b10 ff, where his examples are an "eye" that cannot see and an "axe" that cannot cut. Very roughly, we can construe Aristotle's principle in the following fashion: to apply the term "hand" both to an object that *is* attached to a living body and to one that is *not* attached to a living body is to use the term "hand" *homonymously*, or in two different senses. It is a consequence of this that an object that is part of a living body cannot persist through a change which would involve its separation from this living body (see note 28 for a slightly weaker reading): for example, in a circumstance which we would ordinarily describe as "Joe accidentally cut off his hand at noon", the object (hand, in one sense) that is attached to Joe's body until noon is not numerically identical to the isolated object (hand, in a distinct sense) that is not part of any living body; in fact, the object which is attached to Joe's body until noon *ceases* to exist at noon and a qualitatively similar, numerically distinct object *comes into* existence in the region of space-time next to Joe's feet. (The generation, however, is not *ex nihilo*, following Aristotle's belief

passage concerning "unblended disasters" from *Phlb.* 64d9–e3 quoted above) is not as overwhelming as that which supports the other aspects of Harte's reading; it is, for example, nowhere nearly as unequivocal as the textual evidence we find in Aristotle in favor of his endorsement of the Homonymy Principle.[27] Moreover, as Harte herself freely admits in Chapter 5 of her book, more work would need to be done to spell out the precise content of the *dependency* claim which forms the core of the thesis that wholes are prior to parts and that parts are structure-laden.

In the absence of evidence to the contrary, and in order to have a more or less concrete thesis before us whose plausibility can be evaluated, I will construe the priority of wholes over parts as what in the language of contemporary metaphysics would amount to the following *de re* modal claim, though there may be more to the dependency at issue than what is captured by this modal claim:

Priority of Wholes over Parts:
Objects that are part of a whole are *essentially* part of a whole.[28]

This thesis is intended to be read as the reverse of what is known as *mereological essentialism*, the position associated in contemporary metaphysics most prominently with Roderick Chisholm (e.g., Chisholm 1973, 1975, 1976):

Mereological Essentialism:
Wholes have their parts essentially.

According to mereological essentialism, one and the same whole cannot survive gaining or losing any of its parts. According to the priority of wholes over parts, on the other hand, the reverse situation holds, i.e., to use some odd English:

Reverse Mereological Essentialism:

that every change must have an underlying subject; the subject underlying this particular change are the fire, earth, air and water which keep a *potential* presence within Joe's hand while it existed and which now take on a potential presence within the new, unattached object that has just come into existence.) Both of the objects in question are called "hand", but not in the same sense of "hand", according to the Homonymy Principle. Thus, Aristotle's principle seems to involve at least in part the sort of *de re* modal claim I am about to propose in the main text. But Aristotle would also want to add to the *de re* modal claim a further thesis concerning the connections between the different senses of the homonymous term: for the sense of "hand" that is applied to the unattached object, in his view, is in some way *parasitic* on the sense of "hand" that is applied to the attached object; only the latter is *really* a hand, in the full-fledged sense of "hand", the other object is called "hand" only in an *extended* sense of "hand".

[27] Of course, the lack of direct textual evidence may be overruled by a sufficiently persuasive *inferential* case, based on Plato's other theoretical commitments, in favor of his adherence to an analogue of Aristotle's Homonymy Principle.

[28] Actually, this claim has been left deliberately vague in at least the following way: it is left unspecified whether it is essential to a given object that it be part of the *particular* whole of which it is a part, or simply part of a whole of the same (or some related) *kind*. (Think, for example, of an organ-transplant case in which we may be tempted to say that my heart survives by becoming part of the body of another human being.) For reasons of simplicity, I will adopt the first, stronger reading in what follows; but my arguments will not turn on the differences in strength between these readings.

Reverse mereological essentialism (RME) asserts that one and the same part cannot survive gaining or losing its whole, so to speak, i.e., the whole of which it is part. In other words, according to this thesis, no single object could survive, for example, *becoming* a part of a whole of which it is not already part or *ceasing* to be part of a whole of which it is part; any such change would involve the coming-into-existence and going-out-of-existence of numerically distinct, qualitatively similar objects.

RME is, on the face of it, a strange claim. Consider, for example, a factory which manufactures what we would normally describe as "car parts", i.e., engines and their components, wheels, bodies, chassis, and so on. According to RME, we could, I suppose, continue to *talk* the way we ordinarily do, but when we are strict about what we *mean* by what we say, we would have to admit that, for example, the things we have been calling "carburetors", while they are still inside the factory or on the shelf in the auto-parts store, never themselves become part of any functioning car engine; for, in light of RME, installation amounts to the destruction of one object and the creation of a numerically distinct, qualitatively similar object: a transformation happens at the precise moment at which the installation of the thing we (loosely) call "carburetor" is successfully completed, and at that moment a new thing has come into existence, which we continue to call by the same name. Car mechanics, on this picture, turn out to be very powerful creatures indeed; or, alternatively, the creation and destruction of objects is a much less involved affair than we ordinarily suppose.[29]

Harte tries to motivate RME in Chapter 4 of her book by means of several examples, which are simultaneously intended to provide support for the "wholes as *identical* to structures" model. Harte's first example is a dinner party (the complex whole) and its guests (the parts); her second example is that of a simple

---

[29] This approach to the relation between parts and wholes, among other things, has serious consequences for Plato's distinction between structure and content (more on this below in the next section). For, given the truth of RME, content could not survive the imposition of structure, since what exists prior to the creation of a complex whole is never numerically identical to anything that is part of a newly created whole. It is for this reason, I believe, in combination with the "wholes as *identical* to structures" model, that we often find Harte speaking of Platonic content as something completely *unstructured* or *undifferentiated*, as she puts it in the case of the *Timaeus'* "receptacle" or the Philebean "unlimited". Content, in this sense, is not something that we could actually find in the world; it is only something which, in Harte's view, we can *conceive of* in thought (as is the case with Aristotle's "prime matter"). This way of thinking of content may lend itself to the extreme case of the *Timaeus'* "receptacle", but it is less obviously compatible, for example, with the role of the four elements as content and the possibility of intertransformations between them, which seems to be an important feature of Plato's second creation story; for, in that case, it does sound as though one and the same entity—a particular triangle, say—is at one point part of a fiery pyramid and at another point part of an airy octahedron. In fact, as in the case of Aristotle's analysis of change as always involving an underlying subject, it seems that it is the very persistence of these objects (the triangles) which makes these intertransformations between elements intelligible. The RME-model would also prevent us from saying, for example, in the case of the bathwater, that the very same quantities of water which existed prior to the mixing have survived this process and now compose the bathwater.

sentence (the complex whole), which is "woven together" out of a name and a verb (the parts). (As noted earlier, the second example is also one of Plato's favorite ways of illustrating the prominence of structure in his analysis of wholes, especially in the *Sophist*.) In both cases, we are to think of the *structure* in question as the sort of entity which provides "slots" that can only be filled by entities of a certain kind: in the case of the dinner party, Harte conceives of the structure as the *seating arrangement*, in this case of the "alternate-by-gender" type, which specifies "slots" for men and women, respectively (viz., with every man having a woman to his left and his right, and every woman having a man to her left and her right); in the case of the second example, on the other hand, we are to think of the sentence as a kind of "syntactic space" of a particular kind, which specifies a "slot" for a name and a verb, respectively, as combined in a particular way so as to give rise to an *assertion*. In both cases, the structures in question are conceptualized not as universals, i.e., as repeatable types, but as particulars, i.e., as tokens of the type in question. Since Harte is operating under the "wholes as *identical* to structures" model, she is tempted to *identify* the complex whole in question with the structure, i.e., the dinner party with the seating arrangement, and the sentence with the syntactic space.

Harte's identification of wholes with structures raises numerous puzzling issues. For one thing, the persistence conditions assigned to dinner parties seem not to reflect those we ordinarily assign to them: for, given her picture, one wonders, for example, what happens when one of the guests rises from his or her chair within the seating arrangement or whether the party only starts after everyone has sat down at the table and ends immediately after everyone has risen. Moreover, Harte's conception also runs into difficulties reminiscent of the Pythagorization of the bathwater discussed earlier: for we wonder, for example, how the guests or expressions could really be *part* of the dinner party or the sentence in question, when these complex wholes are already fully exhausted by the structure that specifies the slots, i.e., by the seating arrangement and the syntactic space, respectively. For intuitively, the guests and expressions are what *fills* the "slots" in question, but the structures are merely what *specifies* the "slots". Given that the "wholes as *identical* to structures" model does not make room for a genuine structure/content *dichotomy* or for a cross-kind application of the composition relation, whose relata are the complex whole, its structure and its content, there seems to be nothing left to contribute for those elements in the analysis whose job it is to play the role of content, viz., the guests and the expressions.

But let's focus instead on the consequences of applying the RME model to the parts in question. The result, in the first case, is a Geachian universe populated not only by "surmen", "heralds", "passengers", but also by such entities as "guests". Guests, on this conception, are entities which cannot survive separation from the particular dinner party of which they are part; they are related to *persons* (or *human beings*) in the following way: when a person enters its "slot" in the seating arrangement, a guest comes into existence; and when a person exits its "slot" in the seating arrangement, a guest goes out of existence. What this case illustrates, then, is that the RME model can only be plausibly applied, if at all, to cases in which we are also willing to ascribe to an entity essential membership in a *kind*, but not to cases in which we are dealing with what intuitively are *phase-sortals*, i.e., concepts that denote mere *phases* in the life of a kind of thing. But RME requires more than the ascription of essential kind-membership to the part in question; it also requires a particular way of spelling out the *content* of this ascription: for example, in order for RME to take hold in our earlier example involving the hand, we must be willing to say of the object that is attached to the human body not only that it is *essentially* a hand; we must also be willing to accept that part of what it means to be a hand is that hands cannot occur in isolation from living bodies. (The example of living bodies and their parts may well be the kind of case that is most favorable to the RME model.)

Similarly, in the case of sentences and their constituents, RME also has the unattractive consequence of ruling out the possibility of one and the same name or verb occurring in structures of different kinds: for example, the expression "Socrates", which occupies the name-"slot" in the particular name/verb/assertion structure, "Socrates is flying", according to RME, could not be numerically identical to the expression "Socrates" which occupies the name-"slot" in the particular name/verb/question structure, "Is Socrates flying?".[30] For numerous reasons, this extremely fine-grained approach to the individuation of expressions is not an attractive way to proceed: for the most plausible explanation for a competent speaker's ability to form and interpret a potential *infinity* of sentences is that these complex expressions are built up *compositionally* from a *finite* number of pre-existing building-blocks. The RME model, among other things, would make it very difficult to explain how speakers with finite cognitive powers can be so successful in acquiring language and in using language to communicate with one another.

Regardless of what we may think of the *plausibility* of RME, however, what is most important for present purposes is that RME is in any case *independent* of what we may term the structure-laden nature of *wholes* (as contrasted with the structure-laden nature of their *parts*), i.e., feature (iv) of Plato's analysis, which was the subject of the previous section. For regardless of whether this latter claim is to be understood according to the "wholes as *composed* of structure" model or according to the "wholes as *identical* to structures" model, on both models feature (iv) concerns a property of *wholes*, and as it stands not even one that is explicitly *modal*, though presumably both models may certainly choose to take this property to be *essential* to wholes. Both the "wholes as *composed* of structure"

---

[30] The stronger reading of RME has the even more counterintuitive consequence that one and the same name, "Socrates", could not be a part of two distinct complex wholes, even when these wholes are of the same kind, e.g., "Socrates is sitting" and "Socrates is flying".

model and the "wholes as *identical* to structures" model hold that wholes have the property of being *structured*: on the first model, this comes to the claim that structure is among the *components* of a whole; on the second model, it amounts to the claim that wholes themselves *are* structures. But neither of these claims in and of themselves says anything about the essential properties of the *parts* of a whole. In contrast, the point of RME is precisely to identify a *de re* modal property of the *parts* of a whole.[31]

§V.4.2.3 A Final Word on Content

I want to close with a few remarks on the nature of *content*, which has received less attention in the foregoing discussion than structure, the other member of the structure/content dichotomy. Given Plato's characterization of the "unlimited" in the *Philebus* and the *Timaeus*' "receptacle", there is certainly some temptation to conceive of content as something that is in itself completely devoid of structure. The "wholes as *identical* to structures" model, in combination with the priority of wholes over parts just considered, also lends itself to this reading. For if wholes are identified with structures, then insofar as they can be thought of as having parts at all, these parts are most straightforwardly conceived of as being themselves structures, i.e., sub-structures within a larger structure. (Recall our earlier complaint that the "wholes as *identical* to structures" model does not make room for a genuine structure/content *distinction*.) And insofar as parts are thought of as structure-laden, i.e., as unable to survive separation from the wholes of which they are part, then whatever predates the creation of a complex whole can never be numerically identical to anything that is part of a newly created whole (e.g., by filling one of the "slots" specified by the structure or by

---

[31] In the beginning of Chapter 4 of her book, Harte raises another consideration which is supposed to speak in favor of both the RME model and the "wholes as *identical* to structures" model, which she takes to go hand in hand with one another, and against the competing "wholes as *composed* of structures" model. This is her "special pleading" objection, according to which the "wholes as *composed* of structures" model has a more difficult time explaining why it is the case that composition is *restricted*. If structure is merely a *component* of a whole, so Harte reasons, then why isn't it the case that basically any plurality of objects instantiate some structural property and therefore compose a whole? In contrast, she holds that the alternative approach, which *identifies* wholes with structures, can appeal to the fact that the question of which wholes (i.e., structures) there are in the world is a separate question from the question of how the parts of a whole are related to the whole they compose: the former is a question for the ontologist to solve, the latter is one for which the mereologist is responsible. However, I fail to see the contrast between the two approaches with respect to this issue. Why is it not equally open to the proponent of the "wholes as *composed* of structures" model to let the ontologist (as contrasted with the mereologist) answer the question of which entities the world contains that are suited to the role of being the structural component of some complex whole? As I have mentioned earlier, it seems that some approaches have a more difficult time than others in explaining why composition is not unrestricted; for example, Plato's and Kit Fine's deflationary, mathematical conception of structure opens up a greater need to impose external restrictions on composition than Aristotle's more full-grained conception, as we will see in the next chapter. But these differences do not differentiate between the "wholes as *composed* of structures" model, on the one hand, and the "wholes as *identical* to structures" model (combined with RME), on the other.

fulfilling whatever other role an object must fulfil in order to figure within a structure as one of its parts). The combination of these commitments certainly creates considerable pressure to identify, if only in thought, something which, at least on the most basic level, underlies the imposition of structure and is therefore itself completely devoid of structure; a phenomenon of this kind of course could be described in language, if at all, then only with the greatest of difficulty and primarily in negative terms. (We are reminded here once again of Aristotle's "prime matter".)[32]

But this conception makes content out to be needlessly murky. It also gives rise to an analogue of Putnam's famous objection to the "cookie-cutter" model (Putnam 1987, p. 19), the model subscribed to, in Putnam's view, by the metaphysical Realist (with a capital "R"), who believes that there is a single world, viz., the "dough", which can be sliced into "pieces" in different ways: Putnam recommends that we ask philosophers who subscribe to this view, "What are the 'parts' of this dough?"; when we do so, we will see that the "cookie-cutter" model founders on this question, since no "neutral" description can be found of what the "parts" of the "dough" might be, i.e., one which doesn't already presuppose some particular conceptual scheme. Similarly, we may challenge the proponent of "structureless content" to tell us what the "parts" of his "structureless content" might be, and to do so without already invoking some particular way of *structuring* the content in question.

Instead of the needlessly murky conception of content as structureless, I propose that we think of content simply as a domain of complex wholes that are already themselves structured: when a new whole is created, it is created out of pre-existing wholes, each of which is already structured; and it is created by structuring these pre-existing wholes in some new way. (Of course, if composition is to be restricted, then only *some* new ways of structuring pre-existing wholes

---

[32] Harte often sounds like this when she speaks of content, as she does, for example, in the following passage which concerns the Phileban "unlimited", in connection with the example of musical sound:

Unlimitedness, on my reading, is a property of an *undifferentiated* phenomenon such as sound, the content of a domain of science, conceived in the absence of structure. Limit is the structure that, applied to this content, makes up a distinct domain of science from this undifferentiated phenomenon.

(Harte 2002, pp. 204–5; my italics)

But what does it mean for a phenomenon to be *"undifferentiated"*? And how could anything that is "undifferentiated" really be identified as *sound*, as distinct from, say, light? Whatever actually exists in space-time must exhibit certain characteristics (i.e., temperature, velocity, mass, and so on) to a certain degree; and the range of magnitudes (e.g., wavelength, frequency, etc.) exhibited by sound are different in characteristic ways from those exhibited, say, by light. Even at the level of *thought*, it is not clear how something could be *conceived of* as sound, unless it is conceived of as exhibiting certain magnitudes to a certain degree. Moreover, it seems that, in principle, *any* sound could be incorporated into a musical piece (modulo practical considerations relating to our perceptual apparatus and aesthetic sensibilities); thus, sound in itself is not plausibly thought of as falling into different kinds, musical and non-musical.

will result in the creation of a new object.) This conception of content as already structured is certainly what is suggested by the great majority of examples of complex wholes we have considered in the preceding sections: e.g., sentences that are created by combining names and verbs; musical chords and melodies that are created by combining sounds of different pitches; the bathwater that is created by mixing hot and cold water; health, heat waves and thunderstorms that are created by mixing different contrary qualities, such as hot and cold or moist and dry. It is also the conception of content that is more easily squared with the *Timaeus'* first creation story, in which the four elements play the role of content; given what we know from the second creation story, the elements themselves are already structured, and they further consist of entities that are also already structured (the triangles and cubes).

The need for a kind of content that is itself completely devoid of structure only arises when we entertain the possibility of a *first* level of composition, i.e., a level of composition which consists of entities that are not themselves composed of anything more basic. For if these completely basic, ground-level constituents were to be thought of as themselves structured, then of course whatever would fulfil the role of content in that case could not be of the nature of complex wholes. But whether there is a *first* level of composition is not a question that *philosophy* is qualified to answer. And if it turns out that there is such a level, then the structure/content dichotomy simply breaks down at that point. For the very fact that what we are dealing with is a *first* level of composition, i.e., one whose constituents are completely *basic*, means that we cannot think of these entities as being *composed* of anything: since they are basic, no further analysis of them into anything more basic can be given. Any attempt to apply the structure/content dichotomy, which was specifically designed for the analysis of complex wholes, to these basic entities will result in the sort of predicament that lead to Plato's "receptacle" and Aristotle's "prime matter".

§V.5 CONCLUDING REMARKS

The focus of this chapter has been Plato's structure-based analysis of wholes, in its illuminating reconstruction by Verity Harte, especially Harte (2002). Harte discerns in Plato's mereological writings both a *negative* and a *positive undercurrent*. In the former, Plato evaluates and eventually rejects alternative models of composition, particularly a Lewis-style Composition-as-Identity model associated with the commitment-shy Eleatic philosophers; Plato ultimately finds this model to be untenable because it does not make room for wholes that are genuinely *one* despite their *many* parts. In the positive undercurrent of his mereological writings, Plato is concerned to develop his own substantive stance towards what we would now describe as Peter van Inwagen's "Special Composition Question", the question "Under what conditions do *many* objects compose *one* object?", and to come out against David Lewis' "Axiom of Unrestricted Composition", according to which *any* plurality of objects, no matter how disparate and gerrymandered, composes a further object, their mereological sum. In contrast to Lewis' deflationary conception, Platonic wholes, on Harte's reading, have the following full-blooded features: they are (i) genuinely *unified*; (ii) *ontologically loaded*; (iii) governed by a *restricted* notion of composition; (iv) comprised of the two components of *structure* and *content*; (v) ontologically *prior* to their parts; (vi) *normative* and *teleological* in nature; as well as (vii) inherently *intelligible* and the *proper objects of science*.

A contemporary metaphysician who is simply looking for the *right* analysis of ordinary material objects would presumably want to disassociate himself at least from some of the features of Plato's theory, most notably those in (vi) and (vii). For, with respect to these features, Plato's conception of wholes is, for modern tastes, tied too closely to a centralized teleology. As a result of this association, Platonic wholes turn out to have exclusively positive normative and teleological features and are suffused with intelligibility which guarantees them a place in some rigorous discipline.

In contrast, Plato's emphatically *unified* approach to wholes, as compared to the paradoxical "many-one" entities of the Composition-as-Identity model, is surely an attractive feature of his account and one that any credible contemporary approach would want to incorporate in some fashion. We found in Plato the *beginnings* of a fully general answer to van Inwagen's "Special Composition Question", "Under what conditions do *many* objects compose *one* object?": he develops, sometimes with great care, particular *cases* in which composition takes place and provides a rich and suggestive metaphorical vocabulary by means of which to *describe* the composition relation in these particular cases; he thereby draws attention to domains, such as language and music, in which the dominance of structure is hardly deniable. On the whole, however, we found Plato to be less concerned than Aristotle will turn out to be with the project of how to account, in completely general terms, for the source of unity within a mereologically complex object.

Moreover, Plato's *restricted, ontologically loaded* and *structure-based* conception of composition is fully in line with the conclusions reached in Chapters II through IV, as a result of our discussion of Lewis and Fine. However, Plato's *structure/content dichotomy*, I argue, must be read in a particular way; and this is where my account diverges most from Harte's reading. First, despite the Aristotelian regress in *Met.* Z.17, wholes cannot be *identified* with structures; rather, structure is merely one of the *components* of a whole. The "wholes as *identical* to structures" model makes no room for a genuine structure/content *distinction* and puts the composition relation out of business, except insofar as structures themselves are viewed as mereologically complex. Given Plato's deflationary construal of structure in purely mathematical terms, the "wholes as *identical* to structures" model also results in an overly Pythagorean universe.

Secondly, Plato's structure-laden conception of *wholes* should be divorced from the counterintuitive thesis that the *parts* of a whole are structure-laden as well, since these two theses are in any case independent of one another. Finally, the "wholes as *identical* to structures" model, in combination with the "priority" of wholes over parts, leads to a needlessly murky conception of content, which ought to be abandoned in favor of a conception of content as already structured.

Overall, despite some misgivings with respect to the details, Plato's structure-based analysis of wholes provides an attractive blueprint for a contemporary theory of composition. Most of the features of his account that we can no longer accept are connected to Plato's centralized teleology; once we divorce ourselves from these elements, however, we find in Plato a theory which, in broad strokes, is basically correct: wholes are genuinely *unified*; *ontologically loaded*; governed by a *restricted* notion of composition; and comprised of the two components of *structure* and *content*. And while I have in the foregoing discussion indicated some departures from Harte's reading of Plato, my understanding of Plato's mereology, as well as my own thoughts on parthood and composition, have been deeply shaped by my study of Harte's groundbreaking work in this area: without her tremendous success in extracting from Plato's texts an analysis of parts and wholes that is evaluable from the standpoint of a contemporary metaphysician, most of us would have simply missed the surprisingly compelling model of composition that can be found scattered across some of the most opaque contexts in Plato's writings and that is often hidden beneath metaphorical or mythological terms.[33]

---

[33] One feature of Plato's account I did not discuss in this chapter is his characterization of wholes as "that from which no part is lacking" or "that from which nothing is absent" (see, e.g., *Tht.* 205a4–7 and *Parm.* 137c7–8). This characterization of wholes, along with the association between "part" and "measure", will be seen to figure quite prominently in Aristotle's account.

VI

Aristotle's Refinements of Plato's Theory

§VI.1 INTRODUCTORY REMARKS

In the previous chapter, we explored Verity Harte's illuminating exposition of Plato's structure-based theory of parts and wholes (Harte 2002). Plato's aim in his more mature mereological writings is to develop an alternative to the ontologically innocent, Lewis-style Composition-as-Identity model, put forth in ancient times by the notoriously commitment-shy Eleatic philosophers, the followers of Parmenides and Zeno. As against this deflationary conception of composition, Plato ascribes to wholes the following full-blooded characteristics: they are (i) genuinely *unified*; (ii) *ontologically committing*; (iii) governed by a *restricted* notion of composition; (iv) comprised of the two components of *structure* and *content*; (v) ontologically *prior* to their parts; (vi) *normative* and *teleological* in nature; as well as (vii) inherently *intelligible* and the *proper objects of science*. And while the contemporary reader will no doubt find some elements of Plato's account off-putting or problematic, especially those features that depend on his endorsement of a cosmic (and at times explicitly theological) teleology, the core features of Plato's mereology proper (features (i), (ii), (iii) and (iv)) are nevertheless surprisingly compelling and in outline correct.

Our task now is to examine Aristotle's refinements of Plato's theory of composition. Aristotle is generally sympathetic to the Platonic outlook, but differs over the details. In some cases, Aristotle's more nuanced approach avoids certain of the downfalls of Plato's theory; in other cases, however, the added complexities introduced by Aristotle actually lead to further difficulties of their own. Given that my own account of composition, as it will be presented in Chapter VII, is broadly Aristotelian in spirit, the overarching goal of this chapter, as of the preceding one, will be once again to find inspiration in Aristotle's insights into matters of mereology and to separate those features in his treatment of parts and wholes that are timeless and can be taken over by the modern-day mereologist from those that are best left behind. Those readers who are more interested in the conceptual issues arising from Aristotle's analysis of parthood and composition, and less so in the textual details, may wish to proceed directly from the end of Section VI.3 to the beginning of Section

VI.5, which recapitulates the main conclusions established in the intervening sections.[1]

§VI.2 THE CENTRALITY OF "PART" AND "WHOLE" IN THE ARISTOTELIAN CORPUS

As in Plato's case, Aristotle's works do not include a separate treatise devoted exclusively to the discussion of mereology as such. However, applications of the notions of "part", "whole", and related mereological concepts are ubiquitous throughout the Aristotelian corpus: in his logical writings, as well as in his writings on first and second philosophy (i.e., metaphysics, theology, mathematics and what we would now regard as natural science, i.e., physics, biology, chemistry, psychology, astronomy, and the like); even in his discussions of dialectic and speech as well as in his treatises on moral and political philosophy, the relations of "part" and "whole" are of central importance. As an illustration of Aristotle's use of "part" and "whole" in the logical treatises, consider for example the mereological technical vocabulary he employs in the *Prior Analytics* and the *Posterior Analytics* to distinguish *particular* statements from *universal* statements (viz., κατὰ μέρος or, literally, "with respect to the part" and ἐπὶ μέρους, or, literally, "over" or "by the part", are his technical terms for "particular"; καθόλου or, literally, "according to the whole", is his technical term for "universal"); similar uses of the part relation can be found whenever Aristotle is concerned either with matters of ontology or with the characterization of reasoning and the different forms of verbal expression thereof, as he is, for example, in treatises like the *Topics* and the *Rhetoric*. In the *Politics*, he is of course especially interested in the *parts* of communities and households; in the ethical treatises, with the *parts* of virtue and the moral character. The *parts* of the soul are on the forefront of Aristotle's mind in *De Anima*;[2] the *parts* of living things are everywhere discussed in the biological treatises, e.g., *On Plants*, *History of Animals*, *Movement of Animals*, *Generation of Animals*, and, of course,

---

[1] Aristotle's mereology as such has not received much attention in the literature, although parts and wholes do come up in connection with his theory of substance. Given the already considerable length of this chapter, I cannot in the present context provide an adequate discussion of the secondary literature; the following list provides a small selection of works relevant to the issues discussed in this chapter: Barnes (1986); Bogaard (1979); Bostock (1994); Burnyeat (2001); Burnyeat et al. (1979, 1984); Charles (1992, 1994); Driscoll (1981); Fine (1983, 1992, 1994c, 1995c, 1998); Frede and Patzig (1988); Furth (1985, 1986); Gill (1989); Halper (1989); Hamlyn (1993); Harte (1994, 1996); Haslanger (1994b); Kirwan (1971); Lewis, F. A. (1991, 1994, 1995a, 1995b); Loux (1991); Makin (1988); Mignucci (2000); Reeve (2000); Rorty (1973); Scaltsas (1985, 1994); Shields (1999); Wedin (2000); Witt (1989, 2003).

[2] Though I will suggest at the end of this chapter that we should not take Aristotle's talk of powers as parts of the soul literally in *De Anima*.

Parts of Animals. The *parts* of things that undergo change are his focus in the chemical treatises, e.g., *On Generation and Corruption* and *Meteorology.* The *parts* of time, magnitude, and the like, are at issue in the *Physics*; and those of the heavens in *On the Heavens.* Early remarks on the *parts* of substances can be found in the *Categories*; Aristotle's more mature views on the same topic, i.e., the *parts* of substance in its various possible manifestations as essence, substratum, definition, universal, genus, form, compound, etc., take up large sections of the central books of the *Metaphysics*, especially Book H, as well as the notorious Book Z.

The examples just given all illustrate Aristotle's *applications* of his mereological concepts. With the exception of a few scattered remarks here and there (e.g., in the *Categories*, *Topics*, *Physics*, and *On Plants*), the only extended examination of the concepts, "part", "whole" and related notions *as such* is confined to the *Metaphysics*; and, within the *Metaphysics*, especially to Book Δ, the "Philosophical Lexicon", which unfortunately, as it does in this case, often raises at least as many questions as it answers. Since Aristotle's discussion in *Met.* Δ is his most extensive treatment of mereology as such, it will be most practical in what follows to focus on his remarks there, though it is impossible to make sense of what he says in *Met.* Δ without taking into consideration the views expounded elsewhere. Assuming that the "Philosophical Lexicon" in Book Δ collects together concepts which occupy some sort of privileged role in an understanding of Aristotle's views (on any subject), it is a good indication of the centrality of the mereological concepts, "part" and "whole", to Aristotle's philosophy that the corresponding sections in Δ.25 and Δ.26 implicitly or explicitly rely upon almost every single other entry in Book Δ. The notions "part" and "whole" are also listed by Aristotle in *Met.* Γ.2 as among the attributes of *being qua being* (along with the different senses of "same" and "other", "prior" and "posterior", "genus" and "species", and the like). Since both of the concepts, "part" and "whole", are intimately tied up with that of "one" (τὸ ἕν, also translated as "unity"), it is not surprising that the study of parthood and composition would be included among the responsibilities of those who are concerned with the study of being qua being, given the close connection Aristotle draws in Book Γ between being and unity: in particular, being (τὸ ὄν) and one, he says, are "the same", though they don't have the same definition; there are as many kinds of being as there are of unity; and the primary sense of "one", as of "being", is that which applies to substance, all other uses being somehow parasitic on this primary use.[3]

---

[3] Though this doctrine of the so-called "focal meaning" of "one" as being that which applies to substance seems to contradict what Aristotle says in many other places, when he speaks of the primary sense of "one" as that which applies to *quantity* (τὸ ποσόν, literally, "the how much"): being one in the strictest sense, we are often told, is a kind of *measure* (μέτρον τι), primarily of quantity, and secondarily of quality (see, for example, *Met.* I.1, 1053b4–8). The relation between substance and quantity as well as the different senses of "one" will concern us shortly.

§VI.3 THE PROBLEM OF THE ONE AND THE MANY

Aristotle is of course aware of the problem that puzzled his contemporaries and predecessors, of how something that has *many* parts can at the same time be *one*. He states this problem very clearly in *Physics* I.2, where it is listed as among the questions concerning parts and wholes to be dealt with (somewhere):

There is, indeed, a difficulty about part and whole, perhaps not relevant to the present argument, yet deserving consideration on its own account—namely, whether the part and the whole are *one* or *more than one*, and in what way they can be one or many, and, if they are more than one, in what way they are more than one.

(*Phy.* I.2, 185b11–14)[4]

As we observed in the preceding chapter, Plato's eventual answer to the Problem of the One and the Many—after some early flirtations with the Pluralizing Parts Principle and the accompanying Composition-as-Identity model—is that genuine wholes (i.e., the "good mixtures" as opposed to the "unblended disasters") are unqualifiedly one and not many. In a revealing passage from *Topics* VI.13, to which Harte (1994) draws our attention, Aristotle is inclined to agree with Plato's rejection of the Composition-as-Identity model, at least as an across-the-board theory of composition; in the context of discussing the various ways in which arguments can go wrong by failing to *define* objects properly, Aristotle clearly disassociates himself from the deflationary conception of composition, at least as far as those objects (like houses) are concerned whose existence and identity depends on the *manner* in which their parts are *arranged*, and not merely on the presence of these parts:

In general, too, all the ways of showing that the whole is not the same as [the sum of][5] its parts are useful in meeting the type [of argument] just described; for a man who defines in this way seems to assert that the parts are the same as the whole. The arguments are particularly appropriate in cases where the process of putting the parts together is obvious, as in a house and other things of that sort; for there, clearly, you may have the parts and yet not have the whole, so that parts and whole cannot be the same.

(*Topics* VI.13, 150a15–20)[6]

---

[4] Unless otherwise noted, all translations come from Barnes (1984); and all italics can be assumed to be mine, unless otherwise specified.

[5] The words "the sum of" are added in the translation.

[6] Again, notice Aristotle's appeal to a Leibniz's Law-style argument for the non-identity of wholes and their parts; we came across the same argument already in the context of the regress argument passage from *Met.* Z.17, discussed in the preceding chapter.

Instead, Aristotle recommends that in these cases the proper procedure is to define an object by stating "not merely that it is made *from these things*, but that it is made from them *in such and such a way*" (ibid., 150b20–25).

While these passages from *Topics* VI.13–14 provide a good partial glimpse into what is to follow, they of course do not occur in a context in which it would be appropriate to explore different theories of parthood and composition in great depth, since the aim of the treatise is to teach us, by means of practical advice and rules of thumb, how to "reason from reputable opinions about any subject" and to avoid inconsistencies in the process (*Topics* I.1, 100a20ff). In fact, Aristotle's reaction to the Problem of the One and the Many is subtle and difficult to characterize; it requires us to pay attention, among other things, to his distinction among the different uses of the terms employed in the question "Is a whole one or many, i.e., as many as its parts?": for, in typical Aristotelian manner, something can be said to be *one* (or *many*) in a particular way, but not in another; something can also be said to *be* in a particular way and not in another; and, as it turns out, even the terms "part" and "whole", are spoken of in many ways.

§VI.4 A READING OF THE TEXT

§VI.4.1 One, Divisibility, Part, Quantity and Measure

To be *one*, in Aristotle's view, is at bottom to be *indivisible* (ἀδιαίρετον); this is the core meaning of the term "one", and the common thread that ties together all the different uses of the term he discerns.[7] Terms like "unit", "unified" and "unity", all of which are simply different English renditions tracing back to the single underlying Greek term for "one" (τὸ ἕν), are thus also inseparably linked to the notion of *divisibility* (or the lack thereof). The notion of *divisibility*, on the other hand, immediately takes us (first and foremost)[8] into the domain of

---

[7] See, for example, *Met.* Δ.6, 1016b3–4: "For in general those things that do not admit of *division* (διαίρεσις) are *one* insofar as they do not admit of it, ...". His continuation of the sentence illustrates the *adjectival* use of the term "one", which will also become important when we turn to the notion of "whole" below: ". . . e.g., if something *qua* man does not admit of division, it is one man; if *qua* animal, it is one animal; if *qua* magnitude, it is one magnitude" (ibid., 1016b5–6; Ross' italics); in other words, to be *one* is always to be one *something-or-other*; the "something-or-other" in question supplies the *measure*, by means of which the thing in question is judged to be one, i.e., indivisible. For the connection between "one" and "indivisible", see also *Met* I.1, 1052b16.

[8] To be one, Aristotle says in *Met.* I.1, is to be the first measure of a kind, above all of quantity; from there, the notion is extended to other categories, especially that of quality (see e.g. 1052b18–20). As will become apparent shortly, I take Aristotle to mean by "quantitatively one" roughly what we would nowadays call *numerical identity*; by "qualitatively one", *qualitative identity* or *similarity*, though the precise nature of the relationship between Aristotle's concepts of being, oneness and sameness and our concept of identity is controversial.

quantity and is in turn associated with the notions of *part* and *measure*.[9] For any *division* is always in its barest form at least a division of a quantity into subquantities which are its *parts*; each of these is *one* by some *measure*; and to say into *how much* or *how many* of the measures in question a thing can be divided is to approach the thing from a *quantitative* perspective. (Aristotle views both what can be counted or enumerated, i.e., "plurality" or "number", as well as what can be measured, i.e., "magnitude", as falling into the category of quantity; they are different species of quantity.)[10, 11] In some cases, a division into parts proceeds by means of additional non-quantitative considerations, in which case the door is opened for further comparisons among objects that are not purely quantitative. (The distinction between purely quantitative divisions and divisions that introduce further considerations that are not purely quantitative will be clarified further below.)

To illustrate, consider for example the syllable "ba". To ask, "Is it one or many? And if many, how many?" is, so to speak, to hold a conceptual ruler against the syllable in question and to evaluate it from a quantitative perspective, i.e., from a perspective that yields an answer to a "how much" or "how many" question. But in order for the quantitative evaluation to be executable, first a unit of measurement, i.e., something that counts as one or indivisible in the context at hand, must be supplied: this unit of measurement determines by what principle the division into parts is to proceed. Thus, by means of the measure "letter", "ba" is divisible into *two* parts, "a" and "b", each of which is in turn indivisible, i.e., one or a unit, by the same measure, "letter", since neither "a" nor "b" is itself further divisible into letters; by means of the measure "syllable", on the other hand, "ba" is itself indivisible, i.e., a unit or one, since it does not further consist of parts that are themselves syllables.[12] If, on the other hand, we were to try to divide the letters "a" and "b" into parts by means of the measure

---

[9] See, for example, *Met.* Δ.13, 1020a7–8: "We call a *quantity* that which is *divisible* into two or more constituent parts of which each is by nature a *one* and a "this"." (Though the word "part" is here added in the translation.) For an explicit connection between "part" (μέρος) and the notions of "quantity" and "measure", on the other hand, see for example *Met.* Z.10, 1034b32–33: "Perhaps, we should rather say that 'part' is used in several senses. One of these is 'that which *measures* another thing in respect of *quantity*'." Parts are explicitly identified as measures also in *Phy.* IV.10, 218a6–7, as well as in the entry for "part" in Δ.25. The one itself is called a measure, for example, in *Met.* I.1., 1053a18 et al., as well as in N.1, 1087b33, et al. The terminology of "measure" as connected with parthood is of course familiar already from Plato, especially the sections of the *Theaetetus* mentioned in the previous chapter.

[10] "A quantity is a *plurality* (πλῆθος) if it is *numerable* (ἀριθμητόν), a *magnitude* (μέγεθος) if it is *measurable* (μετρητόν)." (*Met.* Δ.13, 1020a8–10)

[11] In the case of magnitude, the division into parts, each of which counts as one by some measure, concerns such dimensions as depth, width, breadth, height, weight, speed, and the like (see e.g. *Met.* I.1, 1052b24ff).

[12] Illustrations of this kind are used, for example, in *Met.* N.1.

"syllable", I take it the result would be either "0" or "inapplicable", but at any rate not anything that would be regarded as a numerical answer according to ancient conceptions of number. Thus, depending on the way in which the "how much" or "how many" question at issue is formulated, we may, if the question can be answered at all, obtain either the answer "one" or the answer "many" (e.g., "two") with respect to one and the same thing: in this way, "ba" comes out to be *one* with respect to the measure "syllable", but *many* with respect to the measure "letter".

In general, then, an object, for Aristotle, can be one or indivisible *in one way*, i.e., with respect to a particular measure, but not *in another*, i.e., with respect to a distinct measure, without contradiction, as long as the measures in question are distinct. Beyond being one or indivisible *in a particular way*, i.e., with respect to some measure or other, however, it presumably makes no sense to classify something as being *simply* one or indivisible in some absolute or unqualified sense (unless of course we mean by "absolutely one", one with respect to *all* conceivable measures); for a thing cannot be evaluated quantitatively without specifying some unit of measurement by means of which the division into parts is to proceed. In this respect, the term "one" is completely in line with the other implicitly relativized central terms of Aristotle's philosophy, e.g., "being" and "good", just as we would expect given the gist of *Met.* Γ.2 as well as Aristotle's general anti-Platonist tendencies.

These distinctions are helpful in clarifying and sharpening our understanding of the question, "Is it one or many? And if many, how many?", when asked about any particular thing. The original difficulty concerning the One and the Many can now be transformed, with all the requisite qualifications made explicit, into the question of how something that is *many* in *any* respect *at all* can nevertheless manage to be *one* in *any* respect *at all*. How, for example, can "ba" be *one* anything (e.g., syllable) despite the fact that it is also *many* somethings (e.g., letters)? As we observed in the preceding chapter, Plato's answer to this question is "structure" in the sense of what is mathematically expressible (number, ratio, measure, proportion), imposed on content within the context of a teleologically ordered cosmos; our goal in the following sections will be to understand how Aristotle accounts for the (relativized) unity within each thing that is also a (relativized) plurality and what conception of parthood and composition guides his response to the Problem of the One and the Many.

§VI.4.2 Kinds of Measure and Principles of Unity

Given the immediate conceptual connections between "one", "divisibility", "part", "measure" and "quantity", we may read Aristotle's distinction among the different uses of the term "one" (and, correspondingly, "many"), as indicating different sorts of *mereological* constellations.[13] For one thing, these different uses of "one" and "many" in effect yield a broad division among different *kinds* of measure: each kind of measure tells us about a particular respect in which a thing may be one or indivisible into parts and therefore contrasts with other respects in which the very same thing may be many (i.e., divisible into parts). Since the ways of being one or indivisible are thus complemented by ways of being many or divisible, we may expect the different uses of "one" and "many" to resurface again in the different uses of the terms "part" and "whole", as we will in fact observe below. At the same time, each of the different uses of the term, "one", in turn points us towards a particular *principle of unity*, i.e., something within the object which accounts for the fact that it is one (i.e., indivisible) in a particular way, despite the fact that it may be many (i.e., divisible into parts) in other ways. The question of precisely how many ways "one" is spoken of in the different contexts in which Aristotle discusses this topic (especially *Met.* Δ.6, Γ.2, I.1 and N.1) raises difficult interpretive issues; I will try in what follows to be as brief as possible in my discussion of detailed textual matters.

Broadly speaking, something can be one in the following four ways. First, it can be one (1) by being indivisible *in number* (in the way in which Socrates is one by virtue of being one human being). Secondly, something can be one (2) by being indivisible in *kind*; and this either by being (2.1) indivisible *in species* (in the way in which Socrates and Coriscus are one in virtue of each of them being one human being); or (2.2) by being indivisible *in genus* (in the way in which Socrates and Fido are one in virtue of each of them being one animal). Finally, things can be one (3) by being *analogically* indivisible (in the way in

---

[13] I take Aristotle's *mereological* construal of the different uses of "one" (with the possible exception of being one by accident and being one by analogy) to be one of his most central anti-Platonist moves. For among his biggest complaints against Platonic forms is that they are incapable of playing the explanatory and causal roles they are intended to play, since they are too far removed, so to speak, from the objects which they are supposed to reach; moreover, the relation by means of which the connection between Platonic forms and sensible particulars is supposed to be established, viz., that of "participation", in Aristotle's mind, remains too obscure to accomplish this task. By contrast, Aristotle's own ontology is mereologically nested in multiple, complex ways, with the result that the causally and explanatorily active principles typically end up being "in" the objects that depend on them in these ways. In the discussion of the different senses of "in" in *Phy.* IV.3, only two are explicitly identified as mereological; given his remarks in *Met.* Δ and elsewhere, however, I take others to be implicitly mereological as well. As our discussion of Kit Fine's work in Chapter IV brought out, Aristotle's anti-Platonist strategy would in general be aided by a mereological analysis of the relevant senses of "in", since he is otherwise committed to his own population of primitive, mysterious "participation" relations.

which, say, 1:2 and 2:4 are one in virtue of each of them exhibiting the ratio one-half).[14, 15, 16]

Things whose *matter* is one are indivisible in the first way (viz., numerically one). Things whose *formula* (i.e., *definition*) is one are indivisible in the second way (viz., specifically one): thus, the term "human being", as Aristotle would put it, when applied to Socrates and Coriscus, is used "synonymously" or in the same way in both cases (as contrasted, say, with the term's application to a *picture* of a human being). Though he doesn't do so in this particular context, Aristotle

---

[14] As I read it, this fourth kind of unity is one among two varieties of unity which cannot be traced directly to a *mereological* constellation of their own peculiar kind (the second being the accidental unity exhibited by a substance and its accidents, e.g., the musical Coriscus, which will be introduced below); this is why analogies (and accidental unities) are not reflected again in separate entries under "part" and "whole" in Δ.25–26. Since, for this reason, they are not immediately relevant to our purposes, these varieties of being one will not receive much attention in what follows.

[15] This is how Aristotle summarizes the results of his entry for "one" in *Met* Δ.6 at 1016b31ff (though the example illustrating the final kind of unity, being one by analogy, is mine); the exercise of attempting to map this summary onto the remarks that precede it is not entirely straightforward and I won't attempt to carry it out here. (My numbering is different from Ross'.) The listing of the different uses of "one" in Δ.6 is reasonably close to that of *Met*. I.1, though the detailed commentary required to show this would take us beyond the scope of the present inquiry. *Met*. N.1 focuses more on the common core in the meaning of "one" as a measure which underlies all the different uses of the term distinguished in Δ.6 and I.1. In contrast, I take the concerns of Γ.2 to be different from those of Δ.6 and I.1 and closer to those of the *Categories*, in the sense that Aristotle is there primarily interested in uncovering the sorts of ontological *dependence* relations which all non-substances bear to substances. In this context, the use of "one" with respect to substance is primary, because quantities are quantities *of* substances. (More on this below.)

[16] We can now make sense of the terminology we encountered earlier, according to which one is a measure, first and foremost, of quantity and only secondarily of other categories, in particular quality. A division into parts is always, at least, a division of a quantity into its subquantities: in this sense, any division involves objects that are *one in number* (number being a species of quantity); I take the relation of being one in number as corresponding roughly to our current notion of *numerical identity*, i.e., the relation each thing bears to itself and nothing else. Since the relation of being numerically one, which is at issue in sense (1), is explicitly linked to the presence of matter, one wonders if those entities that are not straightforwardly material (the species, genus and ratio) can be numerically one in any way that is not parasitic on the material indivisibility of those objects that fall under them. (Although Aristotle does have a notion of "intelligible matter", which he uses to account for the particularity of objects that are not material in any ordinary sense, this notion seems to be reserved for the objects of mathematics; the precise application of the notion of intelligible matter, however, is also a matter of scholarly controversy.) Senses (2.1), (2.2) and (3), on the other hand, exemplify Aristotle's extension of the notion of one as measure into other categories: senses (2.1) and (2.2), being indivisible in kind, either in species or in genus, yield a notion of one as a measure of *quality* (picking up on Aristotle's classification of species and genera in *Cat*.5 as a certain kind of "qualification"); sense (3), being indivisible by analogy, illustrates the notion of one as measure as applied to the category of *relation*. In contemporary terms, senses (2.1), (2.2) and (3) would all be classified as different sorts of relations of *similarity* or *qualitative identity*.

might also characterize the similarity between Socrates and Coriscus by appeal to the fact that they have the same kind of *soul*, viz., a characteristically *human* soul, which is their form. Things which are indivisible by virtue of a higher category are indivisible in the third way (viz., generically one): again, the term "animal", when applied to both Socrates and Fido, is used synonymously, or with the same definition, in both cases. The similarity between Socrates and Fido may also be traced once more to the similarity between their respective forms, since both have souls that are characteristic of animals (as opposed to plants). Finally, things which are indivisible by virtue of the presence of a single relation are indivisible in the fourth way (viz., analogically one).

These broad varieties of being one yield a certain kind of ordering. Being one in the first way is being one *to a higher degree* than being one in any of the other ways, since being numerically one *entails* being one in all of the other ways, but not vice versa. Similarly, being specifically one *entails* being generically and analogically one, but not vice versa: Socrates and Coriscus, objects that are specifically one, are also automatically one in genus and by analogy, but are not indivisible with respect to their matter (viz., Socrates's body is distinct from Coriscus' body). Thus, the objects that fall into the category of being one in number, by this ranking, are one to the highest degree; those that are one in species, to the second highest degree; and so forth. This ranking is implicitly associated with the following broad division into distinct kinds of measure: objects that are one in sense (3) are indivisible only by means of a measure which falls under the general heading *relation*; those that are one in sense (2.1) and (2.2) are indivisible by means of the previous measure as well as a (qualitative) measure which falls under the general heading, *kind*, i.e., either *species* or *genus*; finally, objects that are one in sense (1) are indivisible by means of all the previous measures as well as the measure *matter*. Thus, an object like Socrates, who is indivisible in matter, species, genus and relation, is indivisible to the highest degree by the ordering suggested in $\Delta.6$.

Some of these broad divisions into different kinds of measure or being one themselves come in different varieties, in particular (1) being one in number, i.e., by virtue of being indivisible with respect to matter. Something can be indivisible in this way either (1.1) *by accident*[17] or (1.2) *by its own nature*. Of

---

[17] (1.1) Musical and Coriscus may be one in the first of these two ways, if being musical is an accident of the substance, Coriscus; similarly, musical and just may be one in this way, if they are both accidents of a single substance, Coriscus.

those things which are numerically one by their own nature, some are so (1.2.1) by being *continuous* (συνεχές). Among the things that are indivisible by virtue of being continuous, some are so (1.2.1.1) *by art*, others (1.2.1.2) *by nature*.[18, 19, 20] Things that are one in this way, by being continuous, *move* together, i.e., their *movements* are *indivisible* in time. Among the things that are continuous, some are so merely by *contact* (i.e., by having their boundaries *touch*), in the way in which, say, a bundle of wood is one; others are so by being "a whole" or "whole", in the way in which, for example, a shoe is one:[21, 22] objects of this kind are indivisible not only with respect to their matter (as are all objects that are numerically one in sense (1)), but also in virtue of having a single *form* (as in the case of those objects in (2.1) which are indivisible in species); the parts

---

[18] (1.2.1.1) A bundle that is made one in virtue of having its parts brought into *contact* with one another by a band, or a piece of wood that is made one by means of glue is one by art. In what follows, I will refer to such things as bundles and glued together pieces of wood as *heaps*, though this use of the term may not exactly correspond to the occurrence of the term (σωρός) we encountered in the context of the regress argument in Z.17. There, Aristotle sounds as though heaps lack a principle of unity altogether and are thus not one in any sense of the term, even the weakest. What the Δ.6 bundles of wood have in common with the Z.17 heaps, however, is that both lack *form* as a unifying principle; since this is the feature I want to emphasize in the present context, I will use the term "heap" accordingly to encompass entities that are one in number, mereologically complex and not unified under a single form, though this leaves open whether the entity in question may nevertheless be unified by some other, weaker principle of unity. I take it that the ontological difference between, say, some pieces of wood that are merely stacked on top of one another without being held together by a band, on the one hand, and some pieces of wood that are stacked on top of one another and held together by a band, on the other hand, is not so significant in Aristotle's eyes as to prohibit us from using the term "heap", in both cases; for, in the terminology of the previous chapter, the band which acts as the principle of unity in the case of the bundle of wood is of the same ontological type as the elements, i.e., the individual wooden sticks, it holds together.

[19] (1.2.1.2) A line, even if it is bent, or a part of a body, e.g., a leg or an arm, is one by being naturally continuous.

[20] "Continuity" is defined elsewhere as the *sharing of boundaries* (see *Cat.*6; *Phy.* V.3; *Met.* K.12). For example, in *Cat.*6, language is defined as a quantity that is *discrete*, i.e., non-continuous, because its parts, the syllables, do not share a common boundary; similarly for number. Examples of quantities that are *continuous*, on the other hand, include lines (whose parts are points); surfaces (whose parts are lines); bodies (whose parts are surfaces); as well as time (whose parts are the past and the future, bounded by the present); and place (whose parts are further places).

[21] It is not entirely clear whether Aristotle thinks that *all* wholes are continuous; given his remarks in the entry for "whole" in *Met.* Δ.26, I gather that he does *not*, since he there lists the universal as a kind of whole, no doubt due to the etymological connection mentioned above between the word for "whole" (ὅλον), and the word for "universal" (καθόλου). He does, however, regard continuity, i.e., the sharing of boundaries among the parts, as a mark of those objects that are wholes to the highest degree.

[22] The status of artifacts within Aristotle's ontology is of course highly controversial, and I will not try to take a position on this complicated question; I am simply helping myself to Aristotle's own examples.

of such objects are arranged in a particular way, as demanded by their form.[23] (Since Aristotle's use of the term "whole" in Δ.6 is actually narrower than his use of the term in the entry for "whole" in Δ.26, I will refer to the Δ.6 wholes as "high-level wholes".)

In sum, then, "one" is spoken of in the following ways:[24]

(1) **One in number:** indivisible in matter
   (1.1)   By accident (musical, Coriscus)
   (1.2)   By the thing's own nature
      (1.2.1)   Continuous: indivisible in movement
         (1.2.1.1)   By art
            (1.2.1.1.1)   Heap: indivisible by contact (bundle of sticks)
            (1.2.1.1.2)   High-level whole: indivisible by virtue of form (shoe)
         (1.2.1.2)   By nature
            (1.2.1.2.1)   Heap: indivisible by contact (ivy/tree-trunk ???)
            (1.2.1.2.2)   High-level whole: indivisible by virtue of form (Socrates)
      (1.2.2)   Discrete (language, music ???)
(2) **One in kind:**
   (2.1)   One in species: indivisible in virtue of form (human beings)
   (2.2)   One in genus: indivisible by higher category (animals)
(3) **One by analogy:** indivisible by relation (ratios)

---

23 I have not explicitly accommodated the use of "one" numbered as (2.b) in Ross' translation of Δ.6, viz., things that are called "one" by having the same *kind* of matter or substratum. In this way, Aristotle says, wine and water are said to be one, respectively; so are oil and wine as well as all things that can be melted (since they consist of a high proportion of water). I do not view this sense of "one" as introducing further distinctions that are not already covered by the remaining uses that are already listed in the main text. It seems, rather, to be a different variety of sense (2), with some elements of sense (1) mixed in; thus, all things that can be melted are one because they ultimately derive from the same *kind* of matter. (See also sense (1) of "from" (ἐκ) in Δ.24.)

24 As this figure brings out, Aristotle's discussion of the different uses of "one" in Δ.6 and I.1 leaves open several questions, indicated above in the form of question marks. For example, he does not explicitly say in these passages whether there are things that are numerically one by virtue of being naturally continuous heaps (and, if so, how the contact among the parts would be enforced in such cases). A possible example for an entity of this kind would be ivy growing around a tree-trunk: the contact is enforced by natural growth; but the entities in question lack a single form. Moreover, he does not explicitly settle whether there may be ways of being one by virtue of a thing's own nature without being continuous (and, again, what the principle of unity in such cases would be). Possible examples of this category include language and music, which he thinks of as *discrete* quantities. Some of these questions will be resolved in the entries for "part" and "whole" in Δ.25 and Δ.26, to which we will turn shortly.

Each of these varieties of unity, in turn, points to a particular *principle of unity*, i.e., something within the object that *makes* it one.[25] In particular, what holds together the parts of an object that is one (in a particular way) may be either (i), in the case of a heap, whatever it is that enforces the *contact* among the parts (e.g., bands, glue, and the like in the case of artificial heaps); or (ii) the presence of a single *form* (as in all other cases except (2.2) and (3)); or (iii) the presence of a higher category, i.e., the *genus* (as in the case of (2.2)); or (iv) the presence of a single *relation* (as in the case of (3)).[26] Some varieties of unity may be brought about either by *art*, as in the case of the bundle or the shoe, or by *nature*, as in the case of the individual human being, Socrates. With the help of additional machinery which has not yet been introduced in Δ.6, Aristotle will eventually introduce a further ranking by means of which objects whose parts are held together *artificially* will come out to be one to a lesser degree than objects whose parts are held together *naturally*; moreover, objects whose parts are held together by the presence of *a single form* will turn out to be one to a higher degree than objects whose unity results from some other source (i.e., through mere contact or through the sharing of a genus or a relation). Aristotle's motivations for this additional ranking will become apparent below. At the same time, we should note that no matter how low the musical Coriscus, the bundle of wood, the shoe and the analogy will eventually place in the final ordering of unities, these entities are nevertheless explicitly listed by Aristotle in Δ.6 as exhibiting particular varieties of unity; correspondingly, principles of unity may be as pedestrian as a bit of glue or as ephemeral as a mathematical ratio.

§VI.4.3 The Ways of Being a Part: *Met.* Δ.25

In the context of considering the different varieties of being one, as they are laid out in Δ.6, we have already encountered several general sorts of measures by means of which divisions into parts may proceed: objects that are one in number are not divisible into parts by any of the measures suggested in Δ.6;

---

[25] In this way, there are obvious connections between the entry for "one" in Δ.6, on the one hand, and, among other things, those in Δ.1, 2, 3, 4, 8 on "principle" (ἀρχή), "cause" (αἴτιον), "element" (στοιχεῖον), "nature" (φύσις), "substance" (οὐσία), on the other.

[26] Even the case of the musical Coriscus may present us with a mereological constellation, depending on how seriously we take Aristotle when he speaks, as he occasionally does, of the accidents of a substance as being *part* of the substance in which they inhere, and this despite the fact that he is, in the *Categories*, at pains to distinguish the relation that holds between substances and their accidents, viz., the relation of *inherence*, from that of parthood. (For textual evidence that Aristotle may regard accidents as parts of their substances, in addition to the passage with which we are currently concerned at *Met.* Δ.6, 1015b25, see also *Phy.* IV.3, where white is apparently said to be in the man as a part, as well as, arguably, *Met.* Δ.11, 1018b33.) His use of "part" as applying to the accidents of a substance may, however, be more of a figure of speech, since it is not listed as one of the official senses of "part" in Δ.25. The principle of unity which holds together the many "parts", if we may call them that, in this case is just whatever holds together the substance of which they are accidents, i.e., the single form.

species are divisible into objects that are one in number; genera are divisible into species; objects that are analogically one are divisible in one or more of the aforementioned ways, i.e., numerically, specifically or generically. Aristotle's entries for "part" and "whole" in Δ.25–26 introduce still further refinements into this already complex picture: for even those objects that were initially classified as being one to the highest degree by the measures introduced in Δ.6 (viz., the musical Coriscus, the bundle of sticks, the shoe and Socrates) as well as the principles of unity themselves (in particular, form) now themselves turn out to be not completely indivisible in every conceivable way.[27] Since the entry for "part" in Δ.25 is relatively brief, I will cite it first in full and then comment on each section in detail (the numbering and italics are Ross'):

We call a part (1) that into which a quantity can in any way be divided; for that which is taken from a quantity *qua* quantity is always called a part of it, e.g., two is called in a sense a part of three. –(2) It means, of the parts in the first sense, only those which measure the whole; this is why two, though in one sense it is, in another is not, a part of three. –(3) The elements into which the kind [εἶδος] might be divided apart from the quantity, are also called parts of it; for which reason we say the species are parts of the genus. –(4) Those into which the whole is divided, or of which it consists—"the whole" meaning either the form [εἶδος] or that which has the form; e.g., of the bronze sphere or of the bronze cube both the bronze—i.e. the matter in which the form is—and the characteristic angle are parts. –(5) Those in the formula which explains a thing are parts of the whole; this is why the genus is called a part of the species [εἶδος], though in another sense the species is part of the genus.

(*Met.* Δ.25, 1023b12–25)[28]

Senses (1), (2) and (3) are more or less familiar to us already from the preceding sections. Since the core meaning of "one" turns out to be "indivisible into parts by some measure, primarily with respect to quantity and secondarily with respect to other categories", we can also expect there to be correspondingly unadorned varieties of parthood, which apply to objects as viewed from a quantitative

---

[27] Form, though it is mentioned only in passing in Δ.6, would be classified as indivisible by all of the measures introduced there that apply to it: it is specifically, generically and analogically one. The notion of being numerically one is explicitly linked by Aristotle in Δ.6 with the presence of matter and hence does not (at least not in any straightforward sense) apply to form, which lacks matter. (In fact, whether form really is completely free of matter is a difficult question and depends on how definitions are viewed; however, it is certainly true that there is at least one official strand within Aristotelian doctrine according to which form is pure actuality and hence lacks matter, which is linked with potentiality.) But Δ.6 does not provide us with any means by which form could be classified as being one *to a higher degree* than the musical Coriscus, the bundle of sticks, the shoe and Socrates. Aristotle actually mentions at 1016a34–35 that form, in the sense of definition (λόγος), *is* divisible into parts, but does not pause to tell us whether there is a way of being one that is peculiar to form and qualifies it as being so to a higher degree than anything else.

[28] We have already encountered sense (4) in the preceding chapter, where this section of Δ.25 was cited to confirm that Aristotle does in fact explicitly identify both the form and matter of which a whole consists as parts of the whole; this in turn was used as evidence against Harte's reading of the regress argument in Z.17 and the accompanying "wholes as identical with structures" model.

perspective. This is the work done by Aristotle's first two senses of "part": (1) "that into which a quantity can *in any way* be divided" and (2) "those [parts] which measure the whole", to which I add, "in a particular, *non-arbitrary*, way", since strictly speaking any division into parts measures the whole in some way or other. Thus, Aristotle begins his exploration of the varieties of parthood by considering two ways in which objects, when viewed from a quantitative perspective, may be divided into parts, i.e., their subquantities, the second being somewhat more restrictive than the first. These first two senses of "part" would be of use primarily to the mathematician or the physicist, i.e., to someone who views objects quantitatively, as unit, number, point, line, surface, plane, solid, magnitude, and the like. (Notice the arithmetical examples.)[29] However, given Aristotle's views on the inseparability of quantities from substances,[30] the objects studied in this way by the mathematician and the physicist are the *very same* objects, when approached from a particular quantitative perspective, as those to which the more loaded uses of "part" apply as well (i.e., the bundles of sticks, shoes, human beings, and the like). Thus, when viewed by the mathematician or the physicist purely as a geometrical solid, say, or as a physical magnitude, any arbitrary division of the quantity associated with the substance, Socrates, into subquantities, by sense (1) itself counts as a part of that quantity; sense (2), while still viewing Socrates in a purely quantitative fashion, imposes further (mathematical or physical) restrictions on what sorts of conditions a subquantity must satisfy (e.g., division by a certain factor) in order to count as a part of the larger quantity.[31]

---

[29] There is, however, also a way of reading sense (2), according to which it is the general heading under which all of the more specialized senses of "part", which are yet to be stated, can be subsumed: for, in a way, senses (3), (4) and (5) all divide certain kinds of quantities into certain kinds of subquantities in non-arbitrary ways; however, they do so by introducing further considerations that are not purely quantitative.

[30] See for example *Met.* Z.1, where the *Categories* doctrine, according to which quantities are quantities *of* substances, is repeated. In *Met.* B.5, such entities as points, numbers, bodies and planes (all of which are normally counted as quantities) are classified as the *boundaries* of substances, and hence as not themselves substances (but see the entry for "substance" in Δ.8, which seems to contradict this by listing such things as numbers, lines, planes and bodies as substances). In Book M, it is argued at length, contra the Platonists, that mathematical objects cannot exist separately and hence are not substances; similar views can be found in Book Λ as well as in *Phy.* II.2: one of Aristotle's main motivations for this belief is that he wants to avoid the result that two numerically distinct bodies or solids may occupy the same place at the same time (see, for example, *Met.* M.2 for considerations of this sort).

[31] The first sense of "part" is the closest thing we find in Aristotle to a CEM-style system; notice, however, that he does not take this notion to provide anything close to an exhaustive mereological analysis of what I have called earlier "ordinary material objects", i.e., such things as the bundles, shoes and human beings that we came across in the last section; it is, after all, only the very first step and the least loaded sense of "part" Aristotle recognizes in Δ.25. However, given his actual/potential distinction (according to which a thing and its matter are numerically identical), as well as his doctrine of the categories (according to which all non-substances stand in dependence relations to substances), Aristotle is not committed to numerically distinct, spatio-temporally coinciding objects: each region of space-time is always occupied *actually* only by a single object; all other ways

With sense (3), Aristotle now moves beyond the purely quantitative perspective, into the domain of quality,[32] to the parts of kinds (εἶδος), i.e., species as well as genera.[33] This sort of division into parts picks up on what I referred to earlier, in the context of the varieties of unity and plurality developed in Δ.6, as senses (2.1) and (2.2), viz., being one in kind, specifically or generically. Thus, the species, human being, has as its parts, the individual human beings, Socrates and Coriscus, who are divisible with respect to their matter (since their bodies are distinct), but indivisible with respect to their form (since both of their souls are characteristically human); the genus, animal, in turn has as its parts the species, human being and dog, which are distinguishable both by their matter (since their bodies are not only numerically distinct but also different in kind) and by their form (since the human soul is different in kind from the canine soul).

This exhausts the portion of Δ.25 which overlaps in content with the varieties of one and many, as laid out in Δ.6; we now move on to the ways in which even those objects which are counted as indivisible by all the measures introduced in Δ.6 may nevertheless be divisible into parts: in particular, those objects that are one in number by being materially indivisible (viz., the musical Coriscus, the bundle of wood, the shoe and Socrates); as well as form itself, which as a principle of unity played a central role in Δ.6 in holding together the parts of other objects (viz., the shoe and Socrates).

The fourth sense of "part" spells out the way in which a *whole* is further divisible into parts. There are apparently two cases to consider: wholes which *are* forms (εἶδος)[34] and wholes which *have* form, i.e., the sorts of objects that Aristotle often refers to as "compounds" (i.e., τὸ σύνθετον, literally, "that which

---

of characterizing the contents of a particular region of space-time are just different ways of viewing this single object. Thus, the only example of a "free-floating" mereological sum, so to speak, in Aristotle's system would be something along the lines of, say, a quantity of water that fills a bathtub; entities of this kind are what he will later (in Δ.26) call "totals" (literally, "alls").

[32] Thus, I read Aristotle's otherwise somewhat puzzling remark at 1023b17, "apart from the quantity" (ἄνευ τοῦ ποσοῦ, literally, "without the quantity"), as his way of notifying the reader that he is now moving from the purely quantitative senses of "part" onto more loaded senses.

[33] Reading "εἶδος" in the purely classificatory way that would be employed, say, by a biologist.

[34] It is actually extremely rare that Aristotle refers to form explicitly as a whole, even though he does fairly frequently speak of the parts of form or essence, in the sense of definition. Even though Aristotle recognizes a more deflationary sense of "whole" (similar to our current modern use of the term), according to which anything that is one (even in the weakest sense) and has parts is a whole, he more frequently uses the term "whole" in a more full-blooded fashion, according to which it means just what it does in sense (4) of "part", viz., something that is unified under a single form. (This is also the sense of "whole" we encountered in Δ.6 and Z.17.) According to the first, deflationary, sense of "whole", even heaps might count as wholes, merely because they have parts and they are one in some, albeit exceedingly weak, sense; but according to the second, more loaded sense, heaps would not count as wholes, since their parts are not unified under a single form. Aristotle would be reluctant to consider forms as wholes according to the second, more full-blooded sense of "whole", since this would seem to get him started on a *regress*: for what, then, is the single form under which the parts of form are unified? On the other hand, we can assume that Aristotle would be equally reluctant to classify forms alongside heaps. We will have occasion

is put together"; or simply τὸ ἐξ ὦν, literally, "that out of them").[35] Only the first case ("wholes as compounds") is really addressed by sense (4); I identify the second case ("wholes as forms") with the remaining sense of "part", sense (5). Those wholes which are explicitly addressed by sense (4) (wholes which have form), illustrated here by means of a bronze sphere and a bronze cube, are said to have as parts both their *matter* (the bronze) and their *form* (the characteristic angle). Notice that Aristotle explicitly takes the form and the matter to be part of the compound *according to a single sense of "part"*;[36] in other words, we do not find in Δ.25, where Aristotle's explicit business is to say in how many ways "part" is spoken of, *two separate* entries along the lines of ". . . and 'part' is spoken of in *one* way as the matter is part of the compound, in *another* as the form is part of the compound".[37]

Finally, we come to the fifth sense of "part", which concerns the mereological structure of what Aristotle calls the "formula" (λόγος): according to this sense of "part", we are told, the genus is part of the species (εἶδος), though we have of course already encountered another sense of "part" (sense (3)), according to which, conversely, the species is part of the genus. I read the current notion of parthood as applying to form (εἶδος), i.e., as filling out the promissory note mentioned in the context of the previous sense of "part", sense (4).[38] What underlies this sense of parthood is Aristotle's doctrine that the "definition" (ὁρισμός), which is the "formula of the essence", is composed of a genus and a differentia. To illustrate, the species or form, human being, according to Aristotle, may be defined as rational animal, i.e., by stating the genus (animal) under which the species in question falls, along with a differentiating characteristic (rational), whose job it is to pick out the

below to return to the mereological status of forms, which turns out to be a central difficulty for Aristotle.

[35] This mereological sense of "out" or "from" (ἐκ) is the counterpart of one of the mereological senses of "in" (ἐν), viz., that according to which the form and the matter are both *in* the compound. See also related senses of "have" (ἔχειν) in Δ.23.

[36] This is in line with my attribution of the Weak Supplementation Principle to Aristotle in the preceding chapter: according to WSP, a whole cannot consist of a single proper part, in the way in which, for example, a singleton set would, if its only member were a part of it.

[37] Form is also spoken of as part of a compound, for example, at *Met.* Z.9, 1034a21–30, and very explicitly at Δ.18, 1022a32: ". . . for the soul, in which life directly resides, is a part of the man". Both matter and form are often spoken of as being "in" the compound in a way that seems quite overtly mereological, as, for example, at Z.8, 1033b13–19. Matter is spoken of as part of the compound, for example at Z.7, 1032b32–33. In general, *Met.* Z.7–9 is a good place to find this kind of language, since Aristotle is there explicitly concerned with the question of how compounds of matter and form are brought into existence from (ἐκ) pre-existing ingredients. (See also Harte 1994 for a helpful discussion of the connections between the entries for "part" and "whole" in Δ.25–26 and the entry for "from" which immediately precedes them in Δ.24.)

[38] Just to remind those readers who are not able to consult the text: the single Greek word "εἶδος" may be translated either as "species" or "kind" (e.g., in sense (3) of "part") or as "form" (e.g., in sense (4) and (5) of "part"); thus, all three uses of the term are found in Δ.25. Besides "εἶδος", Aristotle also uses another term to talk about form, viz., "μορφή", sometimes translated as "shape".

particular species in question from among all the other species (dog, bird, horse, etc.) which fall under the same genus. Definitions play a central role all across the Aristotelian corpus, since they are the primary objects of scientific knowledge.

In sum, then, "part" according to Δ.25 is spoken of in the following five ways:

(1)	**Arbitrary Subquantity:**	A given quantity has among its parts all of the subquantities into which it can be arbitrarily divided.
(2)	**Non-Arbitrary Subquantity:**	A given quantity has among its parts all of the subquantities into which it can be divided in non-arbitrary ways.
(3)	**Species and Genera:**	Species have as their parts objects that are numerically one; genera have as their parts the species that fall under them.
(4)	**Wholes as Compounds:**	Wholes which *have* form have as their parts both the matter and the form of which they consist.
(5)	**Wholes as Forms:**	Wholes which *are* forms have as their parts the parts of their definitions, i.e., the genus and the differentia.[39, 40]

§VI.4.4 The Ways of Being a Whole: *Met.* Δ.26

While much of the content of Δ.26 overlaps with material with which we are already familiar from Δ.6 and Δ.25, Aristotle's entry for "whole" plays an

[39] Why is there no separate entry for the parts of matter? I take it that the sense in which matter has parts is already accommodated by sense (1), since matter, when conceived of in the absence of form, is *infinitely divisible*, i.e., divisible in arbitrary ways, into parts of the same kind. (More on this below.) Aristotle seems to feel that matter, when conceived of in the absence of form, is inherently many (in number). For example, upon the death of a human being, the (now numerically distinct, qualitatively similar) body, when no longer unified by means of a single human form, literally falls apart into many pieces; see, for example, *Met.* M.2, 1077a21–23: "For things in our perceptible world are one in virtue of soul, or of a part of soul, or of something else, reasonably enough; when these are not present, the thing is a plurality, and splits up into parts."

[40] Since the analogy does not correspond to a mereological constellation of its own, it is not represented in Δ.25 as introducing a special sense of "part", i.e., a particular kind of measure, of its own. The musical Coriscus belongs in the same category as Coriscus simply, if we do not take Aristotle's use of "part" as applying to the accidents of a substance seriously. The species, human being, and the genus, animal, belong under sense (3); Socrates and the shoe belong under sense (4), since they both are regarded as wholes which have form. The bundle of wood, though somewhat less straightforward to place than the other examples, is most naturally accommodated either under sense (2), i.e., as providing a non-arbitrary division of a quantity into subquantities or as falling somewhere between sense (2) and sense (3), since this case introduces a division into parts which proceeds not purely by means of quantitative considerations.

Since some of the entities that were viewed as indivisible by any of the measures introduced in Δ.6 now turn out to be divisible by some measure, we may wonder by means of what new *measures* these previously indivisible objects have now become divisible. Given my placement of the bundle of wood under sense (2), the measure by means of which it is divisible is "non-arbitrary subquantity" important role in introducing several new key ideas which supply his account of parthood and composition with its characteristically *normative* and *teleological* flavor; the additional machinery furnished by Δ.26 also allows us to accommodate several categories of objects which we have not yet encountered as well as to draw even more fine-grained distinctions among the categories of objects which have already been recognized in Δ.6 and Δ.25.

§VI.4.4.1 Wholes and Totals

I begin with the second half of Δ.26, which, as is to be expected, takes its subject matter to be certain kinds of *quantities*:

> Again, as quantities have a beginning and a middle and an end, those to which the position [θέσις] does not make a difference are called totals [πᾶν], and those to which it does, wholes [ὅλον], [. . .]. Water and all liquids and number are called totals, but "the whole number" or "the whole water" one does not speak of, except by an extension of meaning. To things, to which *qua* one the term "total" is applied, the term "all" [πάντα] is applied when they are treated as separate; "this total number" [πᾶς οὗτος ὁ ἀριθμός], "all these units" [πᾶσαι αὗται αἱ μονάδες].
>
> (1024a1–10; Ross' italics)

All quantities, according to Aristotle, have what he calls "a beginning, a middle and an end", i.e., a certain *order* in which their parts are arranged, e.g., from first to last. But for some among these quantities it matters (viz., to their existence and identity) *which* part goes *where* in the arrangement of parts (viz., these are the entities for which the *position* (θέσις) of their parts makes a difference); others could have their parts shuffled around and rearranged without thereby ceasing to exist: the former are *wholes*; the latter *totals* (literally, "alls"). I interpret totals as the Aristotelian equivalent of CEM-style mereological sums or aggregates; they should be read as falling exclusively under those senses of "part", (1) and (2), which, when applied to quantities, yield arbitrary or non-arbitrary divisions into subquantities. Aristotle's examples here for the category of "pure" totals are water and all liquids as well as number.[41] He notes that the *adjectival* use of "whole" does not apply to those entities which belong into the category of "pure" totals:

(in this case, "individual wooden stick"). The shoe and Socrates, on the other hand, are divisible by the measure "constituent only separable in thought", since Aristotle believes that the constituents of which the compound consists, matter and form, are never actually found separately but can only be distinguished in analysis. Finally, form is divisible by means of the measure "constituent that figures in the definition", since it is considered to be mereologically complex when approached through the angle of the definitory formula.

[41] What underlies these examples is, first, Aristotle's non-atomic conception of the so-called "simple bodies" (i.e., earth, air, fire and water) and everything that is made out of them on the next higher level of composition (i.e., the so-called "homoiomerous substances", e.g., flesh, bone, marrow, blood, etc., as well as what he calls here the "liquids", i.e., wine, oil, and the like), which he views as being infinitely divisible into parts of the same kind. Secondly, Aristotle conceives of number as an aggregate of discrete "ones" or "units", each of which itself is not a number (since one is not a number, according to the Greek conception). This aggregative conception of number

for example, we do not naturally say, in Greek or English, "the whole water" or "the whole oil".[42]

In sum, then, the second half of Δ.26 introduces the following criterion by means of which to distinguish *wholes* from *totals*: wholes are objects whose identity and existence depends on the *position* (θέσις) of their parts; totals are objects whose parts may be shuffled around and rearranged without affecting the identity and existence of the total in question.[43] Even though Aristotle does not explicitly bring up *form* in the formulation of his criterion, we may infer from what he says in Δ.6 and elsewhere that, for those (high-level) wholes that are unified under a single form, it is in fact their formal component that dictates *which* part must go *where* in the order of the parts; for those objects (e.g., bundles of wood) which are not unified under a single form, if they qualify as (low-level) wholes at all, the order among the parts is enforced by means of whatever principle of unity holds together their parts (e.g., bands or bits of glue).[44]

---

is at work in the last sentence of this section: "To things, to which *qua* one the term 'total' is applied, the term 'all' is applied when they are treated as separate; 'this total number', 'all these units'." Since a number is an aggregate of units, we may refer to these units either separately as "all of them" or "every one of them" (i.e., speaking of the units) or as "all of it" (i.e., speaking of the number). Thus, in the language of Δ.6, even the totals may exhibit a (very weak) sort of unity, since we may at least *speak* of the *many* units as *one* number. Aristotle's point here does not come across in English as naturally as it does in Greek, since we do not share his aggregative conception of number and (connectedly) "number" is used in English exclusively as a count noun (in fact, some might say, "number" is the paradigmatic count noun); thus, English actually permits us to say "this whole number". Given our *atomic* conception of liquids such as water, however, we may substitute, for example, for "all these units" and "this whole number", respectively, "all these water molecules" (i.e., singling out the individual units) and "all this water" (i.e., singling out the total quantity).

[42] Surprisingly, Aristotle also allows for a mixed category: entities which are *both* wholes *and* totals, or which at least "admit of both descriptions", e.g., wax and coat. Since wholes and totals have contradictory characteristics (depending on whether or not the position of their parts makes a difference to their identity and existence), it is difficult to see how one and the same object could be described both as a whole and as a total. He characterizes the "mixed" category as having the following feature: they are objects "whose nature [φύσις] remains the same after transposition [μεταθέσει], but whose form [μορφή] does not" (1024a3–5). (The Greek word "μορφή", translated here as "form", could of course also be translated simply as "shape".) To make sense of this category, as I read it, will require reference to Aristotle's distinction between "actuality" and "potentiality", which is perhaps the most central novel idea introduced in the first half of Δ.26; I will therefore postpone discussion of the "mixed" category until this distinction has been introduced.

[43] Since the criterion for being a whole, offered in the second half of Δ.26, turns on the notion of position (θέσις), there is a connection between Aristotle's entry for "whole" in Δ.26 and his entry for "disposition" (διάθεσις) in Δ.19; this connection is pursued in Harte (1994).

[44] This is not to say that totals lack a single form: if they lack a single form, then the category of totals would have collapsed into the category of what I have been calling "heaps" (i.e., the category into which bundles of wood belong). If, on the other hand, totals have a single form, they nevertheless differ in significant ways from artificial and natural non-heaps: at least in the case of homoiomerous substances such as liquids, every part of the total has *the same* form as the total of which it is a part (though this may not be true of numbers). Although Aristotle seems somewhat reluctant to apply his hylomorphic machinery all the way down to the simple bodies and the homoiomerous substances formed out of them, he does in the end speak in *On Generation and Corruption* of such things as, say, the form of flesh (a ratio or proportion of elements, reminiscent

§VI.4.4.2 Degrees of Wholeness

Up to this point, Aristotle has proposed a means by which to distinguish wholes from a different variety of quantities external to them (viz., the totals), which fail to satisfy even the minimal requirement placed on wholes (viz., that the *position* of their parts must make a difference to their existence and identity). The first half of Δ.26 now introduces additional criteria by which to distinguish among the different varieties of wholes: as in the case of unity, wholeness will similarly turn out to be a notion of *degree*, "wholeness being in fact a sort of oneness" (1023b36). I begin by citing the first half of Δ.26 in full:

We call a whole (1) that from which is absent none of the parts of which it is said to be naturally a whole, and (2) that which so contains the things it contains that they form a unity; and this in two senses—either as each and all one, or as making up the unity between them. For (a) that which is true of a whole class[45] and is said to hold good as a whole (which implies that it is a kind of whole) is true of a whole in the sense that it contains many things by being predicated of each, and that each and all of them, e.g. man, horse, god, are one, because all are living things. But (b) the continuous [συνεχές][46] and limited [πεπερασμένον][47] is a whole, when there is a unity consisting of several parts present in it, especially if they are present only potentially, but, failing this, even if they are present actually. Of these things themselves, those which are so by nature are wholes in a higher degree than those which are so by art, as we said in the case of unity also, wholeness being in fact a sort of oneness.

(1023b26–36)

Aristotle's characterization of wholes in (1) as "that from which is absent none of the parts of which it is said to be naturally a whole" is most easily approached by considering the *adjectival* use of the term "whole", from which its substantive uses, as in "*a* whole", are presumably derived. We have already encountered earlier a similar conceptual connection between the adjectival use of the term "one", and the nominal forms that are based on it (e.g., those that might be rendered into English as "unity", "unit", "the one", "a one", and the like): to

---

of Platonic structure) and the form of water (a certain combination of capacities). If, then, the category of totals should be kept distinct from that of heaps, we must recognize that the job of an object's formal component is not always to indicate a specific arrangement among the parts of an object, in cases in which the object's ability to perform its teleological role does not impose stringent requirements to this effect. Thus, while the job of form, on this more general conception, is always to characterize in teleological terms the particular activity characteristic of the object in question, only sometimes does the performance of this activity require that particular parts occupy specific positions in the order of parts.

45 There is no separate word in the text that corresponds to Ross' "class", only the word used for "universal" (καθόλου), which as mentioned earlier contains the word for "whole" (ὅλου).

46 Aristotle's notion of continuity is reminiscent of Fine's requirement of *spatio-temporal proximity.*

47 This verbal form is related to the noun (πέρας) Plato uses for "limit" in the *Philebus.*

be one, for Aristotle, is always to be one *something-or-other*, where the concept to be supplied indicates the respect in which the object in question is measured to be indivisible. Similarly, to be *a* whole, Aristotle seems to think, is to be a whole *something-or-other*, where again the concept to be supplied determines our expectations as to the *number* and *variety* of parts the object in question will in all likelihood have; these are the parts which *ought* not to be absent or missing, if the object in question is to count as one *whole* something-or-other as opposed to being merely a *partial* manifestation thereof.[48] To illustrate, if I ask you, say, to save the *whole* cake for me, I expect to find the cake in roughly the condition it was in when first taken out of the oven, plus or minus a few crumbs or microscopic particles; once (sufficiently large) pieces of the cake have been eaten or otherwise removed, the object before us is no longer a *whole* cake, though it may have survived these changes, as a partial or *incomplete* manifestation of what once was a whole or *complete* cake.

Aristotle's conception of wholes, as indicated by his characterization in (1) as "that from which is absent none of the parts of which it is said to be naturally a whole", given his other theoretical commitments, immediately leads, as in Plato's case, to a *normative* and *teleological* conception of what it means to be a whole: to be a whole (according to the substantival form of the term) is to be a whole something-or-other (according to the adjectival form of the term), i.e., a whole specimen of a particular kind; and to be a whole specimen of a particular kind is to be a *complete* or *perfect* manifestation of the kind in question, i.e., one that is not missing any of the *important* parts, according to some standard of importance, which members of that kind may normally be expected to have.[49] And while Δ.26 itself does not have more to say on the question of how we would determine the number and variety of parts a given whole *ought* to have, or what the standard of importance might be by means of which the parts of a thing are to be ranked, we may infer from what Aristotle says elsewhere that his answer to this question would refer us to the *characteristic activity* associated with the *kind* to which the object in question belongs; as we know, for example, from his remarks on teleology and hypothetical necessity in contexts like *Phy.* II.8 and *PA* I.1, the number and variety of parts a normal member of a species can be expected to have, respecting the constraints of necessity, are just those which allow it to carry out its characteristic activity *best*.

---

[48] This sense of "whole" is already familiar to us from Plato, who also at times characterizes wholes as "that from which no part is lacking" or "that from which nothing is absent" (see, e.g., *Tht.* 205a4–7 and *Parm.* 137c7–8).

[49] This connection between wholeness and completion comes out, for example, in Aristotle's entry for "complete" (τέλειον) in Δ.16, where he states that "each thing is complete and every substance is complete, when in respect of its proper kind of excellence it lacks no part of its natural magnitude" (1021b20–23). Also relevant in this respect is the entry for "limit" (πέρας) in Δ.17.

The idea that for every whole there is a certain number and variety of parts which it ought not to be missing raises the question of how it nevertheless seems plainly to be possible for many wholes to survive a considerable amount of fluctuation in their mereological make-up. Notice for example that I found it necessary, in this connection, to add the qualification "sufficiently large" in my illustration above to distinguish (in this case merely by size) the sorts of parts whose detachment still leaves us with a whole cake from those whose removal would turn the once complete cake into a partial or incomplete cake. Aristotle is sensitive to the fact that the normative and teleological criterion for wholes he has just proposed in (1) creates the need for the introduction of a hierarchical ordering among the parts of an object; he speaks to this issue in the following chapter, Δ.27, the entry for what he calls "mutilated" (κολοβόν): there, he attempts to propose a criterion, first, for which *objects* can be mutilated by the removal of parts and, secondly, for which among the *parts* of these objects are such that their removal leads to mutilation.[50]

Aristotle's further characterization of wholes in (2) as "that which so contains the things it contains that they form a unity", as it stands, is relatively weak, given the upshot of Δ.6 and Δ.25, since we encountered there a

---

[50] Thus, once we recognize the normative and teleological flavor of Aristotle's conception of wholes, it makes perfect sense that there should be an entry for "mutilated", which otherwise might appear puzzling: Kirwan (1993, p. 177), for example, complains with respect to this entry that "the reason for its inclusion here is a mystery".

The *objects* to which the notion of mutilation applies must be (i) *wholes* by the criterion of the second half of Δ.26 (i.e., the position of their parts must make a difference to their existence and identity); (ii) they must be *continuous* (i.e., their parts must share boundaries); and (iii) they must consist of *unlike* parts. Criteria (i) and (ii) rule out numbers, which are totals, not wholes, and which are discrete, not continuous; criteria (i) and (iii) rule out homoiomerous substances like water and fire, which again are classified in Δ.26 as totals, not wholes, and which consist of like parts. Criterion (ii) rules out musical scales, which apparently are wholes in the sense of (i) (in that the position of their parts makes a difference to their existence and identity) and which consist of unlike parts, but which are discrete, not continuous. This leaves such objects as the cup and the man, wholes that are continuous and consist of unlike parts, as examples of things which can be mutilated by removing certain of their parts.

Among the *parts* of such objects, removal of those which satisfy the following criteria leads to mutilation: (i) the *substance* of the object must remain despite the removal of the part (i.e., the part in question may not be *essential* to the survival of the object in question; a mutilated cup is still a cup); (ii) the portion that remains may not be *equal* to the part that is removed (i.e., an object that has been cut in half is something worse than mutilated); (iii) the part may not be *any chance* part (i.e., a part whose removal is of no consequence whatsoever for the object's ability to carry out its characteristic activity); and, finally, (iv) the part must be such that it cannot be *regenerated*. Aristotle's concern in proposing these criteria is to provide a systematic explanation of why, for example, a cup is (apparently) considered mutilated when its handle is broken off, but not when a hole has been bored through it; and for why a man is considered mutilated when he has lost an extremity, but not when he has lost his hair or some of his flesh. In the interest of space, I will not comment on the success of these criteria; my purpose here was mainly to expose the teleological and normative force inherent in Aristotle's characterization of wholes in (1) as "that from which no (important) parts are missing", and to point out the way in which this criterion creates the need for the otherwise puzzling entry for "mutilated" in Δ.27.

wide variety of objects that are regarded as having parts and as exhibiting some sort of unity, in whatever weak sense of the term. Thus, unless further qualifications are added, Aristotle's characterization of wholes in (2), on its own, does not obviously differentiate among the following entities: artificial heaps such as the bundle of wood; natural heaps such as (arguably) the ivy and the tree-trunk; artificial high-level wholes such as the shoe; natural high-level wholes such as Socrates; discrete quantities like words and musical scales; as well as qualitative classifications of objects that are numerically one such as the species, human being, and the genus, animal.[51, 52] With "wholeness being in fact a sort of oneness", any object that has parts at all and whose parts are held together by means of some principle of unity may be expected to count as a whole, though wholeness, like oneness, will naturally come in degrees depending on the nature of the principle of unity at work.

The relative weakness of the conception of wholes at work in (2) is in fact confirmed in the two-fold distinction that follows, according to which objects that have parts and exhibit some form of unity count as wholes (2.a) "either as each and all one" or (2.b) "as making up the unity between them". The first category is tailored to account for the etymological connection between the word for whole (ὅλον) and the word for *universal* (καθόλου), which Aristotle takes quite seriously. In this sense of "whole", for example, the universal, living thing, counts as a whole because it yields a mechanism for collecting together under a single qualitative heading all of the things of which it is predicated, i.e., man, horse, god, etc. This category of wholes thus corresponds to sense (2) of "one" (being one in kind, either in species or genus) and sense (3) of "part" ("the elements into which the kind might be divided").

Despite the fact that universals are explicitly classified as wholes by (2.a), it is quite obvious that Aristotle regards such entities as being wholes to a lesser degree from that exhibited by category (2.b), viz., wholes that are "continuous" ["συνεχές"] and "limited" ["πεπερασμένον"].[53] For the parts of a universal are

---

[51] The musical Coriscus and the analogy have already been excluded earlier since they were suspected not to present us with a genuine mereological constellation of their own.

[52] Whether the so-called "totals", entities like numbers and liquids, also belong on this list depends on whether or not even these entities are viewed as exhibiting an exceedingly weak sort of unity; the resolution of this question depends on how strongly the "*qua* one" (ὡς ἐφ᾿ ἑνί) in the second half of Δ.26 (at 1024a9) is read. If totals lack unity altogether, this would seem to spell trouble for Aristotle's view in Γ.2 that "being" and "one" are interchangeable, i.e., that to be is always to be one and vice versa. Independently of how this question is resolved, however, totals are of course excluded from whole status in any event, at least by means of the criterion proposed in the second half of Δ.26, since the *position* of their parts does not make a difference to their existence and identity.

[53] "Limit" is defined in Δ.17, first, as a kind of boundary; but from there it is extended to apply also to the form, end, substance and essence of a thing; "limit", Aristotle thinks, has all the same senses as "beginning" or "principle" ("ἀρχή"), but more besides. Compared to its prominence in Plato's *Philebus*, however, the notion of "limit" plays a surprisingly subordinate role

already in and of themselves objects that exhibit some variety of unity ("each and all of them, e.g. man, horse, god, are one"), whereas wholes of type (2.b) are apparently different in this respect, "making up the unity between them". Thus, Aristotle may be read as taking the whole-status of universals as being derivative of that exhibited by those numerically one objects that are being collected together under a single qualitative heading by means of the universal.[54]

Category (2.b), wholes that are continuous and limited, is now subdivided further by means of the single most powerful device in Aristotle's teleological toolkit, which has up to this point not made an appearance, the distinction between what is *actual* and what is *potential*: for among wholes of type (2.b), Aristotle says, some are such that their parts are present in them only *potentially*, while others are such that their parts are present in them *actually*; the former are wholes to a higher degree than the latter.[55] Furthermore, each kind of whole can come about either by *nature* or by *art*; again, the former are wholes to a higher degree than the latter.

Unfortunately, Aristotle is less than generous with examples to illustrate the subdivisions of category (2.b). I take the category of wholes whose parts are present in them only potentially to include our earlier natural and artificial high-level wholes (Socrates and the shoe) which are unified under a single

in Aristotle's metaphysics. Unlike Plato, Aristotle also does not conceive of this notion in purely mathematical terms, but (as its extensions to notions like form, end, substance and essence indicate) as teleologically loaded in the more localized manner that is characteristic of Aristotle's system.

[54] As further evidence for the potentially derivative whole-status of universals, Aristotle also seems to be of two minds as to whether wholes that are not continuous satisfy the completeness criterion. The chapter on mutilation in Δ.27 is restricted explicitly only to wholes which are continuous; however, in Δ.26 itself Aristotle sounds as though *all* wholes satisfy criterion (1). For the sake of simplicity, I will in what follows comply with the terminology of Δ.26 and characterize *all* wholes as being complete, in the sense of unmutilated. In the final analysis, however, it may turn out that this criterion only applies to wholes that are continuous. Similar skepticism might be raised as to whether universals satisfy criterion (3), which concerns the position of the parts of a whole; the answer to this question depends on what sorts of entities Aristotelian universals are taken to be, a question on which I remain entirely neutral.

[55] The primary meaning of "potentiality" (δύναμις), as it is explained, for example, in Δ.12, is the "source of movement or change in another thing or in the same thing *qua* other". An actuality (ἐνεργεία or ἐντελεχεία) is the realization or coming to pass of a change or movement for which a potentiality existed (though this may not reflect the real order of definition); for all change or movement, in Aristotle's view, is from what is potential to what is actual. For example, an architect or builder has the potentiality to build a house, if he can initiate changes or movements which eventually lead to an actual house. In *De Anima*, Aristotle adds a further layer of complexity to his actual/potential distinction: in *DA* II.5, (i) a "*first* potentiality" is defined roughly as the capacity to acquire a capacity (in this sense, all humans are speakers of French); (ii) a "*second* potentiality", which is simultaneously a "*first* actuality", is roughly the result of having acquired a capacity, without currently exercising it (in this sense, only those who have studied French are speakers of French); (iii) finally, a "*second* actuality" is the result of exercising the acquired capacity (in this sense, only those who are currently speaking French are speakers of French). With this added machinery, the soul can now be defined as a first actuality (i.e., a second potentiality) of a natural, organized body having life potentially (in the sense of first potentiality) within it. The intermediary layer of second potentiality/first actuality, at least on the surface, averts the outcome that the soul, which as the form of the organism should come out to be pure actuality, turns into pure potentiality.

form. It is less obvious how to construe the category of wholes whose parts are present in them actually; Aristotle might have in mind here the natural and artificial heaps distinguished earlier, such as the bundle of wood and the ivy around the tree-trunk, whose parts are not unified under a single form.[56, 57]

Although Aristotle does not explicitly bring up form in Δ.26, we know from what he says elsewhere that it is in fact the presence of form which accounts for the fact that those wholes that are unified under a single form have their parts present in them only potentially. In this way, the distinction between actuality and potentiality is closely aligned with Aristotle's "Homonymy Principle", with which we are already familiar from the preceding chapter and according to which a severed hand (say) is a "hand" in name alone. In general, by the Homonymy Principle, no object that is *not* already part of a whole that is unified under a single form can survive *becoming* part of such a whole; and no object that *is* already part of such a whole can survive *ceasing* to be part of it. The reason underlying this radical doctrine is that any such transformation would essentially involve a change in *kind membership* (e.g., a change from being an object that plays a

---

[56] If those wholes whose parts are present in them actually really are the natural and artificial heaps, it is difficult to see how to set this category apart from the category (2.a) universals; for the distinction between the two categories was supposed to be that in the case of (2.a) each of the parts is already one, while in the case of (2.b) the parts together make up a unity. But if each individual wooden stick is actually present in the bundle, and not merely potentially, then how is the bundle of wood different in this respect from, say, the species, human being, or the genus, animal, both of which have as actually existing parts the objects that fall under them? The obvious difference between them is of course that the parts of universals are merely *qualitatively* one, whereas the parts of entities in category (2.b) add up to something that is also *numerically* one. Since Aristotle is not explicit on this point, however, this possible way of spelling out the difference between (2.a) and (2.b) is mere speculation on my part. And while this reading of the difference between (2.a) and (2.b) has the advantage of allowing us to distinguish universals from heaps, it also makes the placement of discrete quantities like words and musical scales in the scheme of Δ.26 more difficult. Since category (2.b) seems to be explicitly restricted to wholes that are *continuous*, it is not clear where words and musical scales should go, if, as seems plausible, not all of them are to be subsumed under the category of totals (as are numbers). In fact, as in Plato, we find linguistic entities (such as syllables) to be among Aristotle's favorite examples for form/matter compounds.

[57] Since form, in the guise of definition, was listed as a particular kind of whole in Δ.25, one might expect there to be a place for form also in Δ.26; but it is not obvious how to accommodate form within the scheme of Δ.26. Since form, if anything, should exhibit a higher degree of unity from that exhibited by other entities, it cannot be assigned to category (2.a); for wholes of type (2.a) apparently exhibit a lesser degree of unity from that of their parts. If category (2.b) really is to be restricted to wholes that are continuous, it is not clear how form is to fit that description, since the parts of definitions don't obviously share boundaries. Even if we relax this requirement (which might be a good idea at any rate, given the difficulty concerning the placement of discrete quantities like words and musical scales), however, it is still not clear whether definitions should be viewed as having their parts present in them *potentially* or *actually*. Since wholes whose parts are present in them only potentially are wholes to a higher degree than those whose parts are present in them actually, one would tend to assign definitions to the former category. However, Aristotle greatly struggles with the question of whether definitions display the same hylomorphic structure as, say, the shoe and Socrates; as mentioned earlier, Aristotle is aware of the potential regress lurking in a straightforwardly hylomorphic conception of definitions and feels conflicting pressures with respect to this question.

certain characteristic role within a living human organism, to being an object which is not tied in this way into the functioning of a living human organism); and no single object could survive such a change in kind membership.[58] Since the very same hand that *is* part of a living human organism could never enjoy an existence separate from the organism of which it is part, its presence within the organism is only *potential*. (For if it were present in the organism *actually*, there would be no reason for it not to be able to exist separately from the whole of which it is part; as a result, however, the whole would be *that* much less unified.)[59] Aristotle's teleological apparatus thus leads to the consequence, which is bound to be surprising from a modern perspective, that those wholes which are unified under a single form do not have any parts at all *actually*; they do so only *potentially*.[60] For this reason, wholes of this kind are wholes to a higher degree than wholes of other kinds, since they are *one* (or indivisible into parts) to a higher degree than other wholes, "wholeness being in fact a sort of oneness".[61]

---

[58] See, for example, Aristotle's remark at 1014b22–26, concerning the distinction between mere "contact" and "organic unity" Δ.4, the entry for "nature" (φύσις): "Organic unity differs from contact; for in the latter case there need not be anything besides the contact, but in organic unities there is something identical in both parts, which makes them grow together instead of merely touching, and be one in respect of continuity and quantity, though not of quality." I take it that the thing which the organically unified parts have in common is *form*; in this sense, then, the human form, for example, is "spread" throughout the human body, and all of the merely potentially existing parts of the body have a share in the same form, despite the fact that they of course each have their own separate jobs to fulfil within the organism of which they are part. If one and the same object could become separated from the living body whose form it shares, the object in question would therefore have to undergo a change in its form; but no single object can persist through a change of this kind.

[59] See, for example, Z.13, 1039a3–11: ". . . a substance cannot consist of substances present in it actually (for things that are thus actually two are never actually one, though if they are *potentially* two, they can be one, e.g. the double line consists of two halves—potentially; for the *actualization* of the halves divides them from one another; therefore if the substance is one, it will not consist of substances present in it); and according to the argument which Democritus states rightly; he says one thing cannot come from two nor two from one; . . ." (Ross' italics). This is one reason why heaps cannot be substances. (In addition to heaps, Aristotle is of course divided with respect to almost all of the items that are listed as wholes in this chapter as to whether they should count as substances and which, among them, are primary; thus, being a whole and being a substance, primary or otherwise, are in general two very different things.)

[60] One might think, not entirely without justification, "so much the worse for the actual/potential distinction", if the parts that make their presence in the human being felt as much as, say, an eye, an arm, a heart, a brain, and so forth, only maintain a potential existence within the organism. Nevertheless, strange as it may sound to modern ears, it is in fact Aristotle's view that wholes that are unified under a single form have no parts actually, but do so only potentially. Aristotle is aware that some might react to this position with surprise or incredulity; he remarks for example at Z.16, 1040b10–16: "One might suppose especially that the parts of living things and the corresponding parts of the soul are both, i.e. exist both actually and potentially, because they have sources of movement in something in their joints; for which reason some animals live when divided. Yet all the parts must exist only potentially, when they are one and continuous by nature,—not by force or even by growing together, for such a phenomenon is an abnormality."

[61] And natural wholes that are unified under a single form are wholes to a higher degree than artificial wholes that are so unified, presumably because the artificial whole, but not the natural whole, will be fashioned out of pre-existing ingredients (though, by the Homonymy Principle,

In sum, then, Aristotle proposes in Δ.26 the following characterization of wholes:

(1)	**Wholes as Complete:**	A whole is a complete or perfect (i.e., unmutilated) specimen of a particular kind.
(2)	**Wholes as Unities:**	Anything that has parts and is one is a whole to some degree.
	(2.a) Universals:	Universals are wholes because they provide a mechanism for collecting together objects that are in themselves already one under a single qualitative heading.
	(2.b) **Continuous and Limited Wholes:**	The parts of continuous and limited wholes together make up a unity.
	(2.b.i) **Single Form:**	Wholes that are continuous and limited are wholes to a higher degree when their parts are present in them only *potentially*.
	(2.b.ii) **No Single Form:**	Wholes that are continuous and limited are wholes to a lesser degree when their parts are present in them *actually*.[62]
(3)	**Wholes vs. Totals:**	Quantities are wholes when the *position* of their parts makes a difference to their existence and identity; totals otherwise.

Given the different criteria for being a whole, and those for being a whole to a higher or lesser degree, we can furthermore rank the different entities which I

---

the pre-existing ingredients even of artificial non-heaps cannot be identical to those objects which eventually function as the matter for the newly created artifact): in the case of a living organism, on the other hand, there is not even a qualitatively similar, albeit numerically distinct, pre-existing heap of flesh, bones, blood, hair, etc., out of which the future human being will be formed; rather, the matter of the human being grows and comes into existence along with the human being himself. The generation of living things is actually a complicated matter for Aristotle and is addressed in more detail in *On the Generation of Animals*; in *Met.* H.4, for example, Aristotle identifies the menstrual fluid contributed by the maternal parent as the material cause of a human being; the semen contributed by the father as the efficient cause; the formal and final cause, i.e., the essence and end, of the human being are also apparently somehow associated with the semen contributed by the paternal parent. In the case of natural and artificial heaps, a different story will have to be told as to why the former are wholes to a higher degree than the latter, presumably having to do with the nature of the relation (e.g., growth versus glue) which holds together the parts in each case.

[62] Each of category (2.b.i) and (2.b.ii) is further subdivided into wholes that are natural and wholes that are artificial, with the former being wholes to a higher degree than the latter.

have used as illustrations throughout this chapter in the following way, starting with highest-degree wholes and ending with quantities that are not wholes at all:

(1) **Wholes as Forms**[63]   (Definition = genus + differentia)

(2) **Wholes as Matter/Form Compounds:** (high-level wholes)
    (2.1) Continuous Compounds:
        (2.1.1) Natural   (Socrates)
        (2.2.1) Artificial   (shoe)
    (2.2) Discrete Compounds:[64]
        (2.2.1) Natural   (???)
        (2.2.2) Artificial   (music, language)

(3) **Wholes as Heaps:**   (lower-level wholes)
    (3.1) Natural Heaps   (ivy/tree-trunk)
    (3.2) Artificial Heaps   (bundle of wood)

(4) **Wholes as Universals**   (human being, animal, living thing)

(5) **Totals**   (numbers, liquids)[65]

§VI.5 SUMMARY OF SECTIONS VI.3–4: THE HIGHLIGHTS

In the preceding sections, I have focused mainly on the entries for "one", "part" and "whole" in Book Δ of the *Metaphysics*, the so-called "Philosophical Lexicon". Despite the relative brevity and density of these texts, the resulting mereology is remarkably subtle and wide-ranging in its application. Before I turn to some conceptual issues which I see as arising from Aristotle's analysis of parthood and composition, I want to restate the highlights of Sections III–IV; I will do so by

---

[63] I rank forms highest in this ordering not because of anything that Aristotle has explicitly said which would justify this ranking, but simply because I take it that this would be his desire and because form is the source of unity for other objects. We will turn to the problematic status of form in Aristotle's mereology shortly.

[64] The category of discrete compounds is not explicitly represented in Δ.26 and is my insertion, based on Aristotle's remarks and his use of examples elsewhere. I'm unsure of what would count as a good example for a naturally formed discrete compound.

[65] Given the distinction between potentiality and actuality, we can now explain the puzzling mixed category of "whole/totals" from the second half of Δ.26 as follows: what Aristotle might have in mind there is that one and the same object can be described both as a total, e.g., as wax or cloth, when we speak of it simply as matter, and as a whole, e.g., as a candle or a coat, when we speak of it as a matter/form compound. Since wholes and totals have contradictory properties (depending on whether or not the position of their parts matters to their existence and identity), some such additional qualification as the different modes of existence, potential versus actual, may be expected to be at work in this category to prevent outright inconsistency. Given this reading, I don't list the whole/totals as a separate category in the scheme of Δ.26, since they do not introduce a kind of entity that is not already covered by the other entries.

showing in what way, using the vocabulary of the preceding chapter, Aristotle's mereology agrees with the main features of the Platonic account, according to which wholes are (i) genuinely *unified*; (ii) *ontologically committing*; (iii) governed by a *restricted* notion of composition; (iv) comprised of the two components of *structure* and *content*; (v) ontologically *prior* to their parts; (vi) *normative* and *teleological* in nature; as well as (vii) inherently *intelligible* and the *proper objects of science*.

(i) *Unity.* Aristotelian wholes, like their Platonic counterparts, are genuinely unified, though we need to qualify Aristotle's answer to the question "Are wholes one or many, as many as their parts?" in two respects. First, the notions "one" and "many", in Aristotle's view, must always be understood as being relativized to a particular *measure*. Aristotle takes the core meaning of "one" to be "indivisible (into parts)" and, correspondingly, that of "many" to be "divisible (into parts)", where a division into parts always proceeds by means of some measure; the measure in question indicates the respect in which the object, which is to be evaluated from a quantitative or other perspective, is judged to be one (indivisible) or many (divisible). The result of this explicit or implicit relativization of the notions "one" and "many" is that one and the same object can be measured to be one or indivisible into parts in one respect, while being measured to be many or divisible into parts in another respect. While it is therefore true to say that Aristotelian wholes are always one or indivisible into parts *in some respect*, they tend to be at the same time many or divisible into parts in other respects. Thus, Aristotle would respond to the initial question posed by the Problem of the One and the Many, "Are wholes one or many, as many as their parts?", in a characteristically qualified manner, by answering, without contradiction, "Wholes are both one and many, as many as their parts", depending on the measure by means of which a particular division into parts proceeds.

Secondly, we saw that Aristotle's answer to the Problem of the One and the Many must be qualified by taking note of the particular *principle of unity* by means of which the parts of a given whole are held together. For wholes, in Aristotle's view, come in many different varieties, almost as many varieties as objects that are one or unified; and wholeness, like oneness or unity, is a notion of *degree*, depending on the strength of the particular principle of unity by means of which the parts of the object in question are held together. Though Aristotle sometimes uses the term "whole" in a stricter sense which applies only those wholes that are unified under a single form, he also allows for a relatively permissive use of the term according to which anything that has parts and is one, in whatever weak sense of the term "one" counts as a whole. This weaker use of the term "whole", on my reading of Aristotle, encompasses entities as varied as the following: Aristotelian forms, in the guise of definitions, whose parts are the genus and the differentia; the entities I have termed artificial or natural "heaps", whose parts are not unified under a single form, e.g., the bundle of wood and (arguably) the ivy growing around a tree-trunk; those I have termed natural or artificial "high-level wholes", which are continuous and whose parts are unified under a single form, e.g., the shoe and Socrates; the so-called "discrete quantities", such as words and musical scales; as well as the "universals", e.g., the species, human being, and the genera, animal or living thing, which provide a mechanism for collecting other objects together under a single qualitative heading. The only entities which seem to be *excluded* from whole status, under this weak construal of the term, are the so-called "accidental unities", e.g., the musical Coriscus, and the analogies, e.g., the relation between 1:2 and 2:4, neither of which indicate a genuinely mereological constellation of their own; as well as the so-called "totals", e.g., numbers and liquids, from the second half of the chapter on wholes in Δ.26, which fail to satisfy even the minimum requirement placed on wholes, viz., that the *position* of their parts must make a difference to their existence and identity. In sum, then, while Aristotle agrees with the Platonic position that wholes are genuinely unified, Aristotle's solution to the Problem of the One and the Many yields an implicitly *relativized* conception of wholes as well as one which allows for *degrees* of wholeness, corresponding to the strength of the principle of unity by means of which the parts of an object are held together: depending on the particular category of entity in question, principles of unity can range from bits of glue or bands holding together individual wooden sticks into the shape of a bundle, to full-fledged and teleologically loaded Aristotelian forms.

(ii) *Ontological Commitment.* As can be gleaned even from Aristotle's early remarks in *Topics* VI.13 cited above, as well as from the regress argument in *Met.* Z.17 discussed in the previous chapter, Aristotle in general agrees with the Platonic account that wholes must be numerically distinct from their parts, insofar as their parts can have a separate existence from the whole at all: since the existence and identity of a whole depends on the manner in which their parts are arranged, Aristotle reasons (by implicitly appealing to a Leibniz's Law-style argument) that a whole cannot be numerically identical simply to its parts, when these parts can also be found in different arrangements. (This much is true, I take it, even of natural and artificial heaps.)

This picture is complicated, however, by the introduction of Aristotle's teleological apparatus, in particular the powerful actual/potential distinction and its accompanying Homonymy Principle, according to which (say) a severed hand is a "hand" in name alone and an "eye" that cannot see is an "eye" only in an extended sense of the term. For the parts of those wholes which are unified under a single form cannot even exist separately from the whole of which they are part, since such a transformation would involve a change in kind membership which no single entity can survive; the parts of such wholes (other than form) maintain a merely *potential* presence within the whole of which they are part, with the surprising consequence that wholes that are unified under a single form, despite appearances, *actually* have no parts at all and are for this reason *that* much more unified.⁶⁶ Since for these wholes the question of the separate existence of their parts does not even arise, Aristotle now takes himself to have the option of holding that the parts of such high-level wholes are not distinguishable from the whole of which they are parts, though their *mode* of existence is different, the parts existing merely potentially within the whole, while the whole is capable of existing actually.⁶⁷ However, the mysterious oneness or sameness between matter/form compounds and their merely potentially existing parts is so teleologically, and otherwise, loaded that, to put it mildly, it is a far cry from the ontological innocence of the Lewis-style or Eleatic approach to mereology; in this sense, then, I take it that we are quite justified in regarding Aristotelian wholes as carrying considerable ontological commitment.⁶⁸

(iii) *Restricted Composition.* A full answer to the question of whether and how Aristotle's mereology utilizes a restricted conception of composition depends in

---

⁶⁶ Although I take it to be part of official Aristotelian doctrine, given the entry for "part" in Δ.25 as well as other passages cited earlier, that form is a proper part of any matter/form compound, it is undeniable that Aristotle also often uses the term "part" to single out merely the potentially existing matter portion of a matter/form compound. It is this use of the term "part" that is most conducive to Harte's reading of the regress argument in Z.17, which takes "part" to be synonymous with "element" (which in turn is identified with "matter"), as well as the accompanying "wholes as identical to structures" model she endorses. Among the numerous passages in which this use of the term "part" is prevalent, see for example *Phy.* VII.5, 250a24–25, where Aristotle states, apparently only focusing on high-level wholes, that "no part even exists otherwise than potentially in the whole"; see also the entry for "cause" (*αἴτιον*) in Δ.2, where Aristotle speaks of the parts as the material causes of the whole; as well as the entry for "prior" and "posterior" in Δ.11, especially 1019a8 ff. However, while I acknowledge that Aristotle often uses the term "part" in this way, I take this usage to be mere shorthand for singling out the *non-formal* parts of a matter/form compound.

⁶⁷ At the same time, however, he also explicitly takes its matter to be merely one constituent of the matter/form compound, the other constituent being form. I will not attempt to explain how, by means of his actual/potential distinction and the accompanying Homonymy Principle, Aristotle takes himself to be able to say, without inconsistency, *both* that matter is a proper part of a matter/form compound *and* that a matter/form compound is not distinguishable from its matter. (As a consequence of this combination of views, the Weak Supplementation Principle, which I earlier ascribed to Aristotle in the context of our discussion of the regress argument in Z.17, would also have be modified to reflect the actual/potential distinction in something like the following way: a whole cannot be composed of a single *actual* or *potential* part.) For relevant discussion, see, for example, *Met.* Z.10, which concerns the ways in which parts and wholes are prior or posterior to one another. I have here merely stated in its starkest outlines what I take to be Aristotle's view, without attempting to elaborate on it. Since, as I indicated already in my discussion of the Platonic account in the previous chapter, I take the teleological content of their respective positions to be conceptually separable from the mereology *per se*, an analysis of Aristotle's theory of parthood and composition need not enter very far into the complexities of the actual/potential distinction or the closely related Homonymy Principle, which would in any case require a book-length treatment of its own. For an interesting discussion of *Met.* H.6, in which the actual/potential distinction is brought to bear, among other things, on the question of the unity of matter/form compounds, see Haslanger (1994b) and Harte (1996).

⁶⁸ For the unity between a thing and its matter, see, for example, *DA* II.1, 412b4–9: "That is why we can dismiss as unnecessary the question whether the soul and the body are one: it is as though we were to ask whether the wax and its shape are one, or generally the matter of a thing and that of which it is the matter. Unity has many senses (as many as 'is' has), but the proper one is that of actuality." Similar remarks can be found, for example, in *Met.* H.6, among other places.

part on how we resolve a difficult issue which I have deliberately not brought up so far, viz., the question of whether Aristotle's system utilizes several distinct notions of parthood and composition and, if so, how many. I will be suggesting below that Aristotle may have to be interpreted as making use of several distinct notions of parthood and composition, to avoid the prospect of having to give up on certain non-negotiable formal properties of the part relation. For now, however, it is sufficient to recall that, among the entities we encountered in the previous sections, the only plausible candidates for a CEM-style unrestricted notion of composition are the mathematician's and physicist's quantities that are governed by sense (1) of "part", according to which any *arbitrary* division of a quantity into subquantities yields a division into parts. All other entities discussed above, it is safe to say, are governed by a restricted notion of parthood and composition of some sort. Sense (2) of "part", for example, explicitly requires that the divisions of a quantity into subquantities that are governed by it must be *non*-arbitrary; moreover, quite obviously not every plurality of objects gives rise to something Aristotle would consider a species or a genus, a matter/form compound, a form, a discrete quantity, or even a heap. Thus, even without committing ourselves explicitly on the precise number of distinct notions of parthood and composition that are at work in Aristotle's mereology and the nature of their restrictions, we may conclude that the great majority of them are restricted.

(iv) *Structure/Content Dichotomy.* One of the most central features of Platonic wholes, as they were characterized in the previous chapter, is their dichotomous nature: they consist of *structure* (which, for Plato, is that which is mathematically expressible: number, measure, ratio, proportion, and the like) and *content* (that on which structure is imposed); both of these components, according to the "wholes as composed of structure" model I endorsed, are to be viewed as *parts* of the whole. Since Aristotelian wholes come in so many different varieties, it is difficult to discern in all of them a single uniform dichotomous nature: even though the parts of all wholes are held together by some principle of unity, it is not equally natural in all cases to take the principle of unity itself to be a *proper part* of the whole in question. (The case of universals comes to mind in this connection; however, perhaps in part for this very reason, these entities were also seen to be assigned a secondary, possibly derivative, whole status.) At the same time, Aristotle's high-level wholes, which are in any event those that are of primary interest to us given the purposes of this discussion, nicely conform to the Platonic picture: those wholes that are unified under a single form quite clearly display the two-fold nature of a Platonic whole, with the structure-role being played this time by Aristotelian *forms* and the content-role being played by Aristotle's concept of *matter*. The matter/form distinction is of course extremely difficult to characterize, and I won't attempt an adequate treatment here. We may be content to characterize matter, in this context, in the same negative terms which were used in relation to Platonic content, as "that on which form may be imposed", noting that Aristotle's conception of matter in general (i.e., with the exception of the controversial "prime matter") seems to conform quite well to the "less murky" conception of content suggested in the previous chapter, according to which content is best thought of as being in itself already structured. The range of entities which can be found to be designated as matter is extremely wide and varied, and often includes entities that are surprisingly "unstuff-like"; the following are representative examples: the four elements (i.e., earth, air, fire and water); the so-called "homoiomerous substances" (e.g., flesh, blood, marrow, hair, and the like); the so-called "anhomoiomerous substances" (e.g., arms, legs, eyes, hearts, brains, and the like); anything that underlies change, as in *Phy.* I (e.g., the musical man who turns unmusical); the premises of an argument; the parts of mathematical objects (e.g., the half line is at times identified as the matter for the whole line); and even the genus, as it appears in the definition (e.g., animal is sometimes, apparently, regarded as the matter underlying the differentia, rational, in the definition of human being as rational animal).[69]

Aristotelian forms, unlike Platonic structure, in most cases cannot be captured in purely mathematical terms.[70] In contrast to Plato's *cosmic* teleology, which sometimes appears to be explicitly theological (at least according to the literal reading of the *Timaeus*), each Aristotelian form, so to speak, already has its own, *localized*, teleological content built into it. If we think of Aristotle's universe as being divided into different *kinds* of entities, each of which contributes to the teleological ordering of the cosmos by performing a certain *characteristic activity* of its own, then we may conceive of Aristotelian forms as having the job roughly of capturing in teleological terms the particular activity characteristic of each object.[71] In most cases, with the possible exception of the so-called "totals", an object's ability to fulfil its teleological role requires that its parts be *arranged* in a certain specific manner; in these cases, the task of form, then, includes a specification of the particular arrangement of parts that is required for the object's ability to carry out its characteristic function. In this vein, for example, a house is defined in *Met.* H.2 as bricks, stones and timbers (the matter) arranged in such

---

[69] Though there is a great scholarly controversy surrounding the question of how literally to take Aristotle when he seems to designate the genus as the matter of the definition; as I mentioned earlier, a straightforwardly hylomorphic conception of definitions, among other things, threatens to give rise to an endless demand for further principles of unity.

[70] An interesting exception to this generalization is the form of homoiomerous substances such as flesh and blood, which in *On Generation and Corruption* is characterized as a *ratio* of elements. Despite the, at least in part, overtly mathematical content of these Aristotelian forms, Aristotle nevertheless seems to want to distance himself at all costs from Platonic structure, as can be seen, for example, in an almost comical passage from *Met.* N.5, whose purpose is to argue that number is never a cause of substance or being in any sense of "cause" (see 1092b8 ff).

[71] I am here trying to remain as neutral as possible with respect to the different scholarly controversies surrounding the nature of form, such as the question of whether Aristotelian forms are to be viewed as universal or particular. My purpose here is merely to point out some general distinguishing features of Aristotelian forms, which differentiate them from Platonic structure, as it was characterized in the preceding chapter.

a way as to provide a covering for bodies and chattels (the form and end). And while Aristotle's teleology, like Plato's, ultimately has a theological component as well (as is laid out in *Met.* Λ), Aristotle's God, whose activity is thought ceaselessly thinking itself, enters into the mereology only in a relatively remote way, by inspiring other objects, as their object of desire, to be as much like him in their activities as they can be, given their own natures.

In sum, then, while we may ascribe to all Aristotelian wholes some principle of unity which holds together their parts, the Platonic dichotomy of structure and content applies most straightforwardly to high-level Aristotelian wholes, whose components are form and matter. Aristotelian forms, however, must be read quite differently from the mathematical conception of structure prevalent in Plato, with each of them already containing their own localized teleological content, tailored to the particular kind of object at issue and its characteristic activity.

(v) *Priority of Wholes over Parts.* Given Aristotle's actual/potential distinction and the closely aligned Homonymy Principle, high-level Aristotelian wholes are ontologically prior to their parts, in the sense distinguished in the previous chapter: no single object can survive either becoming part of a high-level whole of which it is not already part or ceasing to be part of a high-level whole of which it is already part, since such a transformation would involve a change in kind membership which no single object can survive. The same radical doctrine, however, does not obviously apply to other wholes, since it is connected specifically with the presence of form as principle of unity.

(vi) *Normativity and Teleology.* Aristotle conceives of wholes as *complete* or *perfect* (i.e., *unmutilated*) specimens of a particular kind, as is best made explicit by considering the adjectival use of the term "whole" (as in "Please save the *whole* cake for me"). To this extent, all wholes have a certain number and variety of parts which they *ought* not to be missing if they are to be *normal* members of the species to which they belong; these are the parts which, respecting the constraints of necessity, allow each object to carry out its characteristic activity best. In addition, high-level wholes, whose parts are unified under a single form, satisfy further teleological conditions, as brought out by the actual/potential distinction and the accompanying Homonymy Principle, since their parts are incapable of even carrying on a separate existence outside the whole to which they belong. Thus, Aristotle's conception of parthood and composition, like Plato's, is quite explicitly normative and teleological, though they differ on how the details are to be filled in.

(vii) *Proper Objects of Science.* Again, Aristotle's mereology requires a qualified answer to the question of whether wholes are inherently intelligible and the proper objects of science. As he explains primarily in *Posterior Analytics* and certain sections of the *Metaphysics*, the proper objects of scientific knowledge are first and foremost universals with which Aristotelian forms, in the guise of definitions, are sometimes identified. Thus, it is not the form/matter compounds or high-level wholes that are in the first instance the proper objects of science, since they are primarily objects of perception; rather, the proper objects of science are those wholes, i.e., the forms and universals, whose status in Aristotle's mereology was seen in the previous remarks to be problematic in various respects.

To summarize, then, Aristotle's account of wholeness centers on the following three criteria. (1) *Completeness*: Wholes are complete or perfect (i.e., unmutilated) specimens of a particular kind; (2) *Unity*: their parts are held together by some principle of unity of whatever degree of strength; and (3) *Position*: the position of their parts makes a difference to their existence and identity. Wholes are furthermore ranked into higher or lower kinds, depending in part on whether they are *continuous* (in the sense that their parts share boundaries) and whether their parts are held together by the presence of a *single form*. With the proper qualifications added, we may conclude that Aristotelian wholes share the seven characteristic features of Plato's mereology: they are (i) genuinely *unified*; (ii) *ontologically committing*; (iii) governed by a *restricted* notion of composition; (iv) comprised of the two components of *structure* and *content*; (v) ontologically *prior* to their parts; (vi) *normative* and *teleological* in nature; as well as (vii) inherently *intelligible* and the *proper objects of science*. Since Aristotle's wholes come in so many different varieties, not all wholes satisfy all of these characteristics to the same extent; however, it is fair to say that, in every respect other than the epistemological concerns of (vii), Aristotelian high-level wholes, the compounds of matter and form, are closest to the Platonic conception.

§VI.6 DISCUSSION

§VI.6.1 The Formal Properties of Parthood

In the remainder of this chapter, I want to raise in particular two conceptual difficulties which I see as arising from Aristotle's mereology: the first concerns the sheer complexity of Aristotle's system. The preceding sections have shown Aristotle's ontology to be mereologically nested in multiple, complex ways; moreover, the range of entities to be covered by his relatively brief remarks on mereology proper is simply enormous and includes anything ranging from numbers, universals and definitions to liquids, bundles of wood, shoes and human beings. We may wonder whether the ambitious scope and complexity of Aristotle's system is not in itself problematic.

Consider the following difficulty. According to Aristotle's account of parthood and composition, we know that high-level wholes, i.e., matter/form compounds such as Socrates and Coriscus, have among their proper parts their form and their matter. Form, in the guise of definition, in turn is said to be composed of a genus and a differentia; in this case, rational and animal. Thus, by transitivity, Socrates and Coriscus apparently have among their proper parts the genus, animal, and the differentia, rational. However, Socrates and Coriscus, as individual human beings, are also themselves proper parts of the species, human being, which in turn is a proper part of the genus, animal. Thus, it seems to be a consequence of Aristotle's remarks not only that the genus, animal, turns out to be a proper part of Socrates and Coriscus, but also, contra the *asymmetry* of the proper part relation, that Socrates and Coriscus turn out to be proper parts of the genus, animal, as well. At the same time, of course, Aristotle would not want to *identify* Socrates and Coriscus with each other or with the genus, animal, which after all also has among its parts lots of other individual human beings, along with all the other living things that are animals, i.e., the dogs, birds, horses, and the like. Nor should it turn out, by transitivity, that Socrates is a *proper part* of Coriscus or, vice versa, that Coriscus is a proper part of Socrates. Something clearly has to give.

Aristotle has several options at this juncture. First, he could reject certain of the formal properties of the part relation, such as the *transitivity* of parthood or the *asymmetry* of proper parthood. I will not seriously entertain this first option, since (following Simons 1987) I take these to be among the non-negotiable formal core of the part relation.

Secondly, Aristotle could argue that the above line of reasoning turns on *mis-identifying* some of the members of the purported chain of mereologically nested entities, which eventually leads to trouble with the formal properties of parthood. For example, he could propose in this connection that form, in the sense in which it is a proper part of any matter/form compound, is *not* to be identified with definition. Given my remarks in the following section concerning the problematic mereological status of form, I take this second option to be quite plausible, though it is not one Aristotle could endorse lightheartedly, given the epistemic and other pressures he apparently feels, in certain contexts (such as *Met.* Z), to identify form with definition.

Thirdly, Aristotle could resolve the above difficulty by suggesting that the sense of "part" in which, say, form is part of an individual human being is not the same sense as that in which, say, Socrates is part of the species, human being: in other words, according to this proposal, Aristotle might reject the claim that the purported chain of mereologically nested entities identified above is in fact chained together by a single relation of parthood. Although this is a live option, I recommend, given the results of our discussion of Kit Fine's work in Chapter IV, that it is best avoided if other solutions are available, since it ultimately leads to a proliferation of primitive, *sui generis* relations of parthood and composition, whose formal characteristics must be explicitly imposed on them by means of distinct bodies of postulates.

In sum, then, while the objection raised in this section is not fatal to Aristotle's mereology, it does require him to incur certain costs: definitions, matter/form compounds, species, and genera cannot be straightforwardly understood as being ordered by means of a single asymmetric and transitive relation of proper parthood.

§VI.6.2 In Search of the Ultimate Mereological Atom

Finally, I want to turn to an issue to which I have alluded many times already in the preceding sections: the difficult status of *form* within Aristotle's mereology. Like Harte (1994), I take this to be a central, and quite possibly *the* central, problem to which Aristotle's analysis of parthood and composition leads; moreover, it is a problem not just for his mereology proper but for his metaphysics at large.

Form is by no means the only principle of unity Aristotle recognizes, since Aristotelian principles of unity come in many different varieties, ranging from bits of glue, which enforce physical contact, to the qualitative similarities captured by universals. Nevertheless, form was identified in the preceding sections as the most powerful principle of unity, in the sense that those wholes that are unified by form *actually* have no parts at all, but do so only *potentially*; to this extent, such objects are wholes to a higher degree than other objects which are not unified by means of form, precisely because they are *one* (or indivisible into parts) to a higher degree than other objects. It is fair to say, then, that the unity of a high-level whole or matter/form compound is, in this sense, *borrowed* from form: such objects inherit their status as highly unified objects from the forms which act as their principles of unity.

At the same time, however, Aristotle seems to be committed to the view that forms themselves, at least in the guise of definitions, are *mereologically complex*: the parts of form are repeatedly identified as the parts of definition, the genus and the differentia. This of course gives rise to the following difficulty: if form in fact has parts, and all mereologically complex objects that are genuinely unified must have their parts held together by means of some principle of unity, then what, if anything, could act as the *further* principle of unity which holds together the parts of form? Unless this quandary can be put to rest in some way, either by meeting it head-on or by rejecting some of its presuppositions, the unity of form is called into question and, with it, also that of matter/form compounds, which depend on form as their source of unity.[72]

---

[72] Moreover, the problem just described is still with us, even if we ascribe to Aristotle the view (despite his occasional apparent pronouncements to the contrary) that form and definition cannot literally be *identified* (in the contemporary metaphysician's sense of numerical identity): for definitions after all are plausibly construed as *linguistic* entities (comparable to, according to Aristotle, but nevertheless of course different from, say, literary works like *The Iliad*), while forms presumably are not plausibly so construed. In that case, then, it might seem that, since definition and form are not literally identical, we need not expect the mereological structure of the one to mirror exactly that of the other. Unfortunately, Aristotle puts obstacles in the way of this possible

At least in part to blame for Aristotle's ambivalent attitude concerning the mereological status of form is the conceptual connection he sets up right from the start between the notions, "one" and "indivisible into parts": for, given this link, only an object that is a true *mereological atom*, i.e., one that is indivisible relative to *all* conceivable measures by means of which other objects turn out to be mereologically complex, could ever put to rest the continued demand for further principles of unity, by claiming to have its unity in a primitive and underived manner. All other objects are found to be many or divisible into parts by some measure; and we may thus continue to ask about these objects from what source they derive their unity. There is thus, according to my reading, at least a strand within Aristotle according to which he has launched himself on a search for the ultimate mereological atom; and, despite the close ties between form and definition, there is evidence that Aristotle would like this search to end with form: on this view, form, and in general all things which are *without matter*, and which, for this reason, are viewed as *pure actuality*, are *simple*, and therefore lack all mereological and ontological complexity.

This suspicion is confirmed by consulting two crucial texts, which also constitute the most detailed development of *examples* of Aristotelian forms, viz., the discussion of the soul in *De Anima* and that of God in *Met.* Λ. In *Met.* Λ.7, for example, Aristotle is quite explicitly concerned to establish that God, the unmoved mover, is *without parts* (ἀμερής) and *indivisible* (ἀδιαίρετος), as the following passage illustrates:

> It is clear then from what has been said that there is a substance which is eternal and unmovable and separate from sensible things. It has been shown also that this substance cannot have any magnitude, but is *without parts* [ἀμερής] and *indivisible* [ἀδιαίρετος].
>
> (1073a3–7; my italics)

Moreover, Aristotle goes to considerable lengths to argue in *Met.* Λ.9 that the unmoved mover's activity (thought thinking itself) is directed at an object (the unmoved mover himself) which is not *composite* (σύνθετον):

> A further question is left—whether the object of the thought is *composite* [σύνθετον]; for if it were, thought would change in passing from *part* to *part* of the whole. We

escape route by endorsing a fairly strong *correspondence* principle between the *parts* of a definition or formula and the *parts* of the object described by it:

> Since a definition is a formula, and every formula has parts, and *as the formula is to the thing, so is the part of the formula to the part of the thing,* . . .
>
> (*Met.* Z.10, 1034b20–22)

Thus, the recognition that forms and definitions belong to distinct ontological categories (the latter being a linguistic entity, or formula (λόγος), the former being what is properly described by at least some of these linguistic constructions) therefore does not remove the worry concerning the unity of form, since Aristotle holds in addition that the association between forms and definitions requires that the mereological structure of definitions accurately reflect the mereological structure of the objects described by them.

answer that *everything which has not matter is indivisible*. As human thought, or rather the thought of composite objects, is in a certain period of time (for it does not possess the good at this moment or that, but its best, being something *different* from it, is attained only in a whole period of time), so throughout eternity is the thought which has *itself* for its object.

(1075a5–10; last two italics are Ross')

As this passage illustrates, Aristotle's rationale for viewing the unmoved mover as incomposite is quite general and can thus be read as applying to *all* form: form is incomposite and hence indivisible and without parts, he states, precisely because it is completely free of matter, i.e., pure actuality.[73] According to this reasoning, then, it is a thing's association with matter which leads to its mereological complexity.

On the face of it, Aristotle's discussion of the form of *non-divine* living things, i.e, the soul, in *De Anima*, seems to conflict with this reading, since he there does seem to speak quite overtly of the soul as having *parts*. For example, the human soul is said to have as parts the faculties responsible for nourishment and growth, locomotion, perception and thought. However, when we look more closely at the text, we see that, in contexts in which he is being careful about his choice of words, Aristotle in fact expresses some uneasiness concerning the practice of referring to these "powers", "potentialities" or "capacities" (δυνάμεις) of the human body as *parts* of the soul in the strict mereological sense. For example, in *DA* III.9–10, Aristotle explicitly worries that, if the faculties really were to be viewed as genuine parts, the soul would, as a result of this view, be divided into an absurdly large number of parts:

Those who distinguish parts [μέρη] in the soul, if they distinguish and divide in accordance with differences of power [δυνάμεις], find themselves with a very large number of parts, a nutritive, a sensitive, an intellective, a deliberative, and now an appetitive part; for these are more different from one another than the faculties of desire and passion.

(*DA* III.10, 433b1–4)

In fact, as the following passage from *DA* I.5 seems to indicate, one of the reasons for Aristotle's reluctance to consider the faculties of the soul as, strictly speaking, parts of it, is precisely his awareness of the potential regress that would result from a conception of the soul as itself mereologically complex:

Some hold that the soul is divisible [μεριστήν], and that we think with one part and desire with another. If, then, its nature admits of its being divided, what can it be that

---

[73] The current reasoning does not apply to mathematical objects which, according to Aristotle, have a kind of matter (viz., "intelligible matter"). Similar passages to the effect that entities without matter have their unity an underived primitive manner can also be found in *Met.* H.6, though there is some dispute among the commentators as to the exact nature of the entities Aristotle had in mind in this context (e.g., form/essence vs. the highest genera in the categories).

holds the parts together? Surely not the body; on the contrary it seems rather to be the soul that holds the body together; at any rate when the soul departs the body disintegrates and decays. If, then, there is something else which makes the soul one, this would have the best right to the name of soul, and we shall have to repeat for it the question: Is *it* one or multipartite? If it is one, why not at once admit that *the soul* is one? If it has parts, once more the question must be put: What holds *its* parts together, and so *ad infinitum*?

(411b5–14; Smith's italics)

This passage suggests that, despite Aristotle's loose way of speaking of powers as parts, he in fact takes it to be the best remedy against a potential regress of principles of unity simply to let the buck stop with form: if forms are mereologically simple, then the unity of the soul needs no further account, since it has no parts relative to any applicable measure.[74]

In sum, then, according to the reading I have suggested in the preceding paragraphs, both Aristotle's discussion of the unmoved mover in *Met. Λ* as well as, despite first appearances, his discussion of the soul in *De Anima*, confirms the suspicion that form, in contexts in which it is *not* thought of as the object represented in a definition, plays the role of the ultimate mereological atom within Aristotle's system; it is precisely because of its mereological simplicity that form can perform the crucial tasks of putting to rest the potential regress consisting in an endless demand for further principles of unity.

§VI.7 CONCLUDING REMARKS

The focus of this chapter has been Aristotle's theory of parthood and composition, particularly as it is laid out in two brief chapters in the "Philosophical Lexicon",

---

[74] Though this reading goes against the tenor of this passage, Aristotle could also be taken as suggesting another option: that the soul is mereologically complex and in fact contains a part which holds together the remaining parts. At least in the case of the human soul, the most plausible candidate for a part of the soul which could simultaneously act as the principle of unity holding together the remainder of the parts is of course the active intellect, which is discussed primarily in *DA* III.5. In a sense, this possibility merely brings us back to the preceding remarks concerning the incomposite nature of the unmoved mover, as described in *Met. Λ*: for Aristotle conceives of the active intellect as that faculty within us by means of which we most resemble God; though with some hesitation, he sometimes speaks of it as possibly separable from the body (and hence completely free of any association with matter) and is similarly concerned to establish (e.g., in *DA* III.6) that this faculty and its activity are not divisible into parts. This second option is thus not incompatible with my reading, but merely adds another layer of complexity to Aristotle's conception of high-level wholes or matter/form compounds: for it now turns out that those forms, which hold together the parts of a matter/form compound, are themselves hylomorphically complex and contain within themselves another principle of unity, a higher-order form, so to speak, which holds together the parts of the lower-level form. The search for the ultimate mereological atom, then, according to this second reading, does not end until we reach something which is completely free of any association with matter, viz., the higher-level form or principle of unity. Since it is not obvious, however, how we would account for the unity of form in the case of plants and non-human animals, on this reading (since they lack a God-like component in their souls), Aristotle might in fact be better served by taking the first route and letting the buck simply stop with form.

Book Δ of the *Metaphysics*. With the proper qualifications added, we found that Aristotle's account agrees in its main structural features with that developed by Plato, according to whom wholes have the following seven characteristics: they are (i) genuinely *unified*; (ii) *ontologically committing*; (iii) governed by a *restricted* notion of composition; (iv) comprised of the two components of *structure* and *content*; (v) ontologically *prior* to their parts; (vi) *normative* and *teleological* in nature; as well as (vii) inherently *intelligible* and the *proper objects of science*.

But we also encountered several important modifications and refinements Aristotle adds to the Platonic picture, with the result that the mereology Aristotle offers is enormously ambitious in its scope and complexity. To appreciate the intended reach and subtlety of the theory, one need only consider the range of entities that are to be accommodated by the theory and which are assigned a distinct status in it: definitions; shoes and human beings; music and language; ivy growing around a tree-trunk; bundles of wood; universals; as well as liquids and numbers.

Among the many ideas in Plato's writings on parts and wholes which Aristotle must have found attractive are, first, the close connection Plato discerns between the notions "part" and "measure"; and, secondly, the idea, suggested by the adjectival use of the term "whole", that a whole is in some sense not lacking any parts. Both of these ideas are incorporated and expanded by Aristotle into a conception of wholes that has the following main features. Unlike our contemporary usage of the term, a whole in Aristotle's view is not simply any object that has parts; for some mereologically complex objects are what he calls "totals" (e.g., liquids and numbers). Rather, a whole must satisfy the following conditions: (1) *Completeness*: a whole is a *complete* or *unmutilated* specimen of a kind; (2) *Unity*: its parts must be held together and made *one* by some principle of unity; and (3) *Position*: the *position* of the parts must make a difference to the existence and identity of the object in question. Since Aristotle takes the notions of "one" and "many" to be implicitly *relativized*, a single object can be, without contradiction, both one (or indivisible into parts) according to one measure and many (or divisible into parts) according to a distinct measure. Moreover, wholeness in Aristotle's view turns out to be a notion of *degree*, depending on the strength of the particular principle of unity which is at work in holding together the parts of an object, "wholeness being in fact a sort of oneness". The strongest principles of unity are those which result in wholes that are *continuous* (in the sense that their parts share boundaries) and, among those, the champion is *form*: wholes that are unified by a single form achieve such a high degree of unity that, in a particularly radical turn of Aristotle's theory, they in fact do not have any parts at all *actually*, but do so only *potentially*. His distinction between potentiality and actuality is among the main innovations Aristotle brings to bear on the Platonic theory of parthood and composition; along with the closely associated Homonymy Principle, this powerful device accounts for much of the teleological content that characterizes high-level Aristotelian wholes. The one feature with respect to which Aristotle's account departs most strongly from Plato's is in its separation of the mereology from the *epistemology*: being a whole, in Aristotle's view, does not automatically confer upon an entity an epistemically privileged status as inherently intelligible or the proper object of science; in fact, those wholes that have these features tend to be those which are least straightforwardly accommodated by his mereology.

Among the conceptual difficulties to which Aristotle's system gives rise, I singled out the following two in particular. First, due to the fact that his ontology is mereologically nested in multiple, complex ways, Aristotle incurs the risk of either having to abandon some of the non-negotiable formal properties of the part relation or of generating a proliferation of distinct, primitive, *sui generis* relations of parthood and composition, each governed by its own body of postulates. Secondly, even though forms in many ways play the starring role in Aristotle's metaphysics, their mereological status is, to put it mildly, quite unresolved. I suggested that, due to some of his theoretical commitments, Aristotle has launched himself on a search for the ultimate mereological atom, which will put to rest the continued demand for further principles of unity; the best candidate to end this search seems to be form, despite the fact that Aristotle is at the same time driven to view forms, in the guise of definitions, as mereologically complex.

Part Four

An Alternative Structure-Based Theory

VII

Objects as Structured Wholes

§VII.1 INTRODUCTORY REMARKS

It is time now to pull together the theory of parthood and composition which we have in effect been gradually building over the course of the previous six chapters. My strategy in what follows will be, first, to state in general terms the distinguishing features of the theory of parthood and composition which in my view best fulfills the demands we have encountered up to this point. Some of the missing details will be filled in in Chapter IX, when we turn in greater depth to the notion of structure and to some illustrations of particular kinds of structured wholes.

§VII.2 OUTLINES OF THE THEORY

§VII.2.1 Mereological Non-Proliferation: A Single Relation of Parthood

To avoid Fine's proliferation of primitive, *sui generis* relations, whose characteristics must be stipulatively imposed on them by means of distinct bodies of postulates, the present approach assumes a *single* notion of parthood, at least for the domain of material objects. This single notion is taken to satisfy at least the minimal formal requirements Simons views as constitutive of any genuinely mereological operation: proper parthood must be at least a strict partial ordering, governed by a supplementation principle of some kind, which we can for now assume to be the weakest possible one, the "Weak Supplementation Principle" (WSP), until our commitments concerning the Uniqueness of Composition are further clarified. The characteristics of proper parthood, which we can take as our single primitive notion, are thus captured by the following principles:

<u>Axiom 1</u> (Asymmetry):	$x<y \rightarrow \sim(y<x)$
<u>Axiom 2</u> (Transitivity):	$(x<y \ \& \ y<z) \rightarrow x<z$
<u>Axiom 3</u> (Weak Supplementation):	$(x<y) \rightarrow (\exists z) \, (z<y \ \& \ z \!\!\mid\!\! x)$

The *irreflexivity* of proper parthood follows from Axioms 1 and 2. The remaining mereological concepts of proper or improper part, overlap, disjointness, and the like, can be defined in terms of proper parthood in the standard fashion.

Recall that, according to the Weak Supplementation Principle, an object that has a proper part must have at least another proper part disjoint from the first. To make WSP more vivid, it may help to appeal to the notion of a *remainder*: thus, WSP dictates that, if a proper part were to be subtracted from a whole of which it is a proper part, a remainder, i.e., a proper part disjoint from the first, should be left over as a result of this operation of subtraction. Most philosophers are happy to accept a relation of proper parthood governed by WSP for the domain of material objects, as long as the presupposition is satisfied that material objects have only material parts; to these philosophers I now issue a warning that, later on in this chapter, WSP will turn out to play a crucial role in motivating the position that material objects have *formal* parts in addition to their ordinary material parts.[1] Those who object to this use of WSP on the grounds that they were willing to follow me in adopting the conception of parthood outlined above for the domain of material objects only as long as their presupposition was satisfied, should be reminded of the following two points from Chapter I.

First, since not every strict partial ordering can be interpreted as a relation of proper parthood, the question arises of what further formal properties distinguish proper parthood from other non-mereological strict partial orderings such as "is less than"; thus, those who do not regard WSP as minimally constitutive of the notion of proper parthood for material objects owe us an explanation of why we should interpret *their* strict partial ordering as a relation of proper parthood. Secondly, the plausibility of WSP as an additional formal constraint on the relation of proper parthood is further buttressed by the observation that WSP is the weakest possible addition to Axioms 1 and 2 by means of which the following two kinds of models can be ruled out: (i) models consisting of infinitely descending linear chains of objects whose proper parts are themselves proper parts of the objects' proper parts; (ii) models consisting of objects all of whose proper parts overlap each other. I take it that a relation which does not exclude both types of models is too weak to capture the mereological characteristics of ordinary material objects.

§VII.2.2 The Restricted Nature of Composition

One of the main points of departure between the current system and CEM is the Axiom of Unrestricted Composition, also referred to in Simons (1987) as the "General Sum Principle" (GSP):

Unrestricted Composition: Whenever there are some things, then there exists a fusion of those things.

---

[1] For an approach to mereology which also recognizes that material objects have non-material parts in addition to their ordinary material parts, see Paul (2002); in other respects, however, our accounts are quite dissimilar.

<u>Axiom 24</u> (General Sum Principle): $(\exists x) (F(x)) \rightarrow (\exists x)(\forall y) ((y \circ x) \leftrightarrow (\exists z) (F(z) \& (y \circ z)))$

GSP states that for any of the objects that satisfy the predicate in question, there exists a sum of these objects (provided that the predicate has a non-empty extension). Once Axiom 24 is added to Axioms 1, 2 and 3, the resulting system is formally equivalent to CEM and any of the possible weaker, intermediary assumptions concerning the conditional or unconditional existence of sums in finite or infinite models have thereby become redundant.

Composition, according to CEM, is thus not a very involved affair: it takes place whenever there is a plurality, *any* plurality, of objects, no matter what relations obtain or fail to obtain among these objects. In contrast, the current approach takes composition to be *restricted*: it occurs only when certain conditions are satisfied and the conditions in question of course concern, among other things, the *manner of arrangement* exhibited by any given plurality of objects; more generally, they require that the dictates of some particular formal components are satisfied. I will, for now, state the Restricted Composition Principle (RCP) in an overly simplified, timeless fashion which still leaves open many important questions to be addressed further below:

(RCP) <u>Restricted Composition</u> (First Version): Some objects, $m_1, \ldots, m_n$, compose an object, O, just in case $m_1, \ldots, m_n$, satisfy the constraints dictated by some formal components, $f_1, \ldots, f_n$.

Among the questions left open by RCP, for example, is the question of how exactly we ought to think about the formal components of objects. For one thing, RCP does not settle the *ontological category* to which the formal components of objects belong, i.e., whether they are themselves objects, whether they are properties or relations, or whether they belong to some other ontological category still. These questions will be discussed in more detail in Chapter IX below; for now, however, we may think of the formal components associated with a particular kind of whole, following Verity Harte's model as discussed in Chapter V, as the sorts of entities which provide "slots" to be filled by objects of a certain kind: thus, the formal components belonging to a particular kind of whole will generally specify not only the *configuration* to be exhibited by the material components in question, i.e., how these objects are to be arranged with respect to one another; they will also usually specify the *variety* of material components of which the whole in question may be composed, i.e., what sorts of objects can go into the various "slots" provided by the formal components.

RCP also leaves open the nature of the *mechanism* by which these sorts of constraints are imposed on the material components of a particular kind of whole. Clearly, according to the abundant conception of structure adopted by both Plato and Kit Fine, the restriction placed on composition by RCP would amount to no real restriction at all, since any plurality of objects whatsoever can be thought of as exhibiting some mathematical relation and any plurality of objects whatsoever can be thought of as the manifestation of some function-like principle which maps times onto objects. Even an explicitly added requirement of *spatio-temporal proximity* would not be strong enough to exclude pluralities of objects which are intuitively gerrymandered but happen to be connected in space and time: to use an example from van Inwagen (1990a), two people shaking hands, on such an approach, would compose a further object, for as long as they are engaged in the handshake, simply because their hands are touching. On the other hand, the more meaty conception of structure we encountered in Aristotle, according to which the formal components of each whole contribute their own localized teleological content, brings with it such controversial metaphysical machinery as the mysterious actual/potential distinction and its closely aligned Homonymy Principle. Thus, a middle ground of some sort, between Plato's and Fine's deflationary mathematical conception of structure and Aristotle's localized teleological conception, is called for.

§VII.2.3 An Ontology of Kinds

This middle ground, I propose, can be derived from a commitment to an ontology of *kinds*, which will be justified in more detail in the next chapter. According to this conception, a plurality of objects composes a whole of a particular kind, when the objects (material components) in question satisfy the selection requirements set by the formal components associated with wholes of that particular kind, e.g., requirements concerning, for example, the variety, configuration and sometimes even the number of parts out of which wholes of that particular kind may be composed. Due to considerations primarily from the philosophy of biology, which will concern us in the next chapter, the sort of conception of kinds which is assumed here is relatively minimal, in the sense that it presupposes neither that all members of a single kind will always share an *essence*; nor that it will always be possible to provide *necessary and sufficient conditions* for membership in a particular kind.[2,3]

---

[2] Both presuppositions may fail, for example, in the case of kinds which are more appropriately conceived of along the model of Wittgensteinian *family resemblances*, rather than in terms of essences and/or necessary and sufficient conditions for kind membership. Although neither essentialism about kinds nor the across-the-board availability of necessary and sufficient conditions determining kind membership is *presupposed* by the current account, nothing I say here *rules out* that either of these features obtains in at least some cases. Moreover, the question of whether members of a single kind share an essence is of course independent of the question of whether mereologically complex objects in general have *other* sorts of essential properties, i.e., properties which may not determine their membership in a kind but nevertheless belong to them essentially (e.g., origin-related properties, haecceities, and the like). In what follows, I intend to remain neutral on both of these questions.

[3] Despite the fact that the conception of kinds presupposed here is relatively minimal in the respects just outlined, it may perhaps be considered philosophically loaded in other respects. For I do presuppose that the kinds to which we are committed include those that are familiar to us and that these are embedded within a conception of space-time which is similarly familiar to us. If both of these fixed points are varied too much, as they might be, for example, by the sorts of exotic cases

§VII.2.4 Ontology and Mereology

The question of which kinds there are I take to be one that is not answered by the mereologist proper, but by the ontologist at large, in conjunction with other domains, such as science and common sense, which turn out to have something to contribute to the question, "What is there?", or, more specifically, to the question, "What *kinds* of objects are there?". In contrast, I take the mereologist's job to be to devise an appropriate conception of parthood and composition which accurately reflects the conditions of existence, spatio-temporal location and part/whole structure of those objects to which we take ourselves to be already committed as part of the presupposed scientifically informed, commonsense ontology. Thus, mereology, on this conception, does not settle matters of ontological commitment; rather, it presupposes them to be resolved elsewhere within metaphysics or outside of philosophy altogether.

In this division of labor between the tasks performed by mereology proper and ontology at large, my approach differs from the standard conception as well as from Fine's theory of embodiments, both of which view the mereologist as a specialized sort of ontologist, whose job it is precisely to tell us what mereologically complex objects (if any) the world contains. Standard mereology yields the highly *revisionary* answer that for each plurality of objects, no matter how disparate and dissimilar, the world contains a further object, their sum; the result is an ontology which, along with whatever entities are assumed to play the role of individuals, consists of a population of often intuitively gerrymandered composite entities, such as the notorious "trout-turkey", whose existence is not in any way recommended to us by evidence independent of CEM's predictions. Fine answers, in an even more revisionary vein, that for each principle of variable embodiment, which maps times in function-like manner to objects, the world contains a further object, a variable embodiment; since no apparent restrictions are placed on which function-like principles are suitable for this purpose, the result is an ontology that is exponentially even more abundant than that of standard mereology. In contrast, by presupposing that the question, "What mereologically complex objects (if any) are there?" is *descriptively* settled in the course of arriving at a scientifically and commonsensically acceptable ontology of kinds, the present approach assigns to the mereologist proper a more limited set of responsibilities directed at the characterization of those mereologically complex entities whose existence is already confirmed by independent evidence to which the mereologist must hold himself accountable.

presented to us in science fiction stories, then the mereology I am proposing may lose its foothold. In that sense, perhaps, my project may be considered to be conceptually local, in that worlds whose ontology of kinds and whose notion of space-time are very alien from the point of view of our world may require a different metaphysic. (Thanks to Elijah Millgram for bringing this point to my attention.)

§VII.2.5 Form and Matter

Next, I propose that we once more follow Plato and Aristotle in assuming that the world is best described by taking ordinary material objects to be mereologically and ontologically complex in the sense that they are composed of both material and formal components.[4] Given the present, non-teleological, construal of form, I take the primary job of an object's formal components to consist in the specification of a range of selection requirements that must be satisfied by a plurality of objects in order to compose a whole of a particular kind. We may thus think of an object's formal components as a sort of *recipe* for how to build wholes of that particular kind. An object's *material components* or *matter*, on the other hand, may be thought of as the *ingredients* that are called for in the recipe: they are the objects which, in a successful case of composition, in fact satisfy the conditions dictated by the formal components.

In the preceding remarks, we have, among the requirements set by the formal components of ordinary material objects, singled out in particular those that concern the *spatio-temporal proximity* and, more generally, the *manner of arrangement* that must be exhibited by an object's material components.[5] However, as we know from our discussion of Aristotle, formal components may also set additional constraints, for example, concerning the *variety*, and in some cases even the *number*, of material components from which a given whole may be composed. Exactly which requirements are specified by some given formal components of course depends on the kind of object under consideration and cannot be settled in abstraction from particular cases.

To use one of Aristotle's favorite illustrations, an ax, for example, must be made of materials that are sufficiently hard to allow the ax to retain its own material integrity while being able to affect that of other materials on which it is intended to be used; the requirements set by the formal components of an ax are specific enough to rule out, for example, liquids or gases, but they are not so specific as to select, say, a single kind of material, since various sorts

---

[4] There is a debate within Aristotle scholarship as to whether Aristotelian forms are best conceived of as universal, i.e., as shared by members of the same kind, or as particular, i.e., as specific to each object. However, even the forms-as-particulars camp agrees that there are universal forms shared by members of the same kind; the controversy is only over the question whether these universal forms are to be thought of as *constructed* out of particular forms, e.g., via some sort of classification by similarity, or whether, instead, the universal forms are irreducible, and particular forms (if there are such things) are to be thought of as constructed out of them. Since I earlier remained uncommitted on the question of whether each object has associated with it its very own body of essential properties that are specific to that particular object, I will similarly leave open, independently of how this matter is resolved in connection with Aristotle's texts, whether the formal components of objects are first and foremost particular and only derivatively universal.

[5] I take Aristotle's *position* requirement to be included within the manner-of-arrangement condition and will typically not list it separately: according to this requirement, wholes differ from the so-called "totals" in that the position of their parts matters to the existence and identity of the former but not the latter.

of metal and other sufficiently hard materials (such as stone) might do the job equally or comparably well.[6] Moreover, given the sorts of tasks for which an ax is intended to be used, its handle must of course, in some appropriately solid fashion, be attached, i.e., brought into close spatio-temporal proximity, to its blade; someone who is in possession of an unattached ax-blade and an unattached ax-handle may have all the ingredients needed to assemble an ax, but there is as of yet no ax until the handle and the blade have been properly fastened to one another.[7] More specific requirements concerning the variety, number, spatio-temporal proximity and configuration of the material components are set, for example, by the formal components which characterize H_2O molecules: these formal components dictate that a whole of this kind must be composed of a single oxygen atom and two hydrogen atoms, arranged in the particular configuration of chemical bonding, which requires the atoms in question to share electrons. Thus, while an object's formal components need not be very precise in the range of requirements they set for its material components, as is illustrated by axes and other macroscopic objects in our environment, they may in fact in other cases be quite precise, as is illustrated by the case of H_2O molecules just considered.

We can now reformulate RCP in the following, somewhat less open-ended manner, which of course still leaves undecided numerous important questions to be considered in more detail below:

(RCP) Restricted Composition (Second Version): Some objects, $m_1, \ldots, m_n$, compose an object, O, of kind, K, just in case $m_1, \ldots, m_n$, satisfy the constraints dictated by some formal components, $f_1, \ldots, f_n$, associated with objects of kind, K.[8, 9]

---

[6] Given the skepticism I have expressed above concerning the Homonymy Principle, we need not follow Aristotle in thinking that an ax made of, say, porcelain is an ax in name alone; another possibility would be to view such a thing simply as a *bad* or *useless* ax, relative to the purposes for which axes are created and compared to other axes that are available, but an ax nevertheless.

[7] Otherwise, we would be committed to the intuitively highly unattractive view that any given Home Depot store, say, contains among other things many actual houses, roofs, garages, bathrooms, sheds, and so on, simply because it contains all of the, as of yet unassembled, ingredients needed to build these objects. Whether objects, once created, remain in existence in a disassembled state depends on how the question of diachronic identity is resolved; as I point out below, in Section VII.2.10, the present account does not commit itself to any particular account concerning the identity of an object with itself over time.

[8] It is not necessary, in this context, to assume that the constraints dictated by any given formal components are altogether *unique* to the particular kind in question; a case in point might be the relation of chemical bonding which, when applied to distinct varieties of material components, yields wholes of distinct kinds. However, in such cases, the formal components in question will at least differ with respect to some of the *other* constraints they set, for example, concerning the variety or number of material components which may compose a given whole; otherwise, if the formal components of one object agreed in *all* respects with those of another, it is difficult to see on what basis these objects should be associated with distinct kinds at all.

[9] I say "*some* formal components", rather than "*the* formal components", since a given kind may be associated with different sets of selection requirements, e.g., if the kind in question falls into further subkinds or if the kind in question is best described along the lines of the Wittgensteinian family-resemblance model.

RCP, in this formulation, is to be read in light of the two assumptions just taken on board: first, that a mereology for ordinary material objects takes as its starting point a presupposed scientifically informed, commonsense ontology of kinds, which descriptively settles the question of what mereologically complex objects the world contains; and, secondly, that objects of a single kind have associated with them a set of formal components which act as a sort of recipe in specifying the parameters for how a whole of that particular kind may be constructed. Thus, composition, on the present restricted conception of it, takes place, first, only when the resulting whole would belong to a kind whose existence can be accommodated by the presupposed ontology; and, secondly, only when the recipe contained in the formal components associated with wholes of that kind has been followed, in the sense that the candidate plurality of objects is of the right number, variety and configuration to compose a whole of the particular kind under consideration.

§VII.2.6 An Ontology of Structured Wholes

The present approach attributes to *all* mereologically complex material objects the dichotomous nature Aristotle recognizes only in what we have earlier called "high-level wholes", viz., form/matter compounds like Socrates and the shoe.[10] It is a consequence of this approach, then, that the world contains only mereologically complex objects whose composition is not random, in the sense that only candidate pluralities of objects which meet more or less specific selection requirements can compose a whole of a particular kind. To spell out the selection requirements is the job of the *formal components* of a whole; to exhibit them is the job of the *material components*. Thus, all wholes, according to the present approach, are taken to consist of the two components of *structure* or *form*, on the one hand, and *content* or *matter*, on the other.

Content or matter, as we argued at the end of Chapter V, is best viewed as consisting of a domain of objects that are themselves already structured: this conception breaks down only when applied to a "first" level of composition (if there is such a thing), made up of entities that are not further composed of anything; however, since these ground-level entities are presumably not also mereologically complex, a theory which concerns the relation between wholes and their parts does not apply to them and is hence not violated by their non-dichotomous nature.

Structure or form has been tied to an ontology of kinds: each kind of object is taken to have associated with it a set of selection requirements which act as a recipe of sorts in specifying the range and configuration of material components eligible to compose a whole of that particular kind. We have, however, up to

---

[10] The possibility of this simplified ontology is one of the advantages that comes with a non-teleological approach to form.

this point left open the *ontological category* to which the formal components of objects are to be assigned, i.e., whether these entities belong to the category of objects, to that of properties and relations, or to some other category still. These issues will be investigated further and in more detail in Chapter IX.

Since it is of course in part an empirical question whether the world in fact consists of structured wholes of the kind described by the current approach, our only option in justifying the proposed conception of parthood and composition is to extrapolate from known and representative examples what shape a theory of mereologically complex objects must take. The account thus remains open to the following sorts of counterexamples: if a domain, which is deemed a legitimate contributor to the question, "What kinds of objects are there?", finds it necessary to posit a kind of mereologically complex object which lacks any of the structural characteristics that could plausibly be attributed to the presence of formal components within the whole in question, then we would have to conclude that the present theory of parthood and composition has not given an exhaustive characterization of the world's recognized population of mereologically complex objects. But the admission that such select cases of unstructured wholes cannot be ruled out in advance and on purely a priori grounds of course does not amount to anything nearly as strong as the thesis that mereologically complex objects in general are best analyzed in the manner of standard sums.

Standard mereology itself, however, cannot be thought of as providing such independent evidence for the existence of mereologically complex objects which, like sets, are free from the sorts of constraints that could be reasonably attributed to the presence of formal components within these objects: for mereological sums, according to the standard conception, need not satisfy any of the selection requirements concerning the variety, number or configuration of their parts; rather, their composition, as we pointed out earlier, is completely unconstrained and happens whenever there is *any* plurality of objects, regardless of what characteristics these objects bear and how these objects are related to one another. The only evidence a CEM-style theory can muster for the existence of standard sums in the present environment is that the best analysis of ordinary material objects overall is one which identifies these objects with standard mereological sums. But we have already encountered reasons for believing that CEM does not in fact yield the best overall analysis of ordinary material objects: for standard mereology does not have the resources to capture properly the conditions of existence and spatio-temporal location as well as the part/whole structure of ordinary material objects; moreover, its commitment to arbitrary sums leaves us with an ontology populated, among other things, with objects which tend to be excluded from the range of our quantifiers, except while we are engaged in technical metaphysical discussions of parthood and composition, and whose existence is not justified by means of evidence independent of CEM's predictions. Thus, there are no reasons coming from CEM itself to think that the world contains mereological sums, according to the standard conception; and there are plenty of reasons against accepting CEM as the correct tool for the analysis of ordinary material objects. Unless, then, we are independently moved to recognize a category of objects whose composition is as unconstrained as that of standard mereological sums, we may proceed on the assumption, which is in fact confirmed by independent evidence, that the world is instead populated by mereologically complex objects that have the characteristics of structured wholes.[11]

§VII.2.7 The Dichotomous Nature of Wholes

In line with the "wholes as *composed* of structure" model discussed in Chapter V, the present approach adopts a thoroughly *mereological* conception of composition: both the material components and the formal components of a whole, on this view, are taken to be *proper parts* of it. Depending on the ontological category to which the formal components of objects are found to belong, this thoroughly mereological conception of composition may strike us as the most radical aspect of the current approach; it is, however, recommended by the following considerations.

§VII.2.7.1 Material Components as Proper Parts

That the relation between a structured whole and its *material* components is that of parthood I take to be fairly obvious and uncontroversial. For one thing, mereologically complex objects do not come into existence *ex nihilo* and, besides the agency of their creator (where applicable), their material components are intuitively that *from* which these wholes come into existence. Consider, for example, a table which is brought into existence by assembling four legs, a top and an assortment of screws, nuts and bolts, and other hardware. These pre-existing ingredients are of course by themselves not sufficient to bring the table into existence, since they may exist without the table existing (and possibly vice versa, depending on the sorts of changes the table in question can sustain with respect to its material composition);[12] but they are nevertheless what we would point to, besides the agency of the carpenter, as those elements within the

---

[11] Even such objects as heaps of sand or portions of rice, assuming they are in fact to be counted as part of our scientifically informed commonsense ontology, do not conform to the modally rigid profile of standard sums. While we would ordinarily consider a heap of sand which has gained or lost a few grains to be *the same* heap as the earlier one, we would *not* consider it to be the same heap, or a heap at all for that matter, if the sand were to be scattered. Thus, even such "low-level" wholes as heaps of sand or portions of rice exhibit a certain amount of structural complexity and hence deserve to have attributed to them a set of formal components, whose job it is to tell us how the remaining components must be arranged, for the same reasons that motivated us to do so in the case of axes and the like.

[12] More generally, the table and its material components do not share all of their properties and hence, as Aristotle remarks as well, cannot be viewed as numerically identical. This Leibniz's Law-style argument for the numerical distinctness between a whole and its material components is of course not completely uncontroversial and has been argued for separately in Chapter IV (see also Koslicki 2005a for a defense of this reading of Leibniz's Law-style arguments for numerical distinctness). By Leibniz's Law, I mean the following *metaphysical* principle concerning objects,

world of space-time which the process of bringing the table into existence takes as its most obvious starting point. Since the process of assembling the table in the normal case only changes the ingredients' non-essential relational characteristics, there is no reason to think, given the persistence conditions we ordinarily ascribe to these objects, that they cease to exist merely as a result of being rearranged. For example, it seems plainly compatible with the persistence conditions of the two pieces of wood, which we describe (looking towards the future) as a table-leg and a table-top, that the two may come into closer proximity to one another.[13] Thus, unless there is additional evidence to the effect that the pre-existing ingredients are somehow destroyed during the process of assembling the table, it is thus natural to view them as still maintaining a "presence" of some sort within the resulting table; the most obvious way in which their continued "presence" within the resulting table may be understood is by appeal to the notion of parthood.

Furthermore, unless we recognize at least the ingredients as components, i.e., proper parts, of the resulting table, the close connection between the characteristics of the ingredients and those of the resulting table becomes utterly mysterious. To illustrate, if the top, the four legs and the hardware together weigh thirty pounds, and nothing else is added or taken away during the process of assembling the table, then the resulting table can be expected to weigh thirty pounds. Moreover, the connection between the combined weight of the ingredients and that of the resulting table is in no way accidental; for wholes in general inherit such properties as their weight from the material components which compose them. Thus, in explaining the striking similarity between (certain of) the characteristics of the table on (certain of) the characteristics of its ingredients, it is again helpful to appeal to the fact that the ingredients continue to "live on" within the table, as components of it, and are thus able to pass some of their characteristics on to the whole which they come to compose. The relation between these characteristics of the table and the corresponding characteristics of the ingredients then becomes analogous to that between, say, me and my hands: *I* have ten fingers, because *my hands*, which are part of me, do; and it is not the case that together we have twenty.[14]

Thirdly, to deny that even the material components of the table are proper parts of it (while simultaneously holding the objects in question to be numerically

properties and relations: for all objects, x and y, if x and y are numerically identical, then x and y are qualitatively indiscernible. This metaphysical principle is not to be confused with a *linguistic* principle concerning the substitutivity of co-referential expressions, which is often called by the same name and sometimes even taken to be the very same principle as that governing objects, properties and relations. The principle I am calling "Leibniz's Law" is also not to be confused with the much more controversial metaphysical principle known as the "Identity of Indiscernibles", according to which objects that are qualitatively indiscernible are numerically identical; I do not intend to commit myself to the truth of this latter principle and nothing I say forces such a commitment.

[13] This assumption would be disputed by Michael Burke; see note 16 for more details.

[14] The supervenience-like dependence principle that is at work here is explored in more detail in Koslicki (2004a).

distinct) would commit us to a sort of coincidence which, if at all possible, is best avoided. For such a view would force us to subscribe to the thesis that two (or more) numerically distinct material objects, neither of which is a proper part of the other and which share many of their parts, can occupy a single region of space-time.[15] If, on the other hand, its material components are taken to be proper parts of the table, then the sort of coincidence that obtains between them is of the same benign nature as that which holds, say, between a man and his forearm: the man inhabits the region of space-time occupied by his forearm by virtue of having a part, viz., the forearm, which occupies the region of space-time in question; though the two objects are numerically distinct, the sort of spatio-temporal coincidence which obtains between them does not strike us as resulting in any sort of overcrowding. The reason for our relaxed attitude towards this sort of coincidence is that one of the objects in question is a proper part of the other.

Thus, among the overwhelming evidence in favor of taking the material components of a whole to be among its proper parts are the following considerations: (i) first, the pre-existing ingredients, which come to be the material components of a whole, are, besides the agency of its creator (where applicable), the most obvious candidates within the world of space-time for what processes of generation take as their starting point; (ii) secondly, the thesis that the material components of a whole are among its proper parts points the way towards an attractive account of the striking similarities between wholes and their material components, namely one which traces this sort of property inheritance to the more general case of mereological supervenience or dependence, according to which (certain of) the characteristics of a whole derive from (certain of) those of its parts; (iii) finally, the spatio-temporal coincidence between wholes and

---

[15] In fact, many accounts in the literature maintain that numerically distinct, spatio-temporally coincident objects, such as the statue and the clay which constitutes it, share *all* of their parts; see, for example, Thomson (1983, 1998) for a representative version of this widespread view. It is, however, puzzling how the thesis that spatio-temporally coincident objects share all of their parts can be combined with the view that such objects are non-identical, as it frequently is. For consider the relation which obtains, say, between the nose of a statue and the nose-shaped piece of clay which occupies the same region of space-time as it. Surely, the relation between the statue-nose and the nose-shaped piece of clay is exactly the same as that which holds between the whole statue and the whole statue-shaped piece of clay of which they are part, namely just the relation known as *constitution* (i.e., the relation between a thing and what it is made of). But, in that case, it seems that someone who holds that the nose-shaped piece of clay is identical to the statue-nose (i.e., that this is a part they share) should, for the sake of consistency, take constitution generally to be identity. If the nose-shaped piece of clay and the statue-nose it constitutes are distinct, however, then it is not obvious why we should take the piece of clay to have the statue-nose (as opposed to the nose-shaped piece of clay coincident with it) as a part. After all, if the parts in question are distinct, their distinctness presumably has to do, at least in part, with the modal differences between them; but, in that case, it no longer seems plausible to attribute a part to the statue-shaped piece of clay which has the persistence conditions of the statue-nose, as opposed to those of the nose-shaped piece of clay coincident with it. The precise connection between the relation of constitution and the mereological relation of composition, which has been our main concern so far, will be elucidated further below.

their material components can now be assimilated to the benign, mereological manifestation of this phenomenon exhibited, say, by a man and his forearm.

§VII.2.7.2 Formal Components as Proper Parts

There are thus good reasons for wanting to view at least the material components of the table as proper parts of it. But now suppose that it is possible to create a new object out of just a single pre-existing ingredient. A possible illustration of such a scenario may be drawn from cases which exhibit the relation commonly referred to as *constitution*, viz., the relation which is said to obtain between a thing and what it is made of. Suppose, for example, that the world contains objects which belong to the kind, *lump of clay*, and objects which belong to the kind, *statue*; then, nothing seems to stand in the way of creating, for example, a new statue out of just a single pre-existing ingredient, a lump of clay, merely by rearranging the clay's parts. Since a change of this sort is compatible with the persistence conditions we ordinarily attribute to lumps of clay, there is no reason to think that the lump ceases to exist merely as a result of having been rearranged.[16]

What *more*, then, could there be to the statue besides the lump of clay which constitutes it and with which it shares a single region of space-time? It is of course tempting simply to identify the statue and the lump of clay which constitutes it, given that the objects in question occupy exactly the same region of space-time and are strikingly similar to each other in many other respects, such as their weight, shape, texture, color, chemical composition, and so on.[17] On the other hand, we also know that, whenever two objects are constitutionally related,[18] there are some properties with respect to which they appear to differ; e.g., certain modal properties (such as the property of being able to survive squashing) and, typically, certain temporal properties (such as the property of having come into existence after the lump of clay came into existence or before the statue came

---

[16] A possible example of the kind of case I have in mind from the realm of living things would be a zygote which constitutes a human being. As mentioned earlier, this assumption would be disputed by Michael Burke, who has, in a series of papers, argued for the thesis that the lump of clay which constitutes the statue is numerically distinct from the lump of clay which exists before or after the statue exists, since the first lump of clay is *also* a statue (and hence numerically identical with the statue with which it shares a region of space-time) while the latter is *merely* a lump of clay and not also a statue (see especially Burke 1992, 1994a and 1994b). However, I take it to be among of the most powerful objections against this view that it depends on attributing to objects persistence conditions which are radically different from those ordinarily ascribed to them; moreover, it is difficult to see how this shift in the attribution of persistence conditions could be motivated on independent grounds.

[17] Versions of the view that constitution is identity include the following: eliminativism (Unger 1979; van Inwagen 1990a); identity relativized to time (Gallois 1990, 1998; Myro 1986); identity relativized to sort (Deutsch 1998; Geach 1962, 1967; Griffin 1977; Gupta 1980); four-dimensionalism (Cartwright 1975; Forbes 1987; Heller 1984, 1990; Lewis 1983a, 1986b; Perry 1972; Quine 1950; Sider 1997, 2001); contingent identity (Gibbard 1975; Lewis 1968, 1986b); and dominant kinds (Burke 1992, 1994a, 1994b).

[18] An object, x, and an object, y, are *constitutionally related* just in case either x constitutes y or y constitutes x.

into existence). Among the characteristics apparently not shared by the statue and the lump of clay is also the property of being constituted by a lump of clay, which, intuitively, is a property had by the statue but not the lump of clay. By Leibniz's Law, then, we seem to arrive at the conclusion that objects that are constitutionally related must be numerically distinct, since they do not share all of their properties.[19]

Suppose that this Leibniz's Law-style argument for the numerical distinctness of constitutionally related objects is cogent; then, in the case at hand, in which a mereologically complex object consists of just a single material component, the following explanation of their numerical distinctness is actually *dictated* to us by our endorsement of the Weak Supplementation Principle, which was earlier taken to be partially constitutive of the meaning of "is a proper part of": by WSP, we know that the *something extra* which distinguishes the statue from the lump of clay that constitutes it must in fact be an additional *part*; for, according to this principle, an object which has a proper part must consist of *other* proper parts in addition, which supplement the first.[20] Since there is overwhelming evidence

---

[19] Defenders of the thesis that constitutionally related objects are numerically distinct include the following: Baker (1997, 1999, 2000); Doepke (1982); Fine (1982); Johnston (1992); Locke (1975); Lowe (1989, 1995); Oderberg (1996); Simons (1987); Stone (1987); Thomson (1983, 1998); Wiggins (1968, 1980); and Yablo (1987).

[20] In Chapter IV, I cited the following objection to this use of WSP, due to Kit Fine (p.c.). Assume for the sake of the argument (very controversially, of course), that sets have their members (and nothing else) as *proper parts*; then, Socrates and his singleton set would present us with a violation of WSP: for Socrates' singleton set is numerically distinct from Socrates, has Socrates as a proper part, but has no proper parts besides this one. Now consider a set which does satisfy WSP by having more than a single proper part, e.g., the set containing Socrates and Plato. If, so Fine reasons, we found the relation between a set and its members puzzling to begin with, then this mystery presumably is not resolved by the presence of an additional member: for example, the presence of Plato in the two-membered set consisting of Plato and Socrates does not help us understand the relation between a set and its members any better than we already did by considering Socrates and his singleton set. For this reason, Fine suggests, nothing is lost by giving up WSP, which in his view should be rejected in any event on independent grounds (see the example involving continuous time-intervals, to which I reply that such a domain may very well require a partial ordering whose formal properties are quite distinct from those of the parthood relation which governs ordinary material objects).

But Fine's objection turns on the fact that Socrates and Plato are, by the standards relevant to the case at hand, objects of the *same kind*, viz., they are both *members* of the sets in question. I agree that adding more objects of the same kind does not elucidate the relation between a whole and its parts; this of course was also Aristotle's point in the regress argument of *Met*. Z.17. But, according to the present conception, the additional parts which help to explain the nature of the relation between a whole and its remaining proper parts belong to a *different kind*, viz., they are formal components which act as a sort of recipe in specifying the range and configuration of material components eligible to compose a whole of that particular kind. Thus, if the current theory were to be extended to the domain of set theory, it would predict that Socrates' singleton set does not violate WSP, since it has additional parts (though not additional *members*) besides Socrates, viz., its formal components, whose nature is presumably spelled out by reference to the axioms of set theory. Whether this kind of account does in fact properly characterize the mereological properties of sets is of course a difficult question, which would need to be pursued in much greater detail; it does, however, at least in principle hold more promise than to construe the formation of singletons as an utterly mysterious process (see Lewis 1991).

in favor of the thesis that the lump of clay, i.e., its single material component, is a proper part of the statue, we must now look for additional proper parts within the statue besides its single material component: the most likely candidates for these additional proper parts are of course those elements of the whole to which we have been referring as its "formal components". Thus, assuming WSP and the cogency of Leibniz's Law-style arguments for the numerical distinctness of wholes and their material components, we arrive at the conclusion that the formal components of a whole as well must be counted among its proper parts; on the basis of this reasoning, then, I propose the following Neo-Aristotelian Thesis (NAT) concerning the dichotomous nature of mereologically complex objects:

(NAT) <u>Neo-Aristotelian Thesis:</u> The material and formal components of a mereologically complex object are *proper parts* of the whole they compose.

In the more general case, in which a whole consists of more than just a single material component, NAT is not forced upon us directly by our acceptance of WSP in conjunction with the Leibniz's Law-style arguments for the numerical distinctness of wholes and their material components. However, given that we have taken the relation between a whole and its formal components to be that of proper parthood in the special case just considered, in which a whole consists of just a single material component, it is of course natural to extend this hybrid conception to the more general case as well: for there is no good reason to treat the relation between a whole and its formal components any differently, depending on the number of material components of which it consists. Moreover, the extension of NAT to the general case has, among other things, the following advantage.

By means of NAT, we may arrive at an attractive *mereological* solution to the so-called "Grounding Problem", which challenges those of us who believe in numerically distinct, spatio-temporally coincident objects to say what *grounds* the differences between objects that are otherwise so alike.[21] For, given the dichotomous nature of wholes, the differences between a whole and its material components, on this account, may in general be explained by pointing to additional *parts* which distinguish the whole from its material components, viz., its formal components. Without the availability of this sort of explanation for the numerical distinctness between a mereologically complex object and its spatio-temporally coincident material components, it is not clear how else this difference may be grounded; it is not surprising, then, that the Grounding Problem has proven to be quite intractable to those who allow for numerically distinct, spatio-temporally coincident objects which share *all* of their parts (see especially Bennett 2004b for useful discussion of this point).

---

[21] The Grounding Problem is explored, for example, in Sosa (1987), Heller (1990), Burke (1992), Zimmerman (1995), Olson (2001) and Bennett (2004b).

To illustrate, consider again the table. According to the present mereological solution to the Grounding Problem, the numerical distinctness between the table and its material components can be traced to the fact that the table has associated with it additional, formal components, which are not shared by the material components and which act as a sort of recipe in specifying the range and configuration of material components eligible to compose a whole of this kind. The formal components of a table, for example, speak to both the variety of material components from which a whole of this kind may be composed as well as their manner of arrangement: as a result of the process of assembly, which is required to bring the table into existence, the table's material components come to bear an array of functional relational characteristics which they did not exhibit before the assembly, and which they *need* not exhibit, given the persistence conditions we ordinarily attribute to these objects; for example, the legs come to be arranged with respect to the top in such a way that they can now stably suspend the top above the ground, with the result that objects deposited on the newly created table are at a comfortable reaching level for the table's users. The fact that these relational characteristics come to obtain among the table's material components is the most minimal, relevant difference between the state of the world *just before* the table comes into existence and the state of the world *just after* the table comes into existence.[22]

As a consequence of the assumptions already endorsed up to this point, it now *follows* that the world does not contain numerically distinct, spatio-temporally coincident wholes which share exactly the same parts: for NAT, in conjunction with the assumption that objects of distinct kinds have distinct formal components, yields the result that there could not be two or more numerically distinct, spatio-temporally coincident objects which belong to *distinct kinds* and which share all of their parts: rather, it is predicted that such objects will always

---

[22] It might be objected at this point that my account is not really in a better position with respect to the Grounding Problem than those of my competitors. (Thanks to Karen Bennett and other members of the Princeton philosophical community for pushing me on this point.) For if the real philosophical challenge posed by the Grounding Problem is to account for the difference in the *modal profile* present in numerically distinct spatio-temporally coincident objects, then the verdict on whether the Grounding Problem has been solved is still out, until we know more about the formal components from which the mereological difference noted above is supposed to issue. For clearly the nature of an object's formal components, and hence its modal profile, is not dictated by its material components, since these are shared between numerically distinct spatio-temporally coincident objects whose modal profile is not the same. Thus, unless the formal components attributed to an object can help to *explain* why the object has the modal profile that it does (so the objection goes), the difference in parts pointed to above provides a response to the Grounding Problem only in letter but not in spirit. I concede that this objection raises a fair challenge for my account and ask that my readers defer their assessment of whether a difference in parts of the sort noted above can ultimately solve the Grounding Problem until the nature of the formal components has been further clarified in Chapter IX; to that extent, whatever advantage I now claim for my position resulting from its response to the Grounding Problem should be considered *conditional* on whether the promise of explaining the difference in modal profile at issue can be made good on below.

differ with respect to some of their proper parts, viz., their formal components.[23] In other words, violations of the truth of the *Uniqueness of Composition* are ruled out as a consequence of the presupposed ontology of kinds, in conjunction with the hybrid conception of mereologically complex objects:

Uniqueness of Composition: It never happens that two numerically distinct wholes have exactly the same parts.

It is therefore not necessary, given our other commitments, to assume the stronger Uniqueness Principle as Axiom 3 in place of the weaker WSP.

To summarize, then, this section has presented further arguments in favor of a thoroughly mereological conception of composition, based on the following assumptions: (i) that, by Leibniz's Law, wholes are numerically distinct from their material components; (ii) that there is overwhelming evidence in favor of taking the material components of a whole to be among its proper parts; (iii) that it is possible, as in cases of constitution, to create a new mereologically complex object out of just a single material component; and (iv) that the Weak Supplementation Principle is partially constitutive of the meaning of "is a proper part of".[24] On the basis of these assumptions, I argued that the relation between the formal components of a whole and the whole they partially compose must be the same as that between a whole and its material components, viz., that of proper parthood. In the special case described in assumption (iii), in which a mereologically complex object is composed of just a single material component, this conclusion follows directly from the remaining assumptions, (i), (ii) and (iv). The extension to the general case, I suggested, is recommended, first, by considerations of symmetry; secondly, it is recommended by the fact that this strategy may yield an attractive mereological solution to the so-called Grounding Problem, which challenges us to say what grounds the differences between numerically distinct, spatio-temporally coincident objects. On the basis of these considerations, then, I conclude that the dichotomous nature of wholes is correctly captured by NAT. The Uniqueness of Composition is preserved within this system, without having to be assumed as an axiom in place of WSP.

§VII.2.7.3 Material and Formal Components as Proper Parts

In addition to the advantages already cited, the following considerations provide further support in favor of NAT. First, a uniformly mereological conception of composition helps to *clarify* the nature of the relation which obtains between a whole and its formal and material components.[25] Our inquiry into the part/whole

---

[23] I assume that the possibility of *same-kind* coincidence is in any case excluded on the basis of independent considerations (see, for example, Oderberg 1996 for discussion).

[24] Arguments in favor of assumption (ii) have already presented; assumption (i) has been argued for separately in Chapter III; assumptions (iii) and (iv) I take to be pretheoretically plausible.

[25] Recall, in this connection, that we raised a similar point in Chapter IV, in the context of Fine's theory of variable embodiments: unless we are explicitly told, by means of an additional postulate,

properties of ordinary material objects has led us towards a structure-based theory of parthood and composition; given this mereology, the question now arises of how each object is related to its structural component as well as to those of its components which exhibit the structural characteristics in question. Since our overall aim is to give an *account* of ordinary material objects, and to do so without commitment to a proliferation of distinct notions of composition, the relation between a whole and its material and formal components ideally should not be taken as an unanalyzed, non-mereological primitive.[26]

Moreover, the thoroughly mereological approach to composition outlined in NAT contributes to the solution of a long-standing problem in metaphysics, the so-called "Problem of Constitution", which challenges us to give an analysis of the relation that holds between an object and what it is made of, e.g., a statue and the lump of clay which constitutes it. The relation of constitution has resisted straightforward analysis because it confronts us with the following dilemma.[27]

As noted earlier, whenever objects are constitutionally related, the objects in question share a striking number of properties; e.g., a statue and the lump of clay which constitutes it occupy the same region of space-time and they have the same weight, texture, chemical composition, color, and so on. Given the striking similarity between constitutionally related objects, it is tempting simply to identify them. If constitution is identity, then no further explanation for the striking similarity between constitutionally related objects is called for; rather, the difficulty now becomes to explain the apparent differences between them. For whenever objects are constitutionally related, there are also some properties which they appear not to share; for example, certain modal properties (e.g., the property of being essentially a statue) and, typically, certain temporal properties (e.g., the property of having come into existence before the statue came into existence). As noted earlier, among the characteristics apparently not shared by the statue and the lump of clay is also the property of being constituted by a lump of clay, which, intuitively, is a property had by the statue but not the piece of clay. Thus, a satisfying account of the apparent differences between constitutionally related objects must also make room for the powerful intuition that constitution, in the sense in which this notion is of interest to us, is an *asymmetrical* relation, while identity is of course symmetrical.

If, on the other hand, the statue and the lump of clay constituting it are viewed as numerically distinct objects which occupy the same region of space-time, we should expect some elucidation of the intimate relation which holds between these objects. After all, since numerical identity is not a relation that admits

---

what the relation is between a variable embodiment and its principle, Fine cannot claim to have met his goal of providing a "theory of the general nature of material things".

[26] I am here alluding to the strategy taken by David Armstrong; see, for example, Armstrong (1989, p. 91 ff).

[27] My take on the Problem of Constitution is explained more fully in Koslicki (2004a).

of degrees, the statue and the lump of clay constituting it, according to this approach, are as distinct from one another as, say, the Eiffel Tower and the planet Jupiter. How, then, is it that two numerically distinct objects can be so closely related and share so many fundamental properties? Moreover, since distinctness is of course as symmetrical as identity, the thesis that constitutionally related objects are numerically distinct by itself is not enough to account for the asymmetry of the constitution relation.

The Problem of Constitution thus challenges us to provide an analysis of the constitution relation which accounts for both the striking similarities as well as the apparent differences between constitutionally related objects. With the help of NAT, we may offer the following attractive *mereological* analysis of constitution:

(MAC) Mereological Analysis of Constitution: Some objects, $m_1, \ldots, m_n$, *constitute* an object, O, just in case $m_1, \ldots, m_n$ are O's *material components*, i.e., $m_1, \ldots, m_n$ are those among O's *proper parts* which satisfy the constraints dictated by O's *formal components*, $f_1, \ldots, f_n$.

Following MAC, constitution now becomes a *species* of the mereological notion of composition, which in turn is just the reverse of parthood: for constitution, on this approach, is analyzed as the relation which a whole bears to certain *specific* ones among its proper parts, viz., its material components; the relation of composition, on the other hand, holds more generally between a whole and all of its parts, including its formal components: all of its proper parts together *compose* a whole, but only its material components *constitute* it. Among the useful consequences of this approach is that it immediately gives rise to a very straightforward account of the *asymmetry* of the constitution relation: constitution, according to the present approach, is asymmetric because the relation of *proper parthood* is.[28]

The mereological solution to the Problem of Constitution outlined in MAC addresses both the striking similarities as well as the apparent differences between constitutionally related objects in a satisfyingly symmetrical manner. The similarities between constitutionally related objects, on this account, are due to the fact that wholes derive some of their characteristics from their material components. The differences between constitutionally related objects, on the other hand, are due to the fact that wholes inherit other characteristics from their remaining

[28] Most extant solutions to the Problem of Constitution do not have the resources needed to capture the asymmetry of the constitution relation. The four-dimensionalist approach, however, fares even worse than that, since in many cases it in fact *reverses* the directionality of the constitution relation in the following sense (see, for example, Lewis 1986b; Sider 2001): whenever the lump of clay outlives the statue it constitutes, the space-time-worm associated with the statue is only a subportion of the space-time-worm associated with the lump of clay that constitutes it; in other words, four-dimensionalist solutions to the Problem of Constitution actually predict that, in such cases, the *statue* is in fact a proper part of the *lump of clay* which constitutes it, and not vice versa.

proper parts, viz., their formal components.[29] In both cases, however, the presence of certain characteristics within a mereologically complex object can be explained by appeal to a supervenience-like dependence principle of a particular *mereological* variety: according to the present account, the characteristics of a mereologically complex object in general derive either from its material components or from its formal components. In this way, NAT explains in a nicely symmetrical way why mereologically complex objects in general have the characteristics they do, both those which they share with their material components and those with respect to which they differ from their material components. This concludes my case for a thoroughly mereological conception of composition, according to which the material and formal components of a mereologically complex objects are proper parts of the whole they compose.

§VII.2.8 The Hierarchical Nature of Composition

Given that we have assumed a single transitive part-relation for the domain of material objects, it is a consequence of NAT that mereologically complex objects are hybrid all the way through. Consider once again the table which, we said, is composed of some material components (the legs, top and hardware), arranged in the manner dictated by the table's formal components; it is the job of these latter components to specify the variety and configuration which must be exhibited by the material components out of which a whole of this kind may be composed. Consider now a proper part of (a proper part of. . .) one of the table's material components, e.g., a single molecule which might be, say, a proper part of (a proper part of. . .) one of the table's legs. By the transitivity of parthood, the single molecule in question is a proper part of the table as well.

If tables are hybrid objects, consisting of formal and material components, then so are molecules, since the same considerations apply in both cases. For the relation between a molecule and the particles which constitute it is exactly the same as that which holds between a table's material components and the table itself: the molecule and the particles that constitute it occupy the same region of space-time, but they do not share all of their properties (e.g., the particles might exist before or after the molecule exists; they need not constitute the molecule in question; etc.); moreover, it is integral to the existence and identity of the molecule that the particles which constitute it are of a particular variety

---

[29] Given my earlier assumptions concerning the formal components of a given whole, the properties that can be accounted for by means of the mereological-supervenience principle hinted at in the text similarly only include those which a whole shares with at least some of the other objects which belong to the same kind. In the event that an object has associated with it a body of particularized modal properties that are specific to that object, the notion of a formal component could be reconceived to accommodate those sorts of differences as well between a whole and its material components; however, these particularized modal properties of course could no longer have as their source the kinds to which the objects in question belong. I will not speculate as to what (if any) their source might be instead.

and exhibit a particular configuration associated with objects of this particular kind. The same considerations which motivated us to recognize within the table a certain amount of structural complexity, which we traced to the presence of additional components within the table over and above its material components, therefore apply with the same force to molecules as well. More generally, the material components of mereologically complex objects, as well as their material components'... material components, can themselves be expected to exhibit the same dichotomous nature as the wholes of which they are part.

Only objects (if there are any) which lie at the very bottom of the compositional hierarchy, i.e., objects which are not themselves constituted by anything, would present us with an exception to this generalization: if there are any such things, they would be non-hybrid; or, at least, the considerations which led us to ascribe a hybrid nature to such objects as tables would not apply to this special case. For the job of an object's formal components is to specify the variety and configuration that must be exhibited by an object's material components in order for a whole of this kind to exist; but an object that is not constituted by anything has no material components, and hence no proper parts that must be of a certain variety and configuration.

As long as we confine ourselves to the case of mereologically complex objects, however, the considerations which motivated us to adopt NAT are general: they apply to such microscopic objects as molecules just as much as they apply to such macroscopic objects as tables. By NAT, the formal and material components of a molecule are proper parts of the whole they compose; and, by the transitivity of parthood, the molecule's formal and material components in turn are also proper parts of the table which they help to compose. But it is implausible to think that the *molecule's* formal components are among the structural features that are associated with object that belong to the kind, *table*, since considerations involving for example relations between protons, neutrons and electrons and the physical and chemical characteristics that go along with these relations play no role in the primarily functional requirements set on potential table ingredients. For this reason, a distinction between two different sorts of formal components suggests itself: (i) those that are directly associated with the kind to which a whole belongs, which we may term *formal components simpliciter*; and (ii) those that are the formal components *simpliciter* of some of a whole's material components, which we may term *derivative formal components*. Only formal components of the first variety play a role in specifying how the material components of a table, say, must be put together in order for there to be on object of this particular kind; thus, only formal components *simpliciter* are relevant to the Restricted Composition Principle, leading to the following reformulation of RCP:

(RCP) <u>Restricted Composition</u> (Third Version): Some objects, $m_1, \ldots, m_n$, compose an object, O, of kind, K, just in case $m_1, \ldots, m_n$, satisfy the constraints dictated by some formal components *simpliciter*, $f_1, \ldots, f_n$, associated with objects of kind, K.

Thus, the formal constraints operative among the proper parts of a mereologically complex object cannot in general be assumed to transfer to the formal components *simpliciter* associated with the wholes of which they are proper parts, though there may be special cases in which the parts and the whole are structurally isomorphic; nevertheless, by NAT and the transitivity of parthood, both sorts of structural features are among the proper parts of the whole whose material components they organize. In this sense, then, mereologically complex objects, according to the present approach, are hybrid through and through: each mereologically complex object consists of formal and material components, which in turn, if they are themselves mereologically complex, display the same dichotomous structure as the whole they help to compose.

§VII.2.9　Change over Time

Ordinary material objects plainly are capable of persisting through change over time with respect to some of their characteristics. Thus, Socrates may at one time be sitting and at another time standing; and he may have less hair at one time than he does at another. The phenomenon of change over time has turned out to be difficult to account for: it appears to present us with violations of Leibniz's Law, viz., scenarios in which (what looks to be) a single object both has and does not have (what looks to be) a single property. The "Problem of Change over Time" thus consists in the demand for an account of where to locate the obvious sensitivity to time that is manifested in these sorts of property attributions.

The two main rival approaches to the Problem of Change over Time are *three-dimensionalism* (also known as *endurantism*) and *four-dimensionalism* (also known as *perdurantism* or *the doctrine of temporal parts*).[30, 31] According to the four-dimensionalist, the Problem of Change over Time is solved by conceiving of objects as themselves relativized to time: our familiar concrete objects of common sense, on this approach, turn out to have a temporal dimension in addition to their three spatial dimensions. Thus, when one and the same persisting object, O, changes over time with respect to a property, F, it does so by having a temporal part, O_1, at one time which instantiates the single property in question and a

---

[30] For proponents of the four-dimensionalist position, see for example: Armstrong (1980b); Cartwright (1975); Heller (1984, 1990); Jubien (1993); Lewis (1983a, 1986b); Quine (1950, 1960); Russell (1914, 1927); Sider (1996, 1997, 2001). Proponents of the three-dimensionalist position include: Baker (1997, 2000); Burke (1992, 1994a, 1994b); Chisholm (1976); Haslanger (1985, 1989a, 1989b, 1994a); Johnston (1987, 1992); Lowe (1987, 1989); Oderberg (1993, 1996); Simons (1987); Thomson (1983, 1998); van Inwagen (1990b); Wiggins (1968, 1980); Zimmerman (1995). (A more complete list of reference can be found in Sider 2001, p. 3.)

[31] The distinction between "perdurance" and "endurance" comes from David Lewis (e.g., Lewis 1986b, p. 202), who attributes it to Mark Johnston.

distinct temporal part, O_2, at another time which fails to do so; since O_1 and O_2 are numerically distinct objects, there is no contradiction involved in O_1's having F and O_2's lacking F. The three-dimensionalist, on the other hand, builds the sensitivity to time into the property, F, or O's instantiation of it: thus, when a single three-dimensional object, O, changes over time with respect to (what appears to be) a single property, F, the single object in question, according to the three-dimensionalist, has-F-at-t and fails to have-F-at-t′; but for a single object both to have-F-at-t and not to have-F-at-t′ is as non-contradictory as, say, being both large and not blue. (There are different ways for the three-dimensionalist to build the sensitivity to time into the property, F, or O's instantiation of it; but I will not at present enter into the details of this debate.)

Suppose that some three-dimensionalist solution to the Problem of Change over Time is feasible.[32] Then, we may think of the structured wholes at work in the current analysis as enduring, three-dimensional objects which may change over time in various respects without threat of contradiction. One of the ways in which a structured whole may change over time is by tolerating the addition, alteration or loss of some of its material components. The table, for example, given the persistence conditions ordinarily ascribed to objects of this kind, need not be constituted of the same legs, the same top or the same hardware throughout its career; the legs, top and hardware in turn need not be constituted of exactly the same wood and metal throughout their career; and so forth. (Of course, there is a certain amount of fuzziness, brought out by Ship-of-Theseus-style puzzles, in just how dramatically an object can change with respect to its material components; but the difficulties raised by the apparent indeterminacy in an object's criteria of identity over time need not concern us here.)

Similarly, there is of course an endless variety of ways in which the *general* formal requirements that come with wholes of a specific kind may be manifested in particular objects at particular times; and, depending on the persistence conditions which characterize the objects in question, one and the same mereologically complex object may well tolerate a fair share of structural change in this regard. Thus, the material components of which an H_2O molecule consists, viz., the two hydrogen atoms and the single oxygen atom, must always exhibit the relation of chemical bonding, for as long as they compose an H_2O molecule; but the *specific way* in which they exhibit this configuration of chemical bonding may vary over time, without affecting the existence or identity of the whole in question.[33] In light of these considerations, then, we ought to think of the formal components, as they have been described up to this point, as something

---

[32] As noted earlier, the nature of persistence over time, which is at issue in the debate between the three-dimensionalist and the four-dimensionalist, is not among the main topics of the present discussion, which is cast within a three-dimensionalist framework (but see Koslicki 2003a for arguments in favor of this position).

[33] The quantum-mechanical state of an H_2O molecule is such that the bonds (i.e., the shared electrons) between the two hydrogen atoms and the single oxygen atom that compose the H_2O

closer to *determinables*, of which particular *determinates* are represented in a mereologically complex object at each time at which it exists. To what extent structural change is permitted either with respect to the determinable or the determinate manifestation of an object's formal components depends on the persistence conditions that are operative in the particular case at hand.

Given that this discussion is set in a three-dimensionalist framework, we will follow the three-dimensionalist's general strategy of accommodating the phenomenon of change over time by relativizing property instantiation to time in some fashion: in this particular case, the specific instance of this general strategy calls for relativizing the part relation to time. Since we assumed parthood as our single mereological primitive, a temporalized part relation has the effect of temporalizing all other mereological notions that are defined in terms of it as well, e.g., those of composition and constitution. In the following reformulations of the relevant principles, our new primitive relation, $<_t$, is to be read as "is a proper part of at time t"; similarly, $\mathord{|}_t$, reads "is discrete from at time t"; the superscript "T" indicates that the principle in question has been temporalized:

Axiom 1^T (Asymmetry): $x <_t y \rightarrow \sim(y <_t x)$

Axiom 2^T (Transitivity): $(x <_t y \mathbin{\&} y <_t z) \rightarrow x <_t z$

Axiom 3^T (Weak Supplementation): $(x <_t y) \rightarrow (\exists z)(z <_t y \mathbin{\&} z \mathord{|}_t x)$

(RCP^T) <u>Restricted Composition (Fourth Version)</u>: Some objects, $m_1, \ldots, m_n$, compose an object, O, of kind, K, at a time t just in case $m_1, \ldots, m_n$, satisfy at t the constraints dictated by some formal components *simpliciter*, $f_1, \ldots, f_n$, associated with objects of kind, K.

(NAT^T) <u>Neo-Aristotelian Thesis</u>: The material and formal components which compose a mereologically complex object at a time t are at t *proper parts* of the whole they compose at t.

<u>Uniqueness of Composition^T</u>: It never happens that two numerically distinct wholes have exactly the same parts at a single time t.

(MAC^T) <u>Mereological Analysis of Constitution</u>: Some objects, $m_1, \ldots, m_n$, *constitute* an object, O, at a time t just in case $m_1, \ldots, m_n$ are at t O's *material components*, i.e., $m_1, \ldots, m_n$ are at t those among O's *proper parts* which at t satisfy the constraints dictated by O's *formal components*, $f_1, \ldots, f_n$.

These temporalized formulations of the relevant principles are only intended to show *that* the phenomenon of change over time can be straightforwardly accommodated by the present analysis in the standard three-dimensionalist

---

molecule are always vibrating, so that the positions of the atoms in question are not fixed. (Thanks to my chemistry consultant, Andrew Loxley, for discussion on this point.)

fashion; the question of what sorts of changes are possible for particular objects is of course one that cannot be answered without appeal to the persistence conditions specific to the case at hand.

§VII.2.10 Synchronic and Diachronic Identity

If a whole may tolerate changes in both its material and, to some extent, its formal composition, we may wonder what then accounts for its *diachronic* identity, i.e., the identity of an object with itself *over time*. The analogous question concerning an object's *synchronic* identity, i.e., its identity *at a time*, can be answered simply by appeal to the Uniqueness of Composition, which yields one half of a biconditional whose other half is supplied by Leibniz's Law:

Synchronic Identity:

An object, x, and an object, y, are *synchronically identical* at some time t iff x and y share all of their parts at t.

But it is not true that an object, x, and an object y, that are *diachronically identical* must share *all* of their parts *over time*, since the object in question may have changed with respect to its parts in the intervening time. Moreover, the identity of an object with itself over time also cannot be traced simply to the fact that at every time at which the object exists it exhibits some particular manifestation of the same general formal components, since the same will be true of other objects which belong to the same kind.[34]

Since the current approach is not addressed directly to the question of how to account for the identity of an object with itself over time, the resources provided by it by themselves do not yield an account of diachronic identity. Surely, in Aristotelian terms, this phenomenon must in some fashion involve the manner in which each manifestation of a given set of formal components is passed on from one collection of material components at one time to another such collection at another time. If the correct analysis of identity over time is one that appeals to *spatio-temporal continuity*, then this idea may be invoked here as well to account for the connection that must obtain between an object's material components at one time and the same object's material components at a different time. If, on the other hand, spatio-temporal continuity is rejected by the three-dimensionalist in favor of another account of diachronic identity, then presumably we have maintained a sufficient degree of neutrality to be able to make room for such an alternative account.

---

[34] In Fine (1994c), we are confronted with the following sort of puzzle for the Aristotelian: suppose that (through some sort of process of migration) the matter of which Socrates is composed at a certain time, t, is exactly the same as the matter of which Aristotle is composed at a later time, t′. If forms are construed as universal, then Aristotle at t′ is composed of both the same matter and the same form as Socrates was at t; and yet, we nevertheless want to say that the two are numerically distinct. What, then, accounts for their distinctness? Fine's puzzle may be construed as an argument in favor of a particularized conception of Aristotelian forms.

§VII.2.11 Composition as Non-Identity

In the previous sections, we have already aligned ourselves explicitly with the Platonic and Aristotelian models of parthood and composition with respect to feature (iii), the *restricted* notion of composition, as well as feature (iv), the *dichotomous* conception of wholes as composed of *structure* or *form*, on the one hand, and *content* or *matter*, on the other. Next, we similarly follow these ancient mereologies with respect to feature (ii), the *ontologically committing* conception of wholes.

Like Plato and Aristotle, the present approach opposes the Eleatic/Lewisian Composition-as-Identity model and takes composition to be genuinely committing: wholes are in no way to be identified with their parts; rather, a commitment to wholes is a commitment to entities numerically distinct from their proper parts. Moreover, since the present approach does away with standard mereological sums and rules out violations of the Uniqueness of Composition, any given collection of objects composes, if anything, only a single whole; this precludes an allegedly ontologically innocent conception of composition which identifies wholes with the *sums* of their parts, as construed in the standard sense.

The evidence in support of this ontologically loaded conception of wholes is two-fold. First, on the negative side, it is supported by considerations which count against the Composition-as-Identity Thesis.[35] Secondly, on the positive side, the case for an ontologically loaded conception of wholes turns on the cogency of Leibniz's Law-style arguments in favor of the numerical distinctness of wholes and their parts: by Leibniz's Law, wholes and their parts are numerically distinct, because they do not share all of their properties (e.g., for one thing, the parts typically do, but the whole does not, exist prior to the creation of the whole). Arguments of this sort have played a pivotal role in the preceding sections and have been defended separately in Chapter III.

§VII.2.12 The Unified Nature of Wholes

Finally, I want to comment on feature (i) of the Platonic and Aristotelian model of parthood and composition, viz., the genuinely *unified* nature of wholes. As was brought out in our discussion of these ancient mereologies in Chapters V and VI, among the most central concerns of Plato's and Aristotle's mereological writings is the desire to provide a satisfying response to what we have termed the "Problem of the One and the Many", which challenges us to say how an object

---

[35] The contemporary, Lewisian, version of the Composition-as-Identity Thesis was briefly discussed in Chapter II; see also the references cited therein. The ancient, Eleatic, version of the same view is subjected to extensive scrutiny and criticism by Plato and was briefly discussed in Chapter V; see Harte (2002) for a more detailed treatment of what she terms the "negative mereological undercurrent" within Plato's writings.

that is mereologically complex, i.e., has *many* parts, can nevertheless be *one* or *unified* in some fashion. Following some early flirtations with the Pluralizing Parts Principle and the ontologically innocent Eleatic/Lewisian Composition-as-Identity model, Plato's more mature mereology takes wholes to be unqualifiedly one, despite the fact that they have many parts; the element present in the whole which holds together the many parts and which bestows on the object in question its normative and teleological character is "structure" or what is expressible in mathematical terms (number, measure, ratio, proportion, and the like). Despite the rich and suggestive detail the Platonic account offers in terms of which to *describe* particular cases of composition, however, we were reluctant to credit this account with a fully general *solution* to the Problem of the One and the Many, since it does not explicitly address the question, except insofar as it invokes a centralized and seemingly theological teleology, of why particular mathematical relations, when they obtain among pluralities of objects, give rise to genuinely unified wholes, while others apparently do not.

Aristotle goes further in this respect and proposes, first, to *relativize* the notions of unity and plurality, so that a single object can be both one (i.e., indivisible into parts) and many (i.e., divisible into parts) simultaneously and without contradiction, relative to different measures; moreover, wholeness (being a species of oneness), in his view, comes in *degrees*, depending on the strength of the principle of unity operative in particular cases. Aristotle's answer to the question of how something that has many parts can nevertheless be one thus in effect yields a hierarchy or ranking of objects, ranging from the least unified (viz., the so-called "totals", e.g., liquids and numbers) to the most unified (viz., Aristotelian forms); matter/form compounds, heaps and universals comprise the intervening cases. Depending on the ontological category to which an object belongs, the principles of unity at work in holding the parts of these objects together correspondingly differ widely: for example, the principle of unity holding together the parts of a heap may be anything that enforces physical contact, i.e., the sharing of boundaries, among its parts (e.g., a band holding together some wooden sticks); the parts of a universal (e.g., animal or living thing) are held together by the qualitative similarity under which these objects may be grouped; finally, the strongest principle of unity of all is form, which unifies matter/form compounds (e.g. Socrates or the shoe) to such an extent that these objects have no parts at all *actually*, but do so only *potentially*.

Despite the amazingly subtle and ambitious mereology with which this account presents us, we also noted that Aristotle in some ways backs himself into a corner by accepting certain assumptions which he thinks are needed to solve the Problem of the One and the Many. First and foremost among them are the following two: (i) the conceptual connection he sets up right from the start between *unity* and *indivisibility* into parts; and (ii) the principle that a mereologically complex object must always derive its unity from some *source*, which in turn must be unified to a *higher degree* than the object it unifies. These two assumptions together threaten to lead to a never-ending demand for further principles of unity and in the end launch Aristotle on his search for the ultimate mereological atom: for only something that is indivisible relative to every conceivable measure, by claiming to have its unity in a primitive and underived manner, could ever put to rest the potential regress to which (i) and (ii) appear to give rise. I argued in Chapter VI that, with some ambivalence, Aristotle takes form to play the role of the ultimate mereological atom within his system, on the basis of the general principle that things that have no association with matter (and hence are pure actuality) are not divisible into parts by any measure, though this strategy conflicts with other central metaphysical commitments that are dear to him, most notably the association between form and definition, the latter of which is generally assumed by Aristotle to be mereologically complex.

In response to the difficulties to which the Aristotelian account gives rise, I recommend that we ask ourselves, first, whether the assumptions in (i) and (ii) are even particularly plausible and, secondly, whether they are in fact necessary for a solution to the Problem of the One and the Many; once we realize that neither is the case, we will see that the Problem of the One and the Many does not require the drastic measures to which Aristotle finds himself driven. Consider, first, the conceptual connection Aristotle sets up between the notions of unity and indivisibility: according to this conception of unity, something's being *one* according to some measure (i.e., its being one *something-or-other*, where the concept used to fill the slot marked by the phrase "something-or-other" supplies the measure in question) is taken to amount to its being not further divisible into parts according to the measure in question; in fact, the lack of divisibility seems to be identified by Aristotle as the reason for the object's status as a unified thing with respect to the measure at hand. Thus, to illustrate, recall an example we used early on in Chapter VI: "ba" is taken to be *one* (syllable) because it is *indivisible* into parts relative to the measure "syllable"; it is *many* (letters) because it is *divisible* into parts relative to the measure "letter".

And while oneness and indivisibility may line up in this way in very many cases, Aristotle's close conceptual connection between these two notions in fact runs into trouble when applied across the board.[36] For it is not difficult to think

[36] Examples of the sort that follow are also used in Koslicki (1997) and (1999a) to make related points as they arise in the context of the so-called "mass/count distinction", a linguistic distinction marked by a wide range of languages which represents the difference between what we *count* and what we merely *measure*. Count nouns are almost universally regarded as being semantically different from mass nouns in that their referents are indivisible into further parts by means of the measure supplied by the count noun (or the concept associated with the noun): thus, the noun, "human being", for example, which is standardly used as a count noun, applies to objects that are *a* or *one* human being; and, as in Aristotle's case, something's being *a* or *one* human being is taken to coincide with its being not further divisible into parts relative to the measure "human being". The semantic properties in question are sometimes called "atomicity" (since the extension of a count noun is thought to consist of mereological atoms relative to the term in question) and "non-distributivity" (since it is not the case that *every* part of something that satisfies a count noun

of cases in which it is perfectly natural to call something *a* or *one* something-or-other, even when the object in question is further divisible into objects of the same kind: for example, a building may be composed of proper parts which are themselves buildings; a particular pattern may be composed of proper parts which are themselves patterns (in fact, the objects in question may even be instances of the *same* pattern, only on a smaller scale); many strings in the alphabet, {"a", "b"}, are composed of proper parts which are themselves also strings in the same alphabet; a journey may be composed of smaller journeys; and so on.[37] In each case, the fact that an object is further divisible into proper parts which satisfy the same concept is no obstacle to its counting as *one* something-or-other, relative to the measure in question. Given the naturalness and intelligibility of cases of this sort, the connection between unity and indivisibility can at most be regarded as a useful rule of thumb, but not as a conceptual truth which correctly describes the domain of objects to which our practices of counting and individuation are directed.

Consider now the second crucial assumption driving the Aristotelian response to the Problem of the One and the Many, viz., the principle that a mereologically complex object must always derive its unity from some *source* which in turn must be unified to a *higher degree* than the object it unifies.[38] Again, there is at least in principle no reason why something that in itself has a relatively low degree of unity should not be able, when coming into contact with objects of the right kind, to unify these objects to a higher degree than the degree of unity possessed by itself or by any of the participating objects prior to this association. For example, imagine a particular kind of glue which is chemically quite unstable (i.e., in the sense that it has a high propensity to disintegrate into its components), except when it is brought into contact with particular substances, such as wood

itself also satisfies the noun in question, i.e., the noun does not *distribute* over proper parts of what it applies to). For reasons similar to those brought up in the main text, I don't believe that properties like atomicity and distributivity can be used to mark the semantic contrast between mass and count nouns; see Koslicki (1997, 1999a and 2006a) for further discussion.

[37] The example, strings in the alphabet, {"a", "b"}, comes from Cartwright (1994); the case of journeys was brought to my attention by Andrew Loxley; thanks also to Leopold Stubenberg for helpful discussion in connection with the issues brought up in this and the next few paragraphs.

[38] Halper (1989, p. 154) cites in this connection the following passage from *Met. α*, as suggesting a general principle from which it follows that the cause of unity must be unified to a *higher* degree than the objects it unifies:

Now we do not know a truth without its cause; and a thing has a quality in a higher degree than other things if in virtue of it the similar quality belongs to the other things (e.g. fire is the hottest of things; for it is the cause of the heat of all other things); so that that which causes derivative truths to be true is most true. (*Met. α*.1, 993b24–26)

This assumption incidentally is also reminiscent of a similar principle employed in Descartes' cosmological argument for the existence of God, according to which that which causes other objects to have a certain quality must always itself exhibit the quality in question to a higher degree than the objects which derive this quality from it; similar examples are used by Descartes to illustrate the principle in question (e.g., fire must be hotter than the objects which are heated by it, and so on).

or paper, in which case the glue and these substances together result in something whose parts hang together much more tightly than did the parts of either object taken by itself.

Thus, it seems that neither of Aristotle's two central assumptions represents a conceptual truth concerning the connection between the notions of unity and indivisibility into parts. Rather, an object apparently can be *one* something-or-other, relative to some measure, even when it is further divisible into proper parts which satisfy the same measure; moreover, there is no reason in principle to expect that the parts of a mereologically complex object must be held together by a principle of unity which possesses a higher degree of unity than that which it contributes to the whole it unifies. Given these results, then, we ought, first, to separate the notion of oneness or unity from that of indivisibility; and we ought, secondly, to abandon the expectation that principles of unity must themselves either be mereologically simple relative to any conceivable measure or that they be, for whatever reason, otherwise highly unified.

Once we realize that Aristotle's two crucial assumptions are in fact neither particularly plausible nor necessary for the solution of the Problem of the One and the Many, other strategies suggest themselves by means of which we may address the challenge posed by this problem, viz., to say how an object can be *one* despite the fact that it has *many* parts. Among the central innovations introduced by the Aristotelian account of parthood and composition is the move to *relativize* the notion of unity (and, correlatively, that of plurality) to particular measures: to be *one* or *unified*, for Aristotle, is always to be one *something-or-other*, where the concept substituted for the phrase "something-or-other" supplies the measure which is applied to the object in question. Given the presupposed ontology of kinds, to be unified relative to some measure in effect simply amounts to being a particular specimen of a kind: to be unified with respect to the measure "syllable", for example, simply amounts to being *one* syllable, i.e., being *one* specimen of the kind *syllable*.

Now recall the earlier separation we induced between the responsibilities of the mereologist in particular and the ontologist at large: the ontologist at large, in conjunction with whatever other disciplines are relevant to this task, settles questions of ontological commitment, in particular the question, "What *kinds* of objects are there?"; the tasks of the mereologist proper, on the other hand, include that of devising an appropriate theory of parthood and composition which correctly reflects the characteristics of those objects to which we take ourselves to be already committed as part of our presupposed scientifically informed, commonsense ontology. In this and the preceding chapters, we have defended the thesis that the theory which best reflects the conditions of existence and spatio-temporal location as well as the part/whole structure of these objects is one which attributes to them a dichotomous nature, consisting of both formal or structural components, alongside their more ordinary, material, components.

The more restricted conception of mereology, along with the presupposed ontology of kinds and the structure-based theory of parthood and composition, together now yield all the apparatus needed to solve the Problem of the One and the Many. For recall that ordinary material objects were taken to be both mereologically and ontologically complex, in the sense that they are composed of both material and formal components; the primary job of an object's formal components, moreover, is to act as a sort of *recipe* in specifying a range of selection requirements which must be satisfied by an object's material components, whose primary role was compared to that of the *ingredients* called for in the recipe. In a successful case of composition, then, a plurality of objects in fact satisfies the requirements specified by some formal components associated with a particular kind, K; the result of this convergence is a new specimen of the kind in question, i.e., an object that is *one* or *unified* relative to the measure supplied by the particular kind at hand.

Nothing more *needs* to be said or *could* be said to lay to rest the challenge contained in the Problem of the One and the Many. For the mereologist, after all, is not attempting to answer the question of *why* there are objects of a particular kind; depending on the kind under discussion, this question, in any event, is more appropriately directed to some discipline outside of philosophy, such as cosmology.[39] Assuming, on the other hand, that, for whatever reason, there *are* objects of the particular kind in question, then it should come as no surprise that one of them has come into existence, when a particular plurality of objects satisfies the requirements for how to "build" an object of this kind. To illustrate, specimens of the kind H_2O *molecule* come into existence when two hydrogen atoms and one oxygen atom enter into a particular configuration of chemical bonding: objects of this kind are *unified* in the sense that they are *one* specimen of the kind in question, i.e., *one* relative to the measure "H_2O molecule"; their material components hang together to the degree that hydrogen and oxygen atoms, which enter into the relation of chemical bonding, can be expected to do so. That an object which counts as *one* or *unified* relative to

[39] Why, for example, are there H_2O molecules? Presumably, the non-philosopher's answer to this question would make reference to the laws of nature, the Big Bang (or whatever other initial state of the universe turns out to be accepted by our best scientific theory) and the complex intervening processes that led to the formation of molecules. An answer of this kind is directed to the question of what conditions were required to obtain to make the formation of such objects possible and to sustain their continued existence. Neither the mereologist nor the ontologist at large can be expected to have anything of interest to contribute to this question.

the measure "H_2O molecule" has parts at all, poses no threat to its status as a particular specimen of the kind in question: rather, given what we know about the chemical composition of H_2O molecules, nothing could be one specimen of this kind or unified relative to this particular measure without having as parts at least two hydrogen atoms and one oxygen atom. Given that this is just what it means to be an H_2O molecule, there is nothing further that the mereologist proper or the ontologist at large can add to what the scientist has already told us about the chemical composition of objects of this kind. The mereologist *can*, however, be held responsible for the task of devising a theory of parthood and composition which is responsive to the fact that there can be no H_2O molecule, unless a particular plurality of objects satisfies the formal requirements as to number, variety and configuration associated with this kind of whole.[40]

§VII.3 CONCLUDING REMARKS

As I hope to have demonstrated in this chapter, a structure-based neo-Aristotelian mereology for ordinary material objects can be defended utilizing a single relation of parthood with relatively straightforward formal properties. A substantive restriction on composition can be derived from a comparatively minimal and metaphysically neutral ontology of kinds; this commitment to kinds, furthermore, is not expected to spring out of the mereology itself, but is to be justified using independent considerations from other disciplines within or outside of philosophy altogether. One of my central aims in this chapter concerned the thoroughly mereological conception of composition which, I have argued, recommends itself based on Leibniz's Law and the Weak Supplementation Principle. This thoroughly mereological conception of composition brings with it certain advantages: it yields the Uniqueness of Composition as a derived

---

[40] In addition to the neo-Aristotelian regress just discussed, one may wonder also whether my account is susceptible to what one may term a neo-Bradleyan regress of the following sort. Suppose a structured whole, X, consists of two material components, Y and Z, as well as a formal component, F. According to my account, then, Y, Z and F are all proper parts of X; the job of F is to unify Y and Z. But how is it that F is "linked", so to speak, to Y and Z? Is there a need for two further formal components, F* and F+, whose job it is to "link" F to Y and Z, respectively? But this is like asking whether, in order to make a quantity of glue, G, bind together two pieces of paper, P* and P+, we need two further quantities of glue, G* and G+, whose job it is to bind together G with P* and P+, respectively; nothing of the sort is required, if the first type of glue is of the right kind to react chemically with paper. Similarly, to bind together a bundle of sticks with a rope, it is not necessary to bind the rope to each stick with another rope; one piece of rope will do just fine for the whole bundle. Moreover, whether or not the principles of unity are to be regarded as proper parts of the resulting whole, as they are according to my approach, does not in any way affect their power to bind together other elements composing the whole: for example, assume that the screws holding together the four table-legs and the table-top are without question proper parts of the resulting table; their mereological status with respect to the table does not in any way lower their capability of holding together the remaining components of the table.

principle; it generates a, to my mind, satisfying response to the Problem of Constitution; it indicates a promising direction to pursue with respect to the Grounding Problem; moreover, it clarifies the relation between a whole and both its material and its structural components, which otherwise remains opaque. Finally, I have tried to suggest how, on the approach defended here, wholes can be thought of as both ontologically committing and genuinely unified, despite the apparent Aristotelian regress caused by a never-ending demand for further principles of unity.

VIII

In Defense of Kinds

§VIII.1 INTRODUCTORY REMARKS

An important piece of the theory of parthood and composition, which was presented in outline in the preceding chapter, is the restricted composition principle (RCP), which carried with it an as of yet unjustified commitment to an ontology of kinds: a plurality of objects was said to compose a whole of a particular kind, when the objects (material components) in question satisfy the selection requirements set by the formal components associated with wholes of that particular kind, i.e., requirements concerning, among other things, the variety, configuration and sometimes the number of parts out of which wholes of that particular kind may be composed. Such a restriction on composition, of course, only has plausibility if there are independent reasons for thinking that objects really do belong to kinds and that kinds really do pose constraints on the mereological composition of their members.

The aim of the current chapter is to defend this commitment to an ontology of kinds at least for the particular case of *natural kinds*. Although there may well be good reasons to believe in other kinds as well, and the considerations used to motivate a belief in the existence of natural kinds cannot in general be expected to transfer straightforwardly to these other categories, I nevertheless restrict myself for the time being to the special case of natural kinds for the following reasons. First, this focus will make the task at hand more manageable than it would otherwise be, since a more general and in-depth discussion of kinds would surely require its own book-length treatment. Secondly, the literature on natural kinds and natural kind terms is quite developed and wide-ranging, and the interesting results which have been reached by those working in this area can be usefully applied to our present investigation. Thirdly, by examining the special case of natural kinds, I hope at least to provide a model for the sort of reasoning which may be invoked to justify a commitment to a particular class of kinds.

I should also warn the reader right up front that this chapter cannot possibly claim to answer all the interesting questions that arise in connection with natural kinds and natural kind terms. This topic has of course generated a vast literature in the last few decades and interconnects many different areas of philosophy. Rather, I am in this chapter merely, as it were, picking my way through a minefield and selecting the theory of natural kinds and natural kind terms that seems best-suited to advance my overall theory. Many questions, in the course of this discussion, will remain open and await more extensive and in-depth treatment in their own right.

§VIII.2 WHAT ARE NATURAL KINDS?

Kinds are categories or taxonomic classifications into which particular objects may be grouped on the basis of shared characteristics of some sort. Judging from the name, one might expect *natural* kinds (if indeed there are any) to reflect those categories which are, in some sense, present in *nature*; in that case, the intended contrast would presumably be with *artificial* kinds which are, in some sense, created by us and are therefore dependent on human activities, cultures, intentions, goals, interests, conventions, and the like. However, as pointed out by LaPorte (2004) and others, there are kinds that are to be found in nature (e.g., *weed* or *shrub*), which most would agree are too heterogeneous to count as genuine natural kinds; and there are kinds, samples of which may be man-made (e.g., *insulin* or *diamond*), which are nevertheless plausibly viewed as natural. Thus, the "natural"/"non-natural" distinction is more profitably construed as pointing to the contrast between what is *arbitrary* (*heterogeneous, gerrymandered*) and what is not, rather than the contrast between what is to be found in nature and what is man-made (more on this below).[1]

Since very little in this area can be taken for granted pretheoretically, it is best to start off, as is customary, with a list of examples, along with some commentary. Common examples of natural kinds one comes across in the literature include both classifications that are part of our ordinary vocabulary (e.g., *tiger, lemon* and *salt*) as well as ones that are dealt with by the various scientific disciplines, which may or may not have been incorporated into the language of the non-specialist (e.g., *Tyrannosaurus rex, liliaceae,*[2] *jadeite,*[3] *planet, electron* and *hydrogen*), though individual writers disagree over the status of our

---

[1] See LaPorte (2004, ch. 1). Ian Hacking reports that while the expression "Kind" (with a capital "K"), was introduced into English philosophy in 1843 by John Stuart Mill in his *A System of Logic*, the phrase "natural kind" was coined in 1866 by John Venn in *The Logic of Chance*; it was then reintroduced into English philosophy in 1948 by Russell in *Human Knowledge: Its Scope and Limits*. (See Hacking 1991 for more on the history of kinds.)

[2] "*Liliaceae*" is the name botanists use for the family of flowering plants which includes both flowers that are ordinarily referred to as "lily" and ones that are ordinarily referred to as "tulip"; it is one of the examples used in Dupré (1981) and (1993) to indicate the possible mismatch between ordinary and scientific classifications.

[3] For those not familiar with the literature, the kind *jadeite* is an example made famous by Putnam (1975b), who notes that *jade*, which was originally viewed as a single kind of mineral, was later discovered to be composed of stones that belong to two chemically rather heterogeneous kinds, *jadeite* and *nephrite*, which share many superficial similarities.

ordinary classifications vis-à-vis their scientific counterparts; it is controversial, for example, whether classificatory expressions from the vernacular should ever really be counted as genuine natural kind terms.[4] The illustrations that are most prominently discussed in the literature thus typically center on *scientific* classifications, in particular *biological* kinds (i.e., the taxa into which living organisms are grouped, e.g., *Tyrannosaurus rex* and *liliaceae*), *chemical* kinds (e.g., *hydrogen*), as well as *physical* kinds, broadly construed (e.g., *jadeite, planet* and *electron*); but the category of natural kinds may very well also extend to the taxonomic divisions presupposed, for example, in disciplines like *medicine, psychology, economics* or *meteorology* (e.g., *multiple sclerosis, schizophrenia, inflation* and *hurricane*). We can thus take at least some of these scientific classifications to provide us with clear examples of kinds which presumably ought to be counted as natural according to anyone's criteria.

Clear cases on the opposite side of the spectrum, i.e., classifications which we can all agree ought *not* to be counted as natural, include for example classifications of objects under the heading "objects that are currently in my visual field", "children born on a Tuesday" or "objects that can be used either as doorstops or as cleaning supplies".

Beyond these clear cases, however, there is a large and varied array of categories with respect to which there is no general agreement. For example, while classifications based on what Hilary Putnam has called "one-criterion words", such as "bachelor", "janitor" or "hunter", will presumably be fairly universally judged to be non-natural,[5] less widespread agreement can be expected, at least outside the scientific community of the Western hemisphere, with respect to categories such as *prophet, seer, angel, witch, ghost, demon, fairy, Sagittarius,* and the like, which may or may not be viewed as originating from superstitious beliefs, depending on whom one is addressing. (We may also, in this context, think of even more politically charged examples, such as *Aryan* or *Jew*.) Intricate issues furthermore arise with respect to such classifications as *phlogiston* or *aether*, which were once part of respected scientific theories but later came to be regarded as unsuccessful in their attempt to determine a genuine natural kind.[6] Finally, it is not immediately obvious where to place classifications like that of, say, honey, ice-cream and syrup under the heading "sweet", or that of, say, sunflowers, lemons and Tour de France bicycle jerseys under the heading "yellow"; such taxonomies, though admittedly heterogeneous in some respects, would perhaps suggest themselves as natural

---

[4] For discussion of this issue, see for example Dupré (1981) and (1993).

[5] See, for example, Putnam (1962); it will become clear below why these terms are given the name "one-criterion words".

[6] Phlogiston was thought of until the time of Priestley and Lavoisier (roughly the 1770s) as a substance that is *emitted* during the process of burning; it was then realized that burning instead involves the *absorption* of a substance, viz., oxygen. Aether was invoked by various scientific paradigms, e.g., classical Newtonian mechanics, as a medium for the propagation of sound and light; aether theory was not discarded until the early 20th century, with the advent of Einstein's theory of relativity. Both examples have been extensively discussed by historians of science, see especially Kuhn (1962).

based on what is immediately available to us through our perceptual apparatus and on the grounds that objects can be sweet or yellow independently of our doing.[7, 8]

What this series of examples may be taken to indicate is that the distinction before us is not *sharp*, but rather one of *degree*, so that perhaps kinds can ultimately be classified only into *more* or *less* natural ones along a spectrum of some sort, with clear cases on either side and a good bit of indeterminacy in the middle. The idea that a kind could be deemed natural or non-natural in any *absolute* sense, on this conception, would be non-sensical, since the naturalness or non-naturalness of kinds is always only the result of a comparative judgment relative to some set of standards.[9] An approach of this sort would also allow for the possibility, for example, that the classification of pieces of furniture under the heading "chair", though obviously a classification of objects that are man-made, may for all we know in the end count as *more natural* than a classification of objects under the heading "yellow", "sweet", "weed" or "shrub", even though at least the latter two categories are exclusively composed of objects that are found in nature. Moreover, whether ordinary or scientific taxonomic efforts will arrive at a single *unique* classification of particular objects into kinds, or whether instead a *pluralistic* attitude towards divisions into kinds is called for, is also not a question which can be decided on a priori grounds, independently of a thorough investigation into the nature of kinds.[10]

§VIII.3 THE SPECIAL FEATURES OF NATURAL KINDS

What, then, distinguishes natural kinds from non-natural kinds? And what reasons are there for believing in the existence of natural kinds in general and certain specific natural kinds in particular? For those who think that

---

[7] There is a tradition within the literature on natural kinds (the most prominent example of which is Quine 1970), which assumes that a classification of objects under the heading "yellow" or "sweet" *would* count as a natural kind, simply because, according to this conception, *any* predicate which is according to the terminology of Goodman (1954) "projectible" yields a natural kind, and the predicates "is yellow" and "is sweet" lack the objectionable features that are distinctive of a non-projectible predicate, such as Goodman's notorious example "is grue", i.e., "is green until time t and is blue thereafter", where t is some time in the distant future. (The connection between natural kinds, induction and projectibility will be the subject of the next section.) However, this deflationary strand within the tradition on natural kinds, not surprisingly, also leads to a certain degree of skepticism concerning the usefulness of the notion of a natural kind.

[8] Of course, if there is a reliable method available by means of which to distinguish, in Aristotelian manner, *substances* from *non-substances* (i.e., quality, quantity, relation, etc.), this distinction could be usefully invoked at this point to exclude at least some of the disputed cases from the realm of natural kinds, e.g., *yellow thing* or *sweet thing*.

[9] See LaPorte (2004), for example, for a recent proposal sympathetic to the "degree"-conception.

[10] See, for example, Hacking (1991) for a historically motivated pluralistic conception of natural kinds in general; a pluralistic attitude towards biological kinds in particular has been recommended by Philip Kitcher in a series of articles, e.g., Kitcher (1984a, 1984b, 1987 and 1989), as well as by John Dupré, e.g., in Dupré (1981 and 1993).

the "natural"/"non-natural" distinction points to a substantive contrast, i.e., those who take a *realist* rather than a *conventionalist* line on natural kinds (more on this below), the belief in the existence of natural kinds in general is typically motivated on the following grounds, which are no doubt intimately related to one another and which may or may not in the end come to the same thing.

§VIII.3.1 Induction and Projectibility

First, natural kinds are often said to distinguish themselves from other sorts of taxonomic classifications in that they are particularly well-suited for the purposes of providing grounds for legitimate *inductive inferences* concerning the members of the kind in question. Thus, the inference from the premise that all observed samples of copper in the past have been found to conduct electricity to the conclusion that the next observed sample of copper will conduct electricity presumably derives its legitimacy, at least in part, from the fact that samples of copper form a genuine natural kind and that their capacity to conduct electricity follows from or is otherwise in some fashion concomitant upon whatever other characteristics are more or less uniformly associated with particular samples of this kind of metal; thus, the predicate "conducts electricity", in the language of Goodman (1954), can be said to "project" with respect to members of this natural kind, and the inductive extrapolation of this particular feature with respect to future samples of copper is thereby legitimized.[11]

In contrast, the classification of objects under the heading, say, "objects that are currently in my visual field", "children born on a Tuesday" or "objects that can be used either as doorstops or as cleaning supplies", presumably performs rather miserably from the point of view of licensing inductive inferences over as-of-yet unobserved members of these groupings; for, as it is sometimes put, what is "wrong" with classifications of this sort (or, at any rate, what renders them useless for the purposes of prediction and explanation) is precisely that the members of such intuitively heterogeneous categorizations have *no other* characteristics in common (or at least none that are not themselves gerrymandered) besides the feature by means of which the classifications in question are effected, viz., in this case, *currently being in my visual field, being a child that is born on a Tuesday* or *being useable either as a doorstop or as a cleaning supply*.[12] It is this deficiency

---

[11] A large portion of the literature on induction has been devoted to spelling out in more detail the distinction between "projectible" and "non-projectible" predicates. Since I am not currently engaged in the project of providing an account or justification of induction, I will bypass this tricky issue and assume that some acceptable solution to Goodman's "New Riddle of Induction" is available. For more discussion concerning the connection between induction and natural kinds in particular, see for example Forster (1988), Kornblith (1993), Macnamara (1991), Snyder (2005), Stalker (1994) and Whewell (1989), as well as the references therein.

[12] It is of course always possible to construct predicates, besides "is currently in my visual field", "is a child that is born on a Tuesday" or "is useable either as a doorstop or as a cleaning supply",

with which John Stuart Mill, for example, was particularly impressed when he remarks with respect to what he considers to be a phony kind, viz., *white thing*:

> White things are not distinguished by any common properties, except whiteness; or if they are, it is only by such as are in some way connected with whiteness. But a hundred generations have not exhausted the common properties of animals, of plants, of sulphur or phosphorus; nor do we suppose them to be exhaustible, but proceed to new observations and experiments, in the full confidence of discovering new properties, which were by no means implied by those we previously knew.

(Mill 1843, p. 122)[13]

§VIII.3.2 Laws of Nature

Assuming that a legitimate inductive inference consists roughly in extrapolating a particular projectible feature that has been noticed to be uniformly present among the members of a particular kind to as-of-yet unobserved members of the *same* kind, it might seem as though *any* classification of objects into kinds, simply by virtue of the fact that it captures a uniformity of some sort, would have the power to legitimize inductive inferences, as long as some projectible features

---

which apply to all and only the objects in question; however, such predicates most likely would be highly disjunctive and there would presumably be no independent evidence to the effect that these predicates indeed correspond to properties which perform any other interesting role besides that of acting as the unifying "glue" that holds together the members of these intuitively heterogeneous classifications. What this last point brings out, however, is that there is a possible danger of circularity that is deservedly emphasized in Quine (1970). For suppose we were to follow the temptation to spell out the "natural"/"non-natural" distinction for *kinds* by appeal to an analogous distinction for *properties*, so that the natural *kinds* would correspond precisely to those categories into which particular objects are grouped on the basis of shared natural *properties*, and similarly for non-natural kinds and non-natural properties. In that case, of course, no progress whatsoever has been made, unless some independent account of what makes a *property* natural can be given, which does not also appeal to the sorts of considerations in terms of which natural *kinds* are distinguished from non-natural ones. (Quine's dim vision of the whole cycle of notions that he views as being inextricably linked—similarity, property, disposition, causation, natural kind, induction, law of nature, etc.—is in large part due to the fact that he doubts that such an independent account can in fact be given.)

[13] Of course, as Mill points out, there is more we can say about the white things, other than that they are white; and some of the features in question would even be characterized by us, inhabitants of a post-Kripkean era, as non-analytically connected with whiteness, e.g., that white things will emit or absorb light in a particular fashion. To attempt to make precise the exact nature of the contrast Mill sees between, for example, *white things* and *phosphorus*, would take us too far afield, deep into Mill's logic and possibly (as was suggested to me by Elijah Millgram, personal communication) into his moral and political philosophy as well, as would of course the question of the ultimate plausibility of Mill's account; however, the contrast at issue, as the passage quoted above brings out, in some way turns on the fact that members of a genuine natural kind, in Mill's view, have a *possibly inexhaustible* array of *diverse* properties in common, where the force of the diversity in question rests on the fact that the properties in question fail to exhibit an *implication* relation to one another. For more discussion of Mill's account, see Hacking (1991).

are shared among the members of the classification in question. Thus, it remains to be seen why the apparent uniformities that are immortalized in the form of *natural* kinds should be especially noteworthy for their explanatory value.

In this connection, one not infrequently comes across the suggestion that natural kinds, in contrast to their "lesser" relatives, bear the further distinction of figuring in *laws of nature*. Thus, while, for example, the undoubtedly highly useful classification of individual pieces of furniture under the heading "chair" may or may not manage to capture uniformities of some sort,[14] the shared features in question are presumably of a very different sort from those unifying, say, samples of copper; for it is highly unlikely that any useful scientific laws will require an appeal to the category *chair*, in particular, as opposed to that of *material object* (or *body*) in general.[15] In contrast, one does often find universally quantified statements of the form, "All pieces of copper conduct electricity" or "All emeralds are green", described as expressing laws or nomological generalizations, though in this case the laws in question (if indeed they are laws) would be of a relatively high degree of specificity as compared to, say, Newton's First Law, according to which *bodies* in general are said to continue at rest or in uniform motion in a straight line unless acted upon by an impressed force.[16]

---

[14] If Wittgenstein was right about family resemblances, of course, then the uniformities in question may not amount to anything nearly as strong as unique sets of necessary and sufficient conditions.

[15] What about statistical generalizations about chairs, such as "Most chairs have four legs" or "Bauhaus chairs are particularly sought after by furniture collectors"? Why should these not count as laws concerning the kind *chair*? The mere fact that such generalizations are *not exceptionless* alone does not succeed in distinguishing natural from non-natural kinds, since many (or perhaps all) nomological generalizations in the sciences appear not to be exceptionless either. Rather, there are at least two features we can single out at this point to mark the contrast between generalizations concerning chairs and generalizations concerning copper at least in a preliminary fashion. (Thanks to Malcolm Forster, personal communication, for valuable discussion of this and related topics.) For one thing, the generalizations in question can be expected to be *qualitatively* different, in that for instance our knowledge of the properties of copper allows us to make exceedingly *precise numerical* predictions concerning the behavior of copper under various diverse conditions; nothing similar is currently available, or could be reasonably expected ever to be available, in the case of chairs. Secondly, it is perhaps fair to say that no one would feel the need to consult whatever complex statistical generalizations we can formulate concerning chairs to find out what *makes* something a chair; not so in the case of genuine natural kinds like copper, at least if what I take to be the central insight behind the Kripke/Putnam analysis of natural kind terms is correct (more on this second point below).

[16] What distinguishes universally quantified statements that express laws from those that merely report accidental generalizations is of course a question that is notoriously difficult and has a long history in the philosophy of science. The following two features are often emphasized in this context: (i) unlike mere regularities, genuine nomological generalizations are thought of as supporting *counterfactual* reasoning (e.g., reasoning of the form, "If a copper wire *were to be* added to an electrical circuit, it *would* affect the amount of electricity flowing through the circuit in proportion to the width and length of the wire"); and (ii) unlike statements describing mere regularities, genuine nomological generalizations can be true even if they are in fact *uninstantiated*, due to the fact, for example, that the idealized conditions described in the law (e.g., frictionless surfaces or complete vacuums) can never in fact obtain in any actual setting. For more discussion concerning the nature of laws, see for example Aronson, Harré and Way (1995); Cartwright, N.

The connection between natural kinds and the laws governing them, for example, is clearly expressed, though with some degree of hesitation, in Fodor (1974), an essay whose main topic is the issue of reduction between physics and the so-called "special sciences":

> If I knew what a law is, and if I believed that scientific theories consist just of bodies of laws, then I could say that "P" is a kind predicate relative to S if S contains proper laws of the form, "$P_x \rightarrow \ldots y$" or "$\ldots y \rightarrow P_x$": roughly, the kind predicates of a science are the ones whose terms are the bound variables in its proper laws.[17]

Hilary Putnam, with no degree of hesitation whatsoever, makes the connection between scientific laws and natural kinds an important theme from the very beginning in his investigations into the semantics of natural kind terms; the following passage from Putnam (1962), for example, serves as an early illustration of the views developed further in Putnam (1970, 1973, 1975b and 1975c):[18]

> What makes the resemblance [between the *law-cluster term*, "energy", and the *one-criterion word*, "bachelor"] only superficial is the fact that if we are asked what the meaning of the term "bachelor" is, we can *only* say that "bachelor" means "unmarried man", whereas if we are asked for the meaning of the term "energy", we can do much more than give a definition. We can in fact show the way in which the use of the term "energy" facilitates an enormous number of scientific explanations, and how it enters into an enormous bundle of laws.[19]

§VIII.3.3 Causation and Explanation

Thirdly, and no doubt connectedly, natural kinds have been recognized by philosophers and scientists for their prominent role in *explanation*, especially *causal* explanation. Following the classical account of the semantics of natural

(1989); Dretske (1977); Earman (1978); Goodman (1954); Kitcher (1981); Mellor (1980, 1990); Swoyer (1982); and Tooley (1977); the connection between scientific laws and natural kinds in particular is investigated in Riggs (1996).

[17] Fodor (1974, p. 506); page numbers are taken from the reprinted version in Kim and Sosa (2000). Although Fodor does not explicitly restrict his statement here to *natural* kinds, he does speak of natural kinds elsewhere in the essay; given his concern with the relation between physics and the special sciences, I do believe it is fair to read him as having natural kinds in mind in the statement above. Fodor's hesitation is due to the fact that, like Quine (1970), he is skeptical that the cycle of interconnected notions, such as *kind* and *law* (as well as, in Fodor's view, *theory*), could ever be broken into from the outside.

[18] Churchland (1985), for example, also endorses the connection between natural kinds and the laws of nature, but argues that the only genuine natural kinds are those which figure in the most basic laws of nature, such as *mass*, *length*, *duration*, *charge*, *color*, *energy* and *momentum*.

[19] Putnam (1962, p. 53); page numbers to this and all following quotations from Putnam are taken from the reprinted versions of these essays in Putnam (1975a). Thus, Putnam's reason for labeling terms like "bachelor" one-criterion words is that he believes the meaning of these terms is exhausted by a single criterion which can be stated in the form of a qualitative definition; not so in the case of law-cluster terms, whose meaning cannot be divorced from the scientific laws and explanations in which they partake.

kind terms given in Putnam (1975b), for example, we may attempt to capture the connection between natural kind classifications and the causal structure of the world as follows. Although our classifications into purported natural kinds often at first have the character of a Lockean "nominal kind", in that they proceed in terms of "superficial", "phenomenal" qualities, simply because these tend to be the characteristics to which we have pretheoretic and direct perceptual access, the (defeasible) intention behind these classifications is eventually to arrive at a Lockean "real kind", i.e., one which reflects the possibly unobservable, "important physical", i.e., underlying structural, features inherent in the objects classified, even though these characteristics may often be unknown to users of the term in question and are only suspected to be present due to a certain homogeneity in the superficial phenomenal qualities that are exhibited by the members of the alleged natural kind. Thus, while the classification of samples of water into a single natural kind notoriously proceeded at first by way of such superficial phenomenal characteristics as "transparent, potable liquid which fills the rivers and lakes", it was later *discovered* by means of empirical investigation that the samples of this suspected natural kind share the chemical structure of being composed of two parts hydrogen and one part oxygen (modulo impurities and issues concerning isotopes). It is these underlying structural properties which are then thought to reveal the true "nature" or "essence" of water, rather than the superficial phenomenal characteristics with which the kind in question was initially associated by members of the lay community; in fact, these latter characteristics are ultimately recognized to be merely a symptom of (i.e., causally dependent on) the underlying structural properties whose presence may or may not eventually be made known to us by the experts.

A similar proposal concerning the ways in which our classifications into natural kinds may reveal the causal structure of the world can be found in the work of Richard Boyd, who shares the realist leanings of the early Putnam. According to Boyd, natural classifications may be distinguished from non-natural ones along the following lines:

There are natural kinds, properties, etc. whose natural definitions involve a kind of property cluster *together with* an associated indeterminacy in extension. Both the property-cluster form of such definitions and the associated indeterminacy are dictated by the scientific task of employing categories which correspond to inductively and explanatorily relevant causal structures. In particular, the indeterminacy in extension of such natural definitions could not be remedied without rendering the definitions *un*natural in the sense of being scientifically misleading. What I believe is that the following sort of situation is commonplace in the special sciences which study complex structurally or functionally characterized phenomena: (1) There is a family F of properties which are "contingently clustered" in nature in the sense that they co-occur in an important number of cases. (2) Their co-occurrence is not, at least typically, a statistical artifact, but rather the result of what may be metaphorically (sometimes literally) described as a sort of *homeostasis*. Either the presence of some of the properties in F tends (under appropriate conditions) to favor the presence of the others, or there are underlying mechanisms or processes which tend to maintain the presence of the properties in F, or both.[20]

Examples of the sorts of "homeostatic property clusters" Boyd has in mind can be found for instance among living organisms, such as plants and animals, which are so structured as to preserve themselves in the face of changes in the environment, for example, by maintaining their body temperature or the pressure within the cells that constitute them within a certain range of values. Similarly, a structural chemical property like *being composed of two parts hydrogen and one part oxygen*, according to Boyd's account, "tends (under appropriate conditions) to favor the presence of" other properties that are more or less uniformly associated with samples of water, such as *boils at 100 °C* or *freezes at 0 °C*.[21]

On both Putnam's and Boyd's realist conceptions, then, the *success* of our natural kind classifications with respect to explanation and prediction can be traced to the fact that these classifications link up in some intimate fashion with the causal features of the world; this convergence between human taxonomic activity and the causal features of the objects classified in turn explains why our natural kind classifications play the important role that they do in inductive reasoning and in the formulation of scientific laws, as is brought out nicely by the following passage from Kornblith (1993), who endorses Boyd's account of natural kinds as homeostatic property clusters:

Inductive inferences can only work, short of divine intervention, if there is something in nature binding together the properties which we use to identify kinds. Our inductive inferences in science have worked remarkably well, and, moreover, we have succeeded in identifying the ways in which the observable properties which draw kinds to our attention are bound together in nature. In light of these successes, we can hardly go on to doubt the existence of the very kinds which serve to explain how such successes were even possible.

(Kornblith 1993, p. 42)

The conventionalist, in contrast, denies that there are any real "chasms or gaps" to be found among particular objects and instead views the world as consisting simply of degrees of similarity and difference; whatever boundaries are placed among particular objects, on this account, are to be traced to the nominal essences recognized by particular conceptual schemes. Given the sorts of causal avenues that are open to realist approaches, the pressure is certainly on the conventionalist,

---

[20] Boyd (1988, pp. 196–7); see also Boyd (1990, 1991 and 1992), for further discussion. I will not discuss in detail the total of eleven features Boyd proposes to characterize the sorts of property clusters he has in mind; the issue of indeterminacy, however, which is brought up by Boyd in the passage cited above, will concern us again below.

[21] The notion of homeostasis is also investigated in Thalos (2005), where it is traced to its origins within Norbert Weiner's "Systems" or "cybernetics" approach to engineering and the natural sciences.

then, to offer a competing account of the explanatory and predictive successes which potentially reside in kinds like *copper* and which are evidently absent from classifications like *objects that are currently in my visual field*.[22, 23]

§VIII.4 BIOLOGICAL TAXA

Up to this point, we have singled out as particularly noteworthy, among the features which may motivate a belief in the existence of natural kinds, their prominent role in (i) *induction*, (ii) the *laws of nature* and (iii) *causal explanation*. But anyone who is at all familiar with the voluminous literature on the nature of biological species and the higher taxa may have found himself wondering whether my remarks so far have not been more or less tailored to the case of *physical* and *chemical* kinds (though, even there, difficulties arise to which we have not yet attended): it may fairly be asked, then, whether biological taxa, which after all are often taken to be paradigmatic of natural kinds, do not in fact constitute a counterexample to the considerations that have been advanced in the preceding sections in favor of a commitment to natural kinds.[24] For it has been alleged by some that species, and possibly the higher taxa as well, far from providing a paradigm case of natural kinds, are not properly viewed as *kinds* at all, since they are in fact *individuals*, i.e., segments of the phylogenetic tree, concrete spatio-temporally located chunks within the total genealogical nexus of life on Earth, of which individual organisms are *parts* rather than *members* or *instances*. Since, on this conception, biological species are not ascribed the ontological status of kinds at all, it obviously should come as no surprise to find that they do not appear to fit the characteristics of natural kinds straightforwardly.

§VIII.4.1 The Ontological Status of Species

The position according to which biological species are properly conceived of as individuals rather than kinds, also known as the "Species-as-Individuals" thesis

---

[22] The phrase "chasms or gaps" is borrowed from Locke, who (on some readings) denies that, independently of the nominal essences we impose on the world, there are any genuine boundaries to be found among particular objects; for interesting discussion, see Ayers (1981).

[23] I do not at the moment intend to endorse the particular features of Boyd's account of natural kinds, or Putnam's for that matter; I am invoking these two realist approaches merely as examples of how one may go about in expressing the connection between our classifications into natural kinds and the causal structure of the world. Another philosopher whose work we might have naturally pointed to in this connection (as well as in connection with the sorts of consideration raised in the previous two sections) is of course Sydney Shoemaker (see for example Shoemaker 1980).

[24] Much of the discussion on the ontological status of biological taxa focuses on species, rather than the higher taxa, and I will comply with this custom in what follows; the relation between species and the higher taxa is examined, for example, in Ereshefsky (1991), who argues that no principled distinction in ontological terms can be drawn between these different levels of organization.

(SAI), is most prominently associated with the work of Michael Ghiselin and David Hull (see especially Ghiselin 1966, 1969, 1974, 1987 and Hull 1976, 1978).[25] In the most general terms, the arguments advanced by Ghiselin and Hull in support of SAI turn on the fact that species can only fulfill the explanatory roles assigned to them within the theoretical context in which these entities are primarily embedded, viz., that of evolutionary biology, if they occupy the same ontological category as the organisms which constitute them. Very briefly, proponents of SAI have found the following observations to be congenial to their approach.

(i) *Change over Time.* According to evolutionary theory, species are the sorts of entities which can persist through change over time: for example, species come into existence through speciation; they go out of existence by becoming extinct; and, while in existence, they may change their characteristics over time by competing with one another and by evolving through natural selection.

(ii) *Historicity.* Species are historical entities; that is, they are confined to particular regions of space-time within the evolutionary history of life on Earth. As a consequence of their historicity, supporters of SAI have claimed that it is a conceptual truth about species, rather than a contingent matter of fact, that they cannot *re*-evolve: being confined to a particular slot within the evolutionary history of life on Earth, one and the same species cannot come into existence again at a later point in time, regardless of how similar the particular organisms in question may be to one another with respect to their genetic, morphological, physiological and other relevant characteristics.

(iii) *Cohesiveness.* The constituents of species, i.e., the particular organisms that are their members, instances or parts, are functionally interdependent and causally connected by virtue of being related to one another through gene flow and possibly other evolutionary mechanisms (e.g., homeostasis); in this way, species form spatio-temporally continuous and cohesive entities.

(iv) *Absence of Laws.* It has been observed that there are apparently no scientific laws concerning biological species; candidate generalizations in biology like "All swans are white" cannot be assigned the status of scientific laws for several reasons. First, they are not true, since they either have exceptions or may be expected to have exceptions. Secondly, they fail to sustain counterfactual reasoning and hence do not reflect a necessary connection of any sort: for example, it is not the case that if something *were* non-white, then it *would not* be a swan, since the occurrence of non-white swan-offspring need not lead either to inviability or to speciation. Thirdly, given the features already noted especially in (i) and (ii), generalizations about species cannot have the character of laws, since they pertain to particular spatio-temporally located entities which may change their characteristics over time; in contrast, genuine

---

[25] For discussion, see, for example, Crane (2004); Dupré (1993); Ereshefsky (1991); Kitcher (1984a, 1984b, 1987, 1989); LaPorte (1997, 2000, 2004); and Sober (1984).

scientific laws are thought to be fully generalizeable and spatio-temporally unrestricted: they hold for all objects of a given kind and across all regions of space-time.

(v) *Lack of Essences.* The widely discussed "species problem" concerns the question as to which of the various available "species concepts" provides the most plausible criteria of conspecificity, i.e., criteria by means of which organisms are judged to belong to the same species. Candidate species concepts may be based either on *intrinsic* or on *relational* criteria of conspecificity: within the first group, we find, for example, species concepts which appeal to morphological, physiological or genetic measures of similarity; the second, more popular group includes, for example, species concepts based on biological considerations (e.g., interbreeding and reproductive isolation), ecological considerations (e.g., mate recognition within an ecological niche), or phylogenetic considerations (e.g., ancestor–descendant relations).

Biologists and philosophers of biology disagree among one another as to what the correct species concept is; however, it is fair to say that none of the prominent options that are still taken seriously by those familiar with the actual practice of evolutionary biology provide a particularly hospitable climate for essentialism, i.e., the idea that the organisms belonging to a single species share an essence.[26, 27] In this post-Darwinian era, species concepts that are based on intrinsic criteria of conspecificity (see, for example, Sokal and Sneath 1963, and Sneath and Sokal 1973) have been more or less completely abandoned, due to the following considerations: first, the organisms belonging to a single species are, as a matter of empirical fact, observed to exhibit a high degree of variation with respect to their intrinsic features (including, of course, genetic ones); and, secondly, whatever intrinsic similarities may in fact obtain at any given point in time among the organisms belonging to a single species are potentially subject to variation through mutation and other evolutionary processes. Thus, given the broadly Darwinian assumptions that are now generally shared among biologists and philosophers of biology, it seems that no credible candidate can be expected to materialize which could plausibly play the role of an intrinsic essential characteristic or set of characteristics tying together the organisms belonging to a single species.

Species concepts that are based on relational characteristics offer equally little promise for the essentialist. Consider, for example, the following three relational species concepts: (a) Ernst Mayr's famous "biological species concept", according to which species are "groups of interbreeding natural populations that are reproductively isolated from other such groups" (see for example Mayr 1969,

---

[26] By "essence" in this context, I mean simply a characteristic or set of characteristics which one and the same object cannot gain or lose without ceasing to exist.

[27] See, for example, Hull (1965) and Sober (1980) for discussion of the failures of essentialism with respect to biological species.

p. 26); (b) *ecological* species concepts, such as that of Paterson (1985), according to which species are groups of organisms with a shared mate recognition system; or (c) *cladism*, according to which species are lineages of organisms between two speciation events, or between a speciation event and an extinction event (see Ridley 1989). In all three cases, the persistence conditions for species come to depend in part on contingent events that cannot plausibly be viewed as essential to individual organisms, e.g., the occurrence of natural cataclysms and their effects on niche-occupancy or reproductive isolation. In sum, regardless of the merits of any particular species concept, the prospects for essentialism with respect to biological species generally look to be quite dim.[28]

(vi) *Reference to Species.* The nomenclature rules for species suggest that terms referring to species behave in important respects like proper names, at least as they have been characterized by a widely accepted tradition within the philosophy of language (see Kripke 1980). When a biologist coins a new species term with reference to a type specimen, the act in question appears to have the character of an *ostensive* definition: pointing to the type specimen, the biologist may introduce the new species term, as in an initial baptism, to refer to the species of which *that* (viz., the type specimen) is a member.[29] In order for this sort of ceremony to get off the ground, the type specimen in question need not in any sense be *typical* of the species that is being defined in this manner; in other words, the successful introduction of a new species term into the language need not be, and usually cannot be expected to be, tied to a list of purely *qualitative* necessary

---

[28] It is important to be clear that my remarks above only target a particular type of essentialism about species, viz., the sort of view according to which for each species there is a characteristic or set of characteristics, such that the organisms belonging to this species *share* the characteristics in question *and* these characteristics are *essential* to the organisms which exhibit them, i.e., the organisms cannot gain or lose these characteristics without ceasing to exist. However, my remarks above do not conflict with *other* sorts of essentialism about species, for example views according to which certain characteristics belong essentially to *species* directly, rather than to the organisms belonging to them. This latter sort of essentialism is advocated in LaPorte (2004), who argues that species (but not the organisms belonging to them) have certain of their *historical* properties essentially, viz., properties that are analogous to the *essentiality of origins* proposed by Kripke for the referents of proper names. Thus, according to Kripke, it is essential to, say, Queen Elizabeth to have originated from the very zygote from which she in fact originated; if LaPorte is right, then a similar state of affairs obtains for species: it is essential to a species, on this conception, that it originated in exactly the particular slot within the phylogenetic tree of life on Earth in which it in fact originated. This latter sort of essentialism is fully compatible with the idea that particular organisms *fail* to belong essentially to the species to which they in fact belong.

[29] According to Kripke's causal theory of reference, the denotation of an expression is initially fixed by means of some sort of act of dubbing, such as a ceremonial baptism ("This ship will henceforth be known as the 'Titanic'" or "Let *Tyrannosaurus Rex* be the species to which this fossilized specimen belongs") or by means of a stipulation of some sort ("I name whatever object is causing these observed disturbances in the orbit of Uranus 'Neptune'"). Subsequent speakers may then succeed in using the expression in question in the same way as the original baptizers (if, indeed, they *intend* to use the expression in this fashion) by virtue of standing in some appropriate *causal* relation to those who were involved in the original act of dubbing. For critical discussion of the causal theory, see for example Devitt (1981), Evans (1973), Sterelny (1983), Unger (1983).

and sufficient conditions which are perfectly represented by the type specimen and shared among all the organisms belonging to the species in question. The semantic behavior of species terms suggests, then, that these expressions bear certain similarities to, and perhaps belong to the same semantic category as, proper names: on this picture, then, species terms refer *directly* (i.e., not through the mediation of a descriptive condition) and *rigidly* (i.e., to the same entity or entities in every possible world in which they refer at all).

§VIII.4.2 Species as Kinds

If the observations just cited are on the right track, then species have the following characteristics: (i) they may persist through change over time; (ii) they occupy a particular slot within the history of life on Earth; (iii) they form cohesive entities whose constituents are causally connected to one another; (iv) they do not figure in scientific laws; (v) they lack essences; and (vi) they are referred to via name-like expressions. To the supporters of SAI, these considerations indicate that species belong to the ontological category of *individuals*, rather than to competing categories.

But what exactly are the competing ontological categories from which species are *excluded* by virtue of SAI? Several traditional metaphysical dichotomies come to mind in this context, and it is important to be clear on precisely what is being affirmed and denied by the supporters of SAI: of particular relevance to the issues at hand are the dichotomies between (a) *concrete* and *abstract* entities; (b) *universals* and their *instances* (viz., *particulars*);[30] (c) *sets* and their *members*;[31] as well as (d) *wholes* and their *parts*.[32]

Given the emphasis above on space-occupancy, historicity, change over time and causal connectedness, I propose that SAI is most straightforwardly read in

---

[30] As I pointed out in Chapter I (note 1), it is difficult to make precise exactly what is meant by the distinctions in (a) and (b). However, typically "concrete" is understood as entailing space-occupancy and the possession of a certain range of physical properties that we take to go along with space-occupancy (e.g., weight, shape, color, texture or temperature); conversely, abstract entities are considered to exist outside of space and time. The defining feature of universals, on the other hand, is typically taken to be that they are multiply located, i.e., that they are simultaneously present in their entirety in each of their instances (e.g., redness is present in its entirety in each of the red things); correspondingly, particulars are understood as being "non-repeatable", as being wholly present in only a single region of space-time at each time at which they exist. Due to my appeal to such notions as "space-occupancy", "being an instance of" and "being wholly present", nothing I have just said can be taken as particularly illuminating or *definitive* of the "concrete/abstract", "particular/universal" distinctions; at most, these related notions can help us to arrive at a rough grasp of the dichotomies that are at issue.

[31] I am not currently making a distinction between sets, on the one hand, and classes, on the other; thus, for the purposes at hand, the terms "set" and "class" may be taken as synonymous.

[32] This classification of entities is of course not as fine-grained as it could be; however, for the time being, it will be sufficient to consider the options outlined in (a)–(d). Below, when our attention turns more explicitly towards metaphysical and semantic questions, we will have occasion to add further gradations to the categories mentioned above.

the following way: on the negative side, SAI intends to exclude species, first, from the category of *abstract* entities as well as, secondly, from the category of entities which have *members* or *instances*, i.e., *universals* and *sets*; on the positive side, SAI instead intends to assign species, first, to the category of *concrete* entities and, secondly, to the category of entities which have *parts*, i.e., *wholes*. Given this reading, the potentially confusing term "individual", as it is employed by proponents of SAI, should be construed as denoting *concrete particular wholes*, as opposed to entities that are *abstract* by being either *sets* or *universals*.

Without becoming overly embroiled in a lengthy debate over the nature of species, I want to comment briefly on just those metaphysical and semantic points raised by (i)–(vi) that are immediately relevant to the overall mereological purposes of the present discussion. First, on the most general level, it should be pointed out that, unless further potentially controversial assumptions are granted, nothing that has been said up to this point directly impinges on the question of whether species are properly viewed as *kinds*. For notice in this connection that the category of kinds is strikingly absent from the options outlined in (a)–(d), due to the fact that it is in itself a highly complex and substantive metaphysical question to which ontological category *kinds* should be assigned with respect to the dichotomies cited above. When the supporters of SAI deny that species are kinds, they have in mind that kinds can be straightforwardly assimilated to the category of sets; and some of their opponents (e.g., Philip Kitcher) are happy to go along with this presupposition. However, it is far from obvious that this assimilation of kinds to the category of sets is in fact the most attractive metaphysical option available, since at least on the face of it these two categories of entities diverge with respect to their persistence conditions: e.g., sets have their members essentially, while kinds apparently can change their members over time; there is only one null-set, but there apparently can be distinct kinds which lack members, e.g., *unicorn* and *dragon*, and so on. (The ontological status of kinds will be taken up again in more detail below.)

(i) Change over Time; (ii) Historicity; (iii) Cohesiveness. Next, as has been pointed out by a numbers of writers, the dispute over SAI seems to a certain extent to be *terminological*.[33] This is especially the case with respect to features (i)–(iii): for even if species turn out to be abstract entities of some sort, we may nevertheless describe *their* apparent changeability, historicity and cohesiveness in terms of what goes on with the *organisms* constituting them: thus, *species* may be said to evolve, to become extinct or to form cohesive entities, for example, by virtue of the fact that the *organisms* belonging to them adapt to their environment, are wiped out, or are connected via such evolutionary mechanisms as gene flow, and so on. To convince us that anything metaphysically substantive is at stake in

[33] See especially Kitcher (1984a, 1984b, 1987, 1989); and LaPorte (2004).

this particular area of the dispute, the proponents of SAI would need to establish that the sort of maneuver just indicated leads to a genuine loss of expressive power.[34]

(iv) Absence of Laws. Given the connection noted above between the role played by natural kinds in inductive reasoning, the laws of nature and causal explanation, the apparent absence of scientific laws concerning species obviously presents a serious concern for those who want to maintain, in the face of SAI, that biological taxa are paradigmatic of natural kinds after all. Thus, as is pointed out in Lange (1995), while biological generalizations like "All robins' eggs are greenish-blue" were originally cited in Carl Hempel and Paul Oppenheim's classic treatment of scientific explanation (Hempel and Oppenheim 1948) as examples of statements stating scientific laws, the majority of biologists and philosophers of biology, especially those sympathetic to SAI, nowadays would take issue with this classification. As mentioned earlier, the reasons for this communal change of mind are that candidate generalizations in biology apparently (a) are *not exceptionless*; (b) do not sustain *counterfactual reasoning*; and (c) are not sufficiently *universal* in their domain of application. I will address each of these considerations in turn and indicate why none of them, in my view, succeeds in establishing that species are not kinds.[35]

Consideration (a), while no doubt true, does not present a serious worry for those who want to maintain that biological generalizations, despite the fact that they may make reference to particular taxa, nevertheless serve as potential candidates for proper scientific laws: as pointed out earlier, it is doubtful that exceptionless nomological generalizations can be found in *any* area of science, even in those domains which furnish uncontroversial candidates for proper scientific laws, e.g., physics and chemistry; thus, the fact that generalizations in biology admit of exceptions is a feature that is not peculiar to this particular scientific domain.

Consideration (b), if anything, presents a challenge for the supporters of SAI: for it is, first of all, not obviously true that biological generalizations really do fail to sustain counterfactual reasoning; and, secondly, those who maintain

---

[34] With respect to feature (ii), the historicity of species, two further observations are in order. First, it is by no means universally granted that the impossibility of re-evolution in fact has the status of a conceptual truth within biology (see the references already cited for discussion of this point). Secondly, we may note that there is an analogous debate within metaphysics concerning the possibility of *intermittent existence* for concrete particulars: for example, it might be claimed that my trumpet ceases to exist when it is taken apart and its components are placed into the trumpet-case; subsequently, when the components are recombined in the proper way, it might be claimed that the very same trumpet comes back into existence; similarly for watches, bicycles, and other artifacts which can apparently be dis-assembled and re-assembled. Thus, whether or not an entity belongs to the ontological category of concrete particulars does not in itself settle the question of whether it can or cannot, as a matter of conceptual necessity, exist intermittently.

[35] My remarks in the next few paragraphs rely heavily on the very useful discussion of the apparent lawlikeness of biological generalizations in Lange (1995).

this position have a good bit of explaining to do, since we are left to wonder why on their view the activity taking place in any of the special branches of biology, e.g., ecology, physiology, anatomy, behavioral biology, embryology, developmental biology, genetics, etc., should be regarded as anything other than a species of *history*. Suppose, for example, as seems certainly conceivable, that due to environmental or other pressures, robins evolve to lay different-colored eggs, without thereby producing inviable offspring or causing a new species to branch off. Such a scenario does not falsify the *properly qualified* generalization, "*Other things being equal*, robins' eggs are greenish-blue"; nor can the truth of this generalization plausibly be viewed as purely accidental, in the same manner in which notoriously the contents of Nelson Goodman's pockets on VE day are merely accidentally silver (see Goodman 1954, p. 19): for if, say, robins' eggs come to be better camouflaged by being red than by being greenish-blue, then other things are precisely not equal in this case, since this new state of affairs can only obtain if systematic changes in the natural habitat occupied by the species in question have taken place as well. That such shifts in natural habitats and their effects on the species inhabiting them are indeed systematic, and not a purely historical accident, is suggested by the fact that phenomena of this sort are studied in completely general terms by some of the special branches of biology, e.g., ecology; clearly, then, the presumption shared by such fields is that correlations between, say, the features of habitats and the characteristics of the species inhabiting them are at least in principle open to scientific explanation. Moreover, the necessary qualification of biological generalizations by means of *ceteris-paribus* clauses is again not a feature that is peculiar to this particular scientific domain; rather, it is widespread even across those areas of science, e.g., physics and chemistry, from which uncontroversial candidates for scientific laws are drawn.[36]

Finally, turning to consideration (c), it is by no means a settled question whether there is in fact a general requirement in effect which prohibits all proper candidates for scientific laws, on a priori grounds, from making reference to particular regions of space-time or their occupants. If, as pointed out in Lange (1995), such an a priori constraint were operative, then certain generalizations in physics, for example, which were at some point taken seriously and subjected to lively debate, could have been dismissed out of hand on the grounds that they are not of the right *form* to constitute a scientific law. In support of this observation,

---

[36] The line of reasoning just suggested in connection with consideration (b) of course raises the difficult and much debated question of how to account for the sorts of *ceteris-paribus* clauses that are prevalent in scientific reasoning without turning apparently substantive generalizations, such as "Other things being equal, robins' eggs are greenish-blue", into trivial ones, such as "Robins' eggs are greenish-blue, *except when they aren't*"; however, it certainly cannot simply be taken for granted by those who invoke consideration (b) in support of their position that nothing of interest whatsoever can be said to clarify further the force of *ceteris-paribus* clauses, as they occur in biological or other scientific generalizations (see Lange 1995 for useful discussion of this point, who suggests roughly that laws differ from accidental generalizations in yielding reliable inference rules).

Lange cites several historical cases, e.g., P. A. M. Dirac's conjecture, according to which the gravitational-force "constant" is inversely proportional to the time since the Big Bang (see Dirac 1938); various law statements, which were at one point formulated by reference to, say, a metal bar in Paris; or law statements within Aristotelian physics, which make reference to the center of the universe or the moon. Since the history of science seems to suggest that such candidates cannot simply be disqualified from the status of proper scientific laws on purely formal grounds, we also may not hold it against generalizations in biology if they apparently violate the universality constraint.[37]

(v) *Lack of Essences.*   As noted earlier, broadly Darwinian assumptions create a generally hostile environment for essentialism about biological species. Given this biological reality, philosophers working at some remove from the practice of evolutionary biology ought to be reluctant to continue to engage in their Aristotelian custom of presupposing, on a priori grounds, that species do have essences.[38] The metaphysically cautious stance to adopt, then, is one which allows for the possibility that essentialism about biological species either has already been, or at least may be, disproven on the basis of empirical arguments. What follows from this admission? Not SAI, at least not immediately. The admission that essentialism about biological species may have to be abandoned on empirical grounds does not lead to an acceptance of SAI, unless the *further* assumption is granted that something cannot be a natural kind unless it has an essence; and this further assumption may certainly be called into question. However, once it has been conceded that the traditional connection between natural kinds and essences may have to be severed in this fashion due to empirical considerations from evolutionary biology, the proponent of SAI has thereby exacted no small philosophical price from those who want to maintain even in this new climate that biological taxa are after all paradigmatic of natural kinds: for any implicit appeal to essentialism along the way, in motivating our belief in the existence of natural kinds, has of course now become suspect as well. Thus, perhaps the most important lesson we learn from the dispute over the nature of species is that those who are engaged in an analysis of *induction*, the *laws of nature*, and *causal explanation* must be mindful of the possibility that any account of these central philosophical concepts which carries with it an implicit or explicit commitment to essentialism about natural kinds may in the end come into conflict with empirical results from evolutionary biology.

(vi) *Reference to Species.*   Finally, to say that species terms behave in certain respects *like* proper names is of course not to say that they *are* proper names or that the entities denoted by species terms belong to the same ontological type as those referred to by proper names. For species terms may very well share certain semantic properties, in particular those of direct reference and rigidity,

---

[37] See also Earman (1978) for discussion of the alleged universality of scientific laws.
[38] Cases in point are, for example, Lowe (1997) and Wilkerson (1988, 1993, 1995).

with proper names, even if the former belong to the category of *general* terms (i.e., expressions which purport to apply to multiple entities all at once, e.g., "red"), while the latter belong to the category of *singular* terms (i.e., expressions which purport to apply to a single entity only, e.g., "Earth"). In fact, Kripke and Putnam, in their classical treatment of the semantics of natural kind terms (Kripke 1980 and Putnam 1975b), notoriously assign expressions denoting species to the category of general terms; but they do not consider this to be an obstacle to ascribing to these expressions the semantic properties of direct reference and rigid designation. Thus, in order for the apparently name-like behavior of species terms to bear any weight as a consideration in favor of SAI, an additional argument would be required to the effect that species terms can behave semantically as directly referential rigid designators *only if* they are proper names.[39]

In sum, then, I take the preceding discussion of biological species to have established that, contrary to SAI, the observations in (i)–(vi) do not by themselves create sufficient pressure to abandon the thesis that biological taxa are after all paradigmatic of natural kinds; at the same time, however, observation (v) in particular was found to require an important modification of the species-as-kinds view, since the traditional connection between natural kinds and essentialism seems not to withstand empirical evidence from evolutionary biology.

§VIII.5 WHAT SORTS OF ENTITIES ARE NATURAL KINDS?

The ontological category to which natural kinds belong has not as of yet been settled by the arguments of the preceding sections. In connection with our discussion of SAI, we considered several traditional metaphysical dichotomies which come to mind in this context: (a) *concrete* and *abstract* entities; (b) *universals* and their *instances* (viz., *particulars*); (c) *sets* and their *members*; as well as (d) *wholes* and their *parts*.[40] In light of the semantic issues which are about to come to the

---

[39] And while it is certainly not inconceivable that such an additional argument could be given, the proponents of SAI tend not to go this extra mile, since such an excursion into the thicket of philosophical and linguistic debates over the semantic behavior of certain categories of natural-language expressions would involve leaving behind the sorts of concerns that are of direct relevance to biologists and philosophers of biology (but see, for example, Crane 2004 for a discussion of the semantic properties of species terms which takes into consideration the specific concerns driving the literature on SAI).

[40] Given the primarily non-metaphysical nature of the discussion surrounding SAI, it was not necessary earlier to distinguish a separate category for *properties* and their *instances*, since the main ways in which properties are standardly analyzed are already canvassed in (a)–(d): e.g., the Platonist or Aristotelian takes properties to be *universals* of some sort, whereas the trope-theorist and the nominalist tend to regard them as some variety of *particulars*, viz., *tropes*, *sets* or *wholes* (but see also the new possibility opened up for the nominalist by category (e) in the text). In what follows, it will

fore in the following sections, it will come in handy to add a further category (e) of bare *pluralities* of some sort, i.e., entities which may function as the extensions of general terms, but which are different from both sets and wholes in being *many*, rather than *one*.[41]

As noted earlier, the proponents of SAI assign species, and possibly the higher taxa as well, to the category of *concrete particular wholes*, as contrasted with entities that are *abstract* by being either *universals* or *sets*. In fact, however, the arguments that are provided in favor of SAI only support the conclusion that members of a single natural kind cannot be assumed to share an essence; and while this claim is certainly of great significance given the historical precedent, it does not by itself settle the question of what sorts of entities natural kinds are. In what follows, I want to approach the onto-logical question before us by examining the semantic behavior of natural kind terms.

§VIII.5.1 The Semantics of Natural Kind Terms

Saul Kripke's lectures "Identity and Necessity" and "Naming and Necessity" (originally published in 1971 and 1972) had a dramatic impact on much of contemporary analytic philosophy. Among Kripke's most central contri-butions in these lectures is a certain picture of proper names which all but single-handedly dislodged the then commonly accepted descriptivist concep-tion derived from the works of Gottlob Frege and Bertrand Russell. According to Kripke, proper names like "Aristotle" are not tied to a list of descriptive conditions like "the teacher of Alexander the Great", with which they are commonly associated by speakers; rather, (i) proper names are *rigid designa-tors* (i.e., they refer to the very same object in every possible circumstance in which they refer at all); (ii) they are *non-descriptive* (i.e., they are not syn-onymous with a description or a cluster of descriptions associated with them

---

sometimes be convenient to speak of properties and their instances; when I do so, however, I intend not to commit myself to any particular analysis of this ontological category.

[41] I have in mind here nothing more mysterious than simple non-singularized predicate-extensions: thus, if natural kinds are to be understood along the lines of category (e), then we ought to resist the temptation to construe terms like "water" as implicit *singular* terms; rather, they simply denote *many* things simultaneously, viz., any and all samples of water, without thereby denoting a *single* entity (e.g., a set or a whole) that is composed of these many things. Entities which fall into this fifth category have been claimed as the semantic values of plural noun-phrases by the neo-Davidsonian, event-based analysis of plurals advocated in Higginbotham and Schein (1989) and Schein (1993), which takes its inspiration from George Boolos' work on second-order logic (see especially Boolos 1975, 1984, 1985a and 1985b). For the opposing, and on the whole more popular, *objectual* view of plurals, see for example Gillon (1984); Higginbotham (1980); Link (1983, 1987); Lønning (1987); Russell (1903); and Scha (1981); the semantics of plurals is also discussed, with respect to the particular bearing it has on the characteristics of generic sentences, in Koslicki (1999b).

by speakers);[42] (iii) proper names initially acquire their referent by means of an ostensive baptism or a descriptive stipulation, which is subsequently passed on from speaker to speaker via a *causal mechanism* of some sort; (iv) identity statements involving rigid designators like "Hesperus is Phosphorus" are *necessarily* true, if true at all, but their truth is often knowable only a posteriori.[43]

In Kripke's view, the semantic, metaphysical and epistemic approach outlined above also applies to natural kind terms, despite the fact that he viewed these latter expressions as belonging to the category of *general terms* (i.e., terms which purport to apply to multiple objects simultaneously), and not, as proper names, to the category of *singular terms* (i.e., terms which purport to refer to a single entity only):

. . .[M]y argument implicitly concludes that certain *general terms*, those for natural kinds, have a greater kinship with proper names than is generally realized. This conclusion holds for certain for various species names, whether they are *count nouns*, such as 'cat', 'tiger', 'chunk of gold', or *mass terms* such as 'gold', 'water', 'iron pyrites'. It also applies to certain terms for natural phenomena, such as 'heat', 'light', 'sound', 'lightning', and presumably, suitably elaborated, to corresponding *adjectives*—'hot', 'loud', 'red'.

(Kripke 1980, p. 134; my italics)

The resulting analysis of natural kind terms agrees in its central features with that developed independently around the same time by Hilary Putnam, as put forth for example in Putnam (1975b). A natural kind term like "water", according to the Kripke/Putnam approach, is similarly not tied to a list of descriptive conditions commonly associated with it by speakers, such as "transparent, potable liquid that fills rivers and lakes"; rather, in the manner described in (i)–(iv), it designates a natural kind, membership in which is determined by the presence of a presumed underlying common nature or essence, e.g., being composed of

---

[42] Rigidity and descriptiveness by no means exclude each other; thus, for example, the expression "the square-root of two" is both *rigid* and *descriptive*, since it denotes the same number in every possible world, but it does so via the satisfaction of a descriptive condition, "being the square-root of two"; the expression "the President of the United States", on the other hand, is *descriptive* and *non-rigid*, since it designates different people at different times and at different worlds. Finally, if Kripke is right about proper names, then the expression "Aristotle" is both *rigid* and *non-descriptive*, since it designates the same person in every possible world, regardless of whether that person taught Alexander the Great in the scenario under consideration.

[43] Given that prior to Kripke's lectures necessity was generally identified with *analyticity* (i.e., truth in virtue of *meaning*), it came as a great surprise to the philosophical community that there should be statements which obtain in every possible world, but whose truth is not accessible to reason alone. In addition to the controversial category of necessary a posteriori truths, Kripke also made philosophical headlines by allowing for a special class of statements that are apparently *contingent a priori*, such as "The meter stick is one meter long". What makes this category of statements so deeply puzzling is that their truth is supposed to be *both* knowable by reason alone *and* dependent on the contingent features of a particular situation (for critical discussion, see for example Donnellan 1979, Evans 1979 and Salmon 1987/88). Since natural kind terms do not figure in any special way into the concerns raised by statements of this latter kind, I will ignore them in what follows.

two parts hydrogen and one part oxygen, which may or may not be known to competent users of the term and which is open to discovery through science.[44, 45]

As appealing as this conception of natural kind terms undoubtedly is, however, the extension of the central philosophical claims outlined above in (i)–(iv) from the category of *singular terms* to the category of *general terms*, to which natural kind terms apparently belong, has been anything but straightforward.[46] Thus, commentators have found it difficult to say what exactly natural kind terms contribute semantically to the sentences in which they occur and to what extent their semantic contribution parallels that of proper names.[47] In the next section, I want to focus in particular on thesis (i), the alleged *rigidity* of natural kind terms; thesis (ii), their purported *non-descriptiveness*, will be taken up separately below.[48]

---

[44] Thus, in its original formulation, the Kripke/Putnam analysis of natural kind terms also came with substantive metaphysical commitments, viz., that the members of a single natural kind share an essence; moreover, these essentialist claims were thought to follow directly from the *semantics* of natural kind terms (viz., in particular their *rigidity*), in conjunction with certain unassailable *logical* premises (e.g., the necessary identity of each thing with itself). However, given the detailed case built against this alleged connection in Salmon (1981), it is now widely accepted that a metaphysical rabbit cannot be pulled out of a semantic or logical hat alone, in the way that the Kripke/Putnam picture had initially suggested, without importing substantive essentialist assumptions from elsewhere. Based on the considerations from evolutionary biology discussed in the preceding section, we of course already have independent reasons for not wanting to take on board unmotivated essentialist assumptions about natural kinds; I will therefore in what follows simply bracket the essentialism which originally came with the Kripke/Putnam package, to the extent that this is possible, and focus instead on the semantic aspects of their analysis.

[45] Both Kripke and Putnam also initially regarded natural kind terms as *indexical*, like "I", "this", "here" and "now". Putnam, for example, characterized "water" as applying in every possible circumstance to objects which exhibit the same "important physical" (i.e., underlying structural) properties as, or which bear the "same-liquid" relation to, paradigmatic instances of what is called "water" *around here* (i.e., in the *actual* world, by speakers of English). However, even though references to the alleged indexicality of natural kind terms are still common now, it is fair to say that, among those writers who study these issues closely, a consensus of sorts has developed to the effect that Kripke's and Putnam's initial characterization of natural kind terms as indexical was in fact due to sloppiness and that these expressions do not manifest the context-sensitivity and shiftiness of reference that is characteristic of genuine indexicals. The case against the alleged indexicality of natural kind terms is convincingly made in Burge (1982) (for a contrasting picture, though, see Almog 1981); in what follows, I will proceed upon the assumption that natural kind terms are not indexical in the same way as "I", "this", "here", "now", and the like.

[46] I will, in what follows, assume that natural kind terms do in fact belong to the category of *general terms*. This assumption is quite uncontroversial for *singular count nouns*, such as "tiger", as well as for *adjectives*, such as "red", both of which are generally taken to function semantically as predicates. The corresponding argument for *plural count nouns*, to my mind, has been quite convincingly made by the Boolos/Higginbotham/Schein approach to plurals. I have argued extensively elsewhere that a predicative analysis is the correct way to proceed for *mass terms* as well (see Koslicki 1995, 1997, 1999a, 1999b).

[47] For influential early criticisms of the Kripke/Putnam-approach, see for example Donnellan (1983), Forbes (1981), Mellor (1977), Salmon (1981), Schwartz (1980), and Zemach (1976); the semantic characteristics of natural kind terms, which will be our central focus in what follows, are most closely examined in Cook (1980), Cordry (2004), Deutsch (1993), LaPorte (2000, 2004), Linsky (1984), Salmon (1981), and Soames (2002, chs. 9–11).

[48] Based on the preceding remarks, thesis (iv), the classification of certain statements as *necessary a posteriori* truths, must be divorced from the remaining aspects of the Kripke/Putnam package,

§VIII.5.1.1 Rigid Designation

An expression is rigid just in case it denotes the very same object or objects in every possible circumstance in which it denotes anything at all. Thus, for a natural kind term like "water" to be rigid, its denotation would have to remain constant from world to world; but it seems obvious that there could have been more water, less water, different water or no water at all. What, then, if anything, stays the same in the denotation of "water" from world to world, when the particular samples of water may vary? Given the options canvassed above, we may think of the denotation of "water" as either (1) a *set*, or (2) a *whole*, or (3) a *plurality*, or (4) a non-set-like *abstract entity* of some sort, whose identity is not tied to that of the individual water samples.[49] In the first three cases, the term "water" will be classified as non-rigid, since its denotation will change from world to world due to the variation in individual water samples. If, on the other hand, "water" is rigid by virtue of denoting the same abstract entity from world to world, then the initially attractive contrast between natural kind terms like "water" and intuitively descriptive general terms like "bachelor" seems to have been lost: for whatever reasoning leads to the conclusion that natural kind terms like "water" denote the same abstract entity in every possible world presumably would apply no less to terms like "bachelor", with the consequence that even non-natural-kind-denoting general terms will now apparently turn out to be rigid. Either way, rigidity no longer serves as a distinguishing mark of natural kind terms.[50, 51]

since it presupposes essentialism about natural kinds. We may also in the current context disregard thesis (iii), the *causal theory of reference*, since natural kind terms again do not figure in any special way into the concerns that have been raised in connection with this portion of the Kripke/Putnam picture, e.g., the so-called "qua-problem" as discussed in Devitt (1981) or the phenomenon of reference-*change* as discussed in Evans (1973) (see also Unger 1983 for further critical discussion of the causal theory). Thus, our main focus in what follows will be on theses (i) and (ii).

[49] This fourth category may be thought of as including both abstract *particular* and abstract *universal* entities, as long as their identity is conceived of as remaining stable from world to world, despite the variation in individual members of the kind in question. Thus, we may include in this category, among other things, *properties* (depending, of course, on what analysis of properties is adopted); predicate-*intensions* (viz., functions from possible worlds to extensions); as well as other varieties of abstract objects (if there are any such), which fall into neither of the previous two classes.

[50] Faced with this dilemma, some writers, e.g., LaPorte (2000) and (2004), have been willing to come down on the side of claiming that even non-natural-kind-denoting general terms, such as "bachelor", are rigid; the difference between natural kind terms and other general terms, then, obviously must lie elsewhere (e.g., in whether the causal theory applies to them).

[51] As both LaPorte (2000, 2004) and Linsky (1984) emphasize, the second horn of the dilemma just described need not be taken to lead to the outcome that *all* general terms are rigid; for there is still room to draw a distinction between expressions like "the color of the sky", which non-rigidly designates different colors in different worlds (e.g., blue on Earth, red on Venus, etc.), and expressions like "blue", which (arguably) rigidly designates the same color in every possible world. Thus, all we can conclude from the second option (as well as from the first option) outlined above is that rigidity can no longer serve to mark the contrast between natural-kind-denoting general terms, such as "water", and non-natural-kind-denoting general terms, such as "bachelor";

Given that, on either horn of the dilemma just outlined, rigidity has ceased to play the semantic role with which it was formerly endowed, the question now arises as to what pressing reasons there were in the first place for taking natural-kind-denoting general terms to be rigid designators. I want to suggest in what follows that, once the essentialism which came with the original Kripke/Putnam package is bracketed, the central arguments with which this approach presents us establish only that natural-kind-denoting general terms are *non-descriptive*, not that they are rigid.[52]

Salmon (1981) helpfully divides Kripke's and Putnam's central arguments into three categories: (i) the "Modal Arguments"; (ii) the "Epistemological Arguments"; and (iii) the "Semantic Arguments". To illustrate, suppose that in accordance with the traditional descriptivist picture a natural-kind-denoting general term, such as "tiger", is synonymous with a description stating the sorts of characteristics commonly associated with tigers by competent speakers of the language, e.g., "four-legged, meat-eating, cat-like animal with a tawny yellow coat and black stripes". If the descriptivist theory were correct, then the sentence "Something is a tiger just in case it is a four-legged, meat-eating, cat-like animal with a tawny yellow coat and black stripes", should be *analytic*, i.e., both *necessarily* true and knowable a priori; moreover, whether something falls into the extension of the term "tiger" should be determined solely by whether the object in question satisfies the descriptive information associated with the term "tiger", i.e., by whether it is a four-legged, meat-eating, cat-like animal with a tawny yellow coat and black stripes.

The Modal, Epistemological and Semantic Arguments show that the traditional descriptivist picture does not correctly describe the semantic behavior of natural-kind-denoting general terms.[53] For it is not completely out of the question, first, that we might come across entities which are superficially similar to the animals we have been calling "tigers" in all the ways listed above without in fact being tigers (e.g., because the entities in question upon investigation turn out to be robots, or because for other reasons they cannot interbreed with, or have a very different evolutionary history from, the animals we have been calling "tigers"); secondly, it is again not completely out of the question that, due to some mass-hallucination perhaps, the animals we have been calling "tigers" might turn out to lack some or even all of the characteristics we have been ascribing to them. Either way, it is neither *necessarily* true (by the Modal Arguments) that something is a tiger just in case it is a four-legged, meat-eating, cat-like animal with a tawny

---

but this does not mean, of course, that there are no other ways to distinguish these two classes of general terms.

[52] My conclusions here essentially agree with those of Cook (1980), Deutsch (1993), Linsky (1984), Salmon (1981) and Soames (2002, chs. 9–11).

[53] The full version of these arguments would of course have to involve the famous thought experiments, e.g., of the twin Earth variety, which have generated such a tremendous outpouring of interest in the roughly thirty years since the publication of Kripke's and Putnam's seminal texts.

yellow coat and black stripes; nor (by the Epistemological Arguments) is this state of affairs knowable a priori; nor, finally (by the Semantic Arguments), is the denotation of the term "tiger" determined solely by whether an object satisfies the descriptive information commonly associated with this term.

While I do not want to question the plausibility of Kripke's and Putnam's central arguments as directed against the traditional descriptivist picture, the important point for our present discussion is just that, without the use of additional potentially controversial premises, these arguments establish only that natural-kind-denoting general terms are *non-descriptive*, i.e., that they apply to their denotations *directly*, without the mediation of the sorts of descriptive conditions that are commonly associated with them by competent speakers of the language.[54] The Modal, Epistemological and Semantic Arguments leave open, however, first, *to what sorts of* entities natural-kind-denoting terms apply and, secondly, whether they are *rigid*, i.e., whether they apply to the *same* entity or entities in every possible circumstance in which they apply to anything at all.

In some respects, the neutrality of Kripke's and Putnam's central arguments is not as detrimental as it might at first appear to be, since the non-descriptiveness of natural-kind-denoting general terms by itself already accomplishes the important semantic task of marking a contrast between expressions like "water" and non-natural-kind-denoting general terms like "bachelor", "hunter" and "janitor". For when we ask now how it is, on the positive side of the story, that natural-kind-denoting general terms acquire the denotations they in fact have, if not through the sort of semantic mechanism attributed to them by the traditional descriptivist picture, the answer we can extract from the Kripke/Putnam account is the following. The *mechanism* by which natural-kind-term denotations are fixed involves, first, reference to *actual-world samples* and, secondly, an appeal to some sort of *same-kind relation*, whose nature need not be known to competent users of the expression; by contrast, the mechanism by which non-natural-kind-term denotations are fixed is of a *semantic* nature and involves the satisfaction in every possible circumstance of a *descriptive condition* of some sort.

To illustrate, when a natural-kind-denoting general term is first introduced into the language either *ostensively* (e.g., as in "Let *Tyrannosaurus Rex* be the species to which this fossilized sample belongs") or *stipulatively* (e.g., as in "I name whatever substance is absorbed during the process of burning, *oxygen*"), subsequent speakers under normal circumstances intend the expression

---

[54] With the presupposed essentialism operative, we would at least be entitled to conclude that, whatever the exact ontological status of natural-kind-term denotations, at a minimum the essences associated with natural kinds must be preserved from world to world; as is suggested in Cook (1980), the sort of stability provided by the preservation of essences from world to world might be sufficient to recover the rigidity of natural kind terms, regardless of whether natural-kind-term denotations are construed in an extensionalist or intensionalist light.

in question to apply to anything that is *of the same kind* as the initial *actual-world samples* with respect to which the term was first introduced into the language, even if they may have *no idea* what the nature of the same-kind relation in question is. The same story does not correctly characterize how non-natural-kind-denoting general terms are standardly used in the language: it would be quite bizarre to construe the denotation of, say, "janitor" as including whatever is of the same kind as (e.g., has the same occupation as) samples of what are called "janitors" in the actual world, where it may come as a *complete surprise* to us what it means to satisfy the same-kind-relation in question; rather, the denotation of the term "janitor" is much more plausibly conceived of as being tied in every possible circumstance to the satisfaction of some such descriptive condition as "cleaning personnel".[55]

Since the non-descriptiveness of natural-kind-denoting general terms alone does not determine *to what sorts of* entities these expressions apply or whether they are *rigid*, i.e., whether they apply to the *same* entity or entities in every possible world in which they apply to anything at all, nothing at this point forces us to the conclusion that natural-kind-denoting terms *must* be analyzed, along the lines of option (4) outlined above, as denoting the same non-set-like *abstract entity* in every possible world in which they apply to anything at all. Thus, unless independent arguments for this conclusion can be provided, the first three options outlined above have not yet been ruled out, viz., that natural-kind-term denotations are either (1) *sets*, (2) *wholes* or (3) *pluralities*, i.e., non-singularized predicate-extensions. The first two options can be excluded on independent grounds, since they have the unfortunate effect of committing us to an analysis of natural-kind-denoting general terms as implicit *singular* terms;[56] thus, on balance, the central arguments presented by the Kripke/Putnam approach are compatible with option (3), according to which the denotations of natural-kind-denoting general terms are simply traditional predicate-extensions.[57]

---

[55] The thesis that natural-kind-denoting general terms are *non-descriptive* by itself also remains neutral on the question of whether the mechanism by which natural-kind-term denotations are fixed is in fact correctly described by the *causal theory of reference*, though it is often assumed that the former claim immediately leads to the latter.

[56] As noted earlier, I have argued extensively elsewhere that such a view should be avoided with respect to mass terms; others have urged an analogous conclusion for plural count nouns. The case of singular count nouns and adjectives is not really under dispute.

[57] This is not to say, of course, that there may not be *other* reasons for preferring option (4) over option (3); however, as the discussion in Soames (2002, chs 9–11) indicates, the introduction of properties or other abstract entities into the semantics by itself does not suffice to capture the difference in cognitive significance between, say, "Water is water" and "Water is H_2O", since a further story needs to be told as to why the *property* denoted by "water" is not the very same property as that denoted by "H_2O". Regardless of how in the end we deal with versions of Frege's Puzzle, as they arise for natural-kind-denoting general terms, my relatively modest aim in this section was simply to suggest that the *non-descriptiveness* of these expressions alone, which is all that is directly established by Kripke's and Putnam's central arguments, does not settle the ontological category to which natural-kind-term denotations belong.

§VIII.6 INCOMMENSURABILITY AND INDETERMINACY: PHYSICAL AND CHEMICAL KINDS

Earlier in this chapter, we discussed the case of biological taxa in detail, since numerous considerations have been raised in the literature to the effect that biological taxa apparently are not after all paradigmatic of natural kinds; I have spelled out my reasons for thinking that these observations establish at most only that the traditional connection between natural kinds and essentialism seems to clash with empirical results from evolutionary biology. But the case of physical and chemical kinds, such as *hydrogen* and *copper*, which we have all along assumed provides us with clear examples of natural kinds, raises complexities of its own; it is to these that I now turn in the final sections of this chapter.

§VIII.6.1 Impurities and Isotopes: Scientific and Ordinary Classifications

Among the most prevalent criticisms of the Kripke/Putnam approach to natural kind terms, which was raised early on by a number of writers and has enjoyed an afterlife since then, is the observation that our natural kind terms may apparently denote substances of varying chemical compositions, among other things due to the phenomenon of *impurities* as well as the existence of different *isotopes* of what may or may not in the end amount to a single substance. Thus, much of what we in practice refer to as "water" is in fact not pure H_2O, but contains traces of many other elements; moreover, as Zemach (1976, p. 120), for example, points out, heavy water,[58] mineral water, salt water and distilled water are all commonly referred to as "water", as were, at least at one point in time, tears, urine, sweat, saliva and the like, despite the fact that the substances in question obviously form quite a heterogeneous bunch with regard to their chemical composition. As a result, the semantic behavior of terms like "water" appears to be closer than is compatible with the main tenets of the Kripke/Putnam approach to that of

---

[58] The substance called "heavy water" has the chemical structure D_2O (or "deuterium oxide"). Deuterium atoms are classified as an *isotope* of hydrogen, along with the remaining two hydrogen isotopes, 1H and tritium. The *element* hydrogen occupies the first slot in the periodic table and has atomic number one, i.e., atoms which belong under this rubric have a single positively charged particle or proton in their nucleus and their nucleus contains a single electron in its orbit. Unlike other hydrogen isotopes of the variety 1H, however, deuterium atoms also contain in their nucleus, in addition to the single proton, an extra neutrally charged particle or neutron; tritium, the remaining isotope of hydrogen, contains two such additional neutrons in its nucleus. The presence of these extra particles accounts for the fact that deuterium and tritium atoms have greater mass, and therefore exhibit different characteristics from those exhibited by atoms of the variety 1H, whose nucleus lacks the extra particles; for this reason D_2O and T_2O, for example, boil and freeze at different temperatures from H_2O. Again, I am grateful to my chemistry consultant, Andrew Loxley, for clarification on these points.

intuitively descriptive non-natural-kind-denoting general terms like "bachelor", "janitor" and "hunter", which are similarly not tied to a single underlying micro-structure, and it no longer seems defensible under these circumstances to hold that the extension of terms like "water" includes whatever bears a *single* same-kind relation to prototypical actual-world samples with respect to which the term was first introduced.[59]

But the presence of impurities and isotopes does not in itself constitute an argument against the *existence* of natural kinds as such or against the sorts of reasons cited earlier on the basis of which a belief in the existence of natural kinds may be motivated, viz., their prominent role in explanation and prediction; nor does it show that we do not at least sometimes succeed in singling out genuine divisions among natural kinds with our expressions when we intend to do so. Rather, these observations only bring out that we cannot in general expect, as would in any case seem unjustifiably optimistic, that our ordinary or scientific taxonomic vocabulary is entirely successful right away in reflecting true divisions among natural kinds; but it does not thereby follow that there are no such divisions, or that these divisions cannot at least sometimes be accurately reflected in our ordinary or scientific taxonomic vocabulary.

Thus, consider for example a classificatory term from the vernacular, such as "water" (or analogous terms in English or other languages). When this term was first introduced into the language, members of the relevant speech community were no doubt under the impression, due to the *superficial* homogeneity of samples of what they were calling "water" (viz., the transparent potable liquid which fills the rivers and lakes, which also appeared to them to be involved in many of the physical processes exhibited by living organisms, and so on), that these samples all exhibited a single underlying nature which is causally responsible for the similarity in observed superficial characteristics, though what this underlying nature might be was of course completely unknown at the time of the introduction of the term. Competent speakers of the language thus *intended* to use the term "water" as a natural kind term, to pick out all and only samples of what they thought of as a single substance, *water*. Later on, it was *discovered* that not everything that was being called "water" is in fact properly classified as belonging to a single kind of liquid: for example, we now no longer think of tears, urine, sweat and saliva as *kinds* of water, but rather as mixtures which contain water as one among their many ingredients.[60] Moreover, even typical samples of

---

[59] For discussion of these and related points, see for example Aune (1994); Donnellan (1983); Johnston (1997); LaPorte (1996, 2004); Mellor (1977); and Zemach (1976).

[60] It is precisely considerations of this sort which indicate that the Kripke/Putnam approach is on the right track in proposing that terms like "water" are *non-descriptive* and hence function very differently in the language from terms like "janitor": for if "water" were analytically tied to a description of the sort "the transparent potable liquid that fills the rivers and lakes and is implemented in many of the physical processes exhibited by living organisms, ...", then we could never *discover*, as a result of empirical investigation, that some of the transparent potable liquid that

what we *continue* to call "water" (e.g., samples of mineral water, salt water and distilled water as well as the transparent potable liquid that fills the rivers and lakes) have similarly turned out to be mixtures of different ingredients, which tend to be at most *predominantly* composed of two parts hydrogen and one part oxygen; what counts as "predominant", in this context, is of course vague.[61]

The phenomenon of isotopes illustrates that it would be equally unjustifiably optimistic to expect our *scientific* vocabulary to be somehow completely shielded from the potential need to refine or correct proposed taxonomic categories. Thus, whereas it was initially thought that the kind *hydrogen* was ultimate, in the sense of not being divided into further sub-kinds, this assumption turned out to be mistaken, as was revealed by the discovery of hydrogen isotopes: since chemical *elements* are individuated by how they behave in chemical reactions (and this, in turn, is determined by how many protons are in their nucleus and by how many electrons are in the orbit of their nucleus), the three hydrogen isotopes, viz., 1H, deuterium and tritium, are classified as three different varieties of a single chemical element, *hydrogen*.[62] In this case, our attempts at classifying incoming information were mistaken in that we miscategorized a particular variety of object by hitting the wrong taxonomic *level*, i.e., something that we thought was an ultimate kind, upon further examination, turned out to be subject to further subdivisions.[63]

fills the rivers and lakes, say, is not really water; or that, say, tears, urine, sweat and saliva are not properly classified as kinds of water; or that some water (e.g., heavy water), say, is not potable, and so on. But, plainly, not only is it true that we *can* make such discoveries, but such discoveries *have* in fact been made. In contrast, to think that a more thorough understanding of the underlying causal story could convince us that someone whom we describe as a janitor is not cleaning personnel after all, strikes most of us as something along the lines of a category mistake.

[61] The realization that what we commonly call "water" is in fact a mixture of different elements, as discussed for example in Johnston (1997), spells trouble for Kripke and Putnam's original thesis that a statement like "Water is H_2O" is a theoretical *identity* statement, since this statement seems to be true only when interpreted in a weaker fashion, along the lines of "Quantities of water are typically predominantly *composed* of two parts hydrogen and one part oxygen". Since the element *hydrogen* can itself come in different varieties (viz., 1H, deuterium and tritium), I take the property of *being composed of H_2O* to be a distinct property from that of *being composed of two parts hydrogen and one part oxygen*, assuming that the "H" in "H_2O" is interpreted as referring to 1H, as it normally would be, due to the fact that 1H is so much more common than the other two hydrogen isotopes. Thus, on this conception, heavy water is in fact a *kind* of water (since deuterium is a *kind* of hydrogen), and the use of the term "water" in this context is not like that of, say, "dog" in "hot dog".

[62] It is thus confused to think, as is sometimes proposed in the literature, that the phenomenon of isotopes is a real-world analogue of Putnam's XYZ (see, for example, Donnellan 1983, Mellor 1977 and Zemach 1976 for suggestions along those lines); for the different isotopes, which are classified as varieties of single element, are in fact chemically related to one another with respect to those criteria which determine placement in the periodic table (viz., number of protons in the nucleus and number of electrons in the orbit). Thus, Putnam's XYZ case is instead much closer to the case of *jade*, which turned out to be comprised of two chemically unrelated kinds of minerals, *jadeite* and *nephrite*, which are only superficially alike.

[63] Our attempts at classifying objects of course can turn out to be mistaken in a myriad of ways, of which the scenario just cited involving isotopes is just one example. We may also sometimes be

Thus, the phenomenon of impurities and isotopes brings out at most a certain degree of potential mismatch between the ordinary or scientific vocabulary we intend to use to single out what we think of as genuine divisions among natural kinds and the natural kinds themselves, which we may or may not have succeeded in capturing by means of this vocabulary: while of course we intend a certain portion of our language right from the start to reflect correctly the actual varieties among objects with which we are confronted in ordinary life and in the laboratory, seldom if ever are our attempts at classifying these objects completely insulated from any traces of indeterminacy or from the need to make further revisions in our conceptual or linguistic apparatus somewhere down the line.

§VIII.6.2 Meaning-Change and Theory-Change

One of the major attractions of the Kripke/Putnam analysis of natural kind terms was said to be that it contributes to the defense of a *realist* conception of scientific discourse against the constructivist threat posed especially by the views of Kuhn and Feyerabend (e.g., Feyerabend 1962, 1965 and Kuhn 1962). In particular, according to the Kripke/Putnam tradition, scientists do not stipulate but instead discover by means of empirical investigation what the theoretically interesting underlying properties of natural kinds are. In doing so, experts do not change the meanings of ordinary or scientific classificatory terms; rather, they simply fill in hitherto unknown details in what speakers have all along been referring to by means of these expressions. Thus, when scientific theories change, the Kripke/Putnam approach allows that the meanings and reference of natural kind terms nevertheless remain stable; incommensurability between scientific theories and the apparent threat of relativism, which seems to accompany the Kuhn/Feyerabend tradition in the history and philosophy of science, thereby seems to have been averted. It has, however, been argued by a number of

mistaken in graver ways, e.g., by thinking that we have come across a natural kind when in fact we have not; in a case of this latter sort, speakers of the language will have to acknowledge, as a result of further empirical investigation, that a term which was initially intended to function in the language as a natural kind term never in fact successfully played this role, since there never was a natural kind for it to denote. The example of *the common cold* discussed in Putnam (1975b) is meant to illustrate a case of this kind: whereas it was initially thought, because of the similarity in symptoms associated with what we refer to as "the common cold" (e.g., runny nose, fatigue, swollen glands, etc.), that the term in question successfully isolated a single kind of disease or condition, it in fact turned out that the underlying causal story is far too heterogeneous to continue to think of the common cold as a natural kind; one way to tell, for example, that no single natural kind has been isolated is that, if there ever were to be a treatment for the common cold, there would have to be many different vaccines, and not just a single one, since the same group of symptoms in question is caused by a variety of different viruses. Presumably, the much-discussed example of *jade*, which turned out to comprise two completely unrelated minerals, *jadeite* and *nephrite*, belongs under this rubric as well. In contrast, as was suggested earlier, the case of *water* is in fact closer to that of *hydrogen*, since samples of what we continue to call "water" at least share a similar chemical structure, viz., that of being predominantly composed of two parts hydrogen and one part oxygen (where *hydrogen* itself can come in different varieties).

writers that natural kind terms, by virtue of being tied through their *theoretical* content to particular scientific traditions in physics, chemistry and biology and the like, are in fact more susceptible to the specter of meaning-change brought on by scientific revolutions than the Putnam/Kripke line initially let on; this alleged lack of stability in the semantic behavior of natural kind terms is in turn more naturally combined with a traditional *descriptivist* approach to their meaning.[64]

Consider, for example, terms like "mass", "force", "motion", "species" and "phlogiston". If expressions of this sort derive at least some of their content from the theories within which they are embedded, then it is unlikely, for example, that the proponents of Newtonian mechanics could have meant the very same thing by their use of terms like "mass", "force" and "motion" as those subscribing to Einsteinian relativity theory, since among other things the two theories endorse incompatible claims concerning the physical quantities to which they each seem to refer with what sounds like the same term (e.g., according to Newtonian mechanics, mass remains unchanged from one frame of reference to another, while Einsteinian relativity theory predicts that mass increases as the velocity approaches the speed of light). Similarly, pre-Darwinian uses of the term "species" came loaded with creationist assumptions, e.g., to the effect that species include all the descendants of some especially created first pair; while post-Darwinian uses of the term, on the other hand, presuppose that all species have evolved from a common ancestor. Finally, the interesting and complex case of apparently defective terms like "phlogiston" suggests at the very least that earlier theorists cannot have been entirely successful in singling out the very same phenomena (e.g., *oxygen, hydrogen,* etc.) with their vocabulary as, say, their contemporary counterparts. Theoretical terms such as "mass", "force", "motion", "species" and "phlogiston" thus seem to indicate that the Kripke/Putnam approach to natural kind terms is committed to an excessive amount of stability in the meaning and reference of such expressions.

But the apparent threat posed by the phenomenon of incommensurability between competing theories has of course been widely discussed in the literature and numerous responses are available, many of which are in fact compatible with non-descriptivist approaches to the semantics of natural kind terms. For example, Kitcher (1978) suggests that theoretical terms should be analyzed as implicitly *context-dependent*, thus allowing for the outcome that at least some occurrences of terms like "phlogiston" may be regarded as successfully singling out phenomena that would also be recognized by the 20th-century chemist. Field (1973), on the other hand, argues that expressions like "mass", "force" and "motion", as they are used by earlier theories, are *indeterminate* as between distinct uses of these

---

[64] For relevant literature, see for example Boyd (1988, 1990, 1991); Enç (1976); Field (1973); Hacking (1993); Kitcher (1978); Kuhn (1982); LaPorte (1996, 1997, 2004); Lewis (1970); Nola (1980); Papineau (1996); Sankey (1994); and Shapere (1981).

terms recognized by later theories; the crucial theoretical terms at issue, according to Field's proposal, only *partially denote* the physical quantities singled out by later theories and the earlier theories are only *approximately true*: the history of science, on this conception, progresses from less refined theories to more refined theories which may nevertheless address the very same phenomena as earlier theories.[65] Finally, Boyd (1990), for example, like Field (1973), similarly appeals to the notion of *approximate truth* and an accompanying notion of *approximate knowledge* to justify a realist conception of scientific progress in the face of challenges raised by the constructivist.[66]

Moreover, even Kuhn himself (see, e.g., 1982) later came to advocate a much less radical and more localized version of the incommensurability thesis than was originally suggested by his early formulations in Kuhn (1962). According to this more moderate conception, incommensurable theories can in fact be rationally compared, even if not all the terms of one theory can be replaced or eliminated by terms belonging to another, incommensurable theory. The obstacles which stand in the way of completely *translating* the vocabulary of one theory into that of a competing theory will typically be confined to only a cluster of very central related terms (such as "phlogiston", "element" and "principle"), but they will not affect the majority of the remaining terms used by the theorists in question (e.g., "burning", "flame", "candle", "air", "extinguish", "absorb", etc.). In any case, the skillful historian of science can, with sufficient effort, learn to *interpret* the foreign theory as one could learn to interpret a foreign language, which also often cannot be translated word-for-word into one's own language: as a result of this process of emersion, the historian of science learns to "see" the world differently, in the sense of becoming familiar with a different way of parceling up or structuring the world by means of a partially alien system of *taxonomic categories*. It is this incompatibility between competing systems of taxonomic categories to which the incommensurability between theories is ultimately traced in Kuhn's later writings. This more moderate and localized

---

[65] A contemporary version of the indeterminacy approach to biological and chemical kinds has been developed recently in a series of writings by Joseph LaPorte (see especially 1996, 1997 and 2004). To the extent that the meaning of natural kind terms, according to this view, is to some degree a matter of *decision*, LaPorte's indeterminacy solution to the incommensurability thesis goes against the grain of the Kripke/Putnam tradition. Both Field's and LaPorte's views seem to clash with the observation that if, say, the pre-Darwinian creationist had been presented with the post-Darwinian conception of the nature of species, he would surely have decidedly *rejected* this conception (as is in fact still visible today in debates over "intelligent design"); a similar outcome would seem to obtain if the Newtonian had been confronted with an Einsteinian conception of mass, force and motion. Thus, in cases of a straightforward theoretical *disagreement* between the proponents of incompatible theories or in cases in which one theory is *corrected, revised* or *abandoned* in the face of another, it seems exceedingly implausible to hold that the notions endorsed by the now scientifically unfashionable theory are simply indeterminate as between the different alternatives recognized by the competing and possibly contemporary theory.

[66] See also Sankey (1994) for a more recent discussion of the compatibility between the phenomenon of incommensurability between theories and non-descriptivist approaches to the semantics of natural kind terms.

conception of incommensurability certainly allows for a fair amount of stability in the meaning and reference of natural kind terms; in fact, it is hard to see how theory-change could even take place, and how communication across paradigms could be as successful as it plainly is, in the absence of some degree of overlap in taxonomic categories.[67]

§VIII.7 CONCLUDING REMARKS

The aim of the current chapter has been to defend a commitment to an ontology of kinds for the special case of natural kinds; such a commitment plays an important role in motivating and underwriting the structure-based and restricted conception of parthood and composition outlined in the previous chapter. The special case of natural kinds was intended as an illustration of how a commitment to a certain class of kinds in general, or to specific kinds among them, may be generated on the basis of *extra-mereological* considerations: the belief in the existence of natural kinds, for example, may be supported by an appeal to their role in prediction and explanation; particularly noteworthy in this respect is the weight borne by *scientific* natural kinds (e.g., physical, chemical and biological kinds) in (i) inductive arguments, (ii) the laws of nature and (iii) causal explanations. Once such *independent* reasons for believing in the existence of a certain kind of object have been given, we find in general that objects must satisfy more or less stringent mereological constraints in order to count as instances of the kind; as noted in the previous chapter, the types of constraints that are relevant in this context typically concern the *variety*, *configuration* and sometimes even the *number* of material components which must be present in an object in order for

---

[67] One of my aims in this chapter has been to argue that, despite considerations that have been advanced to the contrary, we should not regard biological species as individuals; my arguments to this effect were based mainly on the parallels between biological species and other more readily accepted natural kinds (e.g., those from physics or chemistry) in how these respective pluralities figure in our explanatory and predictive scientific practice. One may wonder, however, whether, by denying that species are individuals, we have thereby affirmed that they are kinds; I acknowledge that this question has not yet been completely settled by anything that was put forth in this chapter and that more remains to be said on this interesting topic. There do appear to be some notable differences between biological species, on the one hand, and these other more readily accepted natural kinds, on the other. Among other things, the essentialist seems to be on better footing with respect to chemical or physical kinds; and it might strike us, furthermore, that there is a difference between scientific terms denoting biological species and those denoting chemical or physical kinds in whether and to what extent their extensions are vague. Unless these apparent asymmetries between biological species and other candidate kinds can be dispelled in some fashion, it may be more desirable to settle for a more unified conception of natural kinds and assign biological species to some other category of pluralities. Alternatively, we might continue to group biological species alongside chemical and physical kinds; in that case, however, it remains to be explained either why, despite appearances, this categorization is less heterogeneous than it might strike us as being or why one should not be troubled by the outcome that the category of natural kinds itself turns out to be heterogeneous. I leave these questions for future inquiry.

it to count as a whole of that particular kind. Similar features are strikingly absent from the notorious Lewisian "trout-turkey" and other intuitively gerrymandered mereological sums, whose existence (if they were to exist) would be justified by nothing other than that it follows from the Unrestricted Composition Principle embraced by standard mereology; consequently, such (alleged) objects, and the pseudo-kinds to which they belong, lack any significance with respect to the sorts of considerations that are invoked in regions outside of mereology to justify our belief in the existence in a particular kind of object. The task of the next chapter will be to clarify further the nature of the structural components which have been identified as the source from which the constraints that are imposed on the mereological composition of objects originate.

IX

Structure

§IX.1 INTRODUCTORY REMARKS

From previous chapters, the view has emerged that mereologically complex objects, in order to be specimens of a particular kind, must satisfy certain structural requirements placed on them by their formal components, e.g., requirements concerning the configuration, variety and sometimes even the number of their material components. The purpose of the present chapter is to gain further insight into the nature of these formal components.

In Chapter V, we encountered Verity Harte's idea of structure as the sort of entity which makes available "slots" that can be filled by other objects, as long as these objects satisfy certain type restrictions; the objects in question, as a result of occupying the slots made available by the structure, will exhibit a particular kind of arrangement or configuration. To illustrate, consider again Harte's example of the "alternate-by-gender" seating arrangement, which may be implemented by the guests at a dinner party. Each slot in the seating arrangement (the structure) imposes type restrictions on its occupant: one slot, for example, requires its occupant to be a man; the slots to either side of this slot require their occupants to be women, though *which* man occupies each man-slot and *which* woman each woman-slot is immaterial to the implementation of the structure in question. (Moreover, assuming that the structure in question issues only the instruction "alternate by gender", then, within reason, such further features as, for example, the exact distance between the guests, and the like, are similarly irrelevant to the question of whether the seating arrangement at issue has been implemented.) As a result of their occupancy of these slots, the guests at the dinner party will be arranged or configured in such a way (assuming that the party is attended by an equal number of men and women) that each man is flanked by a woman on his left and his right side, and each woman is flanked by a man on her left and her right side; the arrangement or configuration specified by the structure in question may be expressed by means of such relations as "sits next to" or "is flanked by".

As will become apparent below, Harte's idea of structure is exactly on the right track: structures are precisely the sorts of entities which make available positions or places for other objects to occupy, provided that these occupants satisfy the type restrictions imposed by the structure on the positions in question; as a result of occupying these positions, the objects in question will exhibit a particular configuration or arrangement imposed on them by the structure. My aim in this chapter will be to develop this idea a bit further, by looking at different areas in which the notion of structure is central; my case studies in what follows will be taken in particular from mathematics, logic, linguistics, chemistry and music. The level of detail provided by these applications of the notion of structure to particular contexts proves to be helpful in extracting what is common to this notion, as it is applied in different domains; moreover, it also helps to bring out how the notion of structure may be tailored in different ways to the interests, concerns and requirements of particular domains.

We will find that what lies at the heart of the notion of structure is ultimately the distinction, already hinted at above, between what is taken as *variable* in a given domain and what is taken as *invariable*, relative to a set of admissible transformations.[1] To illustrate, relative to the structure imposed on the dinner guests by the "alternate-by-gender" seating arrangement, for example, the particular men and women occupying these slots are taken as variable, i.e., their numerical identity is irrelevant to the question of whether the seating arrangement in question has been successfully implemented, as long as the distribution of their gender with respect to one another remains fixed. Thus, all "transformations", which involve only women switching places with other women and men switching places with other men, are admissible in the context at hand, in the sense that they leave the seating arrangement in question intact: such "transformations" result in scenarios which, from the point of view of the structure, look indistinguishable.

Moreover, as we will see in what follows, particular domains, in which the notion of structure is prominent, tend to aim at formulating *laws* whose purpose is to characterize the behavior specifically of those features of the domain which are held invariant under structure-preserving transformations. The numerical identity of those elements, on the other hand, which are taken as variable within a given domain, tends to be irrelevant to the laws governing these domains; the only features of these variable elements which are relevant to the laws in question are their type as well as their distribution relative to the structural elements that are taken as invariant in a given context.

§IX.2 SOME PRELIMINARIES

§IX.2.1 Related Notions

There is a bewildering variety of concepts that are, at least in some contexts, intimately connected to the notion of structure (for a helpful catalogue, see

---

[1] This distinction between what is variable and what is invariable relative to a set of admissible transformations is also at the center of Nozick (2001); it is, however, put to very different philosophical use by Nozick.

Tranöy 1959). The closest synonym to the term "structure" is probably "form", which I have in the preceding sections assumed to be interchangeable with it; I will continue to do so in what follows.

Other concepts, which bear a close conceptual connection to the notion of structure or form and which are already familiar to us by now, are those of a "slot", "place", "position" or "node" within a structure; as well as that of a "configuration" or "arrangement" imposed by the structure on the elements occupying the slots, places, positions or nodes made available by it. Sometimes, depending on the contexts, the configurations or arrangements exhibited by these elements can also be referred to as "pattern"; "model"; "schema"; "type"; "motif"; "formation"; "shape"; "composition"; "texture"; "figure"; or "Gestalt". Similarly, in close vicinity to the idea of "arrangement" or "configuration" stand the notions of "order"; "sequence"; "beginning", "middle" and "end"; "hierarchy"; "organization"; "system" and "network". Depending on how involved the configurations or arrangements exhibited by the elements in a structure are, they can be characterized by means of such notions, for example, as their degree of "complexity". When a structure allows for movement, the configuration or arrangement imposed by the structure on its elements may also be described in such terms as "direction" or "dynamic".

Our investigation into natural kinds in the previous chapter has already revealed the close connection between the notion of structure or form and those of "kind", "species", "group", "class", "membership", and so on; those of "naturalness" and "arbitrariness"; as well as those of "regularity", "uniformity", "law", "causation", "explanation" and "prediction". For, roughly, entities that are structured may be classified into particular kinds, species, groups or classes, of which they are members, based on the regularities or uniformities exhibited by them. These regularities or uniformities, depending on their degree of naturalness or arbitrariness, are correlated with laws, which in turn license causal explanations and predictions.

Chapters IV through VII emphasized the close connection between "structure" or "form", on the one hand, and "unity" or "oneness", on the other: for it is precisely when a plurality of objects satisfies the structural requirements imposed on them by a particular kind that a unified thing, a member of the kind in question, results.

Our investigation into Plato's and Aristotle's mereology brought out the close affinity which, at least in the minds of these philosophers, obtains between the notion of structure, on the one hand, and those of "function", "purpose", "completeness", "completion", and so on, on the other. I have tried, as much as possible, to steer clear of imparting to the mereology proper normative and teleological content that is strictly speaking extraneous to it, though we will find these notions resurfacing in our discussion of musical structure below.

Finally, the notions of "dependence" or "interdependence" (as contrasted for example with "isolation") as well as those of "integration", "priority" and "control", surely also belong into this tightly connected family of concepts, at whose center lie the notions of structure or form. Certainly, Plato and Aristotle recognized these connections and attempted to implement them by means of the controversial doctrine associated with the Homonymy Principle. Exactly the best way to proceed in this area is a question I shall have to leave for future discussions, however, since the present study is nearing its conclusion.

§IX.2.2 Different Grammatical Roles

The term "structure" in English is standardly employed in several different grammatical roles; its four main uses are illustrated in the following examples:

(1) Singular and Plural Count Use:

    a. A group is *a* mathematical *structure*.

    b. Groups are mathematical *structures*.

    c. Groups have *a* mathematical *structure* different from that of metric spaces.

(2) Mass Use:

    a. Groups have *structure*; points do not.

    b. Most of mathematics is concerned with the study of *structure*.

    c. Not much *structure* is theorized to be present in this mathematical object.

(3) Adjectival and Adverbial Use:

    a. Groups are *structured*; points are not.

    b. Isomorphic systems are *structurally* equivalent.

(4) Relative Use:

    The *structure* of groups is described by the axioms of group theory.

First, the term "structure" is used as a *singular* or *plural count noun*; in this use, objects may be described as either *being* structures or as *having* a particular structure. Secondly, we find the term "structure" also occurring as a *mass noun*, as when it has "bare" (i.e., unquantified) singular occurrences or when it occurs next to typical mass quantifiers, such as "much" or "little"; in this use, for example, objects may be said to *have* or to lack *structure*, and they may be said to do so to some degree, e.g., they may have *more* or *less* structure than other objects. Relatedly, "structure" may also have an *adjectival* or *adverbial* use, as when we describe objects for example as being *structured* or as being *structurally* similar to or different from other objects. Finally, also common are *relative* uses of the term "structure", as when we speak of the *structure of* a particular object or collection of objects.

It strikes me, based on the results of the following sections, that the count use of the term "structure" is basic, while the mass, adjectival and relative use of the term are derived from it, in the following sense: each of the domains investigated below, in which the notion of structure plays a crucial role, implicitly or explicitly specifies what it means to be *a* structure within this domain; entities can then be said to be *structured* or to have *structure*, or we can speak of the *structure of* a collection of entities, depending on whether something that qualifies as *a* structure, according to the constraints operative in the particular domain at hand, is embedded in these entities.

§IX.2.3 The Gestalt Theorists: Rescher and Oppenheim

Among the forerunners in the analysis of the concepts of part, whole and structure in modern times are the Gestalt theorists, Nicholas Rescher and Paul Oppenheim, who conceive of wholes as structured in a way that is close to Harte's idea cited above:

A structured whole [. . .] involves three things: (1) its *parts*, (2) a *domain of 'positions'* which these parts 'occupy' (this need not necessarily be spatial or temporal, but may have any kind of topological structure whatever), and (3) an *assignment* specifying which part occupies each of the positions of the domain.

(Rescher and Oppenheim 1955, p. 100)

As an example for a structured whole, in which the three aspects just described can be isolated, Rescher and Oppenheim cite, from the domain of music, a (particular) performance of a musical composition: here, the *domain of positions*, according to Rescher and Oppenheim, consists in the time-interval of the performance; the *parts* of the musical composition are the various tones (as characterized by their pitch, volume and duration), which are played throughout the performance; and the role of the *assignment* is played by the score, which fixes the distribution of these notes throughout the performance.

Rescher and Oppenheim's musical example also serves well to illustrate the notion of *sameness* of structure, also known as *isomorphism*, between structured wholes: for we have already seen above that wholes with the same structure are such that we can define *transformations* between them, which leave intact certain of their structural features, while varying some of their other characteristics. For example, in the case of music, we may speak of a particular kind of transformation known as a *transposition*, in which the *key* of a musical composition is changed by systematically varying the *pitch* of the notes of which it consists, while leaving their volume, duration and other characteristics unchanged; musical pieces which are related to one another in this way, one being the transposition of the other, are structurally isomorphic, in the sense that they have the *same melody*. (We will come back to this example and consider musical structure in more detail below.) Other examples of structural isomorphisms given by Rescher and Oppenheim include temperature charts for an ill person whose graphs have the *same shape*; or poems which have the *same meter*. In each case, melody, shape or meter is the particular structural feature which is held constant or invariant under structure-preserving transformations, which the elements occupying the structure in question, e.g., the particular notes in a musical composition, or the particular words in a poem, are allowed to vary.

§IX.3 SOME CASE STUDIES

§IX.3.1 Mathematical Structure

The language of "isomorphism" and "transformations" employed by Rescher and Oppenheim in their characterization of structured wholes is of course borrowed from the world of mathematics as well as from certain branches of mathematical logic (e.g., model theory), which are concerned with the study of structure. Mathematicians think of structure in the following way: *a mathe-matical structure is an ordered n-tuple consisting of a set of objects* (the universe or domain of discourse) and "a list of mathematical operations and relations and their required properties, commonly given as axioms, and often so formu-lated as to be properties shared by a number of possibly quite different specific mathematical objects" (Mac Lane 1996, p. 174). Familiar and widely studied examples of mathematical structures include groups, metric spaces, topological spaces, rings, fields, orders and lattices.[2]

Once a particular kind of structure is defined by reference to a set of axioms, it is then possible to speak of an object or collection of objects as *having* a particular structure or as *being* structured in a particular way, namely when the object or objects in question satisfy the axioms for that type of structure; "structure" may then also be spoken of in the *relative* sense, as when the objects satisfying the axioms of group theory, for example, are said to have the structure *of* a group. In this manner, the application of the term "structure" in mathematics, in all of its different grammatical roles, is tightly linked with the axiomatic method.

In the language of mathematics, specific structures or structures in general can be compared and contrasted by means of various relations, among which the following are the most basic and important: *embedding, homomorphism* and *isomorphism* (see, for example, Manzano 1999, ch. 1). One structure is *embedded* in another just in case a copy of the former exists as a substructure within the

---

[2] To illustrate, a *group*, G, for example, is a set of elements together with some operation, g, defined over the elements of G, such that g has the following characteristics: the result of applying g to any two elements, x and y, of G yields a specific value, $g(x, y)$, which is itself an element of G and which has the following further properties specified by the axioms of group theory. First, $g(x, y)$ must be *associative*, in the sense that for any three elements, x, y, and z, of G, $g(x, g(y, z)) = g(g(x, y), z)$; secondly, the group G must have a *unit* or *identity* element, a, such that $g(x, a) = x$; and, thirdly, for each element, x, of G, there must be in G an *inverse* element, $f(x)$, such that $g(x, f(x)) = a$. This very general statement of the axioms of group theory comes from Jeffrey (1991, p. 93); I ask the reader to place imaginary corner-quotes around schematic expressions, where appropriate, here and in what follows.

latter.[3] A *homomorphism* is a structure-preserving map which holds invariant the crucial characteristics defined for the structures in question (e.g., in the case of algebraic structures, the identity element, the inverse element and the properties of the binary operations defined over the structures in question).[4] An *isomorphism* between two structures is a particular kind of homomorphism, namely a bijective map, f, such that both f and its inverse, f^{-1}, are homomorphisms. (A function, f, from a set, X, to a set, Y, is said to be *bijective* just in case for every y in Y there is exactly one x in X, such that $f(x) = y$; i.e., there is a *one-to-one correspondence* between X and Y.)[5] Isomorphic structures thus have universes with the same cardinality. In mathematics, structures are often said to be describable only "up to isomorphism", because any two isomorphic structures satisfy the same axioms and thus cannot be distinguished by the theory in question.[6]

§IX.3.2 Logical Structure

In a logically valid argument, the premises are connected to the conclusion via the relation of *logical consequence*: that is, the inference from the premises to the conclusion is logically valid just in case the conclusion is a logical consequence of or follows from the premises. Logically valid arguments have the characteristic of being *necessarily truth-preserving*; thus, a logically valid argument, so the idea

[3] To illustrate, let $\mathscr{S} = <\{SE, TO, M, BU, S\}, N>$ be the structure formed by the Spanish cities Seville, Toledo, Madrid, Burgos, Santander, together with the relation N, being to the north of. Let $\mathscr{F} = <\{SF, LA, SD\}, S>$ be the structure formed by the Californian cities San Francisco, Los Angeles and San Diego, together with the relation S, being to the south of. Then the function, h, which takes San Francisco to Seville, Los Angeles to Madrid and San Diego to Santander, is an embedding of $\mathscr{F}$ into $\mathscr{S}$ (see Manzano 1999, Example 1.62, (2), p. 27).

[4] For example, a homomorphism, f, exists between the set of real numbers with addition and the set of positive real numbers with multiplication, where $f(x + y) = f(x) \cdot f(y)$ and $f(0) = 1$, since the unit element for addition is 0 and that for multiplication is 1; the inverse element for any element, x, in the additive group is $(-x)$, while in the multiplicative group it is (x^{-1}).

[5] For example, the function, h, from the set of even natural numbers, 2N, to the set of natural numbers, N, which sends every even number, x, to $x \div 2$ is an isomorphism between the two Peano structures, $< 2N, 0, s' >$ and $< N, 0, s >$, the former consisting of the set of even numbers, 0, and s' (the operation of adding two), the latter consisting of the set of natural numbers, 0, and the successor relation (see Manzano 1999, Example 1.66, (2), p. 28).

[6] Philosophers of mathematics disagree amongst themselves as to whether all of mathematics can plausibly be construed as being concerned with structural matters; nevertheless, it seems safe to say at the very least that much of mathematical activity is directed at the study of one or another kind of structure. The particular school of thought within the philosophy of mathematics known as "mathematical structuralism" maintains that *all* of mathematics can be characterized as being concerned with the study of structure; moreover, mathematical *objects* (e.g., numbers), according to this tradition, are merely points, nodes or positions within structures; they are themselves featureless, except in relation to the structure in which they occur. For present purposes, it is not necessary to become embroiled in this dispute specific to the philosophy of mathematics (for more discussion, see Parsons 1990, 1995, 2004; Resnik 1975, 1981, 1982, 1988, 1997; Shapiro 1983, 1989, 1997). Suffice it to say that those, like Mac Lane, who hold that not all of mathematics can plausibly be construed as being concerned with structural matters may point to questions like "why are π or e transcendental?" or "how are the prime numbers distributed?", which seem to concern features that are quite specific to particular items in the domain (see Mac Lane 1996, p. 177).

is usually explained in the textbooks, is one in which it cannot be the case that the conclusion is false if the premises are true.

But a logically valid argument must also be necessarily truth-preserving in virtue of its *logical form* or *structure*. For example, in classical sentential logic, the arguments "It is raining and the streets are wet; therefore, it is raining" and "Pigs have learned to fly and all hell has broken loose; therefore, pigs have learned to fly", are classified as being instances of the same general valid inference-*pattern* or argument-*type* or *schema*, represented formally as $p \mathrel{\&} q \models p$; it is precisely because the general argument-schema or inference-pattern in question is designated as logically valid by the inference-rules of classical sentential logic that both of the instances of this general schema are designated as valid as well. In contrast, the arguments "This glass contains water; therefore, this glass contains H_2O" or "Roses are red; therefore, roses are colored" may be necessarily truth-preserving, but they would not be classified as logically valid by standard systems of logic.

Logical structure, and hence logical validity and the logical consequence relation as well, can only manifest itself relative to a particular choice of *logical constants*. Thus, it is only because the two arguments just cited are designated as instantiating the pattern, $p \mathrel{\&} q \models p$, whose only logical constant is "$\&$", that it makes sense to classify the two arguments in question as being of the same type, or as exhibiting the same logical form or structure.[7] Once they have been so classified, their validity can then be traced to the behavior of their only logical constituent, "$\&$".

In contrast, the connection between being water and being H_2O, as well as that between being red and being colored, cannot be traced to the behavior of any standardly recognized logical term: for the class of logical constants is quite limited and includes, in classical sentential and first-order logic, not much more besides the truth-functional connectives ("and", "or", "not", "if . . . then", "if and only if", etc.) as well as the first-order quantifiers ("all" and "some") and identity ("="). Since none of the predicates, "is water", "is H_2O", "is red" and "is colored", would be counted among the logical vocabulary of standard systems of logic, the necessary preservation of truth between the premises and the conclusion of these arguments cannot be traced to the behavior of any logical constant, and the arguments in question are therefore classified as *in*valid by standard systems of logic.

Relative to a particular designation of certain terms in a specified language as *logical*, the differences between two instances of the same valid argument-schema can now be characterized as bearing no relevance to their logical status, since such differences concern merely the *non-logical* vocabulary contained in these arguments. Thus, in the argument-schema mentioned above, the only function of the sentence-letters, p and q, is to mark places which may be filled by any

---

[7] The double turnstile, "$\models$", which is here taken to represent the logical consequence relation, marked in natural language by expressions like "therefore", is part of the meta-language.

well-formed truth-evaluable sentence whatsoever that belongs to the language under consideration; and the validity of instances of this argument-schema is not at all affected by *how* the places marked by the sentence-letters, p and q, are filled in, as long as the substitutions in question respect constraints concerning the grammatical category of the substituted item (e.g., items that can fill the places marked by p and q must be truth-evaluable sentences, as opposed to, say, names or predicates) and as long as the substitutions are done uniformly (i.e., the same truth-evaluable sentence goes into all the places marked by a given sentence-letter). In this way, the interpretation of the non-logical vocabulary contained in a valid argument-schema (i.e., the extensions assigned to these items by the interpretation-function that is part of the semantics of a particular logical system) may *vary*, while the interpretation of the logical vocabulary is taken as *fixed*: the value of the truth-functional connective, "*&*", for example, is always the particular function from pairs of truth-values to truth-values which yields the truth-value, True, as output only when given pairs of true sentences as input and False in all other cases.[8] The primary focus of the inference-rules proposed by particular systems of logic, along with the method for assessing whether a particular inference-pattern is licensed by the rules of the system, is to describe the behavior of the *logical* vocabulary contained in a specified language; the only features of the non-logical terms that are deemed relevant to questions concerning validity are their grammatical category and the positions occupied by these items relative to the logical constants of the language.[9]

---

[8] I am here running together two different conceptions of the logical consequence relation, which, if we were currently engaged in a discussion more specific to the philosophy of logic, should be distinguished: a *substitutional* account, according to which a valid argument is one in which no substitution of non-logical terms for non-logical terms (of the right syntactic category) produces true premises and a false conclusion; and a *model-theoretic* account, according to which no interpretation of the non-logical terms in a valid argument produces true premises and a false conclusion. However, for current purposes, it is not important to decide between these different approaches, since either one would do to spell out the general idea I am interested in illustrating, viz., the distinction between elements that are taken as variable and elements that are taken as invariable within a given context.

[9] Why is "and" considered a logical phrase, while "is water" is not? The nature of the criteria governing the choice of logical constants, and therefore the nature of the logical consequence relation itself, is a disputed matter in the philosophy of logic. Some theorists take the choice of logical constants to be to some extent arbitrary and primarily guided by practical considerations concerning the *goals* of logic as an enterprise (see, for example, Hanson 1997, 2002, and Tarski 1936). According to Hanson, the logical terms of a language are those which tend to be *ubiquitous* (in the sense of occurring across many different domains of discourse) and which preserve the *apriority* of logic. Other writers believe that precise formal criteria can be found which single out a unique class of items as *the* logical constants of a language; according to this perspective, logicality is a kind of content an expression either has or lacks absolutely and intrinsically, and not merely in relation to a particular set of purposes (see, for example, Tarski 1966, and Sher 1991, 2001a and 2001b). According to Sher, logical content amounts to *mathematical* content, in the sense that the logical operators of a specified language are just those whose content is *invariant under isomorphisms*, i.e., insensitive to differences that concern merely the individual elements within and across domains but leave the structural features of the domain intact. How this dispute concerning the criteria governing the choice of logical constants, as well as the nature of the logical consequence

§IX.3.3 Chemical Structure

In chemistry, the notion of structure is employed in the following two central ways: the chemical structure of a compound is given by stating (i) the *types* of constituents of which it consists, i.e., its *formula*; as well as (ii) the *spatial* (i.e., *geometrical* or *topological*) configuration exhibited by these constituents. Philosophers are familiar mainly with the first aspect of chemical structure or "micro-structure", as it is often referred to for example in the literature on natural kinds or on mind/body-supervenience, viz., the sense in which for example the chemical structure of water is given by stating its formula, H_2O. But this use of the term "structure" ignores the fact that the second aspect contained in the idea of chemical structure, viz., the three-dimensional arrangement into which these constituents enter, is equally crucial in characterizing the chemically relevant behavior of a compound. This became apparent in the history of chemistry in connection with the phenomenon of *isomers* or *chiral* ("handed") molecules, compounds which consist of the *same* constituents, i.e., have the same chemical formula, but whose constituents are *differently arranged* and which, as a result of this difference in arrangement, behave quite differently in specific circumstances.[10]

The Swedish chemist Jöns Jakob Berzelius (1779–1848), who introduced the name "isomerism" in 1830, to denote the idea of compositionally identical substances which exhibit different chemical properties, was made aware of the occurrence of this phenomenon by his student, the German chemist Friedrich Wöhler (1800–1882), who discovered that the substances silver cyanate and silver fulminate, despite the fact that they were assigned the same formula, AgCNO, exhibit radically different behaviors under certain conditions: for example, silver cyanate decomposes when heated, while silver fulminate explodes violently in the same circumstances; since both substances were hypothesized to consist of the same constituents, the explanation for this difference in behavior had to lie elsewhere, viz., most plausibly, as was later confirmed, in how their constituents are arranged. This realization, however, depended on the acceptance of atomistic principles in chemistry, which were at the time still regarded as suspiciously "transcendental"; the phenomenon of isomerism itself provided powerful evidence for this approach to chemistry.

The second famous example for isomerism in the history of chemistry was that of tartaric and racemic acid. While, again, these two substances had been

relation itself, is to be resolved is not immediately relevant to the present discussion; what matters for current purposes is only that all participants in the dispute agree *that* logical structure can only manifest itself relative to a particular choice of logical vocabulary, though they disagree on exactly *how* this process takes place.

[10] My main source concerning the phenomenon of isomerism and its role in the history of chemistry in what follows is Le Poidevin (2000).

hypothesized to have the same chemical composition, it was noticed that they exhibit puzzlingly different optical properties: a solution of tartrate rotates a plane of polarized light to the right, while a solution of racemate has no such effect. The explanation of this effect, as was discovered in 1848 by the French chemist and microbiologist, Louis Pasteur (1822–1895), is that the crystals contained in tartaric acid all have the same shape, while those in racemic acid have two asymmetric forms, one the mirror image of the other; the reason that the racemic solution does not rotate a plane of polarized light is that the effects of the "right-handed" molecules contained in it are balanced out by those of its "left-handed" molecules. This behavioral divergence between substances with the same chemical formula could not be explained without appeal to the concept of molecular shape; in particular, the phenomenon of optical isomerism made it necessary to think of molecular shape in a *three-dimensional* manner, to allow for the representation of potential asymmetries which could not be captured in a two-dimensional model.

To illustrate, given the idea of a three-dimensional molecular shape, a carbon atom for example can now be thought of as being located in the center of a tetrahedron, whose four apices, corresponding to the four *valencies* of the carbon atom, can be occupied in different ways by other atoms, thus permitting a number of possible permutations involving the same types of constituents.[11] The four apices of the tetrahedron, in whose center the carbon atom is depicted as lying, thus specify four different positions or places which may be occupied by other constituents which enter into the relation of *chemical bonding* with the carbon atom. Constituents which are chemically bonded to one another in this manner *share electrons*, which really amounts to saying that the electron clouds surrounding the *nuclei* of the atoms in question overlap.[12] Atoms which are connected in this fashion are said to be linked by a *covalent bond*. The atoms of each element have a tendency to form a fixed number of bonds; this tendency to form a fixed number of bonds is known as the atom's *valence*.[13]

---

[11] Much of the information in the following paragraphs is assembled from Ball (2001).

[12] The nucleus of an atom, which is its center, is exceedingly dense and hard, and even though it is approximately ten thousand times smaller than the atom itself, nearly all of the atom's mass is located there. The nucleus of an atom has positive electrical charge and is surrounded by a cloud of electrons with negative electrical charge. The electron clouds of two atoms can overlap without there being any danger of the electrons in question colliding; when this occurs, the atoms in question are said to share electrons and the two electron clouds in question merge into one, encompassing the nuclei of both of the atoms in question.

[13] Due to the rise of quantum mechanics, the second aspect of chemical structure, the idea of molecular *shape*, has lately come under fire: for while quantum mechanics has been phenomenally successful in predicting the ways in which the energy of a molecule may change under different conditions, it does so without attributing a specific three-dimensional configuration to a molecule (see for example Woolley 1978). However, as pointed out in Le Poidevin (2000), the issue of whether the idea of molecular shape is strictly speaking incompatible with the principles of quantum mechanics is reminiscent of disputes concerning *reduction* more generally; for it raises a particular version of the question of how the explanatory principles operative at the level of one scientific

The concept of molecular shape is widely employed across different areas of chemistry and other natural sciences, in particular biochemistry and molecular biology, to characterize the processes exhibited by organic and inorganic compounds. And while molecular shape cannot be thought of in a completely static way, since the constituents of a molecule are always vibrating, most of these molecular motions can be safely ignored from the point of view of the biologist or chemist, because they are either random or average to zero (Ball 2001, p. 119). As Philip Ball remarks, "a molecule's shape is the key to its behavior" (ibid., p. 25): molecular "communication" in general, as Ball puts it, operates according to a "lock and key" model, in the sense that molecules identify and interact with one another by "touch", i.e., through binding events in which receptors latch onto targets with precisely the right shape, like a key fitting into a lock (ibid., pp. 144 ff). Thus, despite the fact that the traditional non-dynamic three-dimensional conception of molecular shape, familiar to most of us from the ball-and-stick models of high-school chemistry, has been found to be subject to various pressures resulting from more recent discoveries at the sub-molecular level, the notion of molecular shape, along with chemical formula associated with a given compound, has not lost its clout as a key explanatory principle in the natural sciences.

§IX.3.4 Musical Structure[14]

Unlike the case of chemistry, the structure or organization we experience when we hear sound as music is plausibly construed as representing merely a *perceived* or *phenomenal* order, i.e., an order which comes into existence through the interaction of sound waves, the physical phenomenon underlying our perception of sound events, with observers of a certain kind, viz., creatures like us who have the necessary cognitive apparatus to appreciate sound as music. However, even this domain seems to be governed by a kind of *virtual* causality, according to which, for example, a tone may be heard as being the result of, or as generating, another; a chord may be heard as resolving another; a passage may be heard as completing another. This experience of virtual causality and movement within a phenomenal space arguably stands out as the crucial feature transforming our acoustic perception of sound into a musical experience of tones; it sets up in the hearer a series of musical expectations, characteristic of our experience of sound as music, concerning the ordering of tones into pitch groups, rhythm, harmony and melody.

Depending on the tradition in which a particular musical composition situates itself, our musical expectations are subject to something like a system of "laws".

theory are related to those operative at a level "below" it. As I am about to illustrate, the usefulness of the concept of molecular shape across a wide range of disciplines has not diminished in light of the success of quantum mechanics.

[14] In what follows, I rely primarily on the conception of music developed in Scruton (1997).

And while the "laws" in this case are perhaps more adequately characterized as retrospective generalizations describing a particular tradition of musical practice, there is no doubt an interesting further story to be told as to why particular traditions or styles of music catch on, whereas others are perceived as esoteric or marginal. For example, the most prominent style of music within the Western tradition is that of *tonal* music; relative to this musical tradition, the "laws" governing our aesthetic expectations are the "laws of tonality", a complex system of rules governing the composition of tonal music.[15]

Violations of these quasi-laws are certainly quite unlike violations of the laws of nature: whereas deviations from the laws of nature are classified as miracles, deviations from the "laws of tonality" may be employed by a skillful composer, even within the tradition of tonal music, to achieve highly successful artistic results. However, unless such violations of the "laws of tonality" are put to use with great care and expertise, they will cause in the hearer a kind of aesthetic confusion or "feeling at sea", which may in turn lead us to judge the composition in question to be either an unsuccessful instance of an already established kind or an unsuccessful attempt at creating a new musical kind or tradition; witness, for example, in this connection the wildly diverging reactions listeners have to *atonal* music in the style of Schoenberg. Negative aesthetic reactions that result from unsuccessful attempts at departing from our musical expectations find expression through a rich evaluative vocabulary consisting of terms like "jarring", "incompetent", "ineffective", "offensive", "disturbing", "off-putting", "uninteresting", "forced", "artificial", and the like.

Despite predictable differences between the phenomenal domain of music and domains like mathematics, logic and chemistry, we nevertheless find striking commonalities between musical wholes constructed out of tones and mereologically complex entities in other domains. Structure, which in the context of music amounts to organization with respect to the principles of pitch, rhythm, melody and harmony, certainly plays an extremely prominent role in music: just as the disciplines of mathematics, logic and chemistry struck us as being predominantly concerned with the study of their respective notions of structure,

---

[15] Tonal music, which is characterized by a privileged tone, the *tonic*, may be described as follows (Scruton 1997, pp. 240 ff): the melodic line of a composition does not feel fully "closed" unless it comes to rest on the tonic; the final move to the tonic standardly has the character of a "cadence", a loosening of tension; octaves are heard as equivalent, i.e., the effect of the tonic is duplicated at the octave; and other tones are heard in relation to the tonic, as more or less distant from it, as tending towards or away from it. Central to tonal music are the notion of a key; the diatonic scale; the distinction between designated and non-designated tones; the circle of fifths; the harmonic scale; the relation between major and minor; a system of triads; polyphony and voice-leading; systematic relations between chords; cadences; the independence of the bass line; modulation; the tonal center and the harmonic "force field" generated by the tonal center; as well as the elements of structure and prolongation emphasized in Schenkerian analysis. While these "tonal laws" of course do not necessitate that a particular musical constituent can only occupy one particular place and no other within a musical composition, they nevertheless pose considerable constraints on what would be judged as a successful artistic creation within the tradition of tonal music.

so the study of music may equally be fairly characterized as centering around the different aspects of musical structure. As in these other domains, a musical whole consists of certain types of elements structured or configured in particular ways relative to the "laws" of composition prevalent in a given style or tradition of music. The types of constituents of which musical wholes consist are tones; their numerical identity is again more or less irrelevant from the point of view of a particular musical structure, modulo of course such musically relevant features as the specific quality with which the tone is produced or the musical instrument which produces it. More complex musical objects may be constructed out of tones when these are grouped either vertically, as chords, or horizontally, as patterns, motifs, melodies and the like. We characterize the types of configurations exhibited by these constituents in part by recourse to a teleologically and normatively loaded vocabulary consisting of such terms as "completion", "resolution", "resting place", and the like; and in part by recourse to a three-dimensional vocabulary invoking space and motion, as when we speak for example of pitches as "high" and "low", or of melodies as "moving up" or "moving down", or as "falling" and "rising". And while arguably the application of the language of causation, movement, lawlikeness, inevitability and completion to the realm of music is merely metaphorical, we nevertheless find that particular styles or traditions of music, through their "laws" of composition, pose considerable constraints on which constituent can go where within the space of positions opened up by a particular musical structure, especially if the result is to be judged as a successful artistic statement within the given style or tradition; in this way, mereological composition in the realm of music is certainly restricted, and not every gerrymandered combination of sounds counts as music relative to a particular style and relative to the parameters of the human perceptual apparatus.

§IX.3.5 Linguistic Structure

Each of the different areas within contemporary linguistic theory speaks to a particular kind of linguistic structure, i.e., a particular way in which larger linguistic wholes may be formed systematically and in principled ways out of smaller linguistic units. Phonology studies phonological structure, the structure of sound experienced as speech, i.e., the way in which phonemes may combine to form larger well-formed units of speech-sound. Morphology studies morphological structure, the structure of words, i.e., the way in which morphemes may combine into larger meaningful units of the language. Syntax studies syntactic structure, the structure of phrases and sentences, i.e., the way in which words may combine to form larger, grammatically well-formed, constructions. Semantics, like syntax, studies the structure of phrases and sentences as well, but it does so with an eye to their meaningfulness, rather than their grammaticality. In what follows, I will confine my remarks to syntax, as an illustrative example of a certain kind of linguistic structure; however, my observations should translate fairly straightforwardly to other kinds of linguistic structure as well.[16]

One of the main insights of the Chomskyan revolution in this field consisted in the discovery that phrases and sentences cannot simply be viewed as linear strings of words. Rather, they are, from the point of view of syntax, grouped into units called "constituents", which are assigned to syntactic categories, like *noun*, *noun phrase*, *inflection*, *inflection phrase*, and so on. Assigning words and groups of words into syntactic categories allows the syntactician to make generalizations about all linguistic entities belonging to a certain type.

When syntactic constituents combine with one another to form larger grammatical constructions, such as phrases and sentences, they enter into hierarchical relationships with one another; these hierarchical arrangements among constituents are represented geometrically by means of the tree diagrams that are so distinctive of Chomskyan syntax. Many syntactic phenomena, such as anaphora (viz., the relation between a pronoun, such as "he" or "himself", and its antecedent, i.e., the nominal phrase from which the pronoun derives its reference), require reference to the spatial organization among the parts of a tree, e.g., its branches and nodes. Moreover, the structural relations which contemporary syntax recognizes as obtaining among the constituents of a phrase or sentence are all defined in terms of which positions in the tree these constituents occupy in relation to one another. For example, the relations of *dominance*, *precedence*, *c-command*, *government*, and *binding*, which took on center stage during the era of GB ("Government and Binding") syntax, are all defined in terms of spatial relations among the parts of a tree, e.g., one constituent being higher up or to the immediate left of another constituent, or one constituent being connected by means of a continuous downward path to another constituent.

In Chomskyan syntax, generalizations about sentence structure, i.e., the hierarchical ordering of constituents with respect to one another, are represented by means of *generative rules*. A system of generative rules for a language, if successful, would explain all the facts concerning grammaticality for that language in the following sense: for all the (infinitely many) possible grammatically well-formed strings of the language, there exists an admissible derivation, licensed by the rules in question, which generates the particular well-formed string; and the derivation of any of the (infinitely many) possible ill-formed strings of the language contains a violation of at least one of the rules of the system, by reference to which the ungrammaticality of the string in question can be explained. Since the inception of generative grammar in the 1950s, several different systems of

---

[16] My main source here is Carnie (2002), whose exposition is quite sensitive to the sorts of metaphysical issues concerning the notion of structure that are of special interest to me for the purposes of the present discussion. However, nothing I say about syntactic structure in what follows should be particularly controversial, at least from within a Chomskyan perspective, and similar information can be found in any comparable introductory syntax textbook that belongs to this tradition.

rules have been proposed, corrected and replaced by various successors, e.g., phrase structure grammar, X-bar theory, case theory, theta-theory, as well as, more recently, the checking theory and economy conditions of minimalism.

By means of this powerful machinery consisting of generative rules, in conjunction with whatever lexical information concerning the particular items occurring in a given sentence turns out to be syntactically relevant, the syntactician can now account for example for the contrast between different types of constructions, such as the following:

Raising Constructions:

(5) John is likely to leave.

Control Constructions:

(6) John is reluctant to leave.

Despite the fact that these two constructions superficially look alike, contemporary syntax ascribes to them very different underlying structures; the differences between raising and control structures can be brought out for example by inserting an expletive pronoun, "it", into these constructions:

(7) It is likely that John leaves.
(8) *It is reluctant that John leaves.

"It" insertion is licensed in raising constructions, but not in control constructions; this distributional divergence alerts us to the fact that the position occupied by "John" in (5) has characteristics that are different from those of the position occupied by the same nominal in (6), even though these differences are superficially invisible in the strings actually uttered in (5) and (6).[17]

---

[17] This difference, very briefly, is explained as follows. In the raising construction in (5), the subject of the sentence, "John", is hypothesized (by the VP internal subject hypothesis) to start out its transformational life initially close enough to the verb to pick up the thematic role, AGENT, from the verb (since, in "John is likely to leave", it is John who does the leaving). However, because the verb in (5) is in infinitival form, "John" cannot pick up nominative case from the verb, since verbs in infinitival form in general cannot assign nominative case to their subjects. Thus, "John" has to move to the subject-position of "is likely", in order to pick up case there. In the control construction in (6), on the other hand, no movement is hypothesized to take place; instead, control constructions are thought to contain an empty category, PRO, which is invisible on the surface of the sentence; the role of this empty constituent is to absorb the theta-role from the verb, "leave". "John", on the other hand, in (6), begins its transformational life already in the subject-position of "is reluctant", from which it gets both a theta-role and nominative case. The data concerning expletive "it" insertion confirms this hypothesis: the expletive "it", which takes case but cannot be assigned a theta-role, can occur in the subject-position of a raising-verb in (7), but not in the subject-position of a control verb in (8). Thus, the underlying structures assigned to (5) and (6) are as follows ("t_i" marks the position of the trace left by the movement of the nominal, "John", with which the trace is co-indexed, into the subject position of "is likely"):

(5)′ John$_i$ is likely [t_i to leave]
(6)′ John$_i$ is reluctant [PRO$_i$ to leave].

Syntactic structure is remarkably like chemical structure. As in the case of chemistry, the syntactic structure of a linguistic compound is given by stating (i) the types of constituents of which it consists; and (ii) the hierarchical arrangements, represented by means of tree diagrams, into which these constituents may enter with respect to one another. The first aspect of syntactic structure is analogous to the chemical formula of a chemical compound; the second to the notion of molecular shape.

A syntactic structure makes available positions or places which may be occupied by particular constituents, if these constituents satisfy the constraints imposed on these positions by the structure in question. As far as the syntax is concerned, it is immaterial for example whether the lexical items "is likely" or "is expected" occupy a particular position within a structure, since both are of the same syntactic category and both give rise to the same type of construction, viz., raising constructions. Thus, the numerical identity of lexical items matters to the syntax only if the lexical differences between these items are syntactically relevant; since the lexical differences between "is likely" and "is expected" are syntactically irrelevant, these two items are indistinguishable from the point of view of the syntax and it is thus (correctly) predicted that one may be substituted for the other without affecting the grammaticality or the syntactic properties of the outcome. Thus, phrases or sentences in which the lexical items occupying the terminal nodes are replaced by other lexical items indiscernible from them with respect to all of their syntactically relevant features are classified by the grammar as structurally isomorphic, i.e., as having the same syntactic structure: for example, "John is likely to leave" and "Sara is expected to eat" are classified as structurally isomorphic and hence as indistinguishable from the point of view of the syntax for the language; the differences between these two strings are "merely" lexical and not also syntactic.

This concludes my investigation of the notion of structure by means of case studies taken from the areas of mathematics, logic, chemistry, music and linguistics. In each case, I have tried to bring out how a particular application of the notion of structure illustrates the general distinction, which lies at the heart of this notion, namely that between what is taken as variable and what is taken as invariable relative to a set of transformations that count as admissible in a particular context.[18] The level of detail provided by these case-studies also allows us to revisit some loose ends left over from the previous discussion, especially Chapter VII, concerning the metaphysical status of structure. At that time, we

---

[18] The account of structure given in this chapter suggests certain similarities between structured wholes which, like molecules, are in my current framework taken to be three-dimensional entities and those, like melodies, which might be more plausibly construed as four-dimensional, event-like entities. Since the emphasis of the current project rests on an investigation of the part/whole structure of ordinary material objects, I will not at present embark on a further exploration of these potential similarities between three-dimensional and four-dimensional structured wholes; this project does, however, strike me as an interesting one to pursue elsewhere.

raised, and deferred to a later occasion, the following two questions: (i) To what ontological category do structures belong? Are they themselves objects, or are they rather properties and relations? And (ii) the Grounding Problem: how is the modal profile of wholes connected to the structures present in them? In the course of responding to these two questions, I will also have occasion to revisit the following issues. (iii) What sorts of mereological constraints do structures place on the wholes they organize? (iv) What sorts of structural features are shared by the members of a single kind? And (v) through what sorts of structural changes can objects persist?

§IX.4 STRUCTURES AS OBJECTS

Although the disciplines investigated above are of course not in the business of explicitly legislating on such metaphysical questions as whether structures belong to the ontological category of objects or to that of properties and relations, we may nevertheless infer some information from the way structures behave in these areas that is helpful in approaching this issue at least in a preliminary fashion. The evidence reviewed above suggests that structures are at least in some contexts treated as objects, rather than as properties or relations. At the same time, even when structures are so treated, they are always also closely linked with certain properties and relations which elements in the domain come to exhibit as a result of occupying the positions made available by the structure in question; but these properties and relations are nevertheless in these contexts not identified with the structures with which they are associated.

A good test case to consider in this connection is that of syntactic structure. The sorts of relations constituents come to exhibit as a result of occupying positions within a syntactic structure are relations like dominance, precedence, c-command, government, binding, and the like. These relations are themselves already steeped in structural notions. For example, a node, A, is said to *dominate* a node, B, just in case A is higher up in the tree than B and you can trace a line from A to B by going only downwards; precedence and c-command can be defined in terms of dominance; binding can be defined in terms of coindexing and c-command; and so on. The basic relation of dominance in terms of which other relations are defined thus itself already presupposes the inherently structural notion of a node, i.e., a position within a syntactic structure, as well as certain geometrical or topological configurations obtaining among these positions, such as one node being higher up in the tree than another or being connected to another node via a continuous downward path.

Moreover, syntactic structures are also capable of being embedded or transformed into other syntactic structures by means of a system of generative rules. For example, the structure exemplified by "John likes Mary" may be embedded within the structure exemplified by "Sarah thinks that John likes Mary", which in turn may be embedded within the structure exemplified by "Bill doubts that Sarah thinks that John likes Mary", and so on. And given a certain structure, e.g., that exemplified by "John hits men", as input, we may generate by means of a set of transformational rules other structures as output, e.g., those exemplified by "Men are hit by John", "Men were hit by John", "Does John hit men?", "Did John hit men?", "Are men hit by John?", "Were men hit by John?", "John doesn't hit men", "John didn't hit men", and so on (see Lasnik 2000, p. 58).

In each case, the operations in question take structures as inputs and yield structures as outputs; the actual sentences or phrases within which these structures are hypothesized to occur are, in a sense, immaterial from the point of view of syntax, except insofar as they are needed to generate the main data of syntactic theory, viz., grammaticality and ungrammaticality judgements from competent speakers of the language. For recall that syntax is interested in deriving generalizations about all constructions of a certain type, irrespective of the lexical items that may occur in a particular manifestation of the structure in question.

Structures thus constitute the primary domain of objects over which syntactic rules and operations are defined. In this respect, syntactic structures resemble structures as they are conceived of by mathematicians: a mathematical structure, as was noted early on in this chapter, is an ordered n-tuple consisting of a set of objects (viz., the universe or domain of discourse), along with a list of mathematical operations and relations as well as the properties required by these operations and relations, often stated in the form of axioms. Like syntactic structures, mathematical structures themselves count as elements within the domain of discourse over which the operations, relations and properties described by the axioms of a particular system are defined; thus, a group, for example, may consist of elements which are themselves groups. In this way, mathematical structures may act as both the inputs and the outputs of the "generative rules" specified by a particular axiom system.

The case of syntax and mathematics, then, suggests that structures at least in some contexts behave as objects, rather than as properties and relations; moreover, these specific contexts also seem to point to the conclusion that the properties and relations which elements in the domain come to exhibit as a result of occupying positions within a structure are merely closely associated with the structure in question and are not to be identified with it. I do not of course take these brief and programmatic remarks to have settled the question of what the ontological status of structure is for good; rather, this section at most provides some starting-points for a separate inquiry. What matters most from the point of view of the current discussion is to have established that a satisfactory account of the mereological characteristics of ordinary material objects requires the invocation of structural components; furthermore, the argument using Leibniz's Law and the Weak Supplementation Principle from Chapter VII, I take it, has provided general support for the thesis that the structural components which organize ordinary material objects are to be counted among the proper parts of the wholes in which they are present. These two central claims do not require a firm decision on the question of whether structures themselves belong to the category of objects or to that of properties and relations, and I will therefore leave this question to be addressed by future research.[19]

§IX.5 THE GROUNDING PROBLEM REVISITED

Recall, from Chapter VII, that the Grounding Problem challenges those of us who believe in numerically distinct spatio-temporally coincident objects to say what *grounds* the differences between objects that are otherwise so alike. In particular, if the present account is going to advance our philosophical position with respect to the Grounding Problem, one would hope that the presence of formal components within a mereologically complex object contributes in some way to explaining the differences in the *modal profile* associated with a structured whole and that associated with the material components which help to compose it.

Given the results of the previous sections, we know that the presence of structure within an object contributes mainly two sorts of constraints which

---

[19] Does the thesis that structures be themselves viewed as objects, rather than as properties or relations, give rise to a regress? For suppose I am right in thinking that the material objects we encounter in ordinary life and scientific practice are structured wholes, whose material components are organized by the presence of formal components within these objects. If it now turns out that structures are themselves objects, does this commit me to the view that within these structures there are further structures, organizing them, and so on, ad infinitum? This is of course just the sort of position Aristotle found himself in, when he was reluctant to attribute parts to his formal components, in the fear that he would then be forced to introduce yet another type of formal component, organizing and unifying the parts of the first ones, and so on. My reply to the threat of a regress is as follows. First, I have argued in response to Aristotle's treatment of the Problem of the One and the Many that we ought to divorce the notion of unity from that of indivisibility: the mere fact that an entity has parts does not itself pose a threat to its unity, if in order to be a specimen of the kind to which the object belongs it is a requirement that the object in question be composed of certain sorts of constituents, organized in a particular way. Secondly, my current project is addressed specifically to the question of how the parts of ordinary material objects are related to the wholes they compose; in the course of this inquiry, it turned out to be necessary to recognize within these objects the presence of structural components. Of course, if these structural components themselves turn out to have parts, then a new version of the question with which I began can be asked for them: how is it that the parts of structures are related to the structures they compose? But to respond to this query would constitute a different project, one that is specifically addressed to the nature of structures, rather than to that of ordinary material objects; and it is a project which deserves its own thorough discussion. Are, for example, the positions which a structure makes available *parts* of the structure? If so, do they play a role within the structure analogous to that played by the material components in a matter/form compound? What exactly is meant by "analogy" in this context? (Again, these questions are reminiscent of the debate engendered by Aristotle's remarks to the effect that one of the parts of a definition, viz., the genus, plays a role analogous or identical to that of matter in a matter/form compound.) If positions turn out to be parts of structures, what other parts besides these might structures have? The answer to these intriguing questions certainly is not obvious and I would be loathe to settle them in a hurry.

must be obeyed by the object's material components, if they are to compose a whole of a particular kind: (i) constraints concerning the *types* of constituents of which a compound consists; and (ii) constraints concerning the topological or geometrical *configuration* or *arrangement* that is exhibited by these constituents. Thus, assuming that my remarks in this chapter are on the right track, whatever work structures can do in accounting for the modal profile of a whole must originate from these two sources.

Consider again the case of the H_2O molecule, whose material ingredients are the two hydrogen atoms and the single oxygen atom that compose it. The structure associated with an H_2O molecule makes available three positions, on which it imposes the following type and configuration constraints. Two of the three positions must be occupied by hydrogen atoms; the remaining one must be occupied by an oxygen atom. Moreover, the occupants of these positions must be configured in such a way that the three atoms form two sides of an imaginary triangle, with the two hydrogen atoms protruding out from the oxygen atom; this configuration is held in place by the fact that the oxygen atom is chemically bonded to the two hydrogen atoms that lie to either side of it.

These structural constraints help to account for a variety of modal differences between an H_2O molecule and its material ingredients, viz., the two hydrogen atoms and the single oxygen atom. For example, it is not similarly true of the two hydrogen atoms and the single oxygen atom that they themselves must consist of the same types of ingredients as the H_2O molecule they help to compose, and that these ingredients must be arranged in the shape of an imaginary triangle in the manner described above. Hydrogen and oxygen atoms of course have their own sorts of ingredients, viz., protons, neutrons, electrons, and so on, configured in their own characteristic way. Moreover, recall from our discussion above that the structural differences between an H_2O molecule and its ingredients will also supply the main explanatory principles by means of which the differences in their behavior in chemical reactions can be accounted for. Thus, generalizations concerning, say, the way in which changes in temperature affect the chemical properties of H_2O molecules, as opposed to that of its ingredients, will centrally appeal to the types of ingredients of which H_2O molecules consist and to their manner of arrangement.

At the same time, the type and configuration constraints imposed on H_2O molecules also leave room for certain kinds of structural changes. For we observed earlier that, given the results of quantum mechanics, the triangular shape attributed to H_2O molecules must be viewed as something like an idealization or approximation: when we say that the electron clouds surrounding the nuclei of the two hydrogen atoms overlap with the electron-cloud surrounding the oxygen atom, no exact position in space-time is being attributed to these constituents; rather, they can merely be expected to be found within particular regions with certain degrees of probability. Thus, the structural constraints associated with the kind *H_2O-molecule* cannot be understood to be so rigid as to rule out the constantly vibrating motion in which the constituents of a chemical compound are found to engage.

§IX.5.1 A Potential Problem Case

Consider a statue that is constructed out of a heap of trash, say, such that the heap of trash itself has a smaller-scale statue as a part; and suppose further that the statue that is part of the heap of trash (let's call it "the small statue") is structurally isomorphic to the statue that is constructed out of the heap of trash (let's call this one "the big statue"). So the small statue is in effect a miniature version of the big statue.[20]

A case of this sort might seem to present a problem for my earlier claim in Chapter VII that my analysis may contribute to a solution to the Grounding Problem. For the Grounding Problem challenges us to account for the differences in modal profile between numerically distinct spatio-temporally coincident objects and I suggested that, following my analysis, we may be able to trace this difference to a mereological difference between the objects in question: the idea was that a structured whole has among its parts some formal components which its material components lack and that this mereological difference proves to be helpful in accounting for the differences in modal profile between a whole and its material components. But in the scenario just considered the whole and one of its material components seem to share exactly the same formal components; moreover, given the transitivity of parthood, the form associated with the small statue is a proper part of the big statue. Thus, it is no longer clear whether the form associated with the big statue can do any work in accounting for the differences in modal profile between the big statue and its material components.

§IX.5.1.1 The Detachability of the Grounding Problem

The first thing to note in response to this potential problem case is that the question of whether my analysis does in fact yield a solution to the Grounding Problem is at least in principle detachable from the analysis itself and the other virtues I claim for it. As far as I can see, the Grounding Problem is a problem for everyone who admits the possibility of numerically distinct spatio-temporally coincident objects and in that sense it is a problem for no one in particular. The main goal of this current project is to make a case for a structure-based conception of parthood and composition and, in the course of doing so, to develop a less deflationary conception of what it means to be an object than what we find in much of contemporary metaphysics; it is a welcome consequence of this approach that it rules out intuitively gerrymandered objects like Lewis' "trout-turkey". A solution to the Grounding Problem, though it would of course

---

[20] Thanks to Cody Gilmore and the members of the UC Davis Philosophy Department for presenting this case to me and for pushing me on the issues that arise in connection with it.

be a welcome by-product, is not strictly speaking required in order to accomplish this more general task. At the same time, it would of course be preferable, other things being equal, if my analysis did generate a solution to the Grounding Problem; or, if it does not, we should at least hope for an account of why the Grounding Problem is not quite as problematic as it might at first strike us as being.

§IX.5.1.2 Giving Up the Transitivity of Parthood

The scenario considered above could be bypassed by giving up the transitivity of parthood; in that case, one could block the big statue from having among its proper parts all of the proper parts of its material components, including in this case the form associated with the small statue. This is a path I am reluctant to embrace, since I would then no longer be sure why the relation I am calling "parthood" should be considered to be genuinely mereological. (I take the sorts of cases like "This page is part of this book; this book is part of this library; therefore, this page is part of this library", which have been thought to challenge the transitivity of parthood, not to be genuine challenges to it.) If the relation which holds between a whole and its formal and material components is not parthood, then we have not made much progress in elucidating the nature of this relation. As I have pointed out in earlier chapters, the Armstrongian option (of taking the relation in question to be primitive and unanalyzed) as well as Kit Fine's option (of introducing multiple *sui generis* relations which have their characteristics stipulatively imposed on them by means of distinct systems of postulates) both strike me as unattractive.

§IX.5.1.3 Individual Forms and Haecceities

A second way out of the scenario raised above would be to argue that the small statue, though structurally isomorphic to the big statue, in fact has as a part its own small-statue form that is numerically distinct from that of the big statue, either by virtue of the fact that forms are individual rather than universal entities or by virtue of the fact that the small-statue form is a haecceity; according to this option, it would again be possible to say that the big statue has a part which its material components lack.

My general worry in relation to this reply is that I find individual forms as well as haecceities to be puzzling entities, for roughly the same reasons. What exactly makes the small-statue form different from the big-statue form, despite the fact that we had assumed the big statue and the small statue to be structurally isomorphic? More likely than not, what individuates and makes these individual forms or haecceities numerically distinct will turn out to have to be taken as primitive: according to an approach of this sort, among the formal properties of the small statue just is something like the property of being identical with this very statue and among the formal properties of the big statue just is something like the property of being identical with that very statue. This option would require us to consider whether primitive thisness is, all things considered, a desirable place at which all further explanation comes to an end and whether a possible solution to the Grounding Problem is worth going in for the sizeable commitments that come with embracing a primitive formal principle of individuation. Up to this point, my aim has been to stay neutral on the question of whether formal components should be considered individual or universal entities; but perhaps one way to read the scenario raised above is that it creates pressure to embrace individuated formal components, assuming, that is, that the desire to provide a solution to the Grounding Problem is assigned a sufficiently high rank relative to other explanatory goals.[21]

§IX.5.1.4 Denying the Existence of Heaps

Finally, the following fourth response to the scenario raised above is also available. Once we have found reasons to deny Unrestricted Composition (and I have of course provided such reasons in Chapter II), we are no longer committed to endorsing the claim that every plurality of objects itself composes something; in particular, we are no longer committed to endorsing the claim that the material components out of which the big statue is constructed themselves compose a single object, a heap, which constitutes the big statue and has persistence conditions different from those associated with the big statue. My analysis predicts that we only have reason to believe in the existence of an object, when that object falls under a kind whose existence can be justified by appeal to independent considerations from outside the mereology. And what pressing non-mereological reasons are there to be committed to the existence of the kind *heap*?

Once we have freed ourselves from our putative commitment to heaps, we might spell out this fourth response further as follows. Arguably, the Grounding Problem does not really apply to the type of case raised above, since the big statue and the small statue which helps to compose it have exactly the same modal profile, given that the two statues were assumed to be structurally isomorphic and assuming for the moment that formal components are conceived of as universal. It is of course true that the big statue has, among other things, modal properties of the following type: it has for example the property that it cannot survive having its material components completely scattered, while its material components can survive being scattered. But the small statue has an analogous modal property: it also has the modal property of not being able to survive having its material

---

[21] A good place to look for the contemporary metaphysician who wants to make use of individual forms or haecceities is the metaphysics of Duns Scotus, who distinguishes between these two explanatory principles; haecceities are taken by Scotus as primitively individuated (see for example Honnefelder 1984 and King 2003). I am grateful to Jan Szaif and Robert Pasnau for helpful discussion of these points.

components completely scattered, while whatever it is that it is composed of might lack this property. And since we have denied Unrestricted Composition, there is no *single* intermediary object which constitutes the big statue and which can survive being scattered while the big statue cannot. It thus seems as though, at the very least, various options are available by means of which a hylomorphic approach may respond to the Grounding Problem and the sort of scenario raised above; I will leave the question of how to decide between these options, and perhaps between others that I have not canvassed in the foregoing remarks, open for future discussion.

§IX.6 CONCLUDING REMARKS

My aim in this chapter has been to isolate and illustrate the general features of the notion of structure by examining the use to which this notion is put in several domains that are particularly focused on the study of structure. My case studies were taken from the disciplines of mathematics, logic, chemistry, music and linguistics, each of which offers a particular application of the general notion of structure tailored to its own purposes.

Each of these areas conceives of *a* structure as the sort of entity which (i) makes available *positions* or *places* for other objects to occupy; and which (ii) places two distinctive sorts of constraints on these positions. The first sort of constraint concerns the *type* of constituent which may occupy the position in question. The second sort of constraint concerns the particular geometrical or topological *configuration* or *arrangement* which must be exhibited by these constituents, as a result of occupying the positions made available by the structure.

In some cases, these two sorts of constraints a structure places on its occupants also conspire to generate restrictions as to the exact *number* of constituents a particular kind of compound must have: for example, the structure associated with H_2O molecules makes available exactly three positions that may be occupied by hydrogen and oxygen atoms respectively, while that associated with the logical connective "and" makes available exactly two positions that may be occupied by any grammatically well-formed truth-evaluable sentence of the language in question. Other structures, however, are more lenient when it comes to the precise number of positions allowed in a particular formation: the musical structure associated with a twelve-bar blues, for example, does not legislate exactly how many notes must occur in a particular manifestation of this structure; moreover, "John is likely to leave" and "John is likely to leave in a hurry" both exemplify the basic pattern of a raising construction, even though the second sentence contains more words than the first.

The two features in (i) and (ii) that have shown themselves to be characteristic of the general notion of structure lead to a distinction between what is taken as *variable* and what is taken as *invariable* within a given context. The numerical identity of the items occupying the positions made available by a structure is generally unimportant to the question of whether the structure in question has been successfully implemented; the individual occupants of these positions are thus *variable* from the point of view of the structure. What matters concerning these items, and what is hence taken as *invariable*, from the point of view of the structure, is only their type and their configuration.

When we say that structural concerns are prominent in a specific discipline, what we mean is that the theories, axioms or laws formulated by the discipline in question focus in particular on capturing the behavior of those elements that are designated as *invariable* within a given context. Logic, for example, focuses in particular on characterizing the behavior of those items that are designated as logical constants relative to a particular language, since their behavior turns out to be the determining factor on which the validity of inferences depends. Perhaps Plato was right in thinking that structure in this way lies at the heart of every science and every rigorous enterprise; certainly, the particular disciplines we have examined in this chapter give rise to this impression.

Conclusion

We began with the observation that any credible account of the notions, part, whole and object, ideally should provide the resources to respect the distinction between, say, a motorcycle in running condition and its disassembled parts; moreover, other things being equal, such an account should also avoid generating objects, such as the mereological sum consisting of the President's left hand and the Eiffel Tower, whose existence is not motivated in any way by independent evidence outside the theory of parts and wholes. And while of course many questions are left unanswered by the particular account I have provided in the preceding pages, I have tried to center my attention around the key element that, in my view, is missing from the arbitrary sums of standard mereology; the key element in question is of course the notion of structure, which has been surprisingly absent from contemporary metaphysics for quite some time now.

You may not agree with me on all the details of my account. In particular, I expect that my thoroughly mereological conception of composition will raise philosophical eyebrows: recall that according to this conception, the structure which dictates how the remaining parts of an object are to be arranged is itself, literally and strictly speaking, a part of the whole it organizes. In some cases, it comes, I think, quite naturally to us to think of structures as themselves parts of the objects they organize. For example, it is not too much of a stretch to think of the syntactic or semantic structure of a sentence as literally part of the sentence in question. But, then again, sentences are (or at least seem to be) abstract objects, and it is perhaps easier to think of structures as parts of abstract objects than to do the same in the case of ordinary material objects. I agree that it takes some getting used to before one can sign on to this way of thinking of objects across the board. For example, it is admittedly awkward at first to think of the shape of a molecule as literally part of the molecule in question. One wants to respond, in this case: "Well, perhaps it is, but surely in a different sense of 'part'!".

To this sort of reaction I have three replies. First, I would like to see where the differences lie between the sense of "part" the imaginary respondent has in mind and the sense of "part" that has been put to use in the previous pages. Once the alternative mereology is on the table, we can get to work in comparing the two systems; before then, my proposal has at least the advantage of providing the sort of detail that is as of yet missing from the respondent's gut reaction. Those who have been persuaded by me or others to leave behind standard mereology, in favor of the thesis that ordinary material objects are structured wholes, must in some way tell us how a whole is related to its structure. If nothing at all is said about this relation, or if some new primitive operation is introduced especially for this purpose, then we have in a deep sense been left in the dark concerning the nature of ordinary material objects.

Secondly, I have in Chapter VII offered a general philosophical argument in favor of the thesis that ordinary material objects have structures among their parts, alongside their more familiar material parts. This "master argument" uses as premises principles, in particular Leibniz's Law and the Weak Supplementation Principle, that will, I think, strike the reader as much less controversial than the conclusion I derive from them. Given my general argument in favor of the thesis that ordinary material objects have structures among their parts, we can thus advance the philosophical discussion beyond a pure stand-off by inviting the imaginary respondent to refine his gut reaction to the point of being able to pinpoint exactly where in my argument I went wrong in thinking that the conclusion follows from the premises. In this way, I hope at least to stimulate fruitful discussion among other philosophers engaged in similar projects.

Thirdly, given our contemporary philosophical tradition, we are, I think, more likely than older generations to be biased against the thesis that objects have structures as parts by the fact that structures, historically speaking, have their origins in Platonic and Aristotelian forms; in this current naturalistic climate, it is of course not particularly fashionable to defend the claim that something as apparently philosophically uncomplicated as, say, a motorcycle is literally and strictly speaking composed of something as apparently philosophically loaded as a structure or form. To take away some of the puzzlement that this position is sure to generate, I have tried to dispel the myth that structures or forms really must be conceived along the lines of their normatively and teleologically loaded historical predecessors. Aristotle already criticized Plato for removing forms so far from the particulars, whose characteristics they were supposed to explain, that they became causally inert and philosophically useless. In reaction to the Platonic model, Aristotelian matter/form compounds became connected in a much more intimate fashion to their explanatory principles, namely, at least on my reading of Aristotle, by having them as parts. But Aristotelian forms are of course still, and rightly so, viewed by most contemporary metaphysicians with suspicion.

When we put our philosophical prejudices aside for a moment, however, and look at what actually goes on in such disciplines as mathematics, logic, linguistics, chemistry and music, we find that the notion of structure lies at the very center of the daily business that is being conducted in these areas. Philosophers may of course debate whether structures really exist, whether they are abstract or concrete, universal or particular, just as they continue to debate similar questions concerning the status of redness, say. But the fact that mathematical, logical, linguistic, chemical or musical structures are central explanatory principles in their respective disciplines cannot genuinely be in doubt; and the work that is actually done by these principles in their respective disciplines is not significantly affected by whether they turn out to be abstract or concrete, universal or particular.

If I sound as though it is my belief that metaphysicians do nothing besides spin their wheels in the dark, that is not my intention. Having just devoted several years of my life to the task of thinking about parts and wholes from the point of view of a metaphysician, I obviously do think that this part of philosophy has important work to accomplish. It merely strikes me that, given the prominence of the notion of structure in the domains that we have considered, metaphysicians cannot get around the fact that *something* must be doing the important explanatory work that seems to be done by the notion of structure in these areas; and this is true *whatever* exactly these entities turn out to be.

Finally, I would like to address at least briefly an important critical reaction to the kind of position I have argued for in this book; this sort of opposition, though it has not come up directly, has I think been touched on indirectly by what I have said in the preceding chapters. The position I have in mind is a kind of *relativism* concerning divisions of objects into parts: according to this position, divisions of objects into parts are ultimately a conceptual matter, grounded in human activity; it is we who divide objects into parts in particular ways, on this view, depending on what happens to be important to us at a given moment. There is thus, on this view, no right way of dividing an object into parts, since on some occasions it might prove useful, say, to speak of Socrates' left half and his right half, while on other occasions it might make more sense to think of him, as an anatomist would, as divided into arms, legs, a head, a torso, and so on. But such divisions of Socrates into parts, according to the relativist, cannot be ranked in accordance to whether they come closer to the way in which Socrates is in fact divided into parts, since no sense can be made of this latter notion.

As in all other areas of philosophy, there is of course something very seductive about a relativistic approach to mereology. And, as in all other areas of philosophy, it is not a straightforward matter at all to provide a satisfying argument against someone who wants to adopt a relativistic stance towards our divisions of objects into parts. Of course, I do not expect to settle the dispute between the relativist and the absolutist in the course of just a few paragraphs. Moreover, I also do not doubt that at least some of our divisions of objects into "parts" proceed in the way imagined by the relativist.

But I do hope that especially my remarks concerning natural kinds in Chapter VIII as well as my remarks concerning structure in Chapter IX have gone some way towards suggesting that the relativist stance does not properly capture the fairly sizeable constraints to which we take ourselves to be responsive in our actual practices of dividing objects into parts in such domains as physics, chemistry, biology, mathematics, logic, linguistics or music. It follows from my approach to mereology that the parts we attribute to a particular object must themselves deserve the status of objects within our ontology; objects fall into kinds and our commitment to particular kinds must be justified by means of evidence from outside the theory of parts and wholes. And so my question to the relativist is: are there reasons for being committed to a kind of object, left half of a human, that are as convincing as the reasons which motivate, say, our belief in the existence of arms, legs, heads, torsos, and so on? Of course, the relativist may respond to this challenge by adopting a more thorough-going relativistic stance not simply towards our divisions of objects into parts, but also towards our classifications of objects into kinds more generally. But in that case we have at least managed to reduce the question of whether we ought to be relativists concerning our divisions of objects into parts to a different, and more familiar, problem, viz., whether we ought to be relativists concerning the notions of object and kind more generally.

Bibliography

Almog, Joseph (1981) "Dthis and Dthat: Indexicality Goes Beyond That", *Philosophical Studies*, 39, 347–81.

Armstrong, David M. (1978) *Universals and Scientific Realism*, vols. I and II, Cambridge, UK, Cambridge University Press.

—— (1980a) "Against 'Ostrich Nominalism': A Reply to Michael Devitt", *Pacific Philosophical Quarterly*, 61, 440–9.

—— (1980b) "Identity Through Time", in *Time and Cause: Essays Presented to Richard Taylor*, ed. Peter van Inwagen, Dordrecht, Netherlands, D. Reidel, pp. 67–78.

—— (1986) "In Defense of Structural Universals", *Australasian Journal of Philosophy*, 64 (1), 85–8.

—— (1988) "Are Quantities Relations? A Reply to Bigelow and Pargetter", *Philosophical Studies*, 54, 305–16.

—— (1989) *Universals: An Opinionated Introduction*, Boulder, CO, Westview Press.

—— (1991) "Classes Are States of Affairs", *Mind*, 100, 189–200.

—— (1997) *A World of States of Affairs*, Cambridge, UK, Cambridge University Press.

Aronson, Jerrold L., Harré, Rom and Way, Eileen C. (1995) *Realism Rescued*, Chicago, Open Court.

Aune, Bruce (1994) "Determinate Meaning and Analytic Truth", in *Living Doubt*, ed. G. Debrock and M. Hulswit, Dordrecht, Netherlands, Kluwer Academic Publishers, pp. 55–65.

Ayers, Michael (1981) "Locke Versus Aristotle on Natural Kinds", *Journal of Philosophy*, 78(5) 247–72.

Baker, Lynne Rudder (1997) "Why Constitution is not Identity", *Journal of Philosophy*, 94, 599–621.

—— (1999) "Unity Without Identity: A New Look at Material Constitution", *Midwest Studies in Philosophy*, XXIII, 144–65.

—— (2000) *Persons and Bodies: A Constitution View*, Cambridge Studies in Philosophy Series, Cambridge, UK, Cambridge University Press.

Ball, Philip (2001) *Stories of the Invisible: A Guided Tour of Molecules*, New York, Oxford University Press.

Barnes, Jonathan (1984) *The Complete Works of Aristotle: The Revised Oxford Translation*, ed. Jonathan Barnes, Volume One and Two, Bollingen Series LXXI.2, Princeton, NJ, Princeton University Press .

—— (1986) "Bits and Pieces", in *Matter and Metaphysics*, Fourth Symposium Hellenisticum, Bibliopolis, ed. Jonathan Barnes and Mario Mignucci, Pontignano, Italy, pp. 224–94.

Baxter, Donald L. M. (1988a) "Identity in the Loose and Popular Sense", *Mind*, 97, 575–82.

—— (1988b) "Many-One Identity", *Philosophical Papers*, 17, 193–216.

Bennett, Karen (2004a) "Global Supervenience and Dependence", *Philosophy and Phenomenological Research*, 68(3), 501–29.

Bennett, Karen (2004b) "Spatio-Temporal Coincidence and the Grounding Problem", *Philosophical Studies*, 118(3), 339–71.

Bigelow, John (1986) "Towards Structural Universals", *Australasian Journal of Philosophy*, 64(1), 94–6.

Bogaard, Paul A. (1979) "Heaps or Wholes: Aristotle's Explanation of Compound Bodies", *Isis*, 70(251), 11–29.

Boolos, George (1975) "On Second Order Logic", *Journal of Philosophy*, 72, 509–27.

—— (1984) "To Be Is To Be a Value of a Variable (or To Be Some Values of Some Variables)", *Journal of Philosophy*, 81, 430–49.

—— (1985a) "Nominalist Platonism", *Philosophical Review*, 94, 327–44.

—— (1985b) "Reading the *Begriffsschrift*", *Mind*, 94, 331–44.

Bostock, David (1979) *Logic and Arithmetic, Vol. 2: Rational and Irrational Numbers*, Oxford, Clarendon Press.

—— (1994) *Aristotle, Metaphysics Z and H*, translated with a commentary, Oxford, Clarendon Press.

Boyd, Richard (1988) "How to be a Moral Realist", in *Moral Realism*, ed. Geoffrey Sayre-McCord, Ithaca, NY, Cornell University Press, pp. 181–228.

—— (1990) "Realism, Conventionality, and 'Realism About'", in *Meaning and Method: Essays in Honor of Hilary Putnam*, ed. George Boolos, Cambridge, UK, Cambridge University Press, pp. 171–95.

—— (1991) "Realism, Anti-Foundationalism and the Enthusiasm for Natural Kinds", *Philosophical Studies*, 61, 127–48.

—— (1992) "Constructivism, Realism and Philosophical Method", in *Inference, Explanation and Other Frustrations*, ed. John Earman, Berkeley, CA, University of California Press, pp. 131–98.

Bunt, Harry C. (1985) *Mass Terms and Model-Theoretic Semantics*, Cambridge, UK, Cambridge University Press.

Burge, Tyler (1982) "Other Bodies", in *Thought and Object: Essays on Intentionality*, ed. Andrew Woodfield, Oxford, Clarendon Press, pp. 97–120.

Burke, Michael (1992) "Copper-Statues and Pieces of Copper: A Challenge to the Standard Account", *Analysis*, 52, 12–17.

—— (1994a) "Dion and Theon: An Essentialist Solution to an Ancient Puzzle", *Journal of Philosophy*, 91, 129–39.

—— (1994b) "Preserving the Principle of One Object to a Place: A Novel Account of the Relations Among Objects, Sorts, Sortals, and Persistence Conditions", *Philosophy and Phenomenological Research*, 54, 591–624.

Burnyeat, Myles (1990) *The* Theaetetus *of Plato*, tr. M. J. Levett, rev. and with an Introduction by Myles Burnyeat, Indianapolis, Indiana, Hackett Publishing Co.

—— (2001) *A Map of* Metaphysics Zeta, Pittsburgh, Mathesis Publications.

Burnyeat, Myles, et al. (1979) *Notes on Zeta*, recorded by Myles Burnyeat and others, Study Aids Monograph No. 1, Sub-Faculty of Philosophy, 10 Merton Street, Oxford.

—— (1984) *Notes on Eta and Theta of Aristotle's* Metaphysics, recorded by Myles Burnyeat and others, Study Aids Monographs No. 4, Sub-Faculty of Philosophy, 10 Merton Street, Oxford.

Carnie, Andrew (2002) *Syntax: A Generative Introduction*, Oxford, Blackwell.

Cartwright, Helen Morris (1996) "On Plural Reference and Elementary Set Theory", *Synthese*, 96(2), 201–54.

Cartwright, Nancy (1989) *Nature's Capacities and Their Measurement*, New York, Clarendon Press.

Cartwright, Richard (1968) "Some Remarks on Essentialism", *Journal of Philosophy*, 65 (20), 615–26.

—— (1971) "Identity and Substitutivity", in *Identity and Individuation*, ed. Milton Munitz, New York, New York University Press, pp. 119–33.

—— (1975) "Scattered Objects", in *Analysis and Metaphysics*, ed. Keith Lehrer, Dordrecht, Netherlands, D. Reidel, pp. 153–71.

—— (1979) "Indiscernibility Principles", *Midwest Studies in Philosophy*, 4, 293–306.

—— (1987) *Philosophical Essays*, Cambridge, MA, MIT Press.

—— (1994) "Notes on Aquinas", unpublished manuscript.

Casati, Roberto and Varzi, Achille (1999) *Parts and Places: The Structures of Spatial Representation*, Cambridge, Massachusetts, MIT Press.

Charles, David (1992) "Aristotle on Substance, Essence and Biological Kinds", in *Proceedings of the Boston Area Colloquium in Ancient Philosophy*, ed. J. J. Cleary and D. Shartin, 7, 227–61.

—— (1994) "Matter and Form: Unity, Persistence and Identity", in *Unity, Identity, and Explanation in Aristotle's Metaphysics*, ed. T. Scaltsas, D. Charles and M. L. Gill, Oxford, Clarendon Press, pp. 75–105.

Chisholm, Roderick (1973) "Parts as Essential to Their Wholes", *Review of Metaphysics*, 26, 581–603.

—— (1975) "Mereological Essentialism: Some Further Considerations", *Review of Metaphysics*, 28, 477–84.

—— (1976) *Person and Object: A Metaphysical Study*, La Salle, Illinois, Open Court Publishing Company .

Churchland, Paul (1985) "Conceptual Progress and Word/World Relations: In Search of the Essence of Natural Kinds", *Canadian Journal of Philosophy*, 15(1), 1–17.

Clarke, Bowman L. (1981) "A Calculus of Individuals Based on 'Connection'", *Notre Dame Journal of Formal Logic*, 22, 204–18.

Cook, Monte (1980) "If 'Cat' Is a Rigid Designator, What Does It Designate?", *Philosophical Studies*, 37, 61–4.

Cordry, Ben S. (2004) "Necessity and Rigidly Designating Kind Terms", *Philosophical Studies*, 119, 243–64.

Crane, Judith (2004) "On the Metaphysics of Species", *Philosophy of Science*, 71, 1–18.

Deutsch, Harry (1993) "Semantics for Natural Kind Terms", *Canadian Journal of Philosophy*, 23(3), 389–412.

—— (1998) "Identity and General Similarity", *Philosophical Perspectives*, vol. 12 (*Language, Mind and Ontology*), ed. J. E. Tomberlin, Atascadero, CA, Ridgeview, pp. 177–99.

—— (2002) "Relative Identity", *Stanford Encyclopedia of Philosophy* (Summer 2002 Edition), ed. Edward N. Zalta, <http://plato.stanford.edu/entries/identity-relative>.

De Laguna, Theodore (1922) "Point, Line, and Surface, as Sets of Solids", *Journal of Philosophy*, 19, 449–61.

Devitt, Michael (1980) "'Ostrich Nominalism' or 'Mirage Realism'?", *Pacific Philosophical Quarterly*, 61, 433–9.

—— (1981) *Designation*, New York, Columbia University Press.

Dirac, P. A. M. (1938) "A New Basis for Cosmology", *Proceedings of the Royal Society (London), Series A*, 165, 199–208.

Doepke, Frederick (1982) "Spatially Coinciding Objects", *Ratio*, 24, 45–60.

Donnellan, Keith (1979) "The Contingent *A Priori* and Rigid Designation", in *Contemporary Perspectives in the Philosophy of Language*, ed. Peter A. French, Theodore E. Uehling, Jr, and Howard K. Wettstein, Minneapolis, University of Minnesota Press, pp. 45–60.

—— (1983) "Kripke and Putnam on Natural Kind Terms", in *Knowledge and Mind*, ed. Carl Ginet and Sydney Shoemaker, Oxford, Oxford University Press, pp. 84–104.

Dorr, Cian (2005) "What We Disagree About When We Disagree About Ontology", in *Fictionalism in Metaphysics*, ed. Mark Eli Kalderon, Oxford, Clarendon Press, pp. 234–86.

Dretske, Fred (1977) "Laws of Nature", *Philosophy of Science*, 44, 248–68.

Driscoll, John (1981) "EIΔH in Aristotle's Earlier and Later Theories of Substance", in *Studies in Aristotle*, ed. Dominic J. O'Meara, Washington D.C., The Catholic University of America Press, pp. 129–59.

Dupré, John (1981) "Natural Kinds and Biological Taxa", *Philosophical Review*, 90(1), 66–90.

—— (1993) *The Disorder of Things: Metaphysical Foundations of the Disunity of Science*, Cambridge, MA, Harvard University Press.

Earman, John (1978) "The Universality of Laws", *Philosophy of Science*, 45, 173–81.

Eberle, Rolf A. (1970) *Nominalistic Systems*, Dordrecht, The Netherlands, D. Reidel.

Enç, Berent (1976) "Reference of Theoretical Terms", *Nous*, 10, 261–82.

Ereshefsky, Marc (1991) "Species, Higher Taxa, and the Units of Evolution", *Philosophy of Science*, 58, 84–101.

Evans, Gareth (1973) "The Causal Theory of Names", *Aristotelian Society Supplementary Volume 47*, 187–208.

—— (1978) "Can There Be Vague Objects?", *Analysis*, 38, 208.

—— (1979) "Reference and Contingency", *The Monist*, 62(2), 161–89.

Feyerabend, Paul (1962) "Explanation, Reduction and Empiricism", in *Minnesota Studies in the Philosophy of Science*, ed. H. Feigl and G. Maxwell, Minneapolis, University of Minnesota Press, vol. 3, pp. 28–97.

—— (1965) "Problems of Empiricism", in *Beyond the Edge of Certainty*, ed. R. G. Colodny, Englewood Cliffs, NJ, Prentice Hall, pp. 145–260.

Field, Hartry (1973) "Theory Change and the Indeterminacy of Reference", *Journal of Philosophy*, 70, 462–80.

Fine, Kit (1982) "Acts, Events and Things", in *Language and Ontology, Proceedings of the Sixth International Wittgenstein Symposium*, pp. 97–105.

—— (1983) "Aristotle on Substance", unpublished manuscript.

—— (1991) "The Study of Ontology", *Nous*, 25, 263–94.

—— (1992) "Aristotle on Matter", *Mind*, 101, 35–57.

—— (1994a) "Compounds and Aggregates", *Nous*, 28(2), 137–58.

—— (1994b) "Essence and Modality", *Philosophical Perspectives*, vol. 8 (*Logic and Language*), pp. 1–16.

—— (1994c) "A Puzzle Concerning Matter and Form", in *Unity, Identity and Explanation in Aristotle's Metaphysics*, ed. T. Scaltsas, D. Charles and M. L. Gill, Oxford, Clarendon Press, pp. 13–40.

—— (1995a) "Ontological Dependence", *Proceedings of the Aristotelian Society*, 95, 269–90.

—— (1995b) "Part-Whole", in *The Cambridge Companion to Husserl*, ed. Barry Smith and David Woodruff Smith, Cambridge, UK, Cambridge University Press, pp. 463–85.

—— (1995c) "The Problem of Mixture", *Pacific Philosophical Quarterly*, 76, 266–369; published in revised form in *Form, Matter, and Mixture in Aristotle*, ed. Frank Lewis and Robert Bolton, Oxford, Blackwell (1997), pp. 266–369.

—— (1998) "Mixing Matters", *Ratio*, 11(3), 278–88.

—— (1999) "Things and Their Parts", *Midwest Studies in Philosophy*, 23, 61–74.

—— (2000) "A Counterexample to Locke's Thesis", *The Monist*, 83(3), 357–61.

—— (2001) "The Question of Realism", *Philosophers' Imprint*, 1(1), <www.philosophersimprint.org/001001/>.

—— (2003) "The Non-Identity of a Material Thing and Its Matter", *Mind*, 112, 195–234.

Fodor, Jerry (1974) "Special Sciences, or the Disunity of Science as a Working Hypothesis", *Synthese*, 28, 77–115; reprinted in *Metaphysics: An Anthology*, ed. Jaegwon Kim and Ernest Sosa, 2nd edn, Oxford, Blackwell (2000), pp. 504–14.

Forbes, Graeme (1981) "An Anti-Essentialist Note on Substances", *Analysis*, 41(1), 32–7.

—— (1987) "Is There a Problem About Persistence?", *Aristotelian Society*, suppl. vol. 61, pp. 137–55.

Forrest, Peter (1986a) "Ways Worlds Could Be", *Australasian Journal of Philosophy*, 64 (1), 15–24.

—— (1986b) "Neither Magic Nor Mereology: A Reply to Lewis", *Australasian Journal of Philosophy*, 64(1) 89–91.

Forster, Malcolm R. (1988) "Unification, Explanation, and the Composition of Causes in Newtonian Mechanics", *Studies in History and Philosophy of Science*, 19, 55–101.

Frede, Dorothea (1993) *Plato: Philebus*, tr. with Introduction and Notes, Indianapolis, Indiana, Hackett.

Frede, Michael and Patzig, Günther (1988) *Aristoteles* Metaphysik *Z*, Text, Übersetzung und Kommentar, vols. 1 and 2, Munich, Germany, Verlag C. H. Beck.

Furth, Montgomery (1985) *Aristotle*, Metaphysics, *Books VII–X*, Indianapolis, Indiana, Hackett.

—— (1986) "Aristotle on the Unity of Form", *Boston Area Colloquium in Ancient Philosophy*, vol. 2, ed. J. Cleary, pp. 243–67.

Gallois, André (1990) "Occasional Identity", *Philosophical Studies*, 58, 203–24.

—— (1998) *Occasions of Identity: A Study in the Metaphysics of Persistence, Change and Sameness*, Oxford, Clarendon Press.

Geach, Peter (1962) *Reference and Generality*, Ithaca, NY, Cornell University Press.

—— (1967) "Identity", *Review of Metaphysics*, 21, 3–12.

Ghiselin, Michael (1966) "On the Psychologism in the Logic of Taxonomic Controversies", *Systematic Zoology*, 15, 207–15.

—— (1969) *The Triumph of the Darwinian Method*, Berkeley, CA, University of California Press.

—— (1974) "A Radical Solution to the Species Problem", *Systematic Zoology*, 23, 536–44.

Ghiselin, Michael (1987) "Species Concepts, Individuality and Objectivity", *Biology and Philosophy*, 2, 127–43.

Gibbard, Alan (1975) "Contingent Identity", *Journal of Philosophical Logic*, 4, 187–221.

Gill, Mary Louise (1989) *Aristotle on Substance: The Paradox of Unity*, Princeton, NJ, Princeton University Press.

Gillon, Brandon (1984) *The Logical Form of Plurality and Quantification in Natural Language*, unpublished PhD dissertation, MIT, Cambridge, MA.

Goodman, Nelson (1954) *Fact, Fiction and Forecast*, 4th edn, Cambridge, MA, Harvard University Press (1983).

—— (1977) *The Structure of Appearance*, 3rd edn, Dordrecht, The Netherlands, D. Reidel.

Griffin, Nicholas (1977) *Relative Identity*, Oxford, Clarendon Press.

Gupta, Anil (1980) *The Logic of Common Nouns*, New Haven, Yale University Press.

Hacking, Ian (1991) "A Tradition of Natural Kinds", *Philosophical Studies*, 61, 109–26.

—— (1993) "Working in a New World: The Taxonomic Solution", in *World Changes*, ed. Paul Horwich, Cambridge, MA, MIT Press, pp. 275–310.

Halper, Edward (1989) *One and Many in Aristotle's Metaphysics: The Central Books*, Columbus, Ohio State University Press.

Hamlyn, David (1993) *Aristotle, De Anima, Books II and III (With Passages from Book I)*, translated with an introduction and notes by David Hamlyn, with a report on recent work and a revised bibliography by Christopher Shields, Oxford, Clarendon Press.

Hanson, William H. (1997) "The Concept of Logical Consequence", *The Philosophical Review*, 106(3), 365–409.

—— (2002) "The Formal-Structural View of Logical Consequence: A Reply to Gila Sher", *The Philosophical Review*, 111(2), 243–58.

Harte, Verity (1994) *Parts and Wholes: Plato, Aristotle and the Metaphysics of Structure*, unpublished PhD dissertation, St Edmund's College, Cambridge, UK.

—— (1996) "Aristotle: *Metaphysics* H.6: A Dialectic with Platonism", *Phronesis*, 41, 276–304.

—— (2002) *Plato on Parts and Wholes: The Metaphysics of Structure*, Oxford, Clarendon Press.

Haslanger, Sally (1985) *Persistence, Change and Explanation*, unpublished PhD dissertation, Berkeley, CA, University of California .

—— (1989a) "Persistence, Change and Explanation", *Philosophical Studies*, 56, 1–28.

—— (1989b) "Endurance and Temporary Intrinsics", *Analysis*, 49, 119–25.

—— (1994a) "Humean Supervenience and Enduring Things", *Australasian Journal of Philosophy*, 72, 339–59.

—— (1994b) "Parts, Compounds and Substantial Unity", in *Unity, Identity, and Explanation in Aristotle's Metaphysics*, ed. T. Scaltsas, D. Charles and M. L. Gill, Oxford, Clarendon Press, pp. 129–71.

Hawthorne, John, Scala, Mark and Wasserman, Ryan (2004) "Recombination, Causal Constraints and Humean Supervenience: An Argument for Temporal Parts?", in *Oxford Studies in Metaphysics*, vol. 1, ed. Dean Zimmerman, pp. 301–18.

Heller, Mark (1984) "Temporal Parts of Four-Dimensional Objects", *Philosophical Studies*, 46, 323–34.

—— (1990) *The Ontology of Physical Objects: Four-Dimensional Hunks of Matter*, Cambridge, UK, Cambridge University Press.

Hempel, Carl and Oppenheim, Paul (1948) "Studies in the Logic of Explanation", *Philosophy of Science*, 15, 135–75.

Higginbotham, James (1980) "Reciprocal Interpretation", *Journal of Linguistic Research*, 1, 97–117.

Higginbotham, James and Schein, Barry (1989) "Plurals", in *Proceedings of the North Eastern Linguistics Society*, vol. 19, ed. J. Carter and R. Dechaine, Graduate Linguistics Students Association, University of Massachusetts at Amherst, pp. 161–75.

Honnefelder, Ludger (1984) "Natura Communis", *Historisches Wörterbuch der Philosophie*, ed. Joachim Ritter and Karlfried Gründer, Basel/Stuttgart, Schwabe & Co. AG Verlag, pp. 494–504.

Horgan, Terence (1993) "From Supervenience to Superdupervenience: Meeting the Demands of a Material World", *Mind*, 102, 555–86.

Hudson, Hud (2000) "Universalism, Four-Dimensionalism and Vagueness", *Philosophy and Phenomenological Research*, 60(3), 547–60.

—— (2001) *A Materialist Conception of the Human Person*, Ithaca, NY, Cornell University Press.

Hull, David (1965) "The Effect of Essentialism on Taxonomy—Two Thousand Years of Stasis (I)", *British Journal for the Philosophy of Science*, 15, 314–26.

—— (1976) "Are Species Really Individuals?", *Systematic Zoology*, 25, 174–91.

—— (1978) "A Matter of Individuality", *Philosophy of Science*, 45, 335–60.

Husserl, Edmund (1900–1) *Logische Untersuchungen*, 1st edn, Halle, Germany, M. Niemeyer.

Jeffrey, Richard (1991) *Formal Logic: Its Scope and Limits*, 3rd edn, New York, St Louis and San Francisco, McGraw-Hill.

Johnston, Mark (1987) "Is There a Problem about Persistence?", *Aristotelian Society*, suppl. vol. 61, pp. 107–35.

—— (1992) "Constitution Is Not Identity", *Mind*, 101, 89–105.

—— (1997) "Manifest Kinds", *Journal of Philosophy*, 94(11), 564–83.

—— (2002) "Parts and Principles: False Axioms in Mereology", *Philosophical Topics*, 30(1), 129–66.

Jubien, Michael (1993) *Ontology, Modality and the Fallacy of Reference*, Cambridge, UK, Cambridge University Press .

Kim, Jaegwon (1990) "Supervenience as a Philosophical Concept", *Metaphilosophy*, 21, 1–27; reprinted in his *Supervenience and Mind: Selected Philosophical Essays*, Cambridge, UK, Cambridge University Press, ch. 8, pp. 131–60.

—— (1993) *Supervenience and Mind: Selected Philosophical Essays*, Cambridge, UK, Cambridge University Press.

Kim, Jaegwon and Sosa, Ernest (eds.) (2000) *Metaphysics: An Anthology*, 2nd edn, Malden, Massachusetts, Blackwell.

King, Peter (2003) "Scotus on Metaphysics", in *The Cambridge Companion to Duns Scotus*, ed. Thomas Williams, Cambridge, UK, Cambridge University Press, pp. 15–68.

Kirwan, Christopher (1971) *Aristotle's Metaphysics, Books Γ, Δ and E*, Oxford, Clarendon Press.

Kitcher, Philip (1978) "Theories, Theorists and Theoretical Change", *Philosophical Review*, 87, 519–47.

Kitcher, Philip (1981) "Explanatory Unification", *Philosophy of Science*, 48, 507–31.

—— (1984a) "Species", *Philosophy of Science*, 51, 308–33.

—— (1984b) "Against the Monism of the Moment: A Reply to Elliott Sober", *Philosophy of Science*, 51, 616–30.

—— (1987) "Ghostly Whispers: Mayr, Ghiselin, and the 'Philosophers' on the Ontological Status Species", *Biology and Philosophy*, 2, 184–92.

—— (1989) "Some Puzzles About Species", in *What the Philosophy of Biology Is*, ed. Michael Ruse, Dordrecht, The Netherlands, Kluwer Academic Publishers, pp. 183–208.

Kornblith, Hilary (1993) *Inductive Inference and Its Natural Ground: An Essay in Naturalistic Epistemology*, Cambridge, MA, MIT Press.

Koslicki, Kathrin (1995) *Talk about Stuffs and Things: The Logic of Mass and Count Nouns*, unpublished PhD dissertation, MIT, Cambridge, MA.

—— (1997) "Isolation and Non-Arbitrary Division: Frege's Two Criteria for Counting", *Synthese*, 112(3), 403–30.

—— (1999a) "The Semantics of Mass-Predicates", *Nous*, 33(1), 46–91; reprinted in *The Philosopher's Annual*, vol. XXII.

—— (1999b) "Genericity and Logical Form", *Mind and Language*, 14(4), 441–67.

—— (2003a) "The Crooked Path from Vagueness to Four-Dimensionalism", *Philosophical Studies*, 114(1–2), 107–34.

—— (2003b) Review of Theodore Sider, *Four-Dimensionalism: An Ontology of Persistence and Time*, in *The Philosophical Review*, 112(1), 110–13.

—— (2004a) "Constitution and Similarity", *Philosophical Studies*, 117, 327–64.

—— (2004b) Review of Verity Harte's *Plato on Parts and Wholes: The Metaphysics of Structure*, *Journal of Philosophy*, 101(9), 492–6.

—— (2005a) "Almost Indiscernible Objects and the Suspect Strategy", *Journal of Philosophy*, 102(2), 55–77.

—— (2005b) "On the Substantive Nature of Disagreements in Ontology", *Philosophy and Phenomenological Research*, 71(1), 85–105.

—— (2006a) "Nouns, Mass and Count", in *Encyclopedia of Philosophy*, 2nd edn, ed. Donald M. Borchert, MacMillan Reference, USA.

—— (2006b) "Aristotle's Mereology and the Status of Form", *Journal of Philosophy*, Special Issue: "Parts and Wholes", ed. Wolfgang Mann and Achille Varzi, CIII(12), 715–36.

—— (2007) "Towards a Neo-Aristotelian Mereology", *Dialectica*, Special Issue: "The Philosophy of Kit Fine", guest editor Kevin Mulligan, 61(1), 127–59.

Kripke, Saul (1971) "Identity and Necessity", in *Identity and Individuation*, ed. Milton Munitz, New York, New York University Press, pp. 135–64.

—— (1980) *Naming and Necessity*, Cambridge, MA, Harvard University Press, originally published in *Semantics of Natural Language*, ed. Donald Davidson and Gilbert Harman, Dordrecht, The Netherlands, D. Reidel, (1972), pp. 253–355 and pp. 763–9.

Kuhn, Thomas S. (1962) *The Structure of Scientific Revolutions*, Chicago, IL, University of Chicago Press.

—— (1982) "Commensurability, Comparability, Communicability", *PSA*, vol. 2, reprinted in Kuhn (2000), pp. 33–57.

—— (2000) *The Road Since Structure*, Chicago, IL, University of Chicago Press.

Lange, Marc (1995) "Are There Natural Laws Concerning Particular Biological Species?", *Journal of Philosophy*, 92, 430–51.

LaPorte, Joseph (1996) "Chemical Kind Term Reference and the Discovery of Essence", *Nous*, 30(1), 112–32.

—— (1997) "Essential Membership", *Philosophy of Science*, 64, 96–112.

—— (2000) "Rigidity and Kind", *Philosophical Studies*, 97(3), 293–316.

—— (2004) *Natural Kinds and Conceptual Change*, Cambridge, UK, Cambridge University Press.

Larson, Richard and Segal, Gabriel (1995) *Knowledge of Meaning: An Introduction to Semantic Theory*, Cambridge, MA, MIT Press.

Lasnik, Howard (2000) Syntactic Structures *Revisited: Contemporary Lectures on Classic Transformational Theory*, with Marcela Depiante and Arthur Stepanov, Cambridge, MA, MIT Press.

Lejewski, Czeslaw (1982) "Ontology: What Next?", in *Language and Ontology*, ed. W. Leinfellner, E. Kraemer and J. Schank, Vienna, Austria, Hölder, Pichler & Tempsky, pp. 173–86.

Leonard, Henry S. (1930) *Singular Terms*, unpublished PhD dissertation, Harvard University.

Leonard, Henry S. and Goodman, Nelson (1940) "The Calculus of Individuals and Its Uses", *Journal of Symbolic Logic*, 5, 45–55.

Le Poidevin, Robin (2000) "Space and the Chiral Molecule", in *Of Minds and Molecules: New Philosophical Perspectives on Chemistry*, ed. Nalini Bhushan and Stuart Rosenfeld, New York, Oxford University Press pp. 129–42.

Leśniewski, Stanislaw (1916) "Podstawy ogólnej teoryi mnogości I" [Foundations of a General Theory of Manifolds], *Prace Polskiego Koła Naukowe w Moskwie*, Sekcya matematyczno- przyrodnicza, 2, Moscow, Russia.

—— (1927–30) "O Podstawach Matematyki" [On the Foundations of Mathematics], *Przeglad Filozoficzny*, vol. 30 (1927), pp. 164–206; vol. 31 (1928), pp. 261–91; vol. 32 (1929), pp. 60–101; vol. 33 (1930), pp. 75–105, pp. 142–70.

Lewis, David (1968) "Counterpart Theory and Quantified Modal Logic", *Journal of Philosophy*, 68, 113–26.

—— (1970) "How to Define Theoretical Terms", *Journal of Philosophy*, 67, 427–46.

—— (1983a) "Survival and Identity", and "Postscripts", in Lewis (1986c), pp. 55–77.

—— (1983b) "New Work for a Theory of Universals", *Australasian Journal of Philosophy*, 61, 343–77.

—— (1984) "Putnam's Paradox", *Australasian Journal of Philosophy*, 62, 221–36.

—— (1986a) "Against Structural Universals", *Australasian Journal of Philosophy*, 64, 25–46, reprinted in Lewis (1999), pp. 78–107.

—— (1986b) *On the Plurality of Worlds*, Oxford, Blackwell.

—— (1986c) *Philosophical Papers*, vol. I, New York, Oxford University Press.

—— (1991) *Parts of Classes*, Oxford, Blackwell.

—— (1999) *Papers in Metaphysics and Epistemology*, Cambridge, UK, Cambridge University Press.

Lewis, Frank A. (1991) *Substance and Predication in Aristotle*, Cambridge, UK, Cambridge University Press.

Lewis, Frank A. (1994) "Aristotle on the Relation Between a Thing and Its Matter", in *Unity, Identity, and Explanation in Aristotle's Metaphysics*, ed. T. Scaltsas, D. Charles and M. L. Gill, Oxford, Clarendon Press, pp. 247–77.

—— (1995a) "Aristotle on the Unity of Substance", *Pacific Philosophical Quarterly*, 76, 222–65.

—— (1995b) "Substance, Predication, and Unity in Aristotle", *Ancient Philosophy*, 15, 521–49.

Link, Gödehard (1983) "The Logical Analysis of Plurals and Mass Terms: A Lattice-Theoretical Approach", in *Meaning, Use and Interpretation of Language*, ed. R. Bäuerle et al., Berlin, De Gruyter, pp. 302–23.

—— (1987) "Generalized Quantifiers and Plurals", in *Generalized Quantifiers*, ed. P. Gärdenfors, Dordrecht, The Netherlands, D. Reidel, pp. 151–80.

Linsky, Bernard (1984) "General Terms as Designators", *Pacific Philosophical Quarterly*, 65, 259–76.

Locke, John (1975) "Of Identity and Diversity", in *An Essay Concerning Human Understanding*, Book II, Ch. XXVII, ed. Peter H. Nidditch, Oxford, Clarendon Press, pp. 328–48.

Lønning, Jan Tore (1987) "Mass Terms and Quantification", *Linguistics and Philosophy*, 10, 1–52.

Loux, Michael J. (1991) *Primary Ousia: An Essay on Aristotle's* Metaphysics Z and H, Ithaca, NY, Cornell University Press.

Lowe, E. J. (1987) "Lewis on Perdurance Versus Endurance", *Analysis*, 47, 152–4.

—— (1989) *Kinds of Being: A Study of Individuation, Identity and the Logic of Sortal Terms*, Oxford, Blackwell.

—— (1995) "Coinciding Objects: In Defense of the 'Standard Account'", *Analysis*, 55, 171–8.

—— (1997) "Ontological Categories and Natural Kinds", *Philosophical Papers*, 26(1), 29–46.

Mac Lane, Saunders (1996) "Structure in Mathematics", *Philosophia Mathematica*, 4(3), 174–83.

Macnamara, John (1991) "Understanding Induction", *British Journal of the Philosophy of Science*, 42, 21–48.

Makin, Stephen (1988) "Aristotle on Unity and Being", *Proceedings of the Cambridge Philological Society*, 214, 77–103.

Manzano, María (1999) *Model Theory*, Oxford, Clarendon Press.

Markosian, Ned (1998a) "Brutal Composition", *Philosophical Studies*, 92(3), 211–49.

—— (1998b) "Simples", *Australasian Journal of Philosophy*, 76(2), 213–28.

Mayr, Ernst (1969) *Principles of Systematic Zoology*, New York, McGraw-Hill

McLaughlin, Brian (1995) "Varieties of Supervenience", in *Supervenience: New Essays*, ed. E. Savellos and Ü. Yalçin, Cambridge, UK, Cambridge University Press, pp. 16–59.

Mellor, D. H. (1977) "Natural Kinds", *British Journal for the Philosophy of Science*, 28, 299–312; reprinted in Mellor (1991), pp. 123–35.

—— (1980) "Necessities and Universals in Natural Laws", in *Science, Belief and Behavior*, ed. D. H. Mellor, Cambridge, UK, Cambridge University Press, pp. 105–25; reprinted in Mellor (1991), pp. 136–53.

—— (1990) "Laws, Chances and Properties", *International Studies in the Philosophy of Science*, 4, 159–70; reprinted (with revisions) in Mellor (1991), pp. 154–69.

—— (1991) *Matters of Metaphysics*, Cambridge, UK, Cambridge University Press.

Menger, Karl (1940) "Topology Without Points", *Rice Institute Pamphlets*, 27, 80–107.

Merricks, Trenton (1999) "Composition as Identity, Mereological Essentialism, and Counterpart Theory", *Australasian Journal of Philosophy*, 77(2), 192–5.

—— (2001) *Objects and Persons*, Oxford, UK, Clarendon Press.

Mignucci, Mario (2000) "Parts, Quantification and Aristotelian Predication", *Monist*, 83(1), 3–21.

Mill, John Stuart (1843) *A System of Logic: Ratiocinative and Inductive; Being a Connected View of the Principles and Evidence and the Methods of Scientific Investigation*, in *Collected Works*, Toronto, University of Toronto Press (1963).

Moltmann, Friederike (1997) *Parts and Wholes in Semantics*, Oxford, UK, Oxford University Press.

—— (1998) "Part-Structures, Integrity, and the Mass-Count Distinction", *Synthese*, 116(1), 75–111.

Myro, George (1986) "Identity and Time", in *The Philosophical Grounds of Rationality*, ed. R. E. Grandy and R. Warner, New York, Oxford University Press, pp. 383–409.

Nagel, Thomas (1998) "Conceiving the Impossible and the Mind-Body Problem", *Philosophy*, 73, 337–52.

Needham, Paul (1981) "Temporal Intervals and Temporal Order", *Logique et Analyse*, 24, 49–64.

Nola, Robert (1980) "Fixing the Reference of Theoretical Terms", *Philosophy of Science*, 47, 505–31.

Nozick, Robert (2001) *Invariances: The Structure of the Objective World*, Cambridge, MA, Harvard University Press.

Oderberg, David (1993) *The Metaphysics of Identity Over Time*, New York, St Martin's Press.

—— (1996) "Coincidence Under a Sortal", *Philosophical Review*, 105, 145–71.

Oliver, Alex (1994) "Are Subclasses Parts of Classes?", *Analysis*, 54(4), 215–23.

Olson, Eric (2001) "Material Coincidence and the Indiscernibility Problem", *Philosophical Quarterly*, 51, 337–55.

Papineau, David (1996) "Theory-Dependent Terms", *Philosophy of Science*, 63, 1–20.

Parsons, Charles (1990) "The Structuralist View of Mathematical Objects", *Synthese*, 84, 303–46.

—— (1995) "Structuralism and the Concept of Set", in *Modality, Morality and Belief: Essays in Honor of Ruth Barcan Marcus*, ed. W. Sinott-Armstrong et al., Cambridge, UK, Cambridge University Press, pp. 74–92.

—— (2004) "Structuralism and Metaphysics", *The Philosophical Quarterly*, 54(214), 56–77.

Parsons, Terence (1979) "Referring to NonExistent Objects", *Theory and Decision*, 11, 95–110.

—— (1980) *Non-Existent Objects*, New Haven, Yale University Press.

—— (2000) *Indeterminate Identity: Metaphysics and Semantics*, Oxford, Clarendon Press.

Paterson, Hugh E. H. (1985) "The Recognition Concept of Species", in *Species and Speciation*, ed. E. Vrba, Pretoria, South Africa, Transvaal Museum, pp. 21–9.

Paul, L. A. (2002) "Logical Parts", *Nous*, 36(4), 578–96.

Perry, John (1972) "Can the Self Divide?", *Journal of Philosophy*, 69, 463–88.

Plantinga, Alvin (1975) "On Mereological Essentialism", *Review of Metaphysics*, 28, 468–76.

Putnam, Hilary (1962) "The Analytic and the Synthetic", *Minnesota Studies in the Philosophy of Science*, vol. 3, ed. Herbert Feigl and Grover Maxwell, Minneapolis, University of Minnesota Press; reprinted in Putnam (1975a), pp. 33–69.

—— (1970) "Is Semantics Possible?", in *Contemporary Philosophical Thought: The International Philosophy Year Conferences at Brockport*, vol. 1 (*Languages, Belief and Metaphysics*), New York, State University of New York Press; reprinted in Putnam (1975a), pp. 139–52.

—— (1973) "Explanation and Reference", in *Conceptual Change*, ed. G. Pearce and P. Maynard, Dordrecht, The Netherlands, D. Reidel, pp. 199–221; reprinted in Putnam (1975a), pp. 196–214.

—— (1975a) *Mind, Language and Reality: Philosophical Papers*, vol. 2, Cambridge, UK, Cambridge University Press.

—— (1975b) "The Meaning of 'Meaning'", in *Minnesota Studies in the Philosophy of Science*, vol. 7, Minneapolis, University of Minnesota Press; reprinted in Putnam (1975a), pp. 215–71.

—— (1975c) "Language and Reality", in Putnam (1975a), pp. 272–90.

—— (1987) *The Many Faces of Realism: The Paul Carus Lectures*, Chicago and La Salle, IL, Open Court.

Quine, Willard van Orman (1950) "Identity, Ostension, and Hypostasis", *Journal of Philosophy*, 47, reprinted in his *From a Logical Point of View*, Cambridge, MA, Harvard University Press, pp. 65–79.

—— (1960) *Word and Object*, Cambridge, MA, MIT Press.

—— (1970) "Natural Kinds", in *Essays in Honor of Carl G. Hempel*, ed. Nicholas Rescher et al., Dordrecht, The Netherlands, D. Reidel, pp. 5–23.

—— (1980) "Soft Impeachment Disowned", *Pacific Philosophical Quarterly*, 61, pp. 450–1.

Ray, Greg (2000a) "Identity and Cumulative Essence", unpublished manuscript.

—— (2000b) "Identity and Fine Objects", unpublished manuscript.

Rea, Michael (ed.) (1997) *Material Constitution: A Reader*, Lanham, MD, Rowman & Littlefield.

—— (1998) "In Defense of Mereological Universalism", *Philosophy and Phenomenological Research*, 58(2), 347–60.

—— (2002) *World Without Design: The Ontological Consequences of Naturalism*, Oxford, Clarendon Press.

Reeve, C. D. C. (2000) *Substantial Knowledge: Aristotle's Metaphysics*, Indianapolis, IN, Hackett.

Rescher, Nicholas (1955) "Axioms for the Part Relation", *Philosophical Studies*, 6, 8–11.

Rescher, Nicholas and Oppenheim, Paul (1955) "Logical Analysis of Gestalt Concepts", *The British Journal for the Philosophy of Science*, 6(22), 89–106.

Resnik, Michael (1975) "Mathematical Knowledge and Pattern Cognition, *Canadian Journal of Philosophy*, 5(1), 25–39.

—— (1981) "Mathematics as a Science of Patterns: Ontology and Reference", *Nous*, 15, 529–50.

—— (1982) "Mathematics as a Science of Patterns: Epistemology", *Nous*, 16, 95–105.

—— (1988) "Mathematics from the Structuralist Point of View", *Revue Internationale de Philosophie*, 42, 400–24.

—— (1997) *Mathematics as a Science of Patterns*, Oxford, Clarendon Press.

Richard, Mark (1987) "Quantification and Leibniz's Law", *Philosophical Review*, 96(4), 555–78.

Ridley, Mark (1989) "The Cladistic Solution to the Species Problem", *Biology and Philosophy*, 4, 1–16.

Riggs, Peter J. (ed.) (1996) *Natural Kinds, Laws of Nature and Scientific Methodology*, Dordrecht, The Netherlands, Kluwer Academic Publishers.

Rorty, Richard (1973) "Genus as Matter: A Reading of *Met.* Z-H", in *Exegesis and Argument*, ed. Lee, Mourelatos and Rorty, *Phronesis*, suppl. vol. 1, 393–420.

Ross, W. D. (1924) *Aristotle's* Metaphysics, Oxford, Clarendon Press.

Russell, Bertrand (1903) *The Principles of Mathematics*, 2nd edn, London, Allen and Unwin.

—— (1914) *Our Knowledge of the External World*, London, Allen and Unwin.

—— (1927) *The Analysis of Matter*, New York, Harcourt, Brace & Company.

—— (1948) *Human Knowledge: Its Scope and Limits*, London, Allen and Unwin.

Salmon, Nathan (1981) *Reference and Essence*, Princeton, New Jersey, Princeton University Press.

—— (1987/88) "How to Measure the Standard Metre", *Proceedings of the Aristotelian Society (New Series)*, 88, 193–217.

Sankey, Howard (1994) *The Incommensurability Thesis*, Aldershot, UK, Avebury.

Savellos, Elias and Yalçin, Ümit (1995) *Supervenience: New Essays*, Cambridge, Cambridge University Press.

Scaltsas, Theodore (1985) "Substratum, Subject, and Substance", *Ancient Philosophy*, 5, 215–40.

—— (1990) "Is the Whole Identical to Its Parts?", *Mind*, 99, 583–98.

—— (1994) *Substances and Universals in Aristotle's Metaphysics*, Ithaca, NY, Cornell University Press.

Scha, Remko (1981) "Distributive, Collective and Cumulative Quantification", in *Formal Methods in the Study of Language*, ed. J. Gronendijk et al., Amsterdam, Mathematical Centre, pp. 483–512.

Schein, Barry (1993) *Plurals and Events*, Cambridge, MA, MIT Press.

Schiffer, Stephen (1987) *Remnants of Meaning*, Cambridge, MA, MIT Press.

Schwartz, Stephen (1980) "Formal Semantics and Natural Kind Terms", *Philosophical Studies*, 38, 189–98.

Scruton, Roger (1997) *The Aesthetics of Music*, Oxford, Clarendon Press.

Shapere, Dudley (1981) "Meaning and Scientific Change", in *Scientific Revolutions*, ed. Ian Hacking, Oxford, Oxford University Press, pp. 28–59.

Shapiro, Stewart (1983) "Mathematics and Reality", *Philosophy of Science*, 50, 523–48.

—— (1989) "Structure and Ontology", *Philosophical Topics*, 17(2), 145–71.

—— (1997) *Philosophy of Mathematics: Structure and Ontology*, New York, Oxford University Press.

Sharvy, Richard (1980) "A More General Theory of Definite Descriptions", *Philosophical Review*, 89, 607–24.

Sharvy, Richard (1983) "Mixtures", *Philosophy and Phenomenological Research*, 44, 227–39.

Sher, Gila (1991) *The Bounds of Logic: A Generalized Viewpoint*, Cambridge, MA, MIT Press.

—— (2001a) "The Formal-Structural View of Logical Consequence", *The Philosophical Review*, 110(2), 241–61.

—— (2001b) "Truth, Logical Structure, and Compositionality", *Synthese*, 126, 195–219.

Shields, Christopher (1999) *Order in Multiplicity: Homonymy in the Philosophy of Aristotle*, Oxford, Clarendon Press.

Shoemaker, Sydney (1980) "Properties, Causation and Projectibility", in *Applications of Inductive Logic*, ed. L. Jonathan Cohen and Mary Hesse, Oxford, Clarendon Press, pp. 291–312.

Sider, Theodore (1993) "Van Inwagen and the Possibility of Gunk", *Analysis*, 53(4), 285–9.

—— (1996) "All the World's a Stage", *Australasian Journal of Philosophy*, 74, 433–53.

—— (1997) "Four-Dimensionalism", *Philosophical Review*, 106, 197–231.

—— (1999) "Global Supervenience and Identity Across Times and Worlds", *Philosophy and Phenomenological Research*, 49, 913–37.

—— (2001) *Four-Dimensionalism: An Ontology of Persistence and Time*, Oxford, Clarendon Press.

—— (2003) "Against Vague Existence", *Philosophical Studies*, 114(1–2), 135–46.

Sider, Theodore and Braun, David (2007) "Vague, So Untrue", *Nous*, 41(2), 133–56.

Simons, Peter (1987) *Parts: A Study in Ontology*, Oxford, Clarendon Press.

Smith, Barry (1982) *Parts and Moments: Studies in Logic and Formal Ontology*, Munich, Germany, Philosophia Verlag.

—— (1997) "Boundaries: An Essay in Mereotopology", in *The Philosophy of Roderick Chisholm*, ed. Lewis E. Hahn, Chicago, IL, Open Court, pp. 533–61.

Smith, Barry and Varzi, Achille (2000) "Fiat and Bona Fide Boundaries", *Philosophy and Phenomenological Research*, 60(2), 401–20.

Sneath, Peter H. A. and Sokal, Robert R. (1973) *Numerical Taxonomy*, San Francisco, W. H. Freeman.

Snyder, Laura (2005) "Confirmation for a Modest Realism", *Philosophy of Science*, 72(5), 839–49.

Soames, Scott (2002) *Beyond Rigidity: The Unfinished Semantic Agenda of* Naming and Necessity, New York, Oxford University Press.

Sober, Elliott (1980) "Evolution, Population Thinking and Essentialism", *Philosophy of Science*, 47, 350–83.

—— (1984) "Discussion: Sets, Species, and Evolution: Comments on Philip Kitcher's 'Species'", *Philosophy of Science*, 51, 334–41.

Sokal, Robert R. and Sneath, Peter H. A. (1963) *Principles of Numerical Taxonomy*, San Francisco, W. H. Freeman.

Sosa, Ernest (1987) "Subjects Among Other Things", *Philosophical Perspectives*, 1, 155–87.

Stalker, Douglas (ed.) (1994) *Grue! The New Riddle of Induction*, Chicago and La Salle, IL, Open Court.

Sterenly, Kim (1983) "Natural Kind Terms", *Pacific Philosophical Quarterly*, 64, 110–25.

Stone, Jim (1987) "Why Potentiality Matters", *Canadian Journal of Philosophy*, 17, 815–30.

Swoyer, Chris (1982) "The Nature of Natural Laws", *Australasian Journal of Philosophy*, 60(3), 203–23.

Tarski, Alfred (1936) "On the Concept of Logical Consequence", in *Logic, Semantics, Metamathematics*, 2nd edn, tr. J. H. Woodger, ed. with an introduction by John Corcoran, Indianapolis, Hackett (1983), pp. 409–20 (article was first published in Polish and German in 1936).

—— (1937) "Appendix E", in *The Axiomatic Method in Biology*, ed. J. H. Woodger, Cambridge, UK, Cambridge University Press, pp. 161–72.

—— (1956) "Foundations of the Geometry of Solids", in *Logic, Semantics, and Metamathematics*, tr. J. H. Woodger, Oxford, Clarendon Press, pp. 24–9.

—— (1966) "What Are Logical Notions?", reprinted and tr. in *History and Philosophy of Logic*, 7 (1986), 143–54.

Teller, Paul (1983) "A Poor Man's Guide to Supervenience and Determination", *Southern Journal of Philosophy*, suppl. vol. 22, 137–62.

Thalos, Mariam (2005) "The Wide World of Systems", unpublished manuscript.

Thomson, Judith Jarvis (1977) *Acts and Other Events*, Ithaca, NY, Cornell University Press.

—— (1983) "Parthood and Identity Across Time", *Journal of Philosophy*, 80, 201–20.

—— (1998) "The Statue and the Clay", *Nous*, 32, 149–73.

Tiles, J. E. (1981) *Things That Happen*, Aberdeen, Aberdeen University Press.

Tooley, Michael (1977) "The Nature of Laws", *Canadian Journal of Philosophy*, 7(4), 667–98.

Tranöy, Knut Erik (1959) *Wholes and Structures: An Attempt at a Philosophical Analysis*, Interdisciplinary Studies from the Scandinavian Summer University, Ejnar Munksgaard, Copenhagen.

Unger, Peter (1979) "There Are No Ordinary Things", *Synthese*, 41, 117–54.

—— (1983) "The Causal Theory of Reference", *Philosophical Studies*, 43, 1–45.

Van Benthem, Johan (1983) *The Logic of Time*, Dordrecht, The Netherlands, D. Reidel.

Van Inwagen, Peter (1981) "The Doctrine of Arbitrary Undetached Parts", *Pacific Philosophical Quarterly*, 62, 123–37.

—— (1987) "When Are Objects Parts?", *Philosophical Perspectives*, 1 (*Metaphysics*), 21–47.

—— (1990a) *Material Beings*, Ithaca, NY, Cornell University Press.

—— (1990b) "Four-Dimensional Objects", *Nous*, 24, 245–55.

—— (1993) "Naive Mereology, Admissible Valuations and Other Matters", *Nous*, 27(2), 229–34.

—— (1994) "Composition as Identity", *Philosophical Perspectives*, 8 (*Logic and Language*), 207–20.

—— (2002) "The Number of Things", *Philosophical Issues* (*Nous* Supplement), 12 ("Realism and Relativism"), 176–96.

Varzi, Achille (2000) "Mereological Commitments", *Dialectica*, 54(4), 283–305.

Venn, John (1866) *The Logic of Chance*, London and Cambridge, UK, Macmillan.

Wedin, Michael V. (2000) *Aristotle's Theory of Substance: The* Categories *and* Metaphysics Zeta, New York, Oxford University Press.

Whewell, William (1989) *Theory of Scientific Method*, ed. Robert E. Butts, Indianapolis, Hackett.

Whitehead, Alfred North (1919) *An Enquiry Concerning the Principles of Natural Knowledge*, Cambridge, UK, Cambridge University Press.

—— (1920) *The Concept of Nature*, Cambridge, UK, Cambridge University Press.

—— (1929) *Process and Reality*, New York, Macmillan.

Whitehead, Alfred North and Russell, Bertrand (1927) *Principia Mathematica*, 2nd edn, Cambridge, UK, Cambridge University Press.

Wiggins, David (1968) "On Being in the Same Place at the Same Time", *Philosophical Review*, 77, 90–5.

—— (1979) "Mereological Essentialism: Asymmetrical Essential Dependence and the Nature of Continuants", *Grazer Philosophische Studien*, 7/8, 297–315.

—— (1980) *Sameness and Substance*, Cambridge, MA, Harvard University Press.

—— (2001) *Sameness and Substance Renewed*, Cambridge, UK, Cambridge University Press.

Wilkerson, T. E. (1988) "Natural Kinds", *Philosophy*, 63, 29–42.

—— (1993) "Species Essences and the Names of Natural Kinds", *Philosophical Quarterly*, 43, 1–19.

—— (1995) *Natural Kinds*, Avebury Series in Philosophy, Avebury, Brookfield, VT.

Williams, Donald C. (1953) "On the Elements of Being", Parts I and II, *Review of Metaphysics*, 7, 3–18 and 171–92.

Wilson, Jessica (2005) "Supervenience-Based Formulations of Physicalism", *Nous*, 39(3), 426–59.

Witt, Charlotte (1989) *Substance and Essence: An Interpretation of* Metaphysics *VII–IX*, Ithaca, NY, Cornell University Press.

—— (2003) *Ways of Being: Potentiality and Actuality in Aristotle's Metaphysics*, Ithaca, NY, Cornell University Press.

Woolley, R. G. (1978) "Must a Molecule Have a Shape?", *Journal of the American Chemical Society*, 100, 1073–8.

Yablo, Stephen (1987) "Identity, Essence and Indiscernibility", *Journal of Philosophy*, 84, 293–314.

Zemach, Eddy (1976) "Comments and Criticism: Putnam's Theory on the Reference of Substance Terms", *Journal of Philosophy*, 73, 116–27.

Zimmerman, Dean (1995) "Theories of Masses and Problems of Constitution", *Philosophical Review*, 104, 53–110.

General Index

abstract; *see also* concrete 4, 9 n.1, 35 n.,
87–89, 214–5, 219–20, 223, 226,
261–3
actual, actuality (Aristotle); *see* potential,
potentiality
aggregate; *see* mereological sum
analytic, analyticity 205 n.13, 221 n.43, 224,
228 n.60
anti-essentialism, anti-essentialist; *see*
essentialism
atomic, atomicity, atomlessness; *see*
mereological atom
argument from vagueness
(Lewis/Sider) 30–40, 71
Aristotelian regress (*Met.* Z.17) 108–111,
120, 125 n.6, 132 n.18, 135 n.28, 137
n.34, 152, 153 n.66–7, 180 n.20
arrangement; *see also* form, structure ix, 5,
74–5, 90, 93, 115–6, 140, 142 n.44,
155, 169, 172, 182, 235–7, 244, 249,
251, 255, 259

Calculus of Individuals; *see also* mereology:
Classical Extensional Mereology
(CEM) 10, 15–7, 23–8, 75
change over time; *see also* persistence, identity:
diachronic and synchronic identity 24–5,
27, 49, 56–7, 67, 189–91
chemical bonding ix, 5, 7, 173, 189, 197, 245
chiral; *see* isomer, isomerism
cladism 213
coincidence, coinciding objects 26–8, 30, 47,
54–60, 67–8, 82 n., 83, 178, 181–3,
254–9
complete, completeness (Plato, Aristotle); *see*
perfect, perfection
composition
    Composition-as-Identity Thesis 7, 29,
    34 n., 40–4, 71, 95–8, 105, 119–20,
    122, 125, 192–3
    composition as non-identity 45–6, 111,
    192
    container-model of composition 78, 96
    ontologically loaded conception 45, 97,
    100, 105, 120–1, 152–3, 192
    restricted composition; *see also* composition:
    unrestricted composition 30–40,
    97–8, 100, 102, 105, 117 n., 118,
    120–1, 122, 151, 153–4, 157, 163,
    168–70, 173, 187, 190, 192, 200

Special Composition Question 7, 95,
    103–4, 119–20
sui generis notions of composition (Fine) 72,
    82–3, 87, 89–90, 93–4, 158
Uniqueness of Composition 4, 17, 21,
    29–30, 42–44, 82 n., 167, 183,
    190–2, 198
unrestricted composition; *see also*
    composition: restricted composition 4,
    7, 17, 24, 28, 29–40, 42–3, 71, 82 n.,
    95, 105, 117 n., 120, 168–9, 234,
    258–9
compositional, compositionality 116
concrete; *see also* abstract 9, 29, 34–8, 59, 63,
    188, 210, 214–5, 219–20, 262–3
configuration; *see also* arrangement, form,
    structure 5, 7, 99, 105 n.11, 169–70,
    173–5, 180 n.20, 182, 186–9, 197–8,
    200, 233, 235–7, 244–5, 248, 252, 255,
    259–60
constitution 6, 30, 46 n., 47, 49, 54–7, 67–8,
    178 n.15, 179–86, 190, 199
contact, continuity, continuous
    (Aristotle) 132–4, 142, 144 n., 145–6,
    148–50, 152, 157, 159, 163, 193
content; *see* structure: structure/content
    dichotomy
control construction; *see* raising construction
conventionalism, conventionalist 204,
    208–10
count noun; *see* mass/count distinction
counterpart theory 5, 30
creation story (*Timaeus*); *see also* receptacle 95,
    97, 99, 119
creationism 231, 232 n.65

dependence; *see also* supervenience 130
    n.15, 136 n.31, 177 n.14, 178, 186,
    237
disjoint, disjointness 11–9, 25, 34, 41–2,
    87–8, 96, 108 n.18, 167–8
distributivity 194–5 n.36
divisibility, divisible; *see* indivisibility, unity
doctrine of temporal parts; *see*
    four-dimensionalism
dominant kinds (Burke) 177 n.13, 179
    n.16–17

Eleatics 95, 119, 122, 153, 192–3
eliminativism 179 n.17

embodiments (Fine); *see also* manifestation of variable embodiments, principles of embodiment 8, 75–90, 93–4, 96 n.5, 102 n., 110 n.23, 171, 183–4 n.25
endurantism; *see* three-dimensionalism
essence, essential property 40, 46, 48, 55, 59, 67–8, 86–7, 89, 106, 111 n.25, 113–7, 124, 137 n.24, 138, 144 n., 145–6 n.53, 149 n.61, 161 n., 170, 172 n.4, 177, 184, 208–9, 210 n.22, 212–5, 218–25, 227, 233 n.
essentialism, essentialist 48, 59–65, 87, 170 n.2, 212–3, 218–9, 222 n.44, 223 n.48, 224, 225 n., 227, 233 n.
essentiality of origins 59, 67, 86, 170 n.2, 213 n.28
mereological essentialism 113–4
evolution, evolutionary 103, 211–9, 222 n.44, 224, 227, 231
existence, intermittent 216 n.34
explanation; *see also* prediction, predictive practice 39, 204, 207–10, 216–8, 228, 233, 237

family resemblance (Wittgenstein) 170 n.2, 173 n.9, 206 n.14
form; *see also* structure 5, 96–7, 172–5, 191–2, 197–8, 200, 235–8, 254, 256–9
Aristotelian conception of form 6, 86, 109–12, 124, 131–42, 145–64, 170, 172 n.4, 191 n.34, 193–4, 262
determinates vs. determinables 189–90
form as proper part of compound 108–11, 120, 135, 153 n.66–7, 176, 179- 86
Kit Fine's conception of form; *see* principles of embodiment, structure: Platonic conception of structure
Platonic conception of form; *see* structure: Platonic conception of structure
simpliciter vs. derivative formal components 187–8
logical form 242
formal components; *see* form
four-dimensionalism 5, 29–31, 71, 188
fusion; *see* mereological sum

General Sum Principle (GSP) 20, 168–9
general term; *see also* singular term 219–28
Gestalt, Gestalt theory 237, 239
Grounding Problem 181–3, 199, 252, 254, 256–9
group theory 240

haecceitism, haecceity 86, 170 n.2, 257–8
heap 3, 6, 101 n.8, 108–11, 132 n.18, 133–51, 154, 176 n.11, 193, 256–9

homeostasis 209, 211
homeostatic property cluster; *see* homeostasis
Homonymy Principle (Aristotle) 112–3, 147–8, 152, 153 n.67, 156, 163, 170, 173 n.6, 238
hylomorphic, hylomorphism; *see also* mereology: neo-Aristotelian approach to mereology 141 n.44, 147 n.57, 155 n.69, 162 n.74, 259

identity; *see also* composition
as definable in terms of parthood 12, 15–6, 18
contingent 47–8, 58–65, 67–8, 179 n.17
crossworld 59
diachronic and synchronic 173 n.7, 189, 191
Identity of Indiscernibles (II) 52, 65, 177 n.12
indeterminate 47, 51–2, 58, 65–6, 67–8
loose and popular vs. strict and philosophical 41–2
relative 47, 56–7, 58, 66–7, 67–8, 179 n.17
temporary 47, 48–50, 61, 67–8, 179 n.17
indeterminacy, indeterminate; *see* vague, vagueness
individual 15–6, 18, 28 n., 53–4, 86–7, 171, 210, 214–5, 233 n., 257–8
individuation 60, 66, 68, 116, 195, 258
indivisibility; *see also* unity 7, 15, 126–51, 159–64, 193–6, 254 n.
induction, inductive inference 203 n.7, 204–5, 208–10, 216, 218, 233
New Riddle of Induction (Goodman) 204 n.11
Inheritance Principle (Fine) 76 n.2, 81
intelligent design; *see* creationism
isomer, isomerism 244–5
isomorphic, isomorphism (sameness of structure) 188, 239–41, 251, 256–8

laws 236–7, 246–8, 260
laws of nature 197 n., 205–7, 209–12, 214, 216–8, 233
scientific laws; *see* laws: laws of nature
statistical generalization 206 n.15
Leibniz's Law 7, 25, 27 n.3, 45–68, 71, 75, 108 n.17, 125 n.6, 152, 176–7 n.12, 180–1, 183, 188, 191–2, 198, 253, 262
limit, limited (Plato) 95 n.3, 97–9, 105–6, 114 n., 117–8, 128, 142, 145–6, 149
link, auxiliary or fundamental (Fine) 79
logic, logical
logical consequence relation 241–3

logical constants or vocabulary 34–5, 38–9, 242–3, 244 n., 260
logical form; *see* form: logical form
logical structure; *see* structure: logical structure

manifestation, of variable embodiment (Fine) 78–88, 96 n.5
manner of arrangement; *see* arrangement
mass/count distinction 106 n.12, 194–5 n.36, 221, 222 n.46, 226 n.56, 238
mass noun; *see* mass/count distinction
material components; *see* matter
matter 6–7, 67, 84, 169–70, 172–4, 176–9, 183–92, 197–8, 200, 233, 235, 254–8
   Aristotelian conception of matter; *see also* matter: prime matter 6, 86, 109, 110–12, 114 n.29, 118–9, 130–3, 135–40, 147–50, 153 n.68, 154–5, 157–8, 160–2, 194, 264
   matter as proper part of compound 110–11, 153 n.66–67, 157–8, 176–9, 183–6
   prime matter (Aristotle) 114 n., 118–9, 155
measure (Plato, Aristotle) 98–9, 101–2, 104–5, 107, 121 n., 124 n., 126–54, 160–3, 193–8
mereological atom 11, 14–5, 19, 37 n., 42, 96, 101, 140–1 n.41, 159–62, 164, 194–5
mereological chain (Fine) 79–80
mereological sum ix, 4, 6–7, 10–16, 19–20, 22, 23–44, 72–5, 76 n.3, 82 n., 83, 90, 93, 95, 108 n.16, 109, 120, 125, 137 n.31, 140, 168–9, 171, 175–6, 192, 234, 261
   analogy between sets and sums 28, 75
   mereological sum, definition 16, 25
mereology
   Classical Extensional Mereology (CEM) 10–22, 23–30, 40–4, 71–2, 82, 93–4, 136 n.31, 140, 154, 168–9, 171, 175–6
   Minimal Extensional Mereology (MEM) 19
   standard mereology; *see* mereology: Classical Extensional Mereology (CEM)
   neo-Aristotelian approach to mereology; *see also* hylomorphic, hylomorphism ix, 6, 8, 71–2, 90, 93–4, 181, 190, 198
music
   atonal music; *see* music: tonal music, tonality
   musical structure; *see* structure: musical structure
   tonal music, tonality 247
mutilated (Aristotle) 144–9, 156–7, 163

names; *see* proper names
natural selection; *see also* evolution 211
Nihilism, Nihilist 9 n.2, 22, 29, 32–3, 96, 98, 103
nominalistic, nominalism 4, 10, 15–6, 28, 29, 35 n., 219 n.40
nomological generalization; *see* laws
non-atomicity; *see* mereological atom
non-distributivity; *see* distributivity
normative, normativity; *see also* teleological, teleology 6, 99–104, 120, 122, 140, 143–4, 151, 156–7, 163, 193, 237, 248, 262
nucleus; *see* product

one, oneness; *see* unity
one-criterion words (Putnam) 202, 207 n.19
ontological commitment; *see also* composition: Composition-as-Identity Thesis, composition: composition as non-identity, composition: ontologically loaded conception of composition 42–3, 171, 196
ordering, partial or strict partial 12, 15, 18, 20 n., 21, 78, 167–8, 180 n.20
ostension, ostensive baptism or definition 213, 221, 225
overlap 11–9, 30, 34, 41, 76 n.3, 80 n., 87, 108 n.18, 167–8

participation (Plato) 95 n.2, 129 n.
particular; *see also* universal 9, 29, 115, 123, 129 n., 130 n.16, 155 n.71, 172 n.4, 186 n., 191 n., 214–5, 216 n.34, 219–20, 223 n.49, 262–3
part, parthood
   as structure-laden 99, 112–7, 121
   formal properties of parthood; *see also* ordering, Weak Supplementation Principle (WSP), part: transitivity 11–2, 20 n.9, 83, 89–90, 94, 154, 157–9, 164, 167–8, 198
   temporal part 5 n.III, 24–5, 27, 29–30, 188–9; *see also* four-dimensionalism
   timeless vs. temporary part (Fine) 76–84, 87, 88, 90
   transitivity of parthood 11–2, 17, 18, 30, 78, 80, 83, 89, 158–9, 167, 186–8, 190, 256–7
   "sparse" and hierarchical conception (Fine) 88–90
   spatial part 5 n.III, 24–5, 30
   vertical vs. horizontal part (Fine) 88–89
perdurantism; *see* four-dimensionalism
perfect, perfection (Plato, Aristotle) 99, 100–3, 107, 143–9, 156–7, 163, 237

persistence 5 n.III, 29, 114 n.29, 189
persistence conditions 84, 86, 94, 108 n.17,
115, 177–9, 182, 189–91, 213, 215, 258
Philosophical Lexicon (Aristotle, *Met.*Δ) 108
n.16, 124, 150, 162
plural
    plural noun-phrases 106 n.12, 220 n.41,
    222 n.46, 226 n.56, 238
    plural quantification 10 n.4
    plurality, bare 96, 101, 103, 220, 223, 226,
    233 n.
pluralism (with respect to natural kinds) 203
Pluralizing Parts Principle (Harte) 95, 125,
193
postulation (Fine) 82 n., 85 n., 86
potential, potentiality (Aristotle) 135 n.27,
136 n.31, 140 n.40, 141 n.42, 142,
146–9, 152–3, 156, 159, 160, 161–3,
170, 193, 194
prediction, predictive practice 39, 204, 206
n.15, 209–10, 228, 233, 237
principle of unity; *see* unity
principles of embodiment (Fine); *see also*
    embodiments, manifestation of variable
    embodiment 78–81, 84–90, 96 n.5, 102
    n.9, 110 n.23, 170–1, 184 n.6
priority, of wholes over parts 99, 112–7, 121,
156
Problem of the One and the Many 7, 125–6,
128, 151–2, 192–8, 254 n.
product 11–9, 82 n.8
projectibility, projectible; *see also* induction,
    inductive inference 203 n.7, 204–5
proper names; *see also* singular terms 40, 59,
213–4, 218–9, 220–6
Proper Parts Principle (PPP) 19, 82 n.
property
    categorical vs. hypothetical (Yablo) 55
    natural vs. non-natural 39, 205 n.12
    normal (Fine) 54–5, 76 n.2
    nuclear vs. extra-nuclear (Parsons) 52–4
    pro tem (Fine) 79–80, 81 n.7
proximity, spatio-temporal 32, 73–5, 90, 93,
142 n.46, 170, 172–3, 177

qua-objects (Fine) 76, 81, 83
quantity (Aristotle) 124 n., 126–8, 133–54,
203 n.8

raising construction 250–1, 259
realism, realist 16, 118, 204, 208–10, 230,
232
receptacle (*Timaeus*) 99, 104–5, 114 n., 117,
119
reference
    causal theory of reference 213 n.29, 221,

223 n.48, 223 n.50, 226 n.55, 229
    n.60, 230 n.
descriptivism, descriptivist theory of
    reference 214, 220–8, 231, 232 n.66
direct reference 40, 214, 218–9, 225
partial reference or denotation 232
relativism, relativist, relativity 85 n., 230,
263–4
rigid, rigid designator, rigidity 40, 59, 176
n.11, 214, 218–26
rigid embodiment (Fine); *see* embodiment

Ship of Theseus 189
set, set-theoretic, set theory 4, 10, 13–21, 28,
51–2, 58, 65, 68, 75, 85 n., 88–9, 93,
138 n.36, 180 n.20, 214–5, 219–20,
223, 226
    null-set 13, 215
singular term; *see also* general term 13–4, 46,
219–26
Species-as-Individuals Thesis (SAI) 210–20
Strong Supplementation Principle (SSP) 19,
82 n.
structuralism, mathematical 241 n.6
structure; *see also* form, arrangement,
    configuration
    structure as providing "slots", "places",
    "positions", "nodes" 115–6, 169,
    235–7
    causal structure 208–10
    chemical or micro-structure 6, 8, 208, 227
    n.58, 228, 230 n., 244–6, 251, 259,
    262–3
    count use of "structure"; *see also* mass/count
    distinction 106 n.12, 238–9
    linguistic structure 6, 8, 100, 114–6, 119,
    248–51, 253–4, 259, 261–3
    logical structure 6, 8, 241–3, 251, 259,
    262–3
    mass use of "structure" ; *see* structure: count
    use of "structure"
    mathematical structure 6, 8, 103, 240–1,
    251, 253–4, 259, 262–3
    musical structure 6, 8, 98, 100–1, 103–4,
    107, 119–20, 133, 144–5, 147
    n.56–7, 150, 152, 163, 236–7,
    239–40, 246–8, 251, 259, 262–3
    ontological status of structure 107, 109,
    111, 160 n., 169, 175–6, 193, 252–9
    Platonic conception of structure 102–4,
    117 n., 120, 128, 129 n., 142 n.44,
    155–7,169–70, 193, 262
    structure/content dichotomy 98–100,
    105–22, 128, 135 n.28, 151, 153
    n.66, 154–7, 163, 174–88,
    192

"wholes as identical to structure" model; *see* structure: structure/content dichotomy
"wholes as composed of structure" model; *see* structure: structure/content dichotomy
variable vs. invariable elements 236, 243 n.8, 251, 259–60
substitutivity 48, 58–9, 61–5, 66, 68, 177 n.12
sum; *see* mereological sum
superabundance, of objects (Fine) 82 n., 83–5, 90, 93
supervenience 43, 177 n.14, 178, 186, 244

teleological, teleology; *see also* normative, normativity 6, 99–104, 120–1, 122, 128, 140, 142 n.44, 143–4, 146, 148, 151–3, 155–7, 163, 170, 172, 174 n., 193, 237, 248, 262
temporary intrinsics 29
three-dimensionalism 5 n.III, 29, 188
total (Aristotle) 108. n.16, 137 n.31, 140–50, 152, 155, 163, 172 n.5, 193
trout-turkey"D 31, 40, 171, 234, 256

unity ix, 4, 6–7, 96–8, 100, 103–5, 108 n.16, 110 n.21, 111, 120, 124, 126, 128–64, 193–9, 237, 254 n.19
universal; *see also* particular 7 n., 9 n.1, 21, 29, 86, 115, 124, 132 n.21, 142 n.45, 145–7, 149–50, 152, 154–7, 159, 163, 172 n.4, 191 n.34, 193, 214–5, 219–20, 223 n.49, 257–8, 262–3
unlimited (Plato); *see* limit, limited

vague, vagueness; *see also* argument from vagueness, identity: indeterminate identity 30–40, 71, 86, 189, 203, 208, 209 n.20, 227–33
valence 245
variable embodiment (Fine); *see* embodiment, manifestation of variable embodiment, principles of embodiment

Weak Supplementation Principle (WSP) 18–9, 80 n., 82 n., 87, 89–90, 108 n.18, 110 n.23, 138 n.36, 153 n.67, 167–8, 180, 183, 190, 198, 253, 262

Index of Names

Almog, Joseph 222 n.45
Aristotle 6, 8, 72, 94, 101 n.8, 102 n.9, 104,
    105, 106 n.13, 107, 108–11, 112–4, 117
    n., 118, 119, 120, 122–64, 170, 172, 173
    n.6, 174, 176 n.12, 180 n.20, 191 n.,
    192–9, 237–8, 254 n., 262
Armstrong, David M. 20, 21, 29, 41–2, 95,
    184 n.26, 188 n.30, 257
Aronson, Jerrold L. 206 n.16
Aune, Bruce 228 n.59
Ayers, Michael 210 n.22

Baker, Lynne Rudder 47, 54–5, 58–61, 68,
    180 n.19, 188 n.30
Ball, Philip 245 n.11, 246
Barnes, Jonathan 123 n.1, 125 n.4
Baxter, Donald L. M. 29 n.5, 41–2
Bennett, Karen 181, 182 n.
Berzelius, Jöns Jakob 244
Bigelow, John 29 n.
Bogaard, Paul A. 123 n.1
Boolos, George 220 n.41, 222 n.46
Bostock, David 10 n.5, 123 n.1
Boyd, Richard 208–10, 231 n., 232
Bradley, Francis Herbert 198 n.40
Braun, David 33 n.9
Bunt, Harry C. 10 n.5
Burge, Tyler 222 n.45
Burke, Michael 177 n.13, 179 n.16–7,
    181 n., 188 n.30
Burnyeat, Myles 97, 123 n.1

Carnie, Andrew 249 n.
Cartwright, Helen Morris 10 n.5
Cartwright, Nancy 206 n.16
Cartwright, Richard 62 n.15–6, 63, 65 n.17,
    179 n.17, 188 n.30, 195 n.37
Casati, Roberto 10 n.5
Charles, David 123 n.1
Chisholm, Roderick 10 n.5, 41, 113, 188 n.30
Churchland, Paul 207 n.18
Clarke, Bowman L. 11 n.5
Cook, Monte 222 n.47, 224 n.52, 225 n.
Cordry, Ben S. 222 n.47
Crane, Judith 211 n., 219 n.39

Darwin, Charles 212, 218, 231, 232 n.65
De Laguna, Theodore 11 n.5
Descartes, René 6, 195 n.38

Deutsch, Harry 47, 56–7, 58, 66–8, 179
    n.17, 222 n.47, 224 n.52
Devitt, Michael 29 n.5, 213 n.29, 223 n.48
Dirac, P. A. M. 218
Doepke, Frederick 180 n.19
Donnellan, Keith 221 n.43, 222 n.47, 228
    n.59, 229 n.62
Dorr, Cian 9 n.2, 40 n.
Dretske, Fred 207 n.16
Driscoll, John 123 n.1
Dupré, John 201 n.2, 202 n.4, 203 n.10, 211
    n.25

Earman, John 207 n.16, 218 n.37
Eberle, Rolf A. 11 n.5
Einstein, Albert 202 n.6, 231, 232 n.65
Enç, Berent 231 n.64
Ereshefsky, Mark 210 n.24, 211 n.25
Evans, Gareth 51–2, 66, 213 n.29, 221 n.43,
    223 n.48

Feyerabend, Paul 230
Field, Hartry 231–2
Fine, Kit 5 n.IV, 7–8, 11 n.5, 20, 47, 54–5,
    58–61, 68, 71–90, 93–4, 96 n.5, 102 n.,
    106 n.13, 110 n.23, 112, 117 n., 120,
    123 n.1, 129 n., 142 n.46, 158, 167,
    169–70, 171, 180 n.19–20, 183–4 n.25,
    191 n., 257
Fodor, Jerry 207
Forbes, Graeme 179 n.17, 222 n.47
Forrest, Peter 29 n.5
Forster, Malcolm 204 n.11, 206 n.15
Frede, Dorothea 99
Frede, Michael 123 n.1
Frege, Gottlob 46, 53, 220, 226 n.57
Furth, Montgomery 123 n.1

Gallois, André 47, 48–50, 58, 61, 67, 179
    n.17
Geach, Peter 47, 56, 115, 179 n.17
Ghiselin, Michael 211
Gibbard, Alan 26, 30, 47–8, 49, 50, 56,
    58–65, 66, 67, 68, 179 n.17
Gilmore, Cody 256 n.20
Gill, Mary Louise 123 n.1
Gillon, Brandon 220 n.41
Goodman, Nelson 10, 15–7, 23–4, 27–8,
    203 n.7, 204, 207 n.16, 217

Griffin, Nicholas 179 n.17
Gupta, Anil 179 n.17

Hacking, Ian 201 n.1, 203 n.10, 205 n.13, 231 n.64
Halper, Edward 123 n.1, 195 n.38
Hamlyn, David 123 n.1
Hanson, William H. 243 n.9
Harré, Rom 206 n.16
Harte, Verity 5 n.IV, 11 n.5, 20, 29 n.5, 41, 94–121, 122, 123 n.1, 125, 135 n.28, 138 n.37, 141 n.43, 153 n.66–7, 159, 169, 192 n.,235, 239
Haslanger, Sally 123 n.1, 153 n.67, 188 n.30
Hawthorne, John 29 n.5
Heller, Mark 179 n.17, 181 n.21, 188 n.30
Hempel, Carl 216
Higginbotham, James 220 n.41, 222 n.46
Honnefelder, Ludger 258 n.
Hudson, Hud 11 n.5, 33 n.10
Hull, David 211, 212 n.27
Husserl, Edmund 11 n.5,15, 20

Jeffrey, Richard 240 n.
Johnston, Mark 5 n.IV, 12 n., 20, 71, 180 n.19, 188 n.30–1, 228 n.59, 229 n.61
Jubien, Michael 188 n.30

Kim, Jaegwon 207 n.17
King, Peter 258 n.21
Kirwan, Christopher 123 n.1, 144 n.50
Kitcher, Philip 203 n.10, 207 n.16, 211 n.25,215, 231
Kornblith, Hilary 204 n.11,209
Koslicki, Kathrin 5 n.III, 9 n.2, 25, 27 n.3, 29, 30 n., 31, 33 n.11, 37, 45 n.1, 55, 76 n.2, 81, 90 n., 94 n., 108 n.15, 176 n.12, 177 n.14, 184 n.27, 189 n.32, 194 n., 195 n.36, 220 n.41, 222 n.46 Kripke, Saul 40, 47–8, 205 n.13, 206 n.15, 213, 219–32 Kuhn, Thomas S. 202 n.6,230–3

Lange, Marc 216–8
LaPorte, Joseph 201, 203 n.9, 211 n.25, 213 n.28, 215, 222 n.47, 223 n.50–1, 228 n.59, 231 n.64, 232 n.65
Lasnik, Howard 253
Lavoisier, Antoine 202 n.6
Lejewski, Czeslaw 11 n.5
Leonard, Henry S. 10, 15–7, 23–4, 27–8
Le Poidevin, Robin 244 n.10, 245 n.13
Leœniewski, Stanislaw 10, 23 Lewis, David 5, 7, 10 n.4, 11 n.5, 17, 20–2, 28–44, 45, 71, 88, 94–7, 105, 119–20, 122, 153,

179 n.17, 180 n.20, 185 n.28, 188 n.30–1, 192–3, 231 n.64, 234, 256
Lewis, Frank A. 123 n.1
Link, Gödehard 220 n.41
Linsky, Bernard 222 n.47, 223 n.51, 224 n.52
Locke, John 180 n.19, 208, 210 n.22
Lønning, Jan Tore 220 n.41
Loux, Michael J. 123 n.1
Lowe, E.J. 12 n., 180 n.19, 188 n.30, 218 n.38
Loxley, Andrew 190 n.33, 195 n.37, 227 n.58

Mac Lane, Saunders 240, 241 n.6
Macnamara, John 204 n.11
Makin, Stephen 123 n.1
Manzano, María 240–1
Markosian, Ned 11 n.5, 33 n.10
Mayr, Ernst 212
Mellor, D. H. 207 n.16, 222 n.47, 228 n.59, 229 n.62
Menger, Karl 11 n.5
Merricks, Trenton 11 n.5
Mignucci, Mario 123 n.1
Mill, John Stuart 201 n.1, 205
Millgram, Elijah 171 n., 205 n.13
Moltmann, Friederike 11 n.5, 12 n.
Myro, George 47, 48–50, 56, 58, 61, 67, 179 n.17

Needham, Paul 11 n.5
Newton, Isaac 202 n.6, 206, 231, 232 n.65
Nola, Robert 231 n.
Nozick, Robert 236 n.

Oderberg, David 180 n.19, 183 n.23, 188 n.30
Oliver, Alex 11 n.5, 20 n., 29 n.5,41
Olson, Eric 181 n.
Oppenheim, Paul 216

Papineau, David 231 n.
Parmenides 95, 122
Parsons, Charles 241 n.6
Parsons, Terence 47, 51–4, 58, 61, 65–8
Pasnau, Robert 258 n.21
Pasteur, Louis 245
Paterson, Hugh E. H. 213
Paul, L. A. 168 n.
Perry, John 179 n.17
Plantinga, Alvin 11 n.5
Plato 6, 8, 72, 93–121, 122–3, 125, 127 n.9, 128, 129 n., 136 n.30, 142 n.44, 142 n.47, 143, 145–6 n.53, 147 n.56, 151, 152, 153 n.67, 154–7, 163–4, 169–70, 172, 180 n.20,192–3, 219, 237–8, 260, 262

Priestley, Joseph 202 n.6
Putnam, Hilary 37, 40, 118, 201 n.3, 202, 206 n.15, 207–10, 219–32

Quine, Willard van Orman 29 n., 48, 179 n.17, 188 n.30, 203 n.7, 205 n.12, 207 n.17

Ray, Greg 83
Rea, Michael 11 n.5
Reeve, C. D. C. 123 n.1
Rescher, Nicholas 12 n., 239–40
Resnik, Michael 241 n.6
Richard, Mark 62 n.16
Ridley, Mark 213
Riggs, Peter J. 207 n.16
Rorty, Richard 123 n.1
Ross, W. D. 108 n.16, 109, 110, 110–1 n.24, 126 n.7, 130 n.15, 133 n.23, 135, 140, 142 n.45, 148 n.59, 161
Russell, Bertrand 10, 52, 53, 188 n.30, 201 n.1, 220

Salmon, Nathan 221 n.43, 222 n.44, 222 n.47, 224
Sankey, Howard 231 n., 232 n.66
Scaltsas, Theodore 11 n.5, 123 n.1
Scala, Mark 29 n.5
Scha, Remko 220 n.41
Schein, Barry 220 n.41, 222 n.46
Schenker, Heinrich 247 n.15
Schoenberg, Arnold 247
Schwartz, Stephen 222 n.47
Scotus, John Duns 258 n.21
Scruton, Roger 246 n.14, 247 n.15
Shapere, Dudley 231 n.
Shapiro, Stewart 241 n.6
Sharvy, Richard 11 n.5
Sher, Gila 243 n.9
Shields, Christopher 123 n.1
Shoemaker, Sydney 210 n.23
Sider, Theodore 5 n.III, 7, 11 n.5, 22, 25, 29 n., 30–40, 50 n.9, 71, 105, 179 n.17, 185 n., 188 n.30
Simons, Peter 3, 7, 10, 11 n.5–6, 12, 15, 17, 18, 19, 20, 21, 23, 26, 80 n., 87, 89, 158, 167, 168, 180 n.19, 188 n.30
Smith, Barry 11 n.5
Sneath, Peter H. A. 212
Snyder, Laura 204 n.11
Soames, Scott 222 n.47, 224 n.52, 226 n.57

Sober, Elliott 211 n., 212 n.27
Sokal, Richard R. 212
Sosa, Ernest 181 n., 207 n.17
Stalker, Douglas 204 n.11
Sterelny, Kim 213 n.29
Stone, Jim 180 n.19
Stubenberg, Leopold 195 n.37
Swoyer, Chris 207 n.16
Szaif, Jan 258 n.21

Tarski, Alfred 10, 243 n.9
Thalos, Mariam 209 n.21
Thomson, Judith Jarvis 7, 11 n.5, 22–8, 43, 71, 75, 178 n., 180 n.19, 188 n.30
Tiles, J. E. 11 n.5
Tooley, Michael 207 n.16
Tranöy, Knut Erik 11 n.5, 237

Unger, Peter 179 n.17, 213 n.29, 223 n.48

Van Benthem, Johan 11 n.5
Van Inwagen, Peter 7, 10 n.4, 11 n.5, 20, 26, 29 n., 41, 95, 98, 103, 104, 105, 119, 120, 170, 179 n.17, 188 n.30
Varzi, Achille 10–1 n.5
Venn, John 201 n.1

Wasserman, Ryan 29 n.5
Way, Eileen C. 206 n.16
Wedin, Michael V. 123 n.1
Weiner, Norbert 209 n.21
Whewell, William 204 n.11
Whitehead, Alfred North 10, 11 n.5
Wiggins, David 11 n.5, 56, 67, 180 n.19, 188 n.30
Wilkerson, T. E. 218 n.38
Williams, Donald C. 29 n.
Witt, Charlotte 123 n.1
Wittgenstein, Ludwig 170 n.2, 173 n.9, 206 n.14
Wöhler, Friedrich 244
Woolley, R. G. 245 n.13

Yablo, Stephen 47, 54–5, 58–61, 68, 180 n.19

Zemach, Eddy 222 n.47, 227, 228 n.59, 229 n.62
Zeno 95, 122
Zimmerman, Dean 11 n.5, 181 n., 188 n.30

Made in the USA
Middletown, DE
13 March 2015